FOUR PHILOSOPHICAL ANGLICANS

Professor Sell explores the lives and ideas of four unjustly neglected Anglican philosophers: W. G. De Burgh (1866–1943); W. R. Matthews (1881–1973); O. C. Quick (1885–1944); H. A. Hodges (1905–1976). This study fills an important gap in the history of twentieth-century philosophical and theological thought. Sell argues that these writers covered a wide range of philosophical topics in an illuminating way, and that a comparison of their respective standpoints and methods is instructive from the point of view of the viability or otherwise of Christian philosophizing. He discusses the challenges these four philosophical Anglicans issued to certain important trends in the philosophy and theology of their day, and argues that some of them are of continuing relevance.

W. G. De Burgh

W. R. Matthews

O. C. Quick

H. A. Hodges

Four Philosophical Anglicans
W. G. De Burgh, W. R. Matthews,
O. C. Quick, H. A. Hodges

ALAN P. F. SELL

WIPF & STOCK · Eugene, Oregon

Wipf and Stock Publishers
199 W 8th Ave, Suite 3
Eugene, OR 97401

Four Philosophical Anglicans
W.G. DeBurgh, W.R. Matthews, O.C. Quick, H.A. Hodges
By Sell, Alan P.F.
Copyright©2010 by Sell, Alan P.F.
ISBN 13: 978-1-4982-2008-8
Publication date 2/17/2015
Previously published by Ashgate, 2010

To Andrew and Jean MacRae

*Faithful friends, and companions in
theological education*

Contents

Preface ix
List of Abbreviations xi

1 Introduction 1

2 William George de Burgh (1866–1943): Reason, Morality and Religion 3

3 Walter Robert Matthews (1881–1973): Experience, Rationality and Revelation 69

4 Oliver Chase Quick (1885–1944): Philosophy, Theology, Ecumenism 143

5 Herbert Arthur Hodges (1905–1976): Christian Philosopher, Believing Sceptic 203

6 Comparisons, Contrasts and Assessment 273

Bibliography 303
Index of Persons 317
Index of Subjects 325

Preface

> I will sometimes go on both sides of the Hedge, though by so doing I be scratcht.
> Richard Baxter, *A Third Defence of the Cause of Peace*, 1681, II, 85.

Baxter's experience, gleaned during a period of doctrinal strife, may be shared by those who take the risk of working in the borderland between philosophy and theology. Happily, the excitement of conversing with past and present thinkers across the frontiers with a view to formulating one's position on significant matters more than compensates for the perils faced. Not a little of my work has been undertaken with a view to introducing into the ongoing conversation philosophers and theologians who have become largely forgotten. They constituted the intellectual hinterland against the background of which better known authors presented their wares. If we look behind the 'big names' we shall not only understand their intellectual context better, but we shall find writers who, although they may never be named on lists of 'set texts', nevertheless had things of importance to say. The four Anglicans treated here are writers of this kind.

I should like to thank the following persons who located sources and/or answered queries during the writing of this book: Ann Davies of The Open University Library; Alice Ford-Smith of Dr Williams's Library, London; R. S. Luhman of The Victoria Institute; Barbara Merrifield, Librarian of The Well at Willen; Margaret Thompson of Westminster College, Cambridge; Jane Walsh of The British Newspaper Library; and Zofia Weaver of The Society for Psychical Research.

Permission to reproduce the image of O. C. Quick has kindly been granted by the Senior Common Room, Christ Church, Oxford, and I am grateful to Judith Curthoys, College Archivist, for her assistance in this matter. Efforts to trace those who own the copyright of the images of W. G. de Burgh (from *Proceedings of the British Academy*, XXIX, 1943), W. R. Matthews (from *Memories and Meanings*, Hodder and Stoughton, 1969) and H. A. Hodges (from *God Beyond Knowledge*, Macmillan,1979) have proved unsuccessful. However, James Rivington of the British Academy, Loreen Brown of Hodder, and Ruth Tellis of Palgrave Macmillan, have no objection to the use of the images reproduced from their publications.

Thanks are also due to Sarah Lloyd of Ashgate Publishing who, once again, has allowed me to enter her list; to Barbara Pretty for her expert attention to the publishing process; and to all involved in the production of this handsome volume.

It goes without saying that this book would not have appeared without the encouragement and support of Karen, my wife; but it must be said.

I dedicate this work with affection and esteem to our friends of many years, Andrew and Jean MacRae, who first introduced us to the delights of the beautiful Annapolis Valley, Nova Scotia, in which Acadia Divinity College is set, and who have been companions on the way ever since.

Alan P. F. Sell
Milton Keynes, UK

List of Abbreviations

DNCBP: W. J. Mander and Alan P. F. Sell, eds, *Dictionary of Nineteenth-Century British Philosophy*, Bristol: Thoemmes Press, 2002.

DTCBP: Stuart Bown, ed., *Dictionary of Twentieth-Century British Philosophy*, Bristol: Thoemmes Continuum, 2005.

ODNB: *The Oxford Dictionary of National Biography.*

Chapter 1
Introduction

In this book the careers of four philosophical Anglicans are sketched, and their writings are discussed. W. G. de Burgh (1866–1943) was the first Professor of Philosophy at the University of Reading; W. R. Matthews (1881–1973) was Dean and Professor of the Philosophy of Religion at King's College, London, before becoming Dean first of Exeter Cathedral and then of St. Paul's; O. C. Quick (1885–1944) held various ecclesiastical appointments before becoming Professor of Theology at Durham University, and then Regius Professor of Divinity and Canon of Christ Church, Oxford; and in 1934 H. A. Hodges (1905–1976) succeeded his older colleague, de Burgh, as the second Professor of Philosophy at Reading. Of all of them it may be said that their primary academic interest was philosophical, though in the case of Quick and Hodges in particular it must be noted that their theological acumen was considerable. The same may be said of de Burgh, though in his case he tried hard, without always succeeding, to remember that he was a philosopher, not a theologian or an apologist, and he did not publish specifically theological works. Taking all of their publications together we find contributions to philosophy, theology, doctrine, psychology, apologetics and spirituality. Reference will be made to all of these.

Pride of place, however, will be given to philosophy, for the reason why these four philosophical Anglicans are of particular interest (and other Anglicans and non-Anglicans[1] might have been chosen) is that they illustrate some of the ways in which committed Christians charted their intellectual course during a period of philosophical upheaval.[2] The idealistic metaphysics in which they had been reared was under strong, if not always justified, attack. Science was held in high esteem by many, and scientific method, its abstractive nature notwithstanding, was deemed by some to be the sole method of arriving at truth. Barthian theology seemed to many to entail a retreat from reason into a circle of revelation, and logical positivists were branding religious, no less than aesthetic and moral, discourse nonsense. Through all of this de Burgh, Matthews, Quick and Hodges managed to keep their heads and maintain their faith. Our purpose here is to see how they went about doing this. This enquiry into their procedures and findings is by no means an antiquarian or a nostalgic exercise. It is offered in the expectation that

---

[1] Robert Franks the Congregationalist comes immediately to mind. See Alan P. F. Sell, *Hinterland Theology. A Stimulus to Theological Construction*, Milton Keynes: Paternoster, 2008, ch. 10 and *passim*.

[2] For an account of this see Alan P. F. Sell, *The Philosophy of Religion 1875-1980*, London: Croom Helm, 1988, Bristol: Thoemmes Press, 1996.

since philosophical ideas cannot be constricted by time or space (which means that heresies as well as truths are long lived) we may find encouragement, rebuke, and certainly stimulus, in the contributions and methods of our intellectual forebears.

Chapter 2
William George de Burgh (1866–1943): Reason, Morality and Religion

[T]hose who are enlightened by religious vision possess an almost uncanny power of handling their own difficulties and those of others with efficiency, and of discerning, in the most unpromising quarters, the signs of God's indwelling Spirit and of a desire for him akin to their own.[1]

W. G. de Burgh could have been speaking of himself. Tall, slim, bespectacled, and of aristocratic features, he had an aloof air but, as we shall see, his students loved him, notwithstanding the dim view he took of some of their attainments and interests. Beneath all was a religiously-grounded optimism which looked for the best in others, and could write off no one. His friend, A. E. Taylor, supplies many of the basic family details:

> William George de Burgh, born at New Wandsworth on 24 October 1866, was the son of William de Burgh, a barrister holding a post at the War Office, and of his wife, Hannah Jane Monck Mason, a great-granddaughter of Samuel Whitbread,[2] and granddaughter of the Lady Grey (great-grandmother to Viscount Grey of Falloden) who was well known in the Evangelical movement of her day.[3] Of his paternal uncles, one, Maurice de Burgh, was Archdeacon of Ness, another, Hubert, became a priest in the Roman Catholic Church. Dean de Burgh, his paternal grandfather, was the builder of the church at Sandymount, Dublin. He was thus of mixed Norman-Irish and Northumberland strain, an 'aristocrat' in the proper sense of a much abused word ... his mother (who lost her own father early) was much attached to her uncle, Sir George Grey, Home Secretary, and to her cousins, in particular to Thomas Baring, Lord Northbrook.[4]

---

[1] W. G. De Burgh, *Towards a Religious Philosophy* (hereinafter TRP), London: Macdonald & Evans, 1937, 50.

[2] For Samuel Whitbread (1720–96), brewer and landowner, and his son, also Samuel (1764–1815), politician, see ODNB.

[3] For Mary, Lady Grey (1770–1858), née Whitbread, half-sister to the politician, enthusiastic distributor of Bibles to seafarers, see ODNB.

[4] A. E. Taylor, 'William George de Burgh, 1866–1943', *Proceedings of the British Academy*, XXIX, 1943, 371–2. For de Burgh see also DTCBP; ODNB; and further references below.

With this pedigree it is all the more significant that de Burgh was able 'to be natural and unconstrained in all company', and that there was no 'trace of social superiority or snobbery' about him.[5]

Encouraged by his mother, daughter of Captain Thomas Monck Mason RN, whom Taylor describes as 'devout and rather "Puritan"', de Burgh enjoyed learning much of the Bible by heart – 'an admirable practice which I could wish to see more common than it appears to-day' declares Taylor, before drily adding, 'it is not so easy to see why, in later life, he took the pleasure he is reported to have done in memorizing much of the information provided by Bradshaw's [railway] *Guide* and Whitaker's *Almanac*. ... Nor do I know how to explain the keen delight which de Burgh has told me he found in the posting of accounts in neatly written columns with carefully ruled lines in red ink.'[6]

When de Burgh was 12, and still at preparatory school, his father died, leaving his mother in some financial difficulty. This was exacerbated by the fact that in 1880 de Burgh failed to secure a scholarship to Winchester College. Helped by a relative, however, he enrolled as a commoner. During the school holidays he went to stay with his Scots cousins, the Burn Murdochs, in Perthshire. There he immersed himself in music and became an ardent walker: 'forty miles, including the climbing of a mountain, is said to have been his idea of a good walk'.[7] He showed no interest in country sports and heartily disliked school games, though he was well versed in cricket and enjoyed watching the game. Among his school friends was the budding philosopher, H. W. B. Joseph, with whom he maintained contact throughout his life.[8]

To his own surprise de Burgh won a classical Postmastership at Merton College, Oxford, and was placed in the second class in Honour Moderations in 1887, and in the first class in *Literae humaniores* in 1889. In addition to Joseph, de Burgh's Oxford classical-philosophical contemporaries included W. R. Hardie, H. H. Joachim and J. A. Smith.[9] On leaving Oxford de Burgh was briefly an assistant master at Derby School, from whence he went to Toynbee Hall, London, where he became Censor of Studies at Balliol House, a residence for male city workers who wished to benefit from social and intellectual pursuits. Named after the academic and social reformer, Arnold Toynbee, and opened in 1884, Toynbee Hall was set in the heart of one of London's poorest areas, noted for its large contingents of

---

[5] Ibid., 372.

[6] Ibid., 372, 373.

[7] Ibid., 374.

[8] For Horace William Brindley Joseph (1867–1943) see DTCBP; ODNB. Joseph outlived de Burgh by just three months.

[9] For William Ross Hardie (1862–1916), Harold Henry Joachim (1868–1938) and John Alexander Smith (1863–1939) see DTCBP; ODNB.

Jewish[10] and Irish[11] immigrants. This was by no means the environment in which an aristocrat of the snobbier sort would have chosen to live. In 1895 de Burgh moved into lodgings in Stepney with his friend Patrick Duncan, who rose from being a lecturer at Toynbee Hall to become the first Governor-General of the Union of South Africa.[12] De Burgh became a lecturer in the University Extension system, a venture originated by the Universities of Oxford, Cambridge and London during the 1870s, the objective of which was to provide lectures on a wide variety of subjects to working-class people in various parts of the country. As an extension lecturer de Burgh 'became eminently successful, though he always rated his own work in this department as a mere retailing of the second-best at second-hand'.[13] In 1896 he was appointed Lecturer in Greek and Latin at the University Extension College in Reading. The first University Extension lectures had been given in Reading in 1885, and the College had been opened in 1892.

On 26 January 1897 de Burgh married Edith Mary, daughter of William Francis Grace, Vice-Consul at Mogador. They had two daughters and a son, and their home at Southern Hill was open to staff and students alike. In the same year philosophy was added to de Burgh's classical brief. In 1902 the institution became a University College, and when, in 1907, its complement of faculties was determined, he became the first Professor of Philosophy and Dean of the Faulty of Letters – positions he held until his retirement in 1934. From time to time he was invited to consider moving elsewhere – to a projected extension college at Worcester, to the Muslim University of Aligarh, to the Principalship of the Training College at Blackheath, London; but de Burgh stuck to his last and was deeply committed to the Reading enterprise. In 1910, on the arrival of P. N. Ure as the first Professor of Classics, de Burgh relinquished that subject.[14] Henceforth he 'managed Philosophy along with one lecturer'.[15] This was still a formidable task, and it is more than likely that de Burgh's own teaching experience informed his observation upon that of his friend, George Dawes Hicks, who at University College, London, traversed the entire field of philosophy '*almost* single-handed. ... Hicks, with characteristic courage and energy, grappled boldly with a problem that

---

[10] Many of whom worked in tailoring, while others became prominent dance band leaders and musicians – Ambrose, Lew Stone, Oscar Rabin, Joe Loss, to name but a few.

[11] Many of whom became dockers.

[12] For Duncan (1870–1943) see ODNB.

[13] A. E. Taylor, 'William George de Burgh', 375.

[14] Percy Neville Ure held his Chair from 1910 to 1946. The researches of Ure and his wife, Annie D. Ure, into Greek ceramics were of international significance, and led to the creation of the fourth most important collection in the United Kingdom. It is housed in the Ure Museum, University of Reading, of which Annie Ure was curator until her death in 1976.

[15] J. C. Holt, *The University of Reading: The First Fifty Years*, Reading: University of Reading Press, 1977, 16.

besets the teaching not only of philosophy but of every subject in all our English Universities, save at Oxford and Cambridge'.[16]

As if the Chair and the Deanship were not enough, de Burgh was prominent in guiding the institution in its early years. Whereas the large civic universities founded in the Victorian period could not have fulfilled their mission had they not admitted students into halls of residence and welcomed many who continued to live at home, the aim from the outset at Reading was to create an institution centred, after the Oxford pattern, in collegiate life. This proved attractive to a number of distinguished scholars who welcomed the relief from the accumulation of regulations with which they had previously been encumbered, were stimulated by the opportunity to create something new, and found the proximity of Reading to both Oxford and London beneficial to their research work. De Burgh was intimately involved in the leadership of the University College, and played an important part during its passage from its status as a College teaching to the London University external degree syllabi, to that of a degree-granting, chartered, university in 1926: the only new university created in the United Kingdom between the two World Wars.

From the outset the University was well blessed in its leadership. Its first Vice-Chancellor, W. M. Childs, was as skilled in the encouragement of potential benefactors as he was austere towards his colleagues and pessimistic in his annual reports;[17] the first Registrar, the Reverend Francis H. Wright, who had held secretarial posts in the University College since 1887, was an able administrator; de Burgh was the trusted academic, and from 1926 until he retired in 1934 he was the first Deputy Vice-Chancellor. It was said of Childs, Wright and de Burgh that they 'formed a kind of inner cabinet'.[18] Of de Burgh's contribution Childs wrote,

> In temperament we were often as far apart as two men whose friendship went back to the careless days of youth could well be. To agree with de Burgh upon a question of policy was serious, for there was apt to follow by contagion a quickening of pace; to disagree was to find out once again that by reason of exuberance, energy of mind, and power of argumentation, he could be, like Dr. Johnson, a 'tremendous companion'. As I call to mind those discussions of long ago, two things stand out, one is his preference for the higher, though not always the more inviting, of two alternatives. The other is his magnanimity under provocation, often surprising in a man whose reactions to words could be vehement. ... Without my colleague's co-operation and advocacy the university

---

[16] W. G. de Burgh, 'George Dawes Hicks 1862–1941', *Proceedings of the British Academy*, XXVII, 1941, 411. For Hicks see also DTCBP; ODNB.

[17] For William Macbride Childs (1869–1939) see ODNB. De Burgh contributed 'Dr. W. M. Childs', to *The Portmuthian*, LVI, 2 July 1939, 36–41.

[18] J. C. Holt, *The University of Reading*, 42.

movement at Reading could neither have been undertaken nor successfully pursued.[19]

Like other staff members, de Burgh acquired books for the library, and he was also involved in appointing members of staff, not least Franklin Sibley, who succeeded Childs as Vice-Chancellor on the latter's retirement in 1929. Sibley recalled that having been interviewed for the post, and having dined with Childs and a few others, during which time no reference to the vacancy was permitted, 'it was not until Saturday morning, when old de Burgh blew in again for a private chat, that the cat came out: and he then begged the question by telling me what I should find and how I should like it etc. etc., giving me some amusing sketches of some of his colleagues'.[20]

De Burgh, like his successor in the Chair of Philosophy, H. A. Hodges, was a deeply committed Christian,

> but they tended to assume that religion was a highly individual matter, to be discussed with, but not imposed on, students. There were others who, whatever their faith, were unlikely to encourage the development of the formal study of Theology. Doris Stenton regarded Theology as an 'easy subject' and fought with vigour and success against the introduction of Biblical Studies into the Faculty of Letters. ... It was simply assumed that the University was a secular, scholarly institution. It has so remained.[21]

Off campus de Burgh did not hide his Christian light under a bushel of academic reserve. He chaired his church's Parish Council, from time to time he gave sermons in local churches, and he served more widely as President of the local branch of the League of Nations.

During World War I de Burgh had time to turn his hand to consistent writing, and he produced his most widely-read work, *The Legacy of the Ancient World*. It was published in 1923, revised in 1947, and reissued in 1953 and 1955. 'I hope all my Honours men will read it,' said John Burnet, Professor of Greek at St. Andrews

---

[19] Quoted by A. E. Taylor, 'William George de Burgh', 380–81.

[20] J. C. Holt, quoting a letter of Sibley to A. E. Morgan of 19 May 1929 (URC, box 256), ibid., 41 n. 2.

[21] Ibid., 82. Doris Stenton was a Lecturer in History and the wife of Frank Stenton, the medieval historian, who was a Research Fellow in the University College from 1908 to 1912, and then held the Chair of History until his appointment as Vice-Chancellor in succession to Sibley in 1946. For Doris (1894–1971) and Frank (1880–1967) Stenton see ODNB. Doris was Frank's student. She graduated in 1916 and married him in 1919. Among other honours she was FBA; but she clearly manifested either that dismissive attitude towards Theology by which some of the brightest advertise themselves as having an intellectual blind spot, or that illiberal attitude which is never more incongruous than when it is displayed by scholars of the *liberal* arts, or both.

University, to A. E. Taylor, 'it is exactly the book I have wanted to see written for many years.'[22] Taylor's verdict on the book was that 'I can conceive no better prophylactic against the current clamour of raucous voices – some of them, *pro pudor*, those of University Professors – shouting for the destruction of "medieval rubbish" than a serious study of *The Legacy of the Ancient World*'.[23] De Burgh also found time to contribute papers to the *Proceedings of the Aristotelian Society*, *The Hibbert Journal*, whose reviews editor was his friend George Dawes Hicks, *Philosophy*, *Theology*, and the *Proceedings of the British Academy*. A number of these received a new lease of life in the books he published following his retirement: *Towards a Religious Philosophy* (1937); *From Morality to Religion* (1938 – his Gifford Lectures at St. Andrews; *Knowledge of the Individual* (1939) – his Riddell Memorial Lectures before the University of Durham; and, posthumously, *The Life of Reason* (1949). He was elected a Fellow of the British Academy in 1938.

To his published works I shall turn shortly. But what of de Burgh the teacher? As to his method we have his own testimony:

> [I]n the case of philosophy, as in that of Art or Religion, it is futile to seek for a definition at the outset; ... Better far to point to an actual philosopher engaged in philosophic thinking, ... A still more helpful answer is to direct [a student] to the classical masterpieces of metaphysics, bidding him catch fragments of the speculative technique of great thinkers by laying his own mind alongside of theirs and entering, as best he can, into the method of their reasoning. If the student, as well he may, rebels against this relegation to the study of back numbers, there is nothing to hinder him from doing the like with the works of contemporary philosophers.[24]

Student responses to de Burgh's teaching are plentiful and illuminating. Of de Burgh one wrote that

> he admired us for our zest in living, our vitality, but he censured us for our ignorance, our disinclination to think and our lack of reverence for the things that are great and the things that are eternal. But he did not stop at generalizations – he cared for us as individuals too. A student was not something to which he taught philosophy. ... His interest made one want to do well. ... In a sense he was always preaching but it was so spontaneous and inevitable that one never felt it intrusive. Who but Billy would have produced the remark: 'Humanism – to love a man just because he is a man – is one thing, but to love him because he

---

[22] A. E. Taylor, 'William George de Burgh', 382.

[23] Ibid., 384. For a less generous review, which does not do justice to de Burgh's intention or achievement, see A. W. Gomme, *The Classical Review*, XXXVIII, November–December 1924, 177–8.

[24] W. G. de Burgh, *The Life of Reason* (hereinafter LR), London: Macdonald & Evans, 1949, 82.

is part of the mystical body of Christ incorporate – why, that's quite a different kettle of fish.'

The same writer continues,

> We most of us heard him on Logic and few of us evaded his famous 'Republic' lectures. ... He lectured to us in his own room in the University. We sat about his fire and he sat in the biggest armchair with his scrappy old notes in one hand and his spectacles in the other. He thundered his stuff out at us and drove it in by repetition. ... When he digressed he was never dull. ... I can remember his eloquence on the possibility of developing an art of smell, or a projected life of Satan, best of all perhaps on 'Washing'. He treated the subject historically, geographically and personally – how staying in Paris he was obliged to wash himself *en arrondissements*. Lectures were a serious matter. He reproved you if you came without a gown. If you omitted to come at all ... he was apt to notice. 'Will you tell Miss Wratislaw that this is the way to Death, Destruction and Damnation?'[25]

Another student writes, 'It is difficult for me ... to express with any degree of adequacy what I owe to Professor de Burgh';[26] yet another: 'To present the author of the *Critique of Pure Reason* as a man and a brother – and a rather jolly one at that – was, I felt, an achievement worthy of emulation. ... This illustrates another of Professor de Burgh's merits. Not only must philosophy be taken seriously, it must be taken gladly. The way to understanding is through liking ...'[27]

In one of his last addresses to the residents of Wessex Hall de Burgh said,

> I suppose that you want me to talk about ancient history, but the fact is that I am tired of ancient history. What I care about is the future. A university could manage quite well without students, but since they insist on coming they should take some responsibility for the university, which *qua* university is interested in nothing but their intelligence. A place with hot and cold water laid on does not exist to train character. If you want to be in a place that will give you that run away to sea or go on the stage. Things that may matter infinitely to you as an individual, like games, religion or friends, don't matter at all to the university. The university is dependent on its members and the present lot of students are a very poor lot by what they might be. ... Beware of false prophets. No one reads the Old Testament nowadays, but if any one of you did, you would know that the

---

[25] Extracts from the Diary of Vera Willis, 1931–34, quoted by J. C. Holt, *The University of Reading*, 86, 92.

[26] Miss Berthen, quoted by A. E. Taylor, 'William George de Burgh', 382.

[27] A. C. Mason, quoted ibid.

mark of a false prophet was that he said nice things to the folk who entertained him. God bless you, my dears!²⁸

Somewhat more formally, in his last address as Dean to the students of the Faculty of Letters he exhorted them thus:

> You have come to a university to have the opportunity of contact, not merely with direct living, but also with what is absolute and enduring in art, literature and the other things that have value. And you have the opportunity of avoiding the mistake of separating off the values and standards as something abstract and remote from the direct experience which you all want to enjoy.²⁹

With the advent of World War II and the dispersal of numerous academics to other duties, de Burgh began teaching at New College, Oxford. During the summer of 1942, however, he suffered a slight stroke whilst rambling alone on the Dorset downs. He recovered sufficiently to resume his teaching at Oxford, but he soon became weaker and was advised to take a complete rest. This he did, and then returned to New College in January 1943. But on 27th of that month he died at Toller Pocorum, Dorset, where he was buried three days later. 'His name,' wrote P. N. Ure, 'ranks among the highest in the history of the great educational movement of the last half century.'³⁰

I

A. E. Taylor wrote somewhat less than the truth when he declared that 'de Burgh was always, in later life, an eminently *well-read* philosopher',³¹ for the qualification 'in later life' is redundant. Attentive readers of de Burgh's works from his earliest book onwards cannot be unaware of the fact that they are in the presence of one who is widely read and who, for the most part, wears his learning lightly. I say 'for the most part', for he does not hesitate to throw in untranslated phrases in Latin, French, and occasionally Greek and German; he has a habit of introducing esoteric learning by optimistically writing, 'As everybody knows ...'; and he will quote lines of poetry without patronizing (or assisting) his readers by divulging the names of their authors. But for the most part his writing is pellucid and free of philosophical jargon.

---

[28] J. C. Holt, *The University of Reading*, 86.
[29] Ibid., 87. Remarks which, presumably, would be incomprehensible to those present-day vice chancellors whose primary objective is that their universities be 'business-facing'.
[30] P. N. Ure, 'Professor W. G. de Burgh. An Appreciation', *The Times*, 1 September 1943, 7.
[31] A. E. Taylor, 'William George de Burgh', 373.

Precisely because of his breadth of learning it will make for clarity if I approach de Burgh's major themes by introducing first his broad judgements concerning major philosophers and philosophical traditions, as well as his attitudes towards the intellectual trends of his own time.

In his first book, *The Legacy of the Ancient World*, de Burgh ranges widely. He traverses early Eastern civilizations – the Egyptian, Babylonian and Persian among them. In particular the book provides ample evidence of de Burgh's grasp of the heritage of Greece and Rome, and this is the aspect of the work on which I shall focus, since to a considerable degree de Burgh's thought was formed by this classical inheritance. Even more significant was the influence upon him of the Judaeo-Christian tradition. However, de Burgh made a not altogether successful attempt to keep this at bay in his philosophical writings for he wished to present himself not as a theologian, still less as an apologist for Christianity, but as a philosopher who was alive to the fact that both the Greek love of rational argument and the Hebrew grasp of moral values and spiritual insights had permeated the bulk of subsequent Western philosophy. Indeed, '[T]he development of the religion of Israel, in the hands of the prophets, into a spiritual monotheism was as original and distinctive a creation of the Hebrew religious genius as the philosophies of Plato and Aristotle were of the intellectual genius of Greece.'[32] But if belief in one God and his moral government of the world was the strength of Hebrew religion, 'Its besetting weakness was the ineradicable presupposition that the divine purpose was concentrated on a single people ... [T]he Hebrew people failed to realize effectively the larger hope of the prophets.'[33] While the Hebrews had a keen sense of God's dealings with them in history and, at their best, gave due place to conscience, the intellectual, universalizing, impulse came from Christianity, itself driven by the missionary imperative and influenced by Greek thought.

By contrast with Hebrew thought, the Greek ambition, epitomized by Plato and Aristotle, was the quest of knowledge and the disinterested pursuit of truth. Behind them lay the contributions of the sixth-century BC philosophers of Miletus, Thales, Anaximander and Anaximenes, who sought by observation and experiment 'to understand the world as a world of rational law, with system and unity of structure'.[34] They went in quest of a primary, permanent, changeless, substance – water, vapour or fire, for example – from which, in accordance with necessary law, were derived the phenomena of sense experience. At the beginning of the fifth century Heraclitus of Ephesus conceived of nature as being in a state of constant flux, such that the world as perceived by sense is ever coming, or ceasing, to be. Meanwhile Pythagoras had developed pure geometry, and had applied mathematics in the direction of showing the independent reality of the physical universe – an idea pursued by Plato in the *Timaeus*. Parmenides and the Eleatics contended that if the real were one and corporeal then the many and motion

---

[32] W. G. de Burgh, *The Legacy of the Ancient World* (Hereinafter LAW), 30.
[33] Ibid., 88, 89. '*Most* of the prophets' would have been more accurate.
[34] LAW, 121.

were illusory. In response to this Empedocles, Anaxagoras and Leucippis of Miletus, founder of the Atomic school, agreed that reality was corporeal, but that it was also many; while Socrates and Plato concluded that the real was one, but that it was a spiritual, not a corporeal, unity. In opposition to the inherited religious traditions, and notwithstanding the resultant ridicule to which they were subjected in Old Attic comedy, the philosophers held to a 'conception of intellectual contemplation (*theoria*) as the highest human activity, akin to the divine', that, 'realized first by the Pythagoreans and developed by Plato and Aristotle, carries us into the very heart of the Hellenic genius'.[35]

From about 450 BC onwards, 'For the first time in history the clear light of reason was directed upon the problem of human conduct.'[36] De Burgh likens the resulting intellectual ferment to the eighteenth-century Enlightenment, stimulated as it was by its central figure, Voltaire. That Enlightenment prepared the ground for Kant; the Greek 'Enlightenment' prepared the way for Plato. It came to be believed that virtue did not depend upon talents, gifts or fortune, but upon acquired theory. Concurrently, the development of rhetoric drew attention to the importance of words as symbols of thoughts; hence to the analyses of such concepts as 'nature' and 'convention' undertaken by the Sophists. The Sophists followed no one party line. Hippias grounded moral duty in eternal, divine, natural law; Thrasymachus taught that might is right; Protagoras, that in the absence of unchanging natural moral principles the conventions of the *polis* should be honoured by the citizen. On which de Burgh comments,

> The tone of these discussions affords a striking parallel to those of the later eighteenth-century enlightenment, embodied in the writings of Rousseau, Tom Paine, and William Godwin; in the preamble to the American Declaration of Independence, and in the manifestoes of the French Revolution; as also to those invoked in our own day by the advocates of the claims of the superman and of the super-state against the restrictions of conventional moral valuations.[37]

If their criticisms of received religious beliefs rendered the Sophists liable to the charge of scepticism, their redirection of thought towards rationality proved to be a boon of lasting importance.

Of Socrates' faith in reason there could be no doubt. To him 'the discipline of philosophy was at the same time the fulfilment of a religious vocation'.[38] His motivating idea was, in his own words, that 'An unexamined life is not worth living.'[39]

---

[35] Ibid., 131.
[36] Ibid., 160.
[37] Ibid., 163. In a note de Burgh cites Euripides's Heracles in *The Mad Heracles* as a superman figure, while he finds the super-state in the Melian dialogue in Thucydides, V. 84 ff.
[38] Ibid., 167.
[39] Ibid., quoting *Apol.* 38.

His conclusion went against the grain of received popular and educated opinion. Whereas Homer, like the Hebrews, had taught that the soul was the life-principle that left the body at death and then dwelt in the under-world in a state of ghostly unconsciousness; and the Orphic and Pythagorean thinkers had maintained that the soul was divine and immortal, and that it escaped from the prison of the body at death; Socrates 'identified the soul with our conscious personality, the self possessed of the capacity for rational activity, both speculative and practical, which, if duly tended, found expression both in scientific knowledge and in moral character. This was a wholly new and revolutionary doctrine',[40] and it aroused the hostility of many.

Socrates' younger contemporary, Plato, was concerned both to know the truth and to reform the conditions of life. 'Both problems,' says de Burgh, 'the speculative and the practical, found for Plato their common solution in philosophy, in a knowledge that should reveal the inner truth of the world as ideal goodness, and form the goal of individual and social action. What is this knowledge? And how can man attain to it? These are the cardinal questions of Plato's philosophy.'[41] In his *Theaetetus* he set his face against the sensation-based relativism flowing down from Protagoras, according to which every passing appearance was true to percipients in the instant of their perceiving it, and developed his doctrine of the two worlds of sensation and of thought. He argued that sense data could be known 'only by the aid of general concepts, apprehended not by the senses but by thought'.[42] In the intelligible world 'there existed in unchanging being, as substantial realities, the Forms or Ideas, the perfect archetypes, "shared in" or "imitated by" their manifold and changing copies in the world of sense. These Forms alone were the proper objects of knowledge.'[43] The supreme Form was the Form of the Good. From the *Phaedo* we learn that Plato was led to this position by his study of mathematical, moral and aesthetic judgements.

De Burgh is anxious to guard against the misunderstanding of Plato. First, the Forms are not thought-abstractions, but substances existing in an objective spiritual world independently of the thinker. Secondly, 'The Form of the Good is not identified by Plato with God. God is ... a living and active soul, the self-moving source of the motion of the heavens and ... the creator of the sensible universe, after the pattern of the Forms and in accordance with mathematical law.'[44] The identification of God with the Form of the Good, de Burgh reminds us, and the equation of the Forms with God's eternal thoughts, was the work of Neoplatonists and medieval thinkers. Thirdly, Plato does not maintain that the sense-world has no truth, but only that 'its partial truth is visible only to the mind that grasps its

---

[40] Ibid., 169.
[41] Ibid., 172.
[42] Ibid.
[43] Ibid., 173.
[44] Ibid., 174.

dependence on the Forms [which] are the true objects of scientific study'.[45] On the more practical side, Plato believes that human souls are made for cooperation, and in *The Republic* he places government in the hands of the philosopher-kings and 'preaches professorial socialism'.[46]

My principal concern in this section is not fully to expound, still less to challenge, de Burgh's exposition of the philosophers to whom he was indebted, but to indicate his responses to them. He was no mere clone of any of his philosophical predecessors. On the contrary, one of the most interesting features of his writings is his determination to think things through for himself and, as he exhorted his students, to lay his mind alongside that of other philosophers. This done, it becomes clear that in many cases his points of departure from, are as significant as his indebtedness to, those who went before. Thus, while deeply appreciative of Plato's philosophical single-mindedness and his elevation of knowledge and morality, de Burgh could not agree with those who suggested that Plato's philosophy,

> because of its other-worldliness and uncompromising idealism [was] more akin to the spirit of Christianity than to that of Greece, which looked to this life and its opportunities for the satisfaction of man's intellectual and moral aspirations. There is truth in this assertion, though the differences are more vital than the likeness. Plato's doctrine of the soul's salvation through laborious intellectual discipline, and of the spiritual direction of society by a scientific aristocracy, carry us a long way from the ideal of a spiritual kingdom to be entered, not by the wise and prudent, but in the spirit of a little child.[47]

Nevertheless, 'Whenever the spirit of man turns from the world of sense and change towards that which is eternal, unchanging, and one, whether it be in intellectual or religious contemplation, it has claimed kinship with the spirit of Plato.'[48]

To de Burgh, Aristotle was the first Platonist, and he regretted that Aristotle's way of pointing out his divergences from Plato had led some latter-day scholars to press the distinction too far. In two sentences he skilfully sums up the principal differences between the thought of Aristotle and Plato:

> Like Plato, [Aristotle] held the contemplative life to be the highest; like Plato, he held that to be most real which is most knowable, and sought reality in the eternal truths which are objects, not of sense, but of thought. But these eternal forms were not in his view denizens of a world remote from that of actual experience; they were the governing principles of the world in which he lived.[49]

---

[45] Ibid., 175.
[46] Ibid., 179.
[47] Ibid., 181.
[48] Ibid., 182.
[49] Ibid., 207.

In other words, for Aristotle the forms do not exist in a super-sensible world; if they did, they could not participate in our world or assist our knowledge of it. Concrete individuals, not universals, have substantial being. Four kinds of causes contribute to the changes that individual substances undergo: the matter, for example, a block of marble – de Burgh illustrates by reference to an artist; the motion that initiates the change: the mind, hand, and tool of the sculptor; the resulting form; and the end sought: the completed statue. In this we have an example of the teleological thrust which runs through all of Aristotle's thought. Though intensely concerned with causation and change, Aristotle does not posit an infinite regress of causes. Rather, God, pure form, is, as Plato held, the eternal unmoved first mover. This God, however, is not the creator, for that would threaten his impassibility; nor is there providence, for God is utterly apart from nature; he is 'pure self-conscious intelligence' and is both the object and subject of his perfect thought.

A further difference from Plato lies in the fact that

> Whereas Plato had insisted uncompromisingly that knowledge of absolute good was essential to true virtue and felicity, and that the goal of man's nature was realized only in a life of devotion to philosophy, Aristotle turns from the search for the Absolute to that for the specific form of human goodness, an end attainable by the good citizen of the Hellenic *Polis* within the compass of his earthly life. ... [Unlike Plato], Aristotle ... distinguishes sharply between knowing and doing, and between theoretical and practical science. He approached the problems of morals in an empirical and inductive spirit.[50]

In morals, Aristotle elevates the practical wisdom of the statesman above the theoretic wisdom of the philosopher, and in this connection the Stoics, Neoplatonists and Epicureans were indebted to him. As for Christian thought at large: 'If Christian speculation on man's ultimate felicity followed naturally in the track of Plato's other-worldliness, it drew freely on Aristotle's ethical teaching in the application of that ideal to man's life on earth.'[51] In de Burgh's estimation Aristotle's great contribution was twofold: he analysed the logic of science and showed how the several sciences were parts of a single whole. Wagging a cautionary finger, he adds:

> The formalism and artificiality of the pseudo-Aristotelian logic of the later schoolmen provoked a natural reaction among the great pioneers of science in the sixteenth and seventeenth centuries, which still cumbers the minds of many who are ignorant of the history of thought.[52] In fact, Aristotle ... would have recognized in Galileo and in Descartes the true fulfilment of his own principles

---

[50] Ibid., 212, 213.
[51] Ibid., 214.
[52] De Burgh was no less concerned to set those straight who misconstrued Plato. See, for example, his review of C. E. M. Joad, *Return to Philosophy, being a Defence of Reason,*

of scientific method. Every fresh epoch in the progress of speculative science has been inaugurated by a reform in logic.[53]

To illustrate the fact that Aristotle's influence was not entirely positive de Burgh cites his distinction between the upper heavens and the sublunary world which 'lay like a burden on astronomers and physicists till the sixteenth and seventeenth centuries'.[54]

But Plato and Aristotle were not alone in influencing subsequent thought. De Burgh cites the importance of the Stoic emphasis upon the human will, and on the assertion of both human freedom and divine providence. Philosophers as different as Descartes, Butler and Kant, he says, were attracted by Stoicism's 'moral elevation and uncompromising idealism'.[55] Indeed, Kant's dictum, 'Nothing is good without qualification but the good will', 'would have been recognized by the Stoic as his own'.[56] Nor did it escape de Burgh's notice that the apostle Paul's home town of Tarsus was a centre of Stoicism, that Paul used Stoic language when speaking of a heavenly citizenship, and that in his apology at Athens Paul quoted the words 'for we also are his offspring' (Acts 17: 28) from Cleanthes' hymn to Zeus. The Epicureans, though of less intellectual interest, served their troubled times by removing the fears of post-mortem existence which had been engendered by traditional religion, and by encouraging a life of simplicity and mutual affection.[57]

In de Burgh's view the speculative system of Plotinus represents 'the supreme effort of the Hellenic genius to realize philosophy as religion'.[58] He judges that whereas the Greek intellectual inheritance was absorbed by the Christian Platonists of Alexandria as they developed their theology, Christianity made no similar contribution to Greek philosophy: 'To minds [like that of the emperor Marcus Aurelius] trained in the atmosphere of the schools, its historic revelation and its democratic message of salvation were alike contemptible.'[59] There were themes common to Stoic and Christian ethics, such as

> the recognition of the unconditional command of duty, and of the intrinsic worth of virtue, austerity of moral discipline and the ideal of a spiritual commonwealth embracing all mankind. But the differences were more radical than the resemblances. For the Stoic, human nature was all-sufficient for salvation. His

---

an Affirmation of Values, and a Plea for Philosophy, London: Faber & Faber, 1935, in *The Hibbert Journal*, XXXIII no. 3, April, 1935, 477.

[53] LAW, 215–16.
[54] Ibid., 216 n. 2.
[55] Ibid., 219.
[56] Ibid.
[57] De Burgh refers to the praise of Epicurus in the opening lines of Books 3, 5 and 6 of the poem, *de rerum natura*, by the Roman noble, Lucretius.
[58] LAW, 338.
[59] Ibid., 342.

faith was only for the wise and strong, who could attain by effort of their own wills the mastery of their souls. It offered a gospel, not of confident hope, but of resignation and detachment. ... Its strength lay in its realization of the meaning of suffering; its weakness in its ignorance of the meaning of love.[60]

Hence the rise in the third century of Neoplatonism: 'The supersensible world, where Plato of old had sought and found true being, was conceived in more concrete form as the dwelling-place of a God who stood in intimate relationship to the souls of men. Herein lies the intrinsic interest, the distinctive appeal of Neo-Platonism.'[61] De Burgh argues that although Plotinus' philosophy seems to take Plato's distinction of the sensible and spiritual worlds as its point of departure, in fact his objective is to overcome the dualism by contending that 'The spiritual alone has true being; the sensible is no alien reality, but an image begotten by the spiritual in its likeness, in accordance with universal law.'[62] Plotinus posits a single scale of being ascending from indeterminate, non-existent matter to the One, the Good; though, as de Burgh elsewhere points out, 'The neo-Platonists ... were careful to guard against predicating "good" univocally of the One and of existing things, and even hesitated to speak of the One as "the source" of values.'[63]

In Neoplatonic doctrine, creation, 'as the act of spirit or soul, is not in time, though the timeless causality is mirrored in the sensible world under the form of a temporal history'.[64] The end for the immaterial human soul is to live 'without loss of identity, but free from the trammels of the body, in the supersensible world'.[65] That world comprises a triad of graded hypostases: the world soul, the divine mind of spirit, and the One, the Father, the Good. De Burgh importantly adds that Plotinus is not a pantheist, for to him the One 'transcends being and all that is'.[66] He sums matters up thus:

> The three *hypostases* that form the Plotinian trinity illustrate how this great thinker gathered up into an original synthesis the rich deposit of earlier philosophy. In the Soul universal we trace the divine world-soul of the Stoics, in Spirit (*Nous*) the self-thinking God of Aristotle's *Metaphysics*, in the One the Platonic Form of the Good. Plotinus came nearer than any of his precursors both to the fusion of religion and metaphysics, and to the reconciliation of the claims

---

[60] Ibid., 343.
[61] Ibid., 344–5.
[62] Ibid., 345.
[63] W. G. de Burgh, *From Morality to Religion* (hereinafter FMTR), London: Macdonald & Evans, 1938, 169 n. He cites Plotinus, *Enneads*, VI.ii.17; VI.viii.8.
[64] LAW, 347.
[65] Ibid., 348.
[66] Ibid., 350.

of the one and of the many to a place in the system of reality. He was the first to give coherent form to a philosophy of emanation.[67]

Neoplatonism fertilized Christian theology, as witness the writings of Augustine, the Greek theologians of the fourth and fifth centuries, and, later, the pseudo-Dionysius. In contrast with Christianity, however, Neoplatonism, like Stoicism, was a doctrine for an intellectual and moral aristocracy, and at its heart was the idea of the perfectibility of the human soul. This approach calls Spinoza to de Burgh's mind:

> There is something in Spinoza of the intellectual aristocrat, looking down from a far height on the vulgar follies of mankind, with pity not unmixed with scorn. This is what parts the spirit of Spinoza from that of Christianity. He was profoundly religious; but his religion was that of the intellect: alike in his life and in his doctrine, he was a saint of rationalism.[68]

By contrast, Christianity brought a gospel of redemption to the sinful soul by the grace of God. Again, whereas Neoplatonists regarded revelation as mythical, symbolic and therefore subordinate, to Christianity revelation was historic. Yet again, to Neoplatonists matter was evil, to Christians evil derived from the abuse by humans of their power of free choice. Finally, while Neoplatonism taught that human beings could 'rise in knowledge and love to his divine original', their God 'could not stoop down to man. The cause abides, in bleak aloofness, unconscious and heedless of what transpires beneath.'[69] Subscribers to this view could only view with horror the impiety of a doctrine which proclaimed the voluntary humiliation of a God who became incarnate. This doctrine 'marks the point of irreconcilable cleavage between the faith of the gospel and the religion and philosophy of Hellenism'.[70] As he further explains,

> No philosophy can be expected to demonstrate its ultimate grounds; we can claim only that they should be such as can account for facts. But the Christian belief that 'God so loved the world', though far from solving all speculative difficulties, goes a long way further towards an intelligible solution. It enables us to build on the analogy of our own experience of creative love, instead of falling back on a blind impulse of emanation.[71]

---

[67] Ibid., 351.
[68] TRP, 60.
[69] LAW, 354.
[70] Ibid., 355.
[71] Ibid., n. 1.

In this affirmation the Christian doctrine of the Trinity is presupposed, and this leads me to note a further distinction between Christianity and Neoplatonism to which de Burgh elsewhere draws our attention:

> God's simplicity is not to be understood to be exclusive of diversity, as is the simplicity of the neo-Platonic One. Christianity affirms the distinction of persons as real within the divine unity. Revelation apart, a bare unity that in no way *unifies* seems a metaphysical monstrosity; and unification implies diversity within the unifying principle. The doctrine of God's simplicity does not preclude a real distinction of characters in His nature.[72]

I may indicate the way in which de Burgh thought that Neoplatonism influenced Christian thinkers by reference to some of his remarks upon Augustine. He reminds us that while Plato's Form of Good was distinguished from the artificer-God who was not a form but a soul, the Neoplatonists identified the Good with 'the primal source of being and value. The way was thus prepared for Augustine's further identification of the Neo-Platonic One with the God of Christian theism.'[73] Again, Augustine identified the One with the God of love who 'goes forth from himself creatively, not obeying a necessary law of his being, but in an eternal act of self-diffusion, imparting to the world of his creation its measure alike of being and good'.[74] So far, so good; but in other respects de Burgh was not so inclined to think well of Augustine's teaching. For example, he presents Pelagius as voicing popular but belated Stoicism in his view that human beings may be saved by their own efforts, and declares that Augustine goes too far in rebutting him when he 'develops the doctrines of sin and grace to extremes in which catholic theology has declined to follow him'.[75] In particular, while concurring in the doctrine of prevenient grace, the Church 'refused assent to [Augustine's] abrogation of human freedom, and to the terrible doctrine that, out of a race doomed to eternal damnation, a few brands have been snatched from the burning by a *fiat* of the divine will'.[76]

'Medieval philosophy,' de Burgh declares, 'was, in no small measure, an induction from the facts of experience.'[77] Repudiating the term 'the dark ages', he instances John the Scot, John of Salisbury, Abelard and Aquinas as indicating that both the ninth and the twelfth and thirteenth centuries enjoyed a revival of learning which anticipated the later Renaissance. Indeed, modern scholarship has made it clear that 'far from uncritically accommodating a garbled and jaded

---

[72] FMTR, 212 n. He refers here to Edwyn Bevan, *Symbolism and Belief*, London: Allen & Unwin, 1938, 320.
[73] FMTR, 146.
[74] Ibid., 197.
[75] LAW, 378.
[76] Ibid.
[77] Ibid., 439.

Aristotelianism to the dogmas of the church, mediaeval thinkers essayed a reasoned synthesis of theology and metaphysics, which can claim to stand among the most impressive yet achieved in the history of thought'.[78] Whereas the Greek thinkers set out from metaphysical assumptions and 'found in philosophy the satisfaction of spiritual desire and the secret of the religious life', medieval thinkers 'started from the presuppositions of theology, and worked their way to metaphysics'.[79] Conscious of the insecurity of society and of the need for stability, thinkers from Anselm to Aquinas elevated authority as 'the rock on which alone the fabric of truth and justice could be reared',[80] whilst at the same time maintaining their claim to intellectual independence. Moreover, in de Burgh's view, 'The dominant note of the mediaeval spirit was not reverence for authority, but other-worldliness. ... To its thinkers and men of action the supersensible world possessed a reality denied to the scene of man's temporal pilgrimage.'[81]

I shall have occasion to return to Aquinas and other medieval thinkers when I come to the principal themes in de Burgh's philosophical writings, but since my purpose in this section of the chapter is to outline his relationship to major trends in his intellectual inheritance, it will not be out of place to quote his summary judgement upon scholasticism as a whole. The great scholastics, he writes,

> set themselves to demarcate ... the respective provinces of faith and reason, qualifying the distinction so far as to leave room (1) for a tract of common ground, and (2) for the rights of reason to essay a progressive clarification – especially in the refutation of objections – to truths of revelation. This demarcation proved in the event to be the first step towards the restriction of reason to scientific inference, and the relegation of faith to non-rational emotion. ... Henceforward science could go freely on its proper task of exploration of the creaturely, untrammelled by theological intrusion; while truths revealed to faith were reserved for the theologian, reason being restricted to the ancillary function of developing inferentially the implications of the faith and of defending them by positive or negative arguments against the sophistical objections of unbelievers.[82]

De Burgh is convinced that the rival claims of reason and faith can be harmonized only if belief in a religious revelation can be shown to be reasonable. To show that this was indeed the case was the principal objective of de Burgh's philosophical endeavour, as we shall see.

---

[78] Ibid., 445.
[79] Ibid., 445–6.
[80] Ibid., 448.
[81] Ibid.
[82] LR, 93, 123.

II

Enough has been said to indicate the most formative aspects of de Burgh's intellectual inheritance. Before coming to his major philosophical themes we shall do well to consider his views on the intellectual environment and educational challenges of his day. These are of interest in their own right, and they also reveal the degree to which he had processed what thinkers from Socrates to the medievals had given him. I use the verb 'processed' advisedly, for de Burgh believed that intellectual progress was not made 'by mere accretion of new to old; the process is one of interpretation, in which new and old alike are modified'.[83]

When seeking to describe de Burgh's approach to life and philosophy the adjective which most quickly comes to mind is 'expansive'. I do not mean by this that he was wantonly hospitable to ideas and attitudes whencesoever they came: this he certainly was not. He was, however, stoutly opposed to what he saw as the damaging narrowness of vision which resulted from some scientific, philosophical and humanistic doctrines. Let us consider each of these in turn.

De Burgh was by no means unimpressed by the advances made through scientific research, experiment and application. 'The practical applications of science', he said, 'to the conditions of human life have, in the last few generations, revolutionised the face of nature and the whole order of social intercourse.'[84] Nevertheless, in January 1940, as World War II was dangerously escalating, he published the first of a two-part article entitled, 'Sources of present world-trouble.' The subtitle is, 'The abuse of knowledge'; the second part, to which I shall come shortly, is subtitled, 'The idol of humanism.' De Burgh sets out from Plato, who insisted that the state would be ruined unless those charged with ruling it grasped the vision of 'the source of all being and value, the Idea or Form of the Good'.[85] Endorsing Plato's conviction, de Burgh fears that 'The advance of modern science has outstripped man's competence to make right use of it.'[86] The development of moral character has not kept pace with the increase in knowledge. The benefits flowing from the Renaissance notwithstanding, de Burgh cautions that

> The progress has been within a determinate field of knowledge, that of the sciences of man and nature. It may well be that the thinkers and poets and saints of the Middle Ages – Bernard and Anselm, Dante and Aquinas – possessed a deeper knowledge of God and of the things pertaining to God's service than any save a few of the philosophers and theologians of the last four hundred years.[87]

---

[83] LAW, 505, n. 1.

[84] W. G. de Burgh, 'Sources of present world-trouble. I. The abuse of knowledge,' *The Hibbert Journal*, XXXVIII no. 2, January 1940, 198.

[85] Ibid., 196.

[86] Ibid., 197.

[87] Ibid., 197–8.

In other words, there has not been progress on all fronts, and de Burgh is especially concerned about the neglect or banishment of the moral-*cum*-spiritual dimension:

> All human knowledge and all human desire take their origin perforce from objects of sense-perception; prolonged effort of thought and will is needed, if man is to rise above what is obviously on a level with his capacities, so as to know and desire the spiritual world which lies beyond.[88]

In this sentence we have a further clue to de Burgh's constructive method. It is not only that he wishes to repudiate the restriction of reason to ratiocination so that important dimensions of experience and life are not omitted; it is also that because of his determination to stick to his philosophical last and refrain from apologetics, and still more from theology, he does not follow through to a detailed discussion of his most cherished convictions, of which he nevertheless leaves us numerous hints. We have already seen, for example, that he found Neoplatonism wanting because it could not accommodate a God who comes humbly to human beings in the person of his incarnate Son. But there is nothing of this gracious resource in the sentence just quoted; it has a 'Pelagian' ring, concerned exclusively as it is with *our* effort of thought and will.

How does de Burgh account for the omission by scientists of what he regards as of paramount importance? We recall his view that Aquinas, for all his insight, nevertheless sowed the seed which others later exploited when he distinguished between natural and revealed knowledge. Some were able to find reasons for dispensing with the latter. But Cartesianism was the proximate cause of the bifurcation:

> The extrusion of mind from physical Nature and the adoption, in the interest of physics, of the Cartesian doctrine of two mutually exclusive substances [mind and matter] rendered hopeless any explanation of the Mind-body relations. The opinion of leading scientists wavered, then as now, between the frank avowal of Materialism, consciousness being relegated to the paradoxical status of an epi-phenomenon, incidental to physical process; and Subjective Idealism, a metaphysical doctrine that in effect reduced the physical to terms of mind (ideas). The former alternative drew support from its acceptance of a physiological explanation of sense perception.[89]

In this connection de Burgh testified as follows:

> I cannot follow Hume or his modern disciples in the view that our knowledge is founded on isolated sense-data, private to the sentient individual and destitute of intrinsic causal connexion. What is apprehended in perception from the outset

---

[88] Ibid., 199.
[89] LR, 40.

is an objective spatio-temporal-causal continuum, from which the so-called *sensa* are detached by an artificial process of abstraction. I hold with Whitehead that awareness of self and awareness of an external world are present, though obscurely, in the simplest act of perception.[90]

It comes as no surprise, therefore, to find that he was no more satisfied by 'Locke's strange doctrine that an idea is the object of the mind when it thinks'.[91] During the Enlightenment, de Burgh remarks, 'Science went forward on its way, trusting in its chosen instruments of mathematical deduction and empirical induction, and asking no questions as to the legitimacy of this amazing marriage.'[92] Small wonder that a number of significant dimensions of life cannot be accommodated within this abstractive method:

> The truth is that religion – and the same applies to morality, art, and all forms of spiritual activity – cannot be understood on the methods of the natural sciences. ... In the sciences 'understanding' is achieved by piecemeal analysis of the object into its constituent factors, each of which is determined by causal antecedents. But a religion is no an aggregate of phenomena, of beliefs and actions, which can be viewed as objects from the outside. It is a life, expressive of a man's entire personality; a life, moreover, that has its source and growth in the experience of a society. It can only be understood by being lived, *i.e.* enjoyed inwardly by a conscious subject.[93]

As he ponders the general approach of scientists in his own day, de Burgh imagines a Greek thinker *redivivus*. To such a person

> the efforts of science, to remould nature after our heart's desire, and of philosophy, to interpret reality as relative, through and through, to human mind; would appear to his astonished vision as the wild audacity of *hubris*. Where [he would ask] lies the spiritual goal of all this striving, the unity of purpose that gives direction and meaning to man's hustling enterprise? He would point in answer ... beyond the realm of becoming to that of being, beyond the temporal to the eternal, beyond the many to the one. *Theoria*, as well as *praxis*, ... is

---

[90] Ibid., 25.

[91] W. G. de Burgh, review of Susan K. Langer, *Philosophy in a New Key*, in *The Hibbert Journal*, XLII no. 2, January 1944, 184.

[92] Idem, *Knowledge of the Individual* (hereinafter KI), London: OUP, 1939, 5.

[93] Idem, review of Edward Westermarck, *Christianity and Morals*, in *Mind*, NS, XLIX, January 1940, 83. The burden of de Burgh's complaint against this able book is that Westermarck cannot account for, and value, the facts of Christian experience on his naturalistic principles. He concludes (p. 84) that if Westermarck 'fails to carry conviction, it is hardly likely that any other champion of naturalism will achieve success'.

essential to enduring satisfaction. Human nature is two-sided; man's effort is both to know things as they are and to discharge his moral obligations.[94]

Scientists who ignore this truth are more than ill-advised; by reason of the immoral uses to which their creations may be put, they can be positively dangerous. In captivity to their narrow field of vision, scientists can be also be culpably ignorant. For example,

> [M]uch baneful prejudice against religion would have been avoided if its critics from the side of science had been careful in the past to observe these two precautions: (1) to direct their weapons against the authoritative exponents of Christianity instead of against its popular travesty, and (2) to cast the beam of anthropomorphism (*e.g.*, in certain interpretations of natural law) out of their own eyes before cavilling at the motes in the eyes of their theological opponents. ... Even to-day, scientists and philosophers show themselves very imperfectly instructed in the nature of the beliefs they hold up for reprobation. ... Yet criticism of religious doctrine calls, as truly as does criticism of scientific theories, for expert knowledge and a first-hand study of the authoritative evidence.[95]

We may note in passing that in the view of the faithful Anglican, de Burgh, the official representatives of the Churches were not best placed to remedy the current intellectual malaise. On the contrary, 'The leaders both of Anglicanism and of nonconformity in this country are not conspicuous examples of intellectual enlightenment. Their qualifications lie rather in their capacity for administration and in the integrity of their Christian life.'[96] In this connection he recalls Lord Haldane's remark concerning two eminent prelates who had visited him: 'they might have been railway magnates'.[97]

When he wrote his first book during World War I, de Burgh was able to welcome a certain *rapprochement* between metaphysics and the physical sciences which gave him some hope that the broken unity of knowledge might be restored. He instanced the coalescence of philosophy and mathematical physics in the work of Bertrand Russell, Samuel Alexander, A. N. Whitehead and Lord Haldane, and

---

[94] LAW, 520.

[95] FMTR, 168 n. 280. Although works by prejudiced scientists may currently be found in heaps in our major book chains, it must in fairness be stated that scientists are not alone in exhibiting such prejudice. Consider, for example, John Stuart Mill, who was not inhibited by the fact that he was not the most competent critic of Christianity (he read the New Testament, and confessed to having read one theological work right through: *On Nature and Grace*, by the Anglican-turned Roman Catholic, W. G. Ward). See Alan P. F. Sell, *Mill on God. The Pervasiveness and Elusiveness of Mill's Religious Thought*, Aldershot: Ashgate, 2004, 6, 179.

[96] TRP, 244.

[97] Ibid., n. 244.

the biological-, physiological- and psychological-*cum*-philosophical writings of Arthur Eddington, James Jeans and Bergson. 'Even Signor Croce,' he continues, 'who insists uncompromisingly on the severance between [philosophy and science], affirms the identity of philosophy and history (i.e. of ideal value and temporal happenings). Yet the ghost of the distinction between the "eternal truths" of mathematics and "matters of fact" (i.e. between values and events) still haunts the sanctuaries (or, shall we say, the graveyards?) of metaphysics.'[98]

With the passage of time, de Burgh's optimism was tempered by changing attitudes among philosophers. Thus, for example, when in 1935 he came to review Russell's book, *In Praise of Idleness*, he was by no means as sanguine as he had been 20 years earlier. Russell here supposed that truth and knowledge are not to be found in religion, metaphysics, or in objects of humanity's emotional aspiration, but in science alone. He upholds the reasoned appeal 'to a universal and impersonal standard of truth', but de Burgh queries whether the arguments of science are completely valid. Later in his book Russell himself endorses the relativity of scientific knowledge, which leads de Burgh to ask how he would distinguish between truth and superstition? 'Can it be', he asks, 'that science, as well as religion and philosophy, devours its own children?' He ends in exhortatory mode: 'If [Russell] would but grapple seriously with this problem of scientific truth, and, speaking no longer with two voices, justify the claim of science to yield knowledge, which, for all its relativity, is yet objective and entitled to the name, he would be rendering fitting service to his generation, service worthy of his great powers of mind.'[99]

But the philosophers who concerned de Burgh most were the logical positivists, whose dogma required, and whose method assumed, the severance of genuinely scientific discourse from metaphysical, aesthetic, ethical and religious language. He levels a number of charges against the positivistic doctrine that only those propositions are meaningful which are in principle capable of empirical verification, or are analytic, and that, accordingly, propositions concerning God's existence, or value judgements, since they fall outside the rubric, are emotive expressions that can be neither true nor false. First, the doctrine runs counter to the facts, for 'Cognition, will and feeling ... are integrated, in varying measure, in every human experience', and this is 'markedly the case in religion'.[100] Thus, for example, 'who can deny that the artist achieves a synthesis of the manifold, or that his synthesis is, in the literal sense, intelligible?'[101] Secondly, the positivistic principle does not conform to its own prescription. 'What verification,' he asks, 'is possible, by sense or by introspection, of the meaninglessness of those sentences which are *ex hypothesi* incapable of verification? Yet the Principle pronounces

---

[98] LAW, 506.
[99] W. G. de Burgh, review of B. Russell, *In Praise of Idleness, and Other Essays*, in *The Hibbert Journal*, XXXIV no. 4, July 1936, 629.
[100] TRP, 37; cf. 242; FMTR, 31.
[101] LR, 67.

them to be meaningless.'[102] If the principle is defended as a linguistic convention which needs no verification, 'with what right can an arbitrary "stipulation" masquerade as a criterion of truth? A truth that rests on an arbitrary criterion is no "truth" at all.'[103] Thirdly, as to A. J. Ayer's 'weak' sense of verifiability, according to which a proposition is verifiable if 'it is possible for experience to render it probable', or if any observations 'are relevant to the determination of its truth or falsehood', the outcome is that 'The issue is not one of demonstrative evidence, but, as in all matters of fact, of probability.'[104] Not surprisingly, although he found some inadequacies in her work, de Burgh applauded Susan Langer for launching 'a protest against the narrow view of reason to which the Logical Analysts (and many other contemporary thinkers on "the meaning of meaning") are still in bondage'.[105]

Not content with scoring particular points against logical positivists and others in the linguistic analytical camp(s), de Burgh, in head-masterly fashion, held forth against the inadequate education of some of his fellow professional philosophers:

> It is ... a matter for regret that so few contemporary students of philosophy approach the subject with a preparation of historical training. If, for instance, the advocates of Logical Positivism had been so prepared, they would surely have been less inclined to limit verifiability to what the physicist intends by that term in the laboratory, and more inclined to admit the claim of much else that is important, not only for living, but for living *well*, instead of ruling it out of the realm of rational knowledge as the offspring of irrational emotion. Humanistic studies, and history in particular, furnish the needed complement to the sciences.[106]

De Burgh here echoes Aristotle's doctrine that the human being's end is not simply to live, but to live well: that is, to realize his or her highest promise. It is certainly not to succumb to the utilitarian doctrine that the measure of happiness is material prosperity.[107] As he drily remarks, 'If earthly happiness were man's proper end, the constitution of nature is very ill-adapted for its attainment.'[108]

It comes as no surprise that de Burgh was by no means content with all that travelled under the banner of 'humanism'. From the Renaissance there flowed a humanism that elevated the individual, and the appeal to private judgement

---

[102] Ibid., 101.

[103] Ibid.

[104] Ibid., 102, quoting A. J. Ayer, *Language, Truth and Logic*, London: Gollancz, 1936, 22–3, 26.

[105] W. G. de Burgh, review of *Philosophy in a New Key*, 183.

[106] LR, 39.

[107] LAW, 502–3.

[108] W. G. de Burgh, 'Sources of present world-trouble. II. The idol of humanism,' *The Hibbert Journal*, XXXVIII no. 3, April 1940, 312.

against the Church's authority – an appeal which is problematic, for '"Private judgment" is strictly a contradiction in terms; if it be "judgment", it is not merely mine, but claims universal validity as truth.'[109] Descartes made the consciousness of the individual the basis of metaphysical construction, and reason was construed (narrowly) on mathematical and scientific lines as 'the faculty of logical ratiocination, which recognizes only "clear and distinct" concepts as proportions, relegating all thinking that is vague, shadowy, and mysterious, to the limbo of irrational feeling and imagination'.[110] Moreover, as previously indicated, this world replaced the other world as the focus of attention. By the nineteenth century Comte was found positing his religion of humanity; anthropocentrism was rife in many quarters, and there was 'a touching confidence in the inborn excellence of human nature, in the perfectibility of man, and in the possibility of unlimited progress'.[111] The obstacle to these was no longer original sin, but the remediable flaws in societal organization. In all of this the objective was happiness construed as economic welfare. De Burgh's case is that this creed neither delivered what it promised, nor was its theoretical basis adequate. Hence his rhetorical question expecting the answer 'No!': 'That there had been progress in knowledge, and in the power that knowledge gives, is beyond dispute, but has there been a corresponding progress in morality?'[112] We have totalitarian states and war – indeed, 'The bane of secularist humanism, and its *reductio ad absurdum*, is the appalling inhumanity of its performance.'[113] Again, we have the evils done to working people through mechanization, and through the ever-accelerating pace of life. Regrettably,

> The passion for movement has even invaded ... religion; churches would be crowded if the preacher taught belief in a suffering and striving God who looked to men for help in His effort for victory over evil. The older views of God as without variability or shadow of turning, and of man's heart as restless until they rest in Him, are no longer congenial to the taste of the modern world.[114]

---

[109] LAW, 490 n. 1.

[110] Ibid., 555.

[111] Ibid. It should be noted that LAW 553–77 comprise Appendix Three which, together with the first two appendices, was added to the book by de Burgh at the end of his life, and was first published in the 1947 edition of the book. In Appendix Three he drew upon the two-part essay, 'Sources of present world-trouble' referred to above. Cf. also TRP, 191–221.

[112] Ibid., 559.

[113] Ibid., 573.

[114] Ibid., 562–3. There were examples of genial liberalism in theology and churchly life – as witness hymns celebrating the fact that *we* are bringing in the Kingdom (which, in fact, is always God's gift).

'The religion that sets its trust in man', he concludes, 'can only be conquered by a religion that sets its trust in God.'[115] The humanistic concepts of fraternity and personality find their true place within a theocentric world-view; severed from that 'they are robbed of all intelligible meaning'.[116]

Anyone who suggested that theocentric humanism which is concerned with the human being's true end, and secular humanism are varieties of the same species, would earn de Burgh's swift rebuke:

> [I]t is an error to regard these two types of humanism, the anthropocentric and the theocentric, as co-ordinate species of a common genus. The position I am maintaining is rather that a secular humanism, since it is grounded on [sic] a mutilation of our nature and experience, is not to be regarded as humanism, but as a travesty of humanism; and that integration with a theocentric world-view, as in a Christian philosophy, is requisite even for the satisfaction of man's cultural aspirations.[117]

De Burgh concludes his reflections on humanism, and spirals back to his intellectual and religious roots, thus:

> Whereas the Platonist taught salvation by philosophical wisdom and the Stoic salvation by self-sufficiency rooted in strength and will, the Christian preached the gospel of redemption through the Incarnate Christ. ... The gulf here is immeasurable. Of the love of God for His creation, and of the consequent obligations upon man to love God with his whole heart and his neighbour as himself, Greek philosophy knew nothing. These are revealed truths inaccessible to unaided reason; but if we bear firmly in mind that the grace which perfects is *praeter*, not *contra*, *naturam*, we can understand how a Christian philosophy, and it alone, enables man to realize his human capacities in full measure as a freeman of an other-worldly commonwealth.[118]

There can be no question that his desire to heal the breach between scientific and other reductionisms and the vision of the good life, was De Burgh's motivating inspiration as he fulfilled with distinction his vocation as a teacher of philosophy. He was interested in a humane education in the broadest sense. He found it ironic that there should be antagonism over the claims of a classical *versus* a scientific education, since the roots of modern science had been fertilized by 'the spirit of Hellenism'[119] with its faith in reason. To the same source humanity owed the

---

[115] Ibid., 565.
[116] Ibid., 571.
[117] Ibid., 575.
[118] Ibid., 576–7; cf. de Burgh's review of Frederick Copleston, *Friedrich Nietzsche, Philosopher of Culture*, in *The Hibbert Journal*, XLI no. 4, July 1943, 384.
[119] LAW, 497.

recovery of 'the title-deeds of its birthright of free thought. The modern world needs, at times, a salutary reminder, that its enjoyment of this liberty is due to those who had learnt their secret from the first champions of reason, and had lit their torches at the ever-burning heath-fires of ancient Greece.'[120] Not, indeed, that humanity's inheritance is entirely of the intellectualist sort: art and religion as well as science and philosophy have had their roots nourished in the soil of ancient Greece; and de Burgh clearly spoke for himself when he wrote, 'No one who has passed his youth under the shadow of some noble cathedral or within the walls of one of our ancient colleges will [deny] the subtle and unconscious influence of the arts on the character and mind of man.'[121]

Lest such words give the impression of a sentimental dreamer, I hasten to recall de Burgh's highly practical, indeed formative, interest in the establishment and development of the University of Reading. He knew quite well that not all youths live in the shadow of noble cathedrals or attend ancient colleges; he had, after all, spent the first years of his working life in the East End of London, educating those who acquired their learning in their spare time. He fully understood the need for the democratization of education, and in this connection he compared modern journalists such as Bernard Shaw and H. G. Wells with the Sophists, since both were concerned to deepen the thought of the populace. 'The problem with present-day education,' he declared, 'is to do for the many what the Sophists claimed to do for the few.'[122] No one knew better than he what a challenge this was: 'we educate the workers; but the very immensity of the task forces us to mechanize the education'.[123] This was but one example of widespread standardization in life – 'even that of a university professor'.[124] Again, at a time when 'practical' has come to mean 'vocational', the burgeoning of subjects of the latter kind, the objective of which is 'earning a material livelihood', inclines many to forget that 'without friendship, morality, religion, and art, life would not for a moment be worth living. The Greeks of ancient days were wiser. They saw clearly that education, to be practical, must take account of these higher humanistic interests.'[125] Warming further to his theme, de Burgh recommends that 'The teacher of to-day has more to learn from the pages of the *Republic* than from all our modern text-books of pedagogy, English, German, American, put together' – as which point he adds the crushing footnote: 'The literature of pedagogy, extending over more than 2,000

---

[120] Ibid.
[121] Ibid., 147, cf. 511.
[122] Ibid., 163 n.
[123] Ibid., 561.
[124] Ibid. What would de Burgh have made of the overtaking of higher education by a managerialism which talks about 'inputs' and 'measurable outputs', 'targets', and of students as 'customers' to whom courses are 'delivered'? I think I can guess.
[125] Ibid., 518.

years, and multiplying to an appalling degree at the present day, contains some half-dozen or so of works that are worth reading.'[126]

Not, indeed, that all was well with Classics. In de Burgh's view the discipline had been misused by its advocates and maligned by its foes.

> Popular opinion ... opposes classical to modern studies, and a scientific to a humanistic ideal of education. This prejudice is mainly due to the facts that in the generations following on from the Renaissance a training in Greek and Latin came to mean the study of philology rather than of literature, history, and thought, and that the ideal set by the great humanists was tarnished with pedantry and antiquarianism. The efforts of teachers were frequently confined to making their pupils compose slavish imitations of classical models.[127]

Nor has the history of thought received the attention that was its due:

> [I]t is not so long ago that teachers were wont to pilot their classes through the Greek philosophy as far as Aristotle, and then, after a cursory reference to the Stoics and Epicureans, stride with seven-league boots over some two thousand years of the life of the human spirit, to plunge with Descartes into the problems of modern metaphysics. The Neo-Platonists and the mediaeval doctors alike were dismissed with a few contemptuous generalities about mysticism, credulity, and superstition. The student left the university, itself a creation of the mediaeval genius, hardly aware of the bare names of Plotinus or Aquinas. Abelard was known only as the hero of Pope's version of the letters of Eloisa. The schoolmen were branded as sciolists who travestied Aristotle's logic and wrangled in futile syllogisms over the problem of universals ...[128]

Lest there be any misunderstanding, it must be emphasized that nothing was viewed with more horror by de Burgh than what he called 'a sterile reversion to the past'. In no uncertain terms he declared, for example, that '"Back to Aquinas," in any sense other than *reculer pour mieux sauter*, is, both for philosophy and for religion, a counsel not of perfection, but of despair.'[129] Indeed, he welcomed the dissolution of the medieval harmony between religion and philosophy because it 'secured liberty of development for both alike'.[130] His recourse to the philosophical heritage was with a view both to challenging the narrowing of vision on the part of many scientists, philosophers and secular humanists which he deplored, and to adumbrating the expansive nature of the education he favoured. Few have held to

---

[126] Ibid.
[127] Ibid., 517.
[128] Ibid., 444.
[129] TRP, 23.
[130] Ibid.

their ideals so firmly or, to recall the comment of one of his students, *preached* them so ardently. It remains to review de Burgh's principal philosophical positions.

III

A close study of de Burgh's works leads to the inescapable conclusion that it would be futile to discuss his ideas in relation to the chronological sequence of his books, for his major doctrines reverberate throughout the entire corpus. This being so, with a view to expounding his argument without interruption, I shall reserve my comments on his work to the concluding section of this chapter.

De Burgh went in quest of the foundations of a religious philosophy in which reason, faith and history would be accorded their due places, and in which the noblest insights and inspirations of morality would find their fulfilment. My phrase 'in quest of the foundations' is important if we would properly understand de Burgh's objective. In the preface to *Towards a Religious Philosophy* he writes, consistently with the first word in his title and, no doubt, remembering his role as philosopher, not apologist or theologian, 'No attempt has been made in these pages to construct a religious philosophy. These studies are rather of the nature of *Prolegomena* to its establishment. They represent different lines of advance towards a common goal.'[131] The lines of advance are along the paths of rationality and morality: reason being understood more broadly than is frequently the case, and morality being shown to lead to, and to be fulfilled by, religion. I shall consider each of these in turn. As we proceed, what might be taken as de Burgh's philosophical *credo* – a *credo* which sets him apart from many of the self-styled 'humble' (though, as he would have thought, stunted) linguistic analysts of his day – rings in our ears: 'Man is, above all things, a metaphysical, that is, and ideal-forming, animal; he seeks for reason everywhere, in history as in nature, and his thirst will not be quenched until he find it.'[132] In the opening pages of *Towards a Religious Philosophy* de Burgh nails his colours to the mast in uncompromising terms:

> [R]eason must cover more than inferential reasoning. The methods of inference are not sovereign, but manifestly instrumental; they furnish the scaffolding for the mind's ascent, but not the goal of its endeavour. ... [R]eason precludes its limitation to processes of logical inference. Its proper end is to know the universe as a single harmonious system. ... It seems to be a paradox of the intellect, that it cannot be satisfied in what satisfies the intellectual alone. ... Unless the claims of man's practical and emotional nature, as well as those of the intellect, found satisfaction, the vision would remain discordant *for the intellect*.[133]

---

[131] Ibid., vi.
[132] LAW, 499. De Burgh's care with the subjunctive is to be noted, and applauded.
[133] TRP, 1, 2.

In a word, de Burgh proposes that 'reason' be given a wider meaning than Aristotle's *nous*, the Scholastics' *intellectus*, or the post-Kantian idealists' *Vernunft*. To him, 'the activity of reason is coterminous with that of thought', and 'reason is active in all conscious apprehension of unity in difference or of difference in unity, whether the order apprehended be that of a mathematical formula, of a law of nature, of an historical pattern, of an ethical principle, of an aesthetic harmony, or of God's immanent purposes in the world of his creation'.[134] Reason does more than apprehend a given reality; it gives 'form and intelligible structure' to 'materials hitherto unsystematized, as is the case in moral action or in the production of a work of art'.[135] Furthermore, 'In every instance, the outcome, whether in *theoria* or in *praxis*, is knowledge; reason, at every stage of its development, is the power to grasp truth.'[136] In maintaining this position de Burgh was in entire accord with his friend, G. Dawes Hicks, whose Hibbert Lectures he reviewed. He quotes Hicks's view that reason is an activity 'involved in all our experiences, and as at the root of all intelligent belief. ... Intellectual activity may ... degenerate into a cold and merely logical process of ratiocination, that seeks to pass all things in heaven and earth through the sieve of its narrow formulae of elimination or excision; but to suffer this logic-chopping faculty, as Carlyle called it, to usurp the name of reason, is simply to trifle with ordinary linguistic usage.'[137]

On more than one occasion de Burgh cites Descartes as the fountainhead of that narrowing of reason that he so deeply regrets, and which he finds flowing down to his own day in the Gifford lectures of Edwyn Bevan.[138] He welcomes the way in which Bergson and William James 'raised the banner of revolt against intellectualism'. Unfortunately, however, 'instead of enlarging the scope of rational activity, they appealed to intuition, as to non-rational powers, distinct from intelligence – *i.e.*, they retained the traditional limitation of intellect and reason to the field of logical inference [thereby handing] over the newly-acquired territory to the supra-rational'.[139]

Positively, de Burgh stands for the coalescence of reason, intuition and faith in the attainment of knowledge.[140] By so doing he is able to critique both those who

---

[134] KI, 7.

[135] Ibid.

[136] Ibid.

[137] W. G. de Burgh, review of Hicks's 'most able and impressive work', *The Philosophical Bases of Theism*, London: Allen & Unwin, 1937, in *Mind*, NS, XLVII, January 1938, 80–81. He quotes op. cit., 159, 129.

[138] See his review of E. Bevan, *Symbolism and Belief*, in *The Hibbert Journal*, XXXVII no. 1, October 1938, 170–71.

[139] FMTR, 302.

[140] He thought, for example, that 'A fuller recognition that faith is integral to reason, not only in religion but in *all* knowledge, would ... have led [Étienne] Gilson to a juster appreciation of Augustine's position in the history of Christian philosophy.' See his review of Gilson's *God and Philosophy*, in *Mind*, LI, July 1942, 280.

unduly narrowed reason's scope and those who so exalted it as to misunderstand the human being's epistemological status *vis-à-vis* reality. He exemplifies the former pitfall by reference to the Arians, who 'defined the relationship of the Son to the Father in terms of the narrow, formal logic which has proved the bugbear of serious metaphysics in every age';[141] while the latter is instanced in Plato's conviction that the philosopher may attain in this life to the direct vision of the absolute reality – a view shared by later disciples of Hegel, and by Spinoza, who declared that 'The human mind has adequate knowledge of the infinite and eternal essence of God.'[142] De Burgh is with the medievals in their denial of the truth of Spinoza's proposition on the ground that the human being

> is only enabled – as Aquinas and Kant alike insist – to apprehend intelligible objects mediately, from a basis of sense-perception. This is why human knowledge is always proximate, admitting of degrees. It is never infallible; not even in the judgments of pure mathematics, which (*pace* the Positivists) are not tautologous, nor in awareness of *sensa* which (*pace* the Positivists) are products of reflective abstraction operating on objects of sense-perception.[143]

The goal of knowledge, however imperfectly attained, remains 'the perfected apprehension, *uno intuiti*, of the one in the many, the many in the one, and of the one and many alike as good. ... We have to recover this enlarged outlook, if philosophy, and the world to which it speaks its message, are to be rescued from unreason.'[144]

As already hinted, this recovery can only come about if due place is accorded to intuition and faith. Let it be understood that this is not the plea of a 'fuzzy' philosopher who wishes to sweep everything into the equation in order to shore up emotional commitments or irrational prejudices. It is, in fact, the view of one who declared that 'What troubles me about the modern world is its mistrust of intellect.'[145] The roots of this mistrust lie in philosophy's past, and even Aquinas was implicated in the downgrade; for in relation to his distinction between reason and faith, 'it never occurred to him to ask, whether faith (and other non-logical operations) was not integral to all rational processes, whether any exercise of rational activity was possible, even in metaphysics and the sciences, without an act of rational faith'.[146] The moral is that if such a one as de Burgh, so committed to reasonableness, invokes intuition and faith, it behoves us to give his argument more than a passing glance. He continues, 'Reasoning apart from intuition is empty;

---

[141] LAW, 370.
[142] LR, 22. De Burgh quotes Spinoza's *Ethics*, II, 47.
[143] Ibid.
[144] FMTR, 302.
[145] TRP, 236.
[146] LAW, 461; cf. TRP, 112.

intuition apart from reasoning is blind. All knowledge implies their union.'[147] He follows Bergson, whom he construes as teaching that intuition is not a blind instinct but, as Butler saw, 'a sentiment of the understanding' and 'a perception of the heart';[148] and he proceeds at once to invoke Pascal, who wrote that

> *le coeur a ses raisons que la raison ne connait point*, illustrating in a single phrase the ambiguity of the term; for him, the heart, like Kant's Practical Reason, was an organ of vision ... giving knowledge of first principles and of God. Reason, taken in its full breadth of meaning is active in all knowing, be it intuitive, or discursive, of facts or value, of objects within the sensible world or beyond it. Its activity is displayed wherever the mind grasps truth, in moral experience, in art, in religion, as well as in science and philosophy; and in the vision not only of truth, but of good.[149]

All of which is to say that inference is ancillary to intuition: we cannot satisfactorily proceed from the part to the whole. We first have intuitive awareness of a whole that defies analytical dissection. And the ideal consummation when analysis has done its work is again intuitive knowledge, the synthetic vision of a totality that is more than the aggregate of its constituents. The inferential function of reason is subordinate to the intuitive all along the line. The root of the error, alike of Descartes and his rationalist disciples, and of Hume's empiricism, lay in their endeavour to interpret the mind's growth in knowledge on the principle of mechanical composition that had proved so amazingly fruitful in the physical sciences. ... Such a method of explanation does violence to the actual nature of the thinking process which is conditioned from the outset by an indeterminate and schematic apprehension of the whole.[150]

In this apprehension reason and faith are joined. De Burgh notes that throughout the history of philosophy there has been the desire 'to posit a unifying principle that transcends logical mediation'.[151] He cites the One of Neoplatonism, and the infinite substance of Spinoza as examples of this, in that such objects are 'apprehensible by no mere discursive process, but by an *amor intellectualis* that is an act at once of reason and faith'.[152] The mutual interaction of faith and reason is such that it makes sense to speak of a faith of reason. That is to say, we may think both in terms of *fides quaerens intellectum* and also of *intellectus quaerens fidem*. Reason seeks understanding, but calls upon faith in the process of so doing.[153]

---

[147] Ibid.
[148] Ibid., 245.
[149] Ibid., 245–6.
[150] LR, 15–16.
[151] TRP, 100.
[152] Ibid.
[153] See W. G. de Burgh, 'Intelligence in quest of faith,' *The Hibbert Journal*, XL no. 3, April 1942, 221; cf. LR, 94.

Not the least reason for the attractiveness of the enlarged view of reason to de Burgh is that it 'carries us back, behind the narrow channel of Cartesian rationalism, to the great traditions alike of Jewish-Christian and of Hellenic thought'.[154] He deeply regrets that 'For four centuries reason and faith have been drifting apart, on roads that lead logically, the one to a philosophy of mind and nature that negates the claims of the supernatural, the other to a religious supernaturalism that negates the claims of mind and nature.'[155]

While, as we have already seen, logical positivists and analytical empiricists would by no means have assented to de Burgh's position, he was not without some allies in swimming against the philosophical tide. E. P. Dickie expressed his concurrence with de Burgh's broadening of the scope of reason;[156] N. H. G. Robinson welcomed his 'impressive and sustained attack against the limitation of reason "to the analytic procedure of logical inference"'.[157] H. P. Owen found de Burgh's statement of his position 'valuable';[158] and A. E. Taylor spoke for them all:

> The point which [de Burgh] ... makes with exceptional clarity, and on which I confess I completely sympathize with him, is that the whole position [regarding religion as a possible source of genuine knowledge] is bound up with the admission that truth, in the widest sense of the word, is not confined to the logical propositional form; there is a wider sense of the word in which we can speak of the truth not only of a religious insight, but of that of sense-perception or of moral divination or of aesthetic intuition.[159]

It is not, however, simply the case that in de Burgh's view our understanding of reason needs to be broadened; reason needs to be supplemented by divine revelation. On its own it will take us only so far. This comes out in de Burgh's discussions of natural theology and theism. As to the former, by 'natural theology' de Burgh does not mean a common factor found in all religions, for 'That would leave us, as it left Spinoza, with a code of abstract ethical precepts *plus* belief in the existence of a yet more abstract Deity.'[160] Rather, 'The nerve of the distinction between Natural and Revealed Theology lies in the fact ... that the latter is imparted directly, in a special communication, by God Himself.'[161] I shall return to revelation shortly, but first I must make clear de Burgh's view that natural theology, though insufficient,

---

[154] TRP, 248.

[155] FMTR, 286.

[156] E. P. Dickie, *Revelation and Response*, Edinburgh: T. & T. Clark, 1938, 77 n.; cf. idem, *God Is Light*, London: Hodder and Stoughton, 1953, 192–4.

[157] N. H. G. Robinson, *Faith and Duty*, London: Gollancz, 1950, 2 n.

[158] H. P. Owen, *The Christian Knowledge of God*, London: The Athlone Press, 1969, 17.

[159] A. E. Taylor, 'William George de Burgh', 386.

[160] LR, 112.

[161] Ibid., 113.

is not redundant. It prepares the way for revelation, and it confirms beliefs already accepted on the authority of divine revelation.

The theistic arguments comprise endeavours to offer such confirmation. In de Burgh's opinion, however, they 'either fail as proofs, or in what they prove, conclude to something other than the God of religion'.[162] Although the arguments are not demonstrative, they 'serve to fortify the faith of the believer, by showing the coherence with what is established on non-religious evidence'.[163] Thus, for example, the cosmological argument, which concludes from the contingency of the world to a causative necessary being yields at best the knowledge that a transcendent, unknowable, absolute exists, but affords no information as to what it is like. For all its faults, the cosmological argument is preferable to the argument from design, which comes to grief on the fact of evil – the rock on which the immanentisms of Spinoza and Gentile founder. The teleological argument is ontological because it implies that 'the universe is responsive to reason's demand for intelligibility, and that the demand can be satisfied only by a purposive system. It is *a priori*, for its claim does not admit of empirical proof.'[164] As for the ontological argument, it 'is really not an argument at all, but an act of intellectual faith, the thinker's vote of confidence in the validity of thought. Moreover, if taken apart from a prior intuition of God by faith, it warrants at best the belief in a metaphysical Absolute.'[165] In connection with the ontological postulate de Burgh finds Kant wanting, and in an important passage he explains that

> The issue is not that of the inference to a personal and transcendent God, so decisively rejected by Kant; but the wider one, to which ... he gave an ambiguous answer, of the conformability of the real to reason. I confess myself unable to understand how, when the nature of this assumption is once realized, it can be disputed by any philosopher. It is, of course, incapable of demonstration, for it is presupposed in the very attempt to prove it. It represents an act of intellectual faith, at once necessary and incontrovertible; for it is affirmed in the attempted act of denial. The intellect cannot question the truth of what it apprehends to be necessary; and the only necessity it recognizes is the necessity of what is intelligible. I would not dwell upon this point here, were it not that it has been obscured by Kant's severance of phenomena from noumena and of the regulative use of reason from the constitutive. The logical outcome of these distinctions is the divorce of knowledge from reality all along the line. Such a radical dualism cannot survive a moment's consideration.[166]

---

[162] TRP, 40.
[163] KI, 43; cf. LR, 90.
[164] TPR, 137.
[165] Ibid., 171.
[166] Ibid., 138.

The fact is that 'Apart from experience, there is no activity of reason; for the function of reason is to discover what is rational in our experience. Even the *a priori* ontology of the dogmatists assumed that man was in possession of the idea of God.'[167] De Burgh will not endorse Kant's bifurcation of reason into the speculative and the practical. Rather, he holds that 'If purposiveness be the highest form of rationality within our experience, we are warranted in holding that reality is purposive; we are not warranted in holding that it is nothing more.'[168] Although the finite purposes observable in nature cannot demonstrate the truth of a teleological system – and in any case Nature cannot be experienced as a whole, they suggest it. Their very limitations 'point beyond nature to a teleology that is both rational and real'.[169] Indeed, 'An infinite purpose and a teleological whole are the same thing';[170] and 'Reason [appealing to both *a priori* and *a posteriori* grounds] conceives the real as a unified system that is, at least, teleological.'[171]

But it is 'The categorical assertion of God's being' that 'marks the difference between the theistic faith of Christianity and the conclusion of any inferential process'.[172] This assertion is made when, as Aquinas saw, the intellect presents data to which the will voluntarily responds, 'not because of compelling arguments in its favour, but as good; the intellect assents to the will's voluntary choice. You cannot, in short, represent these vital decisions as the conclusions of a demonstrative syllogism.'[173] With this deliverance we pass to religion, revelation and faith, preparing ourselves to notice that as with reason, so with faith: the concept is broadened when the reference is to faith in God.

De Burgh affirms that religion is a specific form of the union of subjectivity and objectivity, and that the religious *a priori* may be set alongside those of

---

[167] Ibid., 139.
[168] Ibid., 145.
[169] Ibid., 147.
[170] Ibid., 148.
[171] Ibid., 154. That not all ways of affirming teleology appealed to de Burgh is clear when he takes issue with Hicks's commitment to one pervasive 'pattern of patterns' which constitutes the whole course of nature. 'How,' asks de Burgh, 'is this thorough-going teleology to be reconciled with the real individuality and freedom of finite human minds [which Hicks wishes to defend]? Is it not as fatal to their (relative) independence as any naturalistic doctrine of mechanism?' See his review of G. Dawes Hicks, *The Philosophical Bases of Theism*, in *Mind*, NS, XLVII, January 1938, 85. He refers to Hicks's book, 218–19. Hicks had earlier (p. 118) complained that with their claim to oneness with the wholly Other mystics assert both their self-hood and its annihilation in absorption. De Burgh can tolerate this paradox, for 'if the transcending of the "either-or of the abstract understanding" is held to be an ultimate contradiction, what ... becomes of all the higher experiences for which Prof. Hicks has unlocked the door by his wider view of Reason?' See de Burgh's review, 83.
[172] LAW, 462.
[173] TRP, 219.

morality, art and metaphysics.[174] What distinguishes developed religion from the rest is the 'personal intercourse intrinsic to religious experience'.[175] This cannot be supplied by the Platonic Form of the Good, or Kant's moral law, of the absolute of immanent metaphysics. There is no way from the last to the affirmation of transcendence. It is not the case, however, that de Burgh, while distinguishing religion from philosophy, wishes to disjoin them completely. On the contrary, he seeks a synthesis of them;[176] but in doing so it is necessary to appreciate their differing starting-points:

> Religious knowledge is from the outset directed towards God. Philosophy, on the other hand, like science, takes as its initial data ourselves, the selves of others, and the world revealed through sense, objects with which we are acquainted from infancy ... With religion is it otherwise; it may well be that God's presence is not recognized till late in life, and, again, there are those – often ethically the most virtuous – who remain permanently blind to it. Further, a growing knowledge of God is the directive influence throughout the whole course of the religious life. The moment the thinker's eye is diverted from this compass, his thought ceases to be religious.[177]

Elsewhere de Burgh makes his point in terms of the contrast between *theoria* and *praxis*, regarding philosophy simply as a theoretical activity, religion as a theory-grounded way of life. In so saying he recognizes that he is in disagreement with Plato, the Neoplatonists and Spinoza, as well as with this-worldly religions as Marxism and National Socialism, for all of whom philosophy and religion are one and the same. Philosophy, he repeats, is simply theoretical reflection upon life, 'which it presupposes as other than the activity of thinking "about" it'.[178] Thus,

> In philosophy, the inference to God is problematic, and comes, if at all, as the consummation of a long process of investigation into man and nature. But were the difference between religion and philosophy one merely of objects, there would be no conflict between their claims to knowledge. What is serious is that they differ on common ground.[179]

Both religion and philosophy take all experience as their province; but for the former, as Bonaventure clearly saw, 'nothing can be known for what it really is, save when known as the effect of divine causality'.[180] The particular temptation

---

[174] Ibid., 33.
[175] Ibid., 39.
[176] See LAW, 446.
[177] TRP, 43.
[178] LR, 85.
[179] TRP, 43.
[180] Ibid.

of metaphysics through the ages has been unduly to emphasize universality; that of religion has been so to elevate the personal experience of the individual as to remove it from the sphere of rational inquiry. Temptations aside, there is a case for the adequacy of their positions to be made both by philosophers and religious believers. In reflecting upon this in one of his last essays, de Burgh draws attention once again to the place of faith in the attainment of diverse world views. He recalls that, as an undergraduate,

> I gave my allegiance to the philosophical teachers Green, Nettleship, F. H. Bradley, Bernard Bosanquet and Caird. I recall how even then I was perplexed by the contrast between the confident assurance with which they asserted their Absolutist solution of metaphysical problems and the mistrust they showed towards the dogmas of Christianity, in relegating them unhesitatingly to the realm of appearance. They treated the one as matter of pure reason, the other as matter of pure faith. It seemed to me that in their *salto mortale* from finite experience to an all-inclusive Absolute Spirit, and conversely in the acknowledged mystery of the differentiation of the Absolute in to finite centres of consciousness, faith was called into play to bridge the gulf as veritably as in acceptance of the Nicene creed. The issue at stake is not that of theological faith versus metaphysical reason, but which of the two faiths – the theological or the metaphysical – is the more 'reasonable'. Both alternatives alike are cases of *intellectus quaerens fidem*.[181]

But the greatest point of distinction between philosophy and religion (by which de Burgh normally means Christianity) is not that the latter claims knowledge derived from revelation, because all knowledge is faith in a revelation: it 'presupposes a "given", be the giver God or Nature or whatever may be the mysterious source of sense data. All discovery is revelation, accepted by an act of faith.'[182] The distinction is that in religion the knowledge of the truth is revealed by the personal God to human beings. 'How else', other than by divine revelation, 'could the chasm be spanned that parts our finite minds from the transcendent Creator of the universe?'[183] In what does the revelation consist? In the first place, through revelation we are granted knowledge of God himself. From the standpoint of the human intellect this knowledge is supra-rational, but it is not so intrinsically, for 'the outpouring of the divine mind, eternally at one with the divine volition, ... is intrinsically rational'.[184] In other words, 'The antithesis of faith and reason is relative to human limitations.'[185] Secondly, the knowledge of God, who cannot

---

[181] W. G. de Burgh, 'Intelligence in quest of faith,' 223–4. For Green and Edward Caird *vis-à-vis* Christian doctrine see Alan P. F. Sell, *Philosophical Idealism and Christian Belief*, (1995), Eugene, OR: Wipf & Stock, 2006.

[182] W. G. de Burgh, 'Intelligence in quest of faith,' 223; cf. TRP, 40; LR, 108.

[183] LR, 118.

[184] Ibid., 89.

[185] Ibid.

be comprehended by human reason, is a gift of grace, accepted by faith. It is knowledge of an 'other' who can enter into personal relations with human beings, but 'God – *pace* certain eminent German theologians of our time – is never *wholly* other.[186] His immanence is the necessary complement of His transcendence. He is knowable, even in direct experience, through His presence in ourselves and in the world.'[187] At this point de Burgh invokes Bonaventure.

> whose theologico-philosophical synthesis presents the most profound and far-reaching illustration of the doctrine, the stamp of the creator, His '*imago*' in man's reason, and His footprints (*vestigia*) below the level of human rationality, is discernible in every detain of the Creation. Thus the universe is sacramental, through all the stages of its hierarchical order, presenting everywhere to man's restricted faculties of sense and thought, the outward and visible signs of the divine intention and causality.[188]

De Burgh is well aware that his position turns upon two presuppositions. The first is that truth is not to be limited to the truth of propositions: 'I cannot believe that truth first enters into an experience when it is analysed into subject and predicate or into two or more subjects in relation. Even in sense-perception, the percept must be true or false prior to its formulation in a statement. ... [T]he propositional statement is never, except perhaps in mathematics, an adequate expression of the experience.'[189] Secondly, since in religious experience we are concerned with a transcendent 'other', it follows that 'in all apprehension by a human mind there are degrees of knowledge and of truth'.[190] After all, 'a revelation that was not adjusted to human intelligence would fail to reveal'.[191] Moreover, it is only by maintaining the idea of degrees of truth that Henry Sidgwick's self-confessed failure to grasp the distinction between 'a contradiction that was just a contradiction and the kind that was a vehicle of the profoundest truth' can be overcome; along such lines, as Bradley saw, 'The so-called "real world" ... becomes the home of distinct

---

[186] Almost certainly Karl Barth was uppermost in de Burgh's mind at this point, albeit Barth was Swiss, not German. Cf. TRP, 245; and FMTR, 293 and 24 n. 1: 'If only German theologians, in this as in many other aspects of Christian teaching, would look more constantly westwards across the Rhine!' Elsewhere Barth is named as, for example, in LR, 111 and 93: 'To emphasise, as does Karl Barth, divine transcendence at the expense of immanence is as disastrous for religion as is the pantheist's insistence on immanence to the exclusion of transcendence.'

[187] LR, 91; cf. KI, 44–5.

[188] Ibid., 92.

[189] Ibid., 71.

[190] Ibid.

[191] W. G. de Burgh, 'Intelligence in quest of faith,' 225.

alternatives, and of plain and clear-cut divisions between Yes and No.'[192] De Burgh is forthright:

> In such a world there is no place for an experience which affirms God's transcendence and His immanence, His impassibility and self-manifestation in the temporal process, His omnipotence and the responsibility of finite creatures who are free to resist His will, the utter nothingness of evil and the terrible actuality of human sin. 'Dying, yet behold we live'; the repentant sinner declared righteous in the sight of God; grace and free will; how can these paradoxes, which lie at the very heart of religious experience, and are accepted as sublime truths by the religious consciousness, be other than fatal to religion, if the final appeal to reason be to the disjunctive judgement, the 'either-or' of the abstract understanding? But, if once degrees of truth be admitted, it becomes possible, under certain conditions, to reconcile statements that are apparently inconsistent, without violence to the Principle of Contradiction.[193]

Far from being a matter of *gnosis* for the initiated few, the locus of God's supreme revelation is history. De Burgh reminds us how 'keenly sensitive' the Hebrews were 'to the pressure of historic fact', adding,

> [W]hereas historic crises served the Roman merely as a stimulus to effective action, and the Greek as a stimulus to reflective thought, their significance to the Hebrew prophets and people was primarily ethical and religious. Christianity learnt from Judaism the habit of associating moral values with historic fact, and thus was enabled to mediate between the one-sided interests of Roman statesmanship and Greek philosophy.[194]

It was supremely by the incarnation of Christ, says de Burgh, that 'the ghost of the two-world philosophy that was the stumbling-block of Platonism was finally laid, when the invisible things of God were declared to be made manifest for faith in the visible processes of nature and history, and the spiritual order to be immanent in the temporal'.[195] The fact is that 'The world cannot be redeemed by even the noblest of abstractions ... [and] to stamp the historical factor in religious creeds as inherently mythological is, in the long run, to deny value to religious experience.'[196] Again, in face of Neoplatonists and others who focus supremely on a timeless world of values, de Burgh thunders, 'A Christianity cut adrift from the course of history is no longer a gospel of salvation to all mankind.'[197] De Burgh

---

[192] LR, 105, referring to F. H. Bradley, *The Principles of Logic*, II, 687.
[193] Ibid., 105; cf. KI, 57–8.
[194] LAW, 381 n. 1.
[195] Ibid., 373.
[196] TRP, 34.
[197] LAW, 526.

fully recognizes that 'With the intrusion of what belongs to an other-worldly order the historian [*qua* historian] has no concern. But this is not a refutation of the fact of such intrusion.'[198]

God's revelation in Christ is appropriated by the response of faith. As we have already seen, de Burgh holds that 'Faith is no idiosyncracy of the religious consciousness, but a primary condition of all reasonable life.'[199] When the reference is to belief, as a specific mode of apprehension, faith is distinguished from knowledge because its insight into the truth is defective; and, like opinion, faith/belief may be true or false.[200] Nevertheless, in religion the term 'faith' denotes something broader than, though not in principle contradictory of, intellectual faith. It is not that religious faith seeks to outrun reason: that way lies irrationality. Rather, religious faith 'is determined by its object. It is faith in God, revealed directly in the response of love and worship.'[201] After all, 'Men do not bring with them to the religious experience a ready-made concept of God as the proper object of worship, and then go on to an emotional attitude towards him. They find themselves in the presence of a reality, and know it to be God in the response that it evokes. Conceptual expression follows after.'[202] Such faith is both inferential and experiential, 'if logical inference be taken to include not merely demonstration, but the drawing of conclusions resting on a wide survey of the facts of man's experience and the nature of the universe in which he finds himself'.[203] It is experiential in being faith in a person – at which point de Burgh faults Aquinas for over-intellectualizing faith by thinking of it more as assent to a dogma than trust in a person.[204] The personal knowledge given to religious faith is 'distinct in form and content from the inferential knowledge of metaphysics'.[205] Moreover, 'God is not present simply as the object of man's response, as though *his* love towards *us* called forth *our* love towards *him*; our answering love is the very spirit of God working within us. God is present, so to speak, on both sides of the reciprocal relation. ... The experience itself is a direct participation in God's presence.'[206] Fully aware of the looming charge of circularity, de Burgh continues,

> Let no one object that this is to argue in a circle, that we first explain the response by assuming God's existence, and then use it as evidence for the truth of the assumption. God's existence is not presupposed as a premiss; our sole premiss

---

[198] LR, 104.
[199] LAW, 527 n. 1.
[200] LR, 125.
[201] TRP, 15.
[202] Ibid., 16.
[203] Ibid., 117.
[204] TRP, 21, 18.
[205] Ibid., 31. Cf. W. G. de Burgh, 'Intelligence in quest of religious faith,' 225–6.
[206] FMTR, 259–60. This position met with John Baillie's approval. See his *Our Knowledge of God*, London: OUP, 1939, 234, n. 1.

is the experienced fact of man's love for him, and his existence is given in that *datum*. ... The view I am here suggesting is thoroughly consonant with the great tradition of Christian Platonism. It is not the only point on which the authority of Anselm is to be preferred to the more rigid Aristotelianism of Aquinas.[207]

Clearly, religious faith of the kind to which de Burgh refers is a theological concept (*fiducia*). Indeed, he affirms this in saying that this faith, which presupposes illumination by the Holy Spirit, has its source in God, as does reason, and both yield truth.[208] This is the point at which de Burgh departs most significantly from Aquinas, whom he construes as holding that theology differs most radically from metaphysics and science in that 'The theologian, taking his start from principles of revelation, known by the light of grace infused by the Holy Spirit, works downwards from God to the world of His creation; the philosopher (and the scientist) starts from the creaturely, which is the proper object of human reason, and works upwards to God by principles of rational demonstration.'[209] Here, once again, is the seed of that theology-metaphysics, faith-reason, bifurcation which de Burgh so fervently deplored.

Two further points of importance must briefly be made. First, de Burgh reminds us that although he frequently speaks of the knowledge and experience of individuals, the religious individual is normally a member of a group, so that the experiences of individuals are moulded into a living unity of corporate faith and action, which in turn directs and enriches personal devotion' – and this despite the 'parasitic accretions' that have corrupted the practice of religion throughout history.[210] Secondly, against McTaggart's pronouncement that no one has a right to religion who has not studied metaphysics, de Burgh, his aristocratic inheritance notwithstanding, stands in the line of Aquinas, Kant and, above all William Wallace, from whom he first learned the value of metaphysics, who declared that God 'if he comes at all, comes altogether, sooner perhaps to the day labourer than to the speculative thinker. ... The modern world can only gain religion, and have such vision of God as man can have, when it realizes to the intensest that the wise and foolish equally enjoy his sunlight, that to him nothing is common or unclean.'[211]

---

[207] Ibid., 260.
[208] LR, 122.
[209] LAW, 460.
[210] TRP, 51.
[211] Ibid., 35, quoting J. M. E. McTaggart, *Some Dogmas of Religion*, London: Edward Arnold, 1906, 292–3, and William Wallace, *Lectures and Essays*, 163. Cf. O. C. Quick's lament in *Modern Philosophy and the Incarnation*, London: SPCK, 1915, 7: 'the metaphysician fails to sympathise with the grocer'.

IV

Having sufficiently considered de Burgh's epistemology, we may now turn to his other major concern, namely, the delineation of the route from morality to God. We might take as our 'text' his pronouncement that 'The Moral argument, for which the world is chiefly indebted to Kant, points with peculiar cogency to faith in God.'[212] I shall return to this argument in due course, but first it will be helpful to locate de Burgh in the territory of the moral philosophy of his day. Indeed, he will do this for us:

> There are two lines of approach to Moral Philosophy. There is the broad – some, in their blindness, would call it the easy – way, of treating morality as one among many spiritual activities, with which it is integrated in concrete experience, and of enquiring into its relationships with science, art, religion and metaphysics. And there is the straight and narrow way of isolating ethics as a self-contained field of study, and of determining by the analytic method the meaning and interconnection of its fundamental concepts. The former of these two ways has of late passed out of favour in academic circles, where it is regarded as a primrose path of dalliance that leads to speculative woolliness, *i.e.* to philosophical perdition. In sharp reaction to Bradley, both Moore at Cambridge and Cook Wilson at Oxford taught that the latter was the more excellent way, and most recent writers on ethics, especially at Oxford, have followed this direction.[213]

For his part, de Burgh treads the broad way, albeit with an eye to careful conceptual analysis.

Secondly, it is necessary to note de Burgh's understanding of the nature of moral action, the ethical ideal of goodness, and the distinction to be drawn between religion and morality. He is convinced that what makes an action moral is its rightness. He succinctly states his position in the following terms: '[R]ightness cannot be interpreted as due to intrinsic or consequential goodness; ... an action is moral only when done for its intrinsic rightness, ... action *sub ratione boni* is a type of action distinct from moral action, and ... both types, the moral and the optimific, have ethical value.'[214] In other words, 'There is action inspired by vision, be it of truth or beauty or the happiness of those we know and love, or, in the religious life, by the presence of God; and there is action inspired solely by the consciousness of present obligation. I maintain that, for ethics, each of these ideals is independent and autonomous.'[215] On this matter de Burgh found himself at odds with his friend A. E. Taylor. In an article entitled, 'The right and the good', Taylor had declared

---

[212] TRP, 20.

[213] W. G. de Burgh, review of W. D. Ross, *Foundations of Ethics*, in *The Hibbert Journal*, XXXVIII no. 2, January 1940, 279.

[214] LAW, 538.

[215] FMTR, 40.

that 'the obligatoriness of the best life is a consequence of the fact that it *is* best.'[216] De Burgh replies:

> I readily allow that the embodiment and promotion of good, whether it be consciously intended or not, is one of the chief *primâ facie* grounds for *justification* of dutiful actions; but it is not the sole or complete ground. Even if it sufficed (which I dispute) to constitute an obligation, this would not prove the converse, that an obligation can arise from no other source. What I deny is a *necessary* connexion between the concept of good and that of right. The good inclines to, but does not necessitate, obligation. I hold still to a dualism of ethical first principles, which can only be resolved by passing beyond the field of ethics.[217]

To repeat: in de Burgh's view, the key ethical motivation is the doing of one's duty for duty's sake – a principle which did not come into its own until Kant emphasized it.[218] Moreover, in doing one's duty in a particular circumstance one wills 'duty *universal*, whose content is irreducible to a sum of its particular embodiments. ... This is, to my mind, the inexpugnable [*sic*] core of truth in the ethical theory of Immanuel Kant.'[219] The practical reason – that is, the power of moral discernment in particular situations calling for action – determines both the end and the means of realizing it; the determining principle is an individual's conscience, not an external authority as in the law. Moral acts, whether 'enjoined by an objective moral law or as the realisation of an objective good'[220] are willed for their own sakes. In short, de Burgh agrees with Kant that morality is autonomous and personal, and distinguishes his position from those of Plato and Hume: 'Neither Plato nor Hume found place for practical reason, but on widely different grounds: Plato, because speculative wisdom sufficed for the practical realisation of the rational good; Hume, because the sole function of reason consists in the ascertainment of the means to the satisfaction of non-rational impulse.'[221]

It is integral to de Burgh's case that 'rational action, on the plane of reflective consciousness, is (a) purposive and (b) free'.[222] The intention to act implies an exercise of free volition in regard to a specific purpose, albeit the purpose may

---

[216] A. E. Taylor, 'The right and the good', *Mind*, NS, XLVIII, July 1939, 281 (though in his article, p. 491, de Burgh wrongly gives the month as June).

[217] W. G. de Burgh, 'The right and the good', *Mind*, NS, XLVIII, October 1939, 491.

[218] He does, however, recognize with John Laird that Hobbes had earlier take the same view, see FMTR, 43, n., and he might also have found a harbinger of Kant in this respect in the writings of Richard Price. His point is that whereas Hobbes and Kant stand for the principle of duty, Spinoza, for example, stands for the principle of good.

[219] TRP, 108–9.

[220] LR, 154.

[221] Ibid., 131.

[222] Ibid., 132.

never reach fulfilment, and may be freely modified during the process of enactment, which may be complex and protracted. Purpose implies decision, which may or may not be between alternatives: in this respect 'Purpose is a wider term than choice.'[223] Whereas God's freedom is absolute, that of human beings is not. Rather, 'in our acts of will we are in some measure self-determining ... over and above the causality of nature, by which antecedent events determine their consequences mechanically, there is a causality of freedom, possessed by rational beings, human and other, which renders rational action possible'. This does not mean that a given act results from a combination of natural causality and the causality of freedom,

> for such an analysis would land us back in the realm of mechanical determinism. What we affirm is that the whole volitional process is throughout informed by a spontaneity and initiative, as the self-development of a purpose that demands natural causality as a condition of its effectuation. What is denied is scientific determinism, the doctrine that the act can be resolved without remainder into terms of its causal antecedents, physical or psychical.[224]

De Burgh proceeds to develop his case against determinism. First, there are no *a priori* or *a posteriori* proofs which can substantiate scientific determinism against freedom: 'The belief in determinism ... is generated by unwarranted prejudice in favour of certain *a priori* doctrines, and has no claim to be regarded as reasonable.'[225] Secondly, determinists must believe that both they, and those who question their belief, have been determined to hold their positions. Rational argument is thus ruled out; 'true' and 'false' have no meaning; and 'The determinist ... surreptitiously makes an exception in his own favour, assuming that it is possible for his adversary to be freely convinced of [determinism's] truth.'[226] Thirdly, if it be held that freedom is illusory, the question arises, How did the illusion arise in the human mind? 'The fact of the illusion of freedom is even harder to account for than the reality.'[227] Finally, as with all scientific enquiry, the determinist position assumes an investigator who

> describes and interprets the object from the standpoint of the spectator observing it from without. In an act of will thus regarded, nothing is observable but a temporal succession of discrete psychical states, each of which is itself and distinct from every other, standing in no relation save to that of temporal sequence in accordance with a rule. Any given term in the series is determined through and through by its antecedents, and in similar fashion determines its successor. Freedom only becomes apparent if we view the act from an entirely different

---

[223] Ibid., 135; cf. FMTR, 90–92.
[224] Ibid., 136–7.
[225] Ibid., 137.
[226] Ibid.
[227] Ibid., 138.

angle – viz., from within by introspective intuition, the self, instead of observing the self as an object, entering into the process of its own activity, and finding there not a sequence of distinct and separable states, but phases that interpenetrate and pass into one another, so that the series is self-developing, or ... self-creative.[228]

De Burgh thus holds, 'against Hume and the Naturalists, Positivist and other, that reason is active in determining the ends of conduct, not merely calculative of the means for satisfying natural desire'.[229] This is not to say that desire and rational volition are intrinsically opposed to each other. On the contrary, 'desire provides the matter in which alone the form of the good life can be realised in conduct'.[230]

In substantiating his central claim that moral action is a matter of doing one's duty for duty's sake, de Burgh takes issue with W. D. Ross, for whom 'right' is synonymous with 'duty'. De Burgh denies this on the ground that it is essential in ethics to understand 'right' in terms of its etymology: 'in accordance with rule'. Thus, 'Both right action and utilitarian action imply the exercise of practical reason; they differ in that an act is useful in relation to the end to which it is a means, but right in relation to the rule which it obeys.'[231] An agent may voluntarily adopt a rule and act in accordance with it, but most moral acts are conceived as duties that the agent is obliged to perform. As compared with the sense of moral obligation, the standard of rightness is indeterminate since, as with utilitarian ends, rules may conflict. Furthermore rules are general and insufficiently precise to prescribe specific actions. Yet again, there is the ambiguity of the right thing to be done, where the reference is to 'the efficient handling of the situation', and what ought to be done, where the reference is to the moral law.[232] There follows a paean of praise to Kant:

> The reason why I believe Kant to stand head and shoulders above any other moral philosopher, ancient or modern, is that he held the Moral Law to be at once a transcendent reality and the generative source, in relation to man's changing experience, of particular moral obligations, which, being conditioned by his empirical nature and that of his environment, of necessity fail adequately to express the pure universality of the law.[233]

De Burgh further explains that the moral law is formal, for 'It points to a supersensible order of which [the spatio-temporal process] is the appearance. This is the reason why Kant's formalism, so far from proving a stone of stumbling in

---

[228] Ibid.
[229] Ibid., 139.
[230] Ibid., 144.
[231] Ibid., 156.
[232] FMTR, 45 n. 2.
[233] LR, 157; cf. FMTR, 52.

his ethical theory, is rather its crowning glory.'[234] He adds the cautionary remark that duty universal is an abstract moral principle; it is not a religious principle, for duty cannot be worshipped. The fulfilment of our duty does, however, give us 'an insight into the moral order, and an assurance of the stability of moral value.'[235]

His praise of Kant notwithstanding, de Burgh regrets the confusion of right and duty in both Kantian and in contemporary ethics.[236] He also draws attention – expressing himself in biblical language – to the paradox of moral experience, namely, that 'while 'ought' implies 'can', duty universal is for ever beyond our power of fulfilment. ... To the end of our endeavour we remain unprofitable servants; we have *not* done that which it was our duty to do.'[237] Were it otherwise, 'morality would no longer exist as morality. It would be *aufgehoben* in another and a richer mode of experience. Thus, in proclaiming the universality and transcendence of the moral principle, Kant was virtually heralding the euthanasia of the moral life.'[238]

So much for de Burgh's elevation of the concept of duty. What, now, of the ethical ideal of goodness? Here again he tempers his praise of Kant:

> Apart from the religious postulate, Kant's *ethics* begins and ends with duty. He is torn in two directions whenever he approaches the concept of good. Either he subsumes all action *sub ratione boni* under the rubric of Psychological Hedonism, or – when he treats the concept of good seriously – he confuses the distinction between morality and religion.[239]

In de Burgh's opinion, purposive activity 'points forward to that of value', and 'Value comes clearly into view when we pass to consider ... human experience. Man is an ideal-forming animal, whose thought and conduct alike are guided by standards of truth and goodness.'[240] In this fact he finds a link between Christianity and Platonism: 'Widely different as are the knowledge of the Christian religion and that of the Platonic philosophy, they are at one in that for both (a) the supreme good is the supreme reality, (b) this supreme good is knowable, (c) this knowledge is indissolubly bound up with love.'[241] De Burgh cautions us, however, against the pitfall of thinking of the good as the end of moral action. Indeed, in opposition to Aristotle, he contends that 'The category of means and end ... is very inadequate to

---

[234] FMTR, 57.
[235] TRP, 14.
[236] See his review of R. G. Collingwood, *The New Leviathan*, in *The Hibbert Journal*, XLI no. 1, October 1942, 91.
[237] FMTR, 52–3, repeated, 67.
[238] Ibid., 69.
[239] W. G. de Burgh, 'The right and the good', 497.
[240] TRP, 107.
[241] LAW, 356 n. 2.

the interpretation of human conduct';[242] it involves an abstraction, for 'The end is throughout immanent in the so-called "means", which are therefore never merely "means" at all. Nor is the end a result, supervening late in time upon its antecedents; it is rather the form that gives unity and coherence to the whole process.'[243] In any case, 'Ideal good is transcendent of any finite embodiment.'[244]

Although de Burgh is anxious to distinguish moral action from action *sub ratione boni*, they are not absolutely unlike one another, for both are rational: 'As particular duties are willed as manifestations of duty universal, so particular goods are willed as expressions of universal good.'[245] What most clearly differentiates the two kinds of action is the spontaneity of action for the good, over against the 'discipline and conflict in the life of duty. ... The desire for good ... knows nothing of the constraint of obligation. The object judged to be good by the understanding, elicits a willing response from the heart.'[246] Indeed, 'If this aspiration after the ideal were present everywhere in full measure, and if it were capable of unbroken sustainment, there would be no place left for moral action.'[247] As things are, '*Theoria* is primary over *praxis*, the vision of the ideal over the process of its actualization.'[248] As to the judgement that a thing is good, this is not simply a matter of self-satisfaction, as Green and Bradley imply, and there are no grounds for interpreting the end in terms of the self. The contrary argument, says de Burgh, 'has given rise to more nebulous vapourising, in the pulpit and elsewhere, during the last forty years, than any other ethical theory of modern times'.[249] He articulates his complaint more temperately, thus:

> 'The rational soul,' writes Green, 'in seeking an ultimate good necessarily seeks it as a state of its own being.' If this means merely that ultimate good must lie within my capacity of attainment, and that in attaining it I find satisfaction, the statement is true but unilluminating; if it means that the nature of the good that satisfies me consists in my satisfaction, it is palpably false. The seemingly edifying principle proves to be egoism in disguise, and loses all claim to moral authority.[250]

---

[242] FMTR, 81.
[243] Ibid., 82.
[244] Ibid., 83.
[245] Ibid., 84.
[246] Ibid., 86, 87.
[247] Ibid., 87.
[248] Ibid.
[249] TRP, 183.
[250] TRP, 184. De Burgh refers to T. H. Green, *Prolegomena to Ethics*, Oxford: Clarendon Press, 1883, 370. See further on de Burgh *versus* Green, Alan P. F. Sell, *Philosophical Idealism and Christian Belief*, 149–50. A. E. Taylor stands with de Burgh on this point. See his 'William George de Burgh,' 389–90 where, on the latter page he writes, 'When all is said, the deity of Green, against his own will, remains, if we are to be quite

The upshot is that while the self may indeed be realized in the life dedicated to the good, this 'is no evidence that self-realization constitutes the goodness of the ideal'.[251]

De Burgh is well aware that in setting his face against the derivation of 'ought' from 'good' he is swimming against the tide of moral philosophy, ancient and modern. His contention is, however, that 'the case for the dependence of "ought" on "good" rests ... on the ascription to what is good of the character that it "ought to be"',[252] He questions this ascription, 'being convinced that all obligation relevant to morality is obligation to *do* (*thunsollen*), and that the term "ought to be" (*seinsollen*), however common in ordinary speech, is either a misnomer or a veiled expression of the *thunsollen*'.[253] The view he repudiates is advanced in two forms. First, in utilitarianism, whether hedonistic or ideal, the doctrine is that that ought to be done which is conducive to good. This position is open to the objection that it furnishes no criterion of what really ought to be done. How do we know what is really good? Moreover, if we are to trust our intuition in this matter, why may we not trust it in regard to our duty? Again, utilitarianism has no answer to the question, 'Why *ought* I to promote good when I don't want to?'[254] Above all, 'Success in securing good cannot be the criterion of morality. The difference must lie, as Kant insisted, in the act of will';[255] and 'reference to sanctions, whether human or divine, is irrelevant to the ethical issue'.[256]

Secondly De Burgh argues against utilitarianism that 'The appeal to good as the ground of obligation is contrary to moral experience.'[257] He does not deny that human beings desire the good. His point is that moral beings also desire to do the right, and that the one desire is not reducible to the other, not least because 'desire stirred by apprehension of good is spontaneous, not commanded.'[258] Even the faith that right will ultimately triumph and that it is conducive to good, 'is grounded on the intrinsic rightness of the action, not the rightness on the conduciveness to good'.[259]

The crucial philosophical issue is whether there is a necessary connection between the concepts of 'ought' and 'good'. De Burgh answers that whereas '"Ought" ... is a unitary notion, with one and the same meaning in all instances of

---

candid, an only half-baptized Aristotelian God; Green has not taken the conception of God which the Christian Church brought with it from the study of the Bible to its subsequent study of the Greek philosophers with sufficient *metaphysical* seriousness.'

[251] Ibid., 89. De Burgh refers again to the same page in Green's book as given in the previous note.
[252] FMTR, 111–12.
[253] Ibid., 112.
[254] Ibid., 118.
[255] Ibid.
[256] Ibid.
[257] Ibid.
[258] Ibid., 138.
[259] Ibid., 122.

obligation; ... "good" is applied analogically, not univocally, to the various orders of goods.'[260] Again, whereas 'the concept of good is not necessarily grounded on that of obligation [because "an apprehended good may already be in existence", or "I may be indifferent or even averse to its actualization"]. Moral goodness, ... is so grounded.'[261] The upshot is that if there is any relation between the concepts of 'ought' and of value it must be synthetic, 'for no mere analysis of good reveals the "ought" as an essential element'.[262] Only in the case of moral goodness is there a necessary connection between the imperative of moral obligation and ethical value, and even then the connection 'is not by way of derivation of duty from good, but conversely by derivation of good from duty. ... For moral goodness means the goodness that comes to the agent by his doing of duty for duty's sake.'[263] One does not justify a moral act by reference to any value that it produces; rather, the doing of one's duty for its own sake will prove to be of value. We may believe that 'the temporal order of nature and history is but the shadow of the new heaven and the new earth, of whose goodness the righteous act must needs be a manifestation. But the belief cannot appeal to philosophy for proof of its validity; philosophy can at most supply evidence confirmatory of an assurance of religious faith.'[264]

Having distinguished moral action from action *sub ratione boni*, the former being concerned with *praxis* for its own sake, the latter with *praxis* as consummated in *theoria*, de Burgh grants that these are 'rather abstract moments in practical experience than self-contained and isolable courses of action. A single act may indeed exhibit one motive to the exclusion of the other, ... one or other may be predominant over a whole life; but in no man is either motive entirely absent.'[265] The fact is that 'Moral action presupposes that the actions which produce it have been motivated by the desire to do duty for duty's sake', while 'not only moral goodness, but goodness in every form, whether as beauty or as knowledge or as love ... is a potential source of obligation.'[266] But whereas there may be more than one moral motive to action, 'The *moral* worth ... depends solely upon the moral motive', and 'the value of an act, prompted by love in conjunction with a sense of duty, may be enhanced, and not diminished, by what Kant would describe as its impurity.'[267]

Just as duty can be willed only by willing particular duties, so good can be desired only as it is embodied in particular goods. Finite goods do not cover the entire field of goodness, and are limited to 'a finite set of spatio-temporal

---

[260] Ibid., 136–7.
[261] Ibid., 137.
[262] Ibid., 140–41.
[263] Ibid., 143.
[264] Ibid.
[265] Ibid., 92.
[266] Ibid., 94, 95.
[267] Ibid., 96.

happenings'.[268] Other goods are 'finite in the sense that they are mutually exclusive as specific types of goodness', are not limited to the temporal process of human history, and are infinite. These are 'knowledge, beauty, moral perfection, love of our fellows, and, if we included religious good, the reciprocal love of God and man. Each of these goods is infinite, in that it provokes and responds to a desire for perfection, which no finite achievement can fully satisfy.'[269] There follows a sentence which encapsulates the heart of de Burgh's position: 'Reason demands that beauty, perfection of character and love should be synthesized in the ideal of perfect goodness'; and this over against specialists engaged in particular enquiries, who may affirm the principles 'of materialism or physical determinism, which have a restricted or purely methodological application, as though they were laws holding of all experience'.[270] As to the ideal of perfect goodness: de Burgh has conceded that it can never be realized by finite creatures; but this raises the question how an ideal can be unrealized and yet real. Ethics cannot answer the question it raises: 'Alike by its inner contradictions and by the other-worldly references implicit in its principles, ethics points beyond its own borders to the fields of metaphysics and religion.'[271]

More than one reference having been made to the relations of morality and religion, it is now time to investigate this aspect of de Burgh's thought. Far from wishing easily to absorb morality in religion, or *vice versa*, de Burgh wishes clearly to demarcate their respective territories. During the course of delivering his Gifford Lectures at St. Andrews he discovered that some of his hearers argued that morality was, throughout, implicitly religious. The following note appended to his published lectures supplies his rebuttal:

> It is true, indeed, that grace knows no limits, and that it perfects, and does not contradict, nature. But the distinction, though relative, must be preserved. To regard thinking men of high intellectual competence and unquestioned moral integrity ... as virtually religious despite their conviction of the contrary; this is surely to confuse the issue at the outset. We must remember Plato's warning against jumping overhastily to principles of unification, to the neglect of intermediate differences. To give full weight to relative distinctions is one of the chief marks that differentiate philosophical from unphilosophical thinking.[272]

---

[268] Ibid., 103.

[269] Ibid., 105.

[270] Ibid., 106.

[271] Ibid., 110. For de Burgh's reflections 'On historical greatness and moral goodness', see LAW, 539–53.

[272] Ibid., 2 n. In this connection John Baillie's reference to those who believe in the bottom of their hearts whilst denying with the top of their heads comes to mind. See his *The Sense of the Presence of God*, London: OUP, 1962, 76–87. Cf. also Karl Rahner's reference to 'anonymous Christians' in *Theological Investigations*, London: Darton, Longman

Undeterred, de Burgh insists that the crucial distinction 'is found to rest on the fact that [religion] is not merely practical [though it is that], but essentially a form of knowledge, and that its knowledge is of God'.[273] 'Even in practice', however, 'the conduct inspired by religion differs, in motive and in expression, from morality. No purely ethical imperative could have prescribed to the poor widow the casting of all she had into the treasury, or to the prodigal's father the killing of the fatted calf.'[274] Furthermore, 'religion ... demands the consecration of man's whole nature to its service'.[275] and in religious experience God is not an impersonal or super-personal absolute, but 'Thou' – one who enters into 'personal communion with the worshipper'.[276] At all levels of religious experience we find the conjunction of cognitive, emotional and practical factors. As to the last, 'religion enjoins modes of conduct' – worship, prayer and observance of sacraments, conceived not as formal acts but as expressions of living faith – 'that fall outside the range of moral duty'.[277] Whereas the proper sphere of morality is that of human life and relationships, religion 'is directed God-wards, alike in *theoria* and in *praxis*; its interest in this world and in man is motived [*sic*] by the desire to realize the divine will. ... [Hence] Morally wrong acts appear as sins [whereas "for the purely moral consciousness there is only vice"[278]], moral virtues as the fruits of the Spirit.'[279] Consistently with this, and in one of his very few references to the Dane, de Burgh writes, 'Kierkegaard rightly held that the experience of penitence marks the point of transition from morality to religion';[280] and on his own account he later declares that 'Moral humiliation proves to be the gateway to religious humility.'[281] By *virtus acquisita* 'man's life is ordered with a view to temporal welfare', by *virtus infusa*, as 'exemplified by the theological triad, faith, hope, and love', it is ordered 'with a view to eternal felicity'.[282] In a word, 'the essence of morality lies in *praxis*, that

---

& Todd, 1969, ch. 6. For my response to these see Alan P. F. Sell, *Aspects of Christian Integrity* (1990), Eugene, OR: Wipf & Stock, 1998, 120.

[273] TRP, vi; cf. 25.
[274] Ibid., 37.
[275] Ibid.
[276] Ibid., 46.
[277] Ibid., 159.
[278] FMTR, 37.
[279] TRP, 159.
[280] FMTR, 26 n.
[281] Ibid., 147.
[282] TRP., 161. De Burgh invokes Aquinas and the medieval doctors in support. He regrets that when A. A. Bowman 'speaks of morality as the "practical content" of religion (II, 391), and tells (II, 137) us that "the jurisdiction which religion claims over the moral life is of such a nature as to leave morality very much what it is outside that jurisdiction", he ignores the vital difference that the infusion of the religious motive entails both in the content of saintly conduct and in the spirit in which it is performed'. See his review of

of religion in *theoria*.'[283] Another way of expressing the distinction is to say that in morality knowledge is for the sake of action; in religion the reverse is the case, because 'The religious life in essence is the life eternal, which is to know God. Such is the burden of every religious revelation, which stakes its all on the truth of its claim to give this knowledge.'[284] De Burgh is convinced that 'moral *praxis* would be enriched and ennobled by the infused virtue that has its source in the *theoria* of religious revelation, the *theoria* which is the knowledge of God'.[285] Finally, on its practical side religion, as distinct from morality, is motivated by the love of the God who is known to the believer in personal experience, and who is worshipped by the believer. Thus, 'Differences of motive give rise not only, within the sphere of ethics, to the distinction of moral action from action directed towards the good, but also to the distinction between both those types of ethical conduct on the one hand and the conduct characteristic of religion on the other.'[286]

So much for the distinction between morality and religion. What, now, of the transition from the former to the latter? In no uncertain terms de Burgh declares that 'moral experience, when thought out, implies the belief in an other-worldly reality, transcendent of the world of spatio-temporal events'.[287] 'Man', he continues, 'is a creature of two worlds, the temporal and the eternal ... the one the object of rational enquiry, the other of moral or religious faith.'[288] At once, however, he adds a footnote in which he denies advocating a two-world metaphysic and resists a final dualism. Indeed,

> such a dualism is very far from my thoughts. If it be urged that the 'other world' is but 'this world' fully understood, I readily assent; but on two conditions. Within 'this world' must be found a place, not only for the ever incomplete stream of historical occurrences, but also for the abiding presence of a super-human and super-temporal power, whence the course of history derives its origin and value; and the 'right understanding' must not be restricted to what is clearly

---

Bowman's *Studies in the Philosophy of Religion*, in *The Hibbert Journal*, XXXVII no. 2, January 1939, 339.

[283] Ibid., 164.

[284] Ibid., 166. H. Barker is thus wide of the mark in saying that 'If *knowledge* were the *goal* of religion, there would surely be no distinction in principle between religion and metaphysics. The relation of religious knowledge to the goal of religion is more truly indicated, *e.g.*, in the concluding words of the prayer of St. Chrysostom, "granting us in this world knowledge of thy truth, and in the world to come life everlasting".' But for de Burgh, the knowledge of God *is* life eternal. See Barker's review of *From Morality to Religion*, in *Mind*, NS, XLVIII, April 1939, 222.

[285] TRP, 177; cf. LAW, 538.

[286] FMTR, 33.

[287] LAW, 552.

[288] Ibid., 553.

and distinctly known by inference and analysis, but must include therewith the assurance of a reasonable faith.[289]

The limitations of morality itself suggest reasons why we should move beyond it to religion. Morality solely concerns human actions, but there are values other than the practical, truth and beauty among them. Every value presses an absolute claim upon our allegiance, and 'when the claims conflict, no single claimant, not even morality, has the right to decide the issue. Religion alone can give a final judgement, for religion knows no departmental limits. It embraces the whole personality of the worshipper, his mind and heart and will; and God, the object of worship, is the Alpha and Omega, the source of all being and of all value, compassing with His presence the whole universe of reality.'[290] Plato's principle of goodness and Kant's moral law are abstract and impersonal, while Stoicism's appeal is to the moral aristocracy. God, however, is personal, and his loving reach extends to all his creatures. Not, indeed, that religion's representatives on earth have always lived and acted as if this were the case. De Burgh pulls no punches when lamenting the *chronique scandaleuse* of ecclesiastical history',[291] while at the same time lamenting the (perennial) fact that 'scientists and philosophers show themselves very imperfectly instructed in the nature of the beliefs they hold up for reprobation'.[292]

De Burgh further tantalizingly suggests in his Gifford Lectures that religion resolves the following tensions in morality: (a) the fact that the moral law remains formal and defies embodiment in any empirical content; (b) the dilemma that 'if evil be illusory, the ethical struggle is a mockery: if it be real, how can good maintain its primacy?'; (c) the question, 'How can the freedom of choice, essential to moral responsibility, be reconciled with the freedom of inner necessitation, when the will responds with unhesitating spontaneity to the vision of ideal good?'[293] I say that he 'tantalizingly suggests' this resolution because he immediately proceeds to hint that the solution in each case turns upon the truth of the doctrine of the incarnation, and then says that to elucidate this would entail an apologetic for the Christian revelation which would be in defiance of Lord Gifford's trust. Instead he contents himself with showing that the dualism of the ethical ideals of duty and good 'can be reconciled by any form of theism that accepts the belief that God is love', and assures us (perhaps with a Trust-circumnavigating twinkle in his eye?) that his 'references to specifically Christian doctrine will be solely for purpose of illustration'.[294] He reiterates the position we have already outlined, namely, that

---

[289] Ibid., n. 553.
[290] Ibid., 564; cf. idem, 'Sources of present world-trouble, I,' 205.
[291] FMTR, 277–8.
[292] Ibid., 279.
[293] Ibid., 187.
[294] Ibid., 188. In the interests of balance I note that not all were impressed by de Burgh's approach. In his review of de Burgh's Gifford Lectures in *Ethics*, L no. 1,

'God is revealed to religious faith as the ground alike of goodness and of the moral law.'[295] Indeed, the so-called moral *argument* for God's existence, which became prominent following Kant's argument that 'moral experience ... requires the postulate of God as moral governor of the universe',[296] is in fact an 'inference from the reality of moral values to their source in God'.[297] If we would affirm God's nature as good, we can adduce only the evidence of religious experience, for 'Neither the moral argument, nor any other based upon non-religious sources, suffices to justify the assurance. Nay, more: none of these arguments avails, of itself, to give *any* positive knowledge of God's nature.'[298] Nevertheless the moral argument 'bears out the truth of the principle ... that it is only by the conjunction of religious experience with that drawn from non-religious sources, that the foundation can be secured for a reasonable faith in God'.[299]

V

There can be no question that de Burgh's philosophical writings were informed by close acquaintance with the classical inheritance, the Judaeo-Christian tradition in general, and patristic and medieval thought in particular. The name of Kant recurs frequently, though it is noticeable that those of Locke, Hume and Price and the moral sense philosophers do not. It has also been shown (not least by the references in my footnotes) that two major themes reverberate throughout his works: the necessity of understanding that reason has to do with more than ratiocination, and that it always includes an intuition of first principles; and the need of morality to find its completion in religion.

In the course of developing his broad themes de Burgh incorporates discussions of a number of particular topics. I shall simply note two of particular interest which have not so far been mentioned. The first concerns Aquinas's theory of analogical predication. De Burgh reminds us that, according to Aquinas, the *via remotionis* clears God of defects and limitations, but yields no positive knowledge of him.

October 1939, 118–19, G. Stanley Whitby writes, 'The effort is an impressive one, but whether or not the plan is basically sound, the synthesis is certainly premature and artificial, and one of the main reasons for the failure lies in De Burgh's attempt to tie ethics to the apron strings of religion. Although it is the reverse of the author's intention, the book tends to heighten the conviction, already held in certain circles, that the next great advance will come, not from religion, but from ethics, and that it will shed a new light on the essentials of religion.' Seventy years on, one cannot suppress the suspicion that if de Burgh's synthesis was premature, the new light from ethics is long delayed.

[295] Ibid., 205.
[296] TRP, 156.
[297] FMTR, 159.
[298] Ibid., 169.
[299] Ibid., 182.

In view of this, and of the fact that in this life the direct vision of God's essence is denied to us, Aquinas, in quest of knowledge of God gained by reason, not revelation, resorts to analogy. By this means we may ascribe to God such predicates grounded as goodness, wisdom and being. De Burgh rightly points out that 'the difficulty in this argument lies in the difference in the terms of the analogy, when compared with all other analogies in our experience',[300] and he does not think that Aquinas resolved the problem with his suggestion of proportionality, namely, 'as the goodness or wisdom of man is to man, so is the goodness or wisdom of God to God'.[301] For the real issue is 'whether we are warranted in *any* application of the term "goodness" to God. ... [T]he assumption that the finite effect must bear a resemblance to an infinite cause ... is precisely what needs justification.'[302] Hence, 'The *via analogica* seems to fade out, if we press the reservations, into the *via remotionis*; if we press the analogy, into anthropomorphism.'[303] The nub of the problem is that Aquinas applies 'the distinctions of Aristotelian logic to matters that are too high for them'.[304] It seems to me that to this point de Burgh's case is unanswerable.[305]

De Burgh understands that in writing as he did, Aquinas was keen to repudiate the 'menace of Pantheism [which] was rife in thirteenth-century Christendom';[306] but he thinks that his zeal in this regard led him on occasion to emphasize God's transcendence at the expense of immanence, and for this reason de Burgh turns to thinkers who adopted a more Platonist approach. He explains, in a carefully articulated passage that must be quoted in full, that

> The special point I have in mind is the indwelling in man of the Holy Spirit, the Spirit of the love of God. Is the relation between God's love for man, as manifested by the presence of the Spirit of God within the soul, really different in kind, and not merely in degree, from the response evoked by that presence in man's love of God? Is not the term 'love' in each case univocal? I am not thinking of the love which is God Himself, the Spirit as uniting Father and Son, in the perfect simplicity of the divine unity; nor of the imperfect judgments by which we grope, darkly for all the aid of grace and revelation, to express the truth of the divine essence. Still less am I thinking of the relation between God's love

---

[300] Ibid., 171.

[301] Ibid., 171–2.

[302] Ibid., 172.

[303] Ibid. Elsewhere de Burgh concurs with C. C. J. Webb in thinking that the analogical theory of being as expounded by Gilson leads to an ultimate Creator-creature dualism, 'that may prove to be as perilous to the interests of religion as the Monism of Spinoza'. See his review of Gilson's *God and Philosophy*, in *Mind*, NS, LI, July 1942, 280.

[304] Idem, Review of E. Bevan, *Symbolism and Belief*, 169.

[305] See further TRP, 123–7; Alan P. F. Sell, *Confessing and Commending the Faith*, 238–46.

[306] FMTR, 172.

of man and man's love of his fellow human beings. I am thinking – in terms, be it understood, of Christian religious teaching – of God's love as communicated by grace to man, and of man's response, inspired also by grace, in love to God. In this relationship, God's grace informs both terms of the relation. It is not a simple antithesis of infinite and finite, the Creator and the creature. On the one side we have the infinite assuming finitude, in the perpetual re-enactment of the Incarnation in the souls of men; on the other side we have the finite, in process of regeneration and transformation by grace into a veritable participation in infinitude. 'God became man' – we may add, and ever becomes man – 'in order that man may be made divine'. This is historic Catholic teaching ... There is nothing in it to warrant inference to a Pantheistic theory of the absorption of the finite individual in God.[307]

There would seem to be much to be said for de Burgh's view that in the usage described, 'love' is an univocal term, and that 'God's grace informs both terms of the relation.'[308] This is consistent with the biblical view that God's grace is prevenient, that the initiative in salvation rests with him, that love to God is engendered in us by the Spirit, and that our response of faith is a response enabled by grace, so that none may boast (Ephesians 2: 8-9). On the other hand, to speak of 'the perpetual re-enactment of the Incarnation in the souls of men' may unintentionally diminish the once-for-all-ness of *the* Incarnation, and, when the phrase is applied corporately, may also encourage believers to think that the Church is the continuation of the Incarnation. Given that the Church comprises saints (that is, members) who are also sinners, this latter view fully merits the protest of P. T. Forsyth who, while not denying that Christ indwells Christians and the Church, declared that 'It is regenerated human nature in which Christ dwells. But that cannot be a prolongation of His Incarnation, wherein there was no regeneration.'[309] Furthermore, even though de Burgh explains that 'the spiritual union is one of quality, not of substance',[310] talk of our being made divine may lead the unwary in the direction of *theosis* construed pantheistically; in which case the rebuttal comes concisely from J. H. A. Bomberger: 'Man is not deified by regeneration. In it

---

[307] Ibid., 173–4.

[308] H. P. Owen queries de Burgh's assertion that 'love precludes all thought of obligation' and gives the reference, FMTR, 66. Owen says that this contradicts 'the New Testament's formulation of Christian *agape* in such terms as "Thou *shalt* love thy neighbour as thyself" and "Beloved, if God so loved us, we *ought* to love one another"'. See *The Moral Argument for Christian Theism*, London: Allen & Unwin, 1965, 66.

[309] P. T. Forsyth, *The Church and the Sacraments* (1917), London: Independent Press, 1947, 83. See further, Alan P. F. Sell, *Testimony and Tradition. Studies in Reformed and Dissenting Thought*, Aldershot: Ashgate, 2005, 195.

[310] Ibid., 177.

men become Christians, but are not made Christs.'[311] As de Burgh himself writes, 'The gulf between [God's] self-being and our created being remains unbridged. But the experience of love carries us behind the limits of propositional statement. It is of the essence of divine love to be self-diffusive.'[312]

My second illustration of a topic to which de Burgh devotes passing attention concerns the nature of Christian ethics. The term 'Christian ethics', he declares, is 'much-used and often-abused'.[313] Its 'proper application is to those elements in secular morality which had their origin in Christianity, and survive as ideals of conduct independently of their former religious associations'.[314] Among secularists who espouse such ideals are Bertrand Russell and Aldous Huxley. I find this definition distinctly odd. It suggests, paradoxically, that if we wish to know what Christian ethics are we must have recourse to secularists who have repudiated the root and allegedly display (how much of?) the fruit. De Burgh contrasts his definition with a more usual one, namely, that Christian ethics refers to the teaching of Jesus and 'the way of life professed, on the basis of that teaching, by his followers'.[315] Against this *praxis*-orientated view de Burgh insists that Jesus'

> life, and the principles he laid down for his disciples, were rather the expression of religious *theoria*. ... The Sermon on the Mount, which is often loosely spoken of as though it were a manual of social ethics, contains few precepts that can be brought under that heading; and of these almost all are regulative of motives rather than of actions. Even in those injunctions which are directly relevant to man's temporal conduct, the appeal is to an authority that is super-sensible and eternal, to the will of 'our Father which art in heaven'.[316]

I should go even further and say, against those who declare, 'We have no time for doctrine, but we do like the teaching in the Sermon on the Mount', that the Sermon poses the Christological question in a clamant way, as R. W. Dale saw:

> Who is this that places persecution for *His* sake side by side with persecution for righteousness' sake, and declares that whether men suffer for loyalty to him or for loyalty to righteousness they are to receive their reward in the divine Kingdom? Who is it that places His own authority side by side with the authority of God? ...

---

[311] J. H. A. Bomberger, 'Regeneration', *Proceedings of the Second General Council of the Alliance of the Reformed Churches holding the Presbyterian System*, Philadelphia, 1880, 552. See further, Alan P. F. Sell, *Confessing and Commending the Faith*, 70–76, where I conclude that 'much that is positively intended by *theosis* is ... better, and less problematically, expressed by the doctrine of sanctification'.

[312] FMTR, 150.

[313] Ibid., 263.

[314] Ibid.

[315] Ibid.

[316] Ibid., 264.

Who is it that in that sermon assumes the awful authority of pronouncing final judgment on men? ... Who is he? That question cannot be silenced when words like these have once been spoken.[317]

In all of this we have that blend of *theoria* and *praxis* which, I should have thought, de Burgh would have been pleased to designate 'Christian ethics' (and which, together with the careful analysis of Christian ethical discourse, is so sadly lacking in much of the issue-driven Christian social ethics of the present time[318]). What inhibits him is his conviction that ethics is one thing, religion another, and that in Christianity 'the *virtus infusa* lifts ... conduct above the purely moral plane'.[319] No doubt it does, but, however motivated by the Spirit and empowered by grace, it does not thereby cease to be moral conduct. In his last book de Burgh withdraws from his blanket denunciation of the term 'Christian ethics': 'Keep the cherished term "Christian ethics", if you wish; provided only you underline the word "Christian" and recognise that the Christian religion prescribes a way of life which, as a higher form of rational praxis, carries us far beyond the prescripts of mere morality.'[320] There is a further point which de Burgh does not raise, namely, that in addition to acknowledging its roots in *theoria*, 'Part of the business of Christian ethics is to keep doctrine ethical.'[321] I therefore conclude that 'Christian ethics' is best understood not as a residue of uprooted *praxis* by which at least some secularists appear to live, but as the outworking in theory (both doctrinal and metaethical) of what is involved in the practice of the Christian way of life.

These considerations lead us directly to de Burgh's distinction between 'ought' and 'good'. The distinction is encapsulated in this bold declaration: 'if I act as duty would prescribe from any other motive, such as love or gratitude, my action is not wrong – far from it – but it has no *moral* worth'.[322] His point is that there are values other than moral values, and that an act may exemplify one or more of these. But he also grants that while a single act may exhibit the deontological motive to the exclusion of the good, and while 'one or other [motive] may be predominant over a whole life ... in no man is either motive entirely absent'.[323] Nevertheless, where duty is concerned the obligation is to be met regardless of questions of value. This leads de Burgh to introduce a more than somewhat disquieting illustration:

I have to choose ... between saving from fire an unknown infant or a masterpiece by Rembrandt. If I acted, as I probably should, without reflection, I should save

---

[317] R. W. Dale, *Christian Doctrine* (1894), London: Hodder and Stoughton, 1903, 166–7.

[318] See Alan P. F. Sell, *Testimony and Tradition*, ch. 9.

[319] FMTR, 265.

[320] LR, 160. How despising, even uncharitable, the little word 'mere' can sound.

[321] Robert Mackintosh, *Christian Ethics*, London: T. C. and E. C. Jack, 1909, 11.

[322] FMTR, 55.

[323] Ibid., 92.

the baby [the babies of Reading emit a collective gurgle of relief]. The issue, however, is not how I should act on impulse, but of the justification of the act in the light of duty. Again, I have no doubt that my duty would be to save the baby [more happy infant gurgles]; but, religion apart, I would be hard put to it to justify the obligation on grounds of value. There is, I suppose, a possibility that the infant may prove of untold benefit to humanity; but the probability is rather in favour of his turning out an average specimen, whose influence upon the world will be slight either for good or ill. On the other hand, we *know* that the Rembrandt is a work of a very high order of value. This is no matter of probability, it is a matter of knowledge. If we are to determine our duty by the standard of goodness, there can, I think, be only one answer: that we ought to save the picture.[324]

While we must take de Burgh's word that, apart from religious considerations, he would find it hard to justify saving the baby on grounds of value, it is odd that he cannot recall to mind those secularists allegedly living on Christian ethical residue who could quite easily save the baby on the ground of the value and sanctity of human life, quite apart from any religious reference. Nor is it easy so to tease out the often mixed motives prompting such any such act of rescue as to pronounce with confidence that the act had no moral worth. The illustration raises the question of the viability of the wedge de Burgh drives between duty and good.

A. E. Taylor's response to his friend's distinction was that 'I cannot satisfy myself that the divergence between a morality of the *summum bonum* and a morality of the Categorical Imperative is as radical as de Burgh maintains.'[325] Others took the matter up in greater detail. H. D. Lewis's point is that 'in one sense, everyone ought to act according to his lights, in another sense, the sense in which the deluded fanatic is doing what is wrong, he ought not'.[326] Even non-fanatics can and do act rightly in accordance with their consciences, whilst in another sense which does not affect the estimation of moral worth, what they do is wrong. A. C. Ewing remarks, 'I seem, to myself to be able to see clearly that, other things being equal, the fact that something would be good carries with it an obligation to produce it, while Professor de Burgh seems to himself to see equally clearly that it does not. ... [His account] brings out effectively the fundamental opposition between two typical rival outlooks in ethics, but I am not satisfied that the different characteristics attributed to each view need go together. It does not seem to me that a philosopher who derives the ought from the good need understress or explain away the occurrence of moral struggle or suppose that to know one's duty is to do it.'[327] Later in the same paper Ewing expresses his point in other words, to which de Burgh replied as follows:

---

[324] Ibid., 140.
[325] A. E. Taylor, 'W. G. de Burgh', 388.
[326] H. D. Lewis, *Morals and Revelation*, London: Allen & Unwin, 1951, 50.
[327] A. C. Ewing, Review of FMTR in *The Hibbert Journal*, XXXVII no. 3, 1939, 497.

> Dr. Ewing criticises my solution as leading to a dilemma. 'Why', he asks, 'ought we to act in accord with God's intentions? Because God is good? If so, we can, after all, derive obligation from the good. Or simply because God commands us to do so? If obligation cannot be derived from the good, still less could it be derived from a mere command.' I accept unreservedly the first alternative. That is one reason why I was at pains to justify the ascription of goodness to God. But (I contend) it is only on the ground of religion that we can overcome the dualism of ethical principles.[328]

Most perceptively of all, N. H. G. Robinson diagnoses the situation in which de Burgh limits the scope of duty by the recognition of the desire for a rational good thus:

> de Burgh is driven to the recognition of the two moral principles, action from a sense of duty and action from desire of a rational good, as two quite different ethical principles, simply because consciously or unconsciously he has adopted a rigouristic [sic] conception of duty. In a personal note he tells us that 'a life worth living has always presented itself to me as a task to be faced rather than as an ideal end to be desired and enjoyed'. On the other hand, he recognises that 'there are many ... who ... are chiefly moved to act by a vivid and growing consciousness of ideal good ... without thought of moral obligation'. Now the guiding principle behind this distinction is the presence or absence of direct desire. The two types of action are distinguished because in one case inclination points directly in the direction of the 'moral' action, whereas in the other case it does not.
>
> Yet surely this is an error. ... This rigouristic [sic] conception of duty is the notion of a self-defeating principle, for if essentially duty resists desire it still requires desire for its own defiant existence. Moreover, it is the case that in fact, although duty may often be in the face of contrary desire, it is not essentially so. The formula of duty is not that I ought to do act A provided that I have no desire to do it or even provided that I have a desire not to do it, but that I ought to do it whether I want to or not.
>
> Once all this is recognized it proves the inadequacy of a rigouristic [sic] conception of duty; and that in turn means that the chief obstacle has been removed which prevents a recognition of the comprehensive character of the principle of duty.[329]

It is interesting to observe that whereas de Burgh was only too keen to take a more comprehensive view of reason and of faith, he drew the line at duty. In view of his own testimony on the matter one may be forgiven for suspecting the influence of

---

[328] W. G. de Burgh, 'The right and the good', 494, citing Ewing's paper above, 499.
[329] N. H. G. Robinson, *The Claim of Morality*, 293–4. Robinson quoted FMTR, 71.

temperament on his decision. The suspicion is increased when de Burgh speaks of 'an idiosyncracy rather than ... a rational experience', and writes:

> The saint[330] ... is tempted, in the ardour of his love for God and his assurance of redemption, to fancy himself already one of the elect ... Mine is the contrary temptation, to fall into the extreme of Calvinistic heresy and imagine that I have been predestined to eternal damnation. Of course, I know that the fear is irrational. God is not like that. But I can never quite rid myself of the suspicion. For, like all perversions, it is the perversion of a truth. If the moral law is the final tribunal, we all stand – of this I am sure – justly condemned. Religion indeed, gives hope of forgiveness; on the one condition of the integrity of our repentance. But who can be perfectly sure of his integrity? Hence of the peace and joy of religion, I know but little. I like religious services, especially sermons, but that is quite another story. I suppose that it is because of this deficiency that the Catholic doctrine of Purgatory has always strongly appealed to me.[331]

This from one who also knows that salvation is by God's grace alone, not by something as fluctuating as our integrity (that would be a doctrine of works indeed); and who, after citing Bernard of Clairvaux's words, *Tu te amas in nobis*, and referring to relevant Pauline and Johannine texts, can declare that 'the real presence of the divine Spirit [is] exhibited, veritably, and not simply by analogy, not even by resemblance, in the experience within the individual of the mutual love of God and man'.[332]

Turning now to the broader question, we must ask how viable is the move from morality to religion, by which de Burgh set such store? De Burgh's case is that morality finds its completion in religion. I could wish that he had made it clearer that there is not a seamless passage from the one to the other. On the contrary, there is a logical discontinuity between the intimations of morality – and, as he recognizes, of the theistic arguments – and what, borrowing from J. L. Stocks, de Burgh calls a 'total assertion', namely, 'the apprehension of a unitary whole which is more than the sum of its constituent parts'.[333] The definition is elaborated later thus: 'a judgment passed, not on this or that tenet or practice, or on any collective body of particular doctrines, but on the proffered scheme of thought and life in its entirety, including both its speculative Weltanshauung and its effects on individual character and history'.[334] Moreover, the judgement passed is of the nature of a judgement of faith and, said de Burgh, recourse was had to such a judgement by Absolute idealists no less than by upholders of the Nicene Creed.

---

[330] He here thinks in ecclesiastical, not in biblical terms.

[331] FMTR, 75. For some reflections on 'the extreme of Calvinistic heresy' see Alan P. F. Sell, *Enightenment, Ecumenism, Evangel*, 325–38.

[332] Ibid., 179.

[333] LR, 14, citing J. L. Stocks, *Reason and Intuition*, London: OUP, 1939, 38 ff.

[334] LR, 120; cf. 203.

Where Christianity is concerned, we recall that de Burgh recommended an understanding of 'faith' that encompasses the logic-surpassing, but not irrational, trustful, enabled, response (*fiducia*) to the God who had lovingly made himself known in revelation, and supremely in Christ. There is thus more to faith than the Neoplatonic intellectual intuition or Aquinas's assent to dogma,[335] and than my faith that the sun will rise tomorrow. This is borne out by many passages in which de Burgh speaks of the importance of religious experience. God is known 'on the strength of his self-revelation, as the object of a reasonable faith';[336] and by the same token he is known as personal. Believers have 'an assurance of God by direct acquaintance'.[337] In this connection he is right to protest against Dawes Hicks's parody of Schleiermacher's view to the effect that the religious experience is a matter of feeling devoid of cognitive import,[338] though in a later work he levels the charge on his own behalf and sweeps Pietists and Methodists into an emotion-mongering bundle in a quite uncritical way.[339] Again, in claiming that 'The experiencing and the experienced are given together'[340] he raises, but does not address, the complex question of the language of encounter in theology, and pursues it no further.[341]

Among questions raised by the positing of world-and-life views are the following: Are they chosen or otherwise come by? What of the clash of world views? De Burgh does not address these matters and, as to the latter, he wrote in a society in which it was easier to assume than it is today that Christianity is the pre-eminent religion. Even in his own time, however, G. H. Langley asked of him, 'How is it possible to obtain an assurance that any particular interpretation of religious experience is sufficiently universal to become central in a theocentric world-view? In seeking a satisfactory interpretation Professor de Burgh turns to the great religious thinkers of the Middle Ages, but it must be borne in mind that this interpretation would not be accepted by spiritual masters belonging to

---

[335] See TRP, 17, 18.

[336] TRP, 54.

[337] Ibid., 110.

[338] FMTR, 149 n. See Alan P. F. Sell, *Confessing and Commending the Faith*, 338. The point is that in the eighteenth century 'feeling' meant more than 'emotion' and much more than 'cosy glows'. In Schleiermacher's thought the feeling of absolute dependence has an objective reference to God, and this has cognitive, not simply emotional, content.

[339] LR, 18–19; cf. TRP, 39.

[340] Ibid.

[341] Though in fairness it must be added that, intellectual time-lags being what they are, it was not until the 1950s that C. B. Martin and R. W. Hepburn brought the insights of analytical philosophy to bear upon encounter discourse. See C. B. Martin, 'A religious way of knowing', in A. G. N. Flew and A. MacIntyre, eds, *New Essays in Philosophical Theology*, London: SCM Press, 1955; R. W. Hepburn, *Christianity and Paradox*, London: Watts, 1958. See also Alan P. F. Sell, *Confessing and Commending the Faith*, 342–4.

other religious communities.'³⁴² We shall in due course find that H. A. Hodges paid considerably more attention to the logic of world views than did his Reading predecessor.

Undeterred, de Burgh affirms that 'The crudest revelation of God generates of necessity an outlook on men and things, a world-view, which as the mind develops, ripens into a theocentric philosophy.'³⁴³ His entire purpose is summed up in the desire to provide a prolegomenon to such a philosophy: a prolegomenon because, as he insists, he wishes to write philosophy, not theology or apologetics. In the event, however, as we have seen time and again, he cannot keep theology at bay and his tone is frequently apologetic. Thus he has much to say on the distinctiveness of Christianity, the foundation of which, he says, is the personality of Jesus.³⁴⁴ This Jesus is the Son of God, and 'the personal relationship of God to man is rendered possible only through the distinction of persons within the divine unity; the middle wall of partition between God and man being broken down by the Father's Incarnation in the person of the Word made flesh'.³⁴⁵ He further explains that 'The strength of the Christian doctrines of the Incarnation and of the Holy Spirit, and their reasonableness, lie precisely in the affirmation that this personal relationship between the Creator and the creature is rendered possible, by act of grace, through the indwelling of the transcendent "Other" in finite man.'³⁴⁶ He affirms the Trinity;³⁴⁷ he asserts Christ's resurrection;³⁴⁸ as we have already seen he distinguishes between sin as a breach of relations with God, and evil; for all its faults, he upholds the place of the Church,³⁴⁹ and he will not rule out hell on moral grounds.³⁵⁰ Indeed, de Burgh offers so much theology that one would have liked to have heard more. For example, the characteristically Anglican emphasis upon the Incarnation seems to swamp the rare references to atonement;³⁵¹ the impassibility of God is asserted rather than defended;³⁵² and when, in contending that to hold that evil is a positive reality is to assert ultimate dualism he counters, 'Philosophy

---

³⁴² G. H. Langley, Review of TRP, *The Hibbert Journal*, XXXV no. 4, July 1937, 636.
³⁴³ FMTR, 150.
³⁴⁴ LAW, 319.
³⁴⁵ FMTR, 202; cf. 221.
³⁴⁶ LR, 92; cf. 116–17.
³⁴⁷ For example, LR, 168.
³⁴⁸ For example, KI, 54.
³⁴⁹ For example, LAW, 336 n; TRP, 51; FMTR, 195 n.
³⁵⁰ FMTR, 76 n.: '[T]hose who reject hell on *moral* grounds are in a singularly weak position. If all is to be well in the end for everybody, the moral significance of our present life is seriously lessened. It ceases to be really a state of probation. Such sentimental optimism, however, is of a piece with the prevalent laxity of thought in regard to the moral responsibility of the individual.'
³⁵¹ De Burgh thought that Aquinas' view of religion was not sufficiently incarnational. See TRP, 112.
³⁵² For example FMTR, 166.

and religion are monistic, or they are nothing',[353] he tends in an intellectualist direction which sidesteps P. T. Forsyth's adverse verdict on monists: 'For want of the dualism that a holy love implies, their moral world flattens, and the moral practice of their successors must succumb.'[354] To place the quotations side by side is to indicate the need of careful consideration of the differences between, and the possible relations of, ontological and moral dualism; and of both in relation to the tenability or otherwise or monism.

It seems to me that de Burgh's failure to keep theology and apologetics at bay is not a product of carelessness on his part, it is a function of his method. I, like others whom I have mentioned, am in entire sympathy with his refusal to restrict reason to ratiocination, and to associate it with the intuition of first principles. But if the intuited first principals concern the God of Christianity who, as lovingly revealed is not an undifferentiated Absolute, or Being, then to expound them is to talk and write theology. De Burgh's professional *cum* departmental embargo simply will not work. To put it otherwise: he knows that neither theistic arguments nor moral insight will carry a person all the way to religious faith. Furthermore, in his late criticism of Gilson he asks,

> is there a place for theology as distinguished from philosophy in a philosophy that is genuinely Christian? God is not a 'clear and distinct' concept, nor is Creation intelligible to human understanding; the difference between these beliefs and that in the Trinity or the Incarnation is one, not of kind, but of degree. If reason be extended to cover a reasonable faith, all alike are capable of inclusion in its synthesis.[355]

Why not, then, instead of attempting to work up to religion, begin with the claims of faith as revealed by God supremely in Christ, and show where and how they endorse, and even fulfil, the best insights of metaphysics and morality. In neither case can copper-bottomed demonstration result, but the latter approach would leave the Christian philosopher freer to announce his or her convictions and to show their coherence with, or points of departure from, other facets of intellectual life. The synthesis of Christianity with philosophy, which he sought on the ground that, its revelational character notwithstanding, the religion's affirmations are intrinsically reasonable,[356] would more readily be achieved (albeit not necessarily to the satisfaction of all philosophers or theologians).

There are hints in his writings that this is the course he would have taken had he lived to present his Christian philosophy[357] and not merely its prolegomena.

---

[353] FMTR, 223.

[354] P. T. Forsyth, 'Monism', a paper printed for the London Society for the Study of Religion, 1909, 10.

[355] W. G. de Burgh, review of É. Gilson, *God and Philosophy*, 280.

[356] TRP, 42; cf. KI, 56.

[357] See Clement C. J. Webb's remarks, LR, xii.

For if, finally, we ask, What form does de Burgh think that a Christian philosophy would take? we find that his answer does not set out from theistic arguments, nor from morality, and then work up to religion. He begins with the experience of God:

> On the evidence of religious experience, clarified by rational criticism, and fortified by speculative arguments which, though not ... demonstrative, yet confirm what it lies beyond their power to prove; such a philosophy acknowledges the theistic postulate and the theocentric world-view that follows from it, as the objects of a reasonable faith. It posits as the supreme reality a God, who is not merely, like the Hegelian Absolute, individual Spirit, but is known to mankind in personal communion through his own act of self-revelation. By thus manifesting himself in love, the supreme reality is revealed also as the supreme good. The reality of the world, the scene of man's temporal life, and therewith the worth of human achievement in civilization, are secured by the doctrine of creation, resting on the distinction between self-caused and created being. Man's other-worldly destiny, to which his sense of guilt and impotence and his infinite desire for perfection alike bear witness – facts which no philosophy, however optimistic, can explain away – is presented as a realizable ideal through the agency of supernatural providence and supernatural grace. *Le grandeur et la misère de l'homme* achieve their synthesis in the scheme of divine redemption.[358]

For a further indication of that of which we have been deprived we may turn to the concluding sentences of his posthumous book:

> My own experience, over more than half a century, has carried me, as a student and teacher of philosophy, into the realm of theory rather than into that of action. If therefore I have any qualification to write as an advocate of the Christian faith, it is the speculative aspect, and not the practical, that falls within my narrow competence. [In a footnote he adds, 'Though no one can set himself to discuss these high matters except with a sense of diffidence or incompetence']. Believing as I do that in that faith alone lie the hope and promise for the world, I cannot, when I look back on that experience and what I have learnt from it, question the urgency of the obligation to use what strength remains to me in the closing years of life in drawing from it the materials for a constructive argument to the truth of the Christian Gospel, and for an answer to the speculative difficulties which, still after nineteen centuries, hinder so many acute and earnest thinkers from yielding to it their assent.[359]

Those poignant words both announce de Burgh's unrealized intention and confirm our loss.

---

[358] TRP, 211.
[359] LR, 207.

Chapter 3
Walter Robert Matthews (1881–1973): Experience, Rationality and Revelation

Of the four Anglicans considered in this book, Walter Robert Matthews, who became Dean of St Paul's, unquestionably had the highest profile nationally. The only one of the four not to have been educated at Oxford or Cambridge, he was lauded as '[T]he most distinguished graduate from the Faculty of Theology' of King's College, London;[1] and he is the only one of the four to have left a full-scale autobiography.[2]

Matthews was born in a small house in Bushey Hill Road, Camberwell, London, on 22 September 1881, and christened at All Saints Church, Blenheim Grove.[3] He was deeply affected by the death on 24 March 1902 of his younger brother, Hubert, aged 18; twins, Olive and Edgar completed the family. Matthews's father, Philip Walter Matthews, a Protestant with deep suspicions of popery, rose from being a bank clerk at a company which was absorbed into Barclays Bank to the position of Chief Inspector at the Bankers' Clearing House. He believed in self-help, and improved his own education by attendance at public lectures held in the district, and through membership of a Shakespeare Society and an Essay Club. Matthews's mother, Sophia Alice Self, who could read and speak French, fostered in Matthews a love of reading and, 'though she would have laughed at the idea that she could be either a poet or a philosopher, if I have any aptitude for either of these exercises, I attribute it to her ... from my early childhood she encouraged me to talk about "God, freedom and immortality" in childish parables and symbols ...'[4] With this we may, perhaps, associate his self-estimation: 'I really seem to have been insufferably dreamy when a boy.'[5] His infant teacher, Miss Batstone, tried in vain to secure Matthews for her Baptist fold, while a dedicated Anglican layman named Brown, theologically conservative and enthusiastically

---

[1] Sydney Evans in F. M. L. Thompson, ed., *The University of London and the World of Learning 1836-1986*, London: The Hambledon Press, 1990, 155.

[2] The autobiography is entitled, *Memories and Meanings* [hereinafter, MM], London: Hodder and Stoughton, 1969. See also DTCBP; ODNB; *Who Was Who, 1971–1980*; H. P. Owen, *W. R. Matthews: Philosopher and Theologian*, London: The Athlone Press, 1976; and references to follow.

[3] MM, 13. This Church was, and according to its website remains, within the Anglican evangelical tradition.

[4] Ibid., 18.

[5] Ibid., 22.

evangelical, challenged him to witness for Christ, whilst at the same time holding that 'There are only two things which keep revolution from this country, religion and beer.'[6] In the circles in which the young Matthews moved were a number who were convinced that the Pope was Antichrist, and that the 'Puseyites' were plotting to overthrow the Church of England.

Matthews proceeded to Miss Rose's Academy for the Sons and Daughters of Gentlemen, and thence to Wilson's Grammar School, Camberwell. During Matthews' time there the Headmaster was the Reverend Mr Macdowell. Consequent upon presenting three sermons he had preached in Camden Church and then paid to have translated into Latin to the Regius Professor, Macdowell was awarded the Doctorate of Divinity of the University of Oxford. Matthews wryly surmizes that the Professor 'no doubt read them and found no heresy in them', and remarks that later in life A. C. Headlam 'confided to me his plans to make the doctor's degree a real credential of scholarship'.[7] The teacher who influenced Matthews the most was Percy Nunn, later Professor of Education and Director of the Institute of Education of the University of London.[8] On one occasion an Anglo-Catholic junior master, St Cedd, accompanied Matthews to hear an address by the ardent Protestant, John Kensit. Matthews recalls that

> When Mr. Kensit made what seemed to me an outrageous sweeping statement about nuns in general, St. Cedd shouted 'That's a lie!', whereupon two or three muscular stewards pushed us not at all gently out of the hall and down some stone steps, which I remember were hard when you fell down them. Since then I have made it a rule to conduct my theological disputes on paper.[9]

On leaving school Matthews found employment at Westminster Bank, and there he remained for five years. He read widely in his spare time – especially in religion and politics, and had conversations with his oldest friend, Sidney Marsh, on questions of belief and Christian practice in the contemporary world. Matthews was grateful for the way in which Herbert Spencer introduced him to epistemology, and to Darwin for raising the questions of the authority of Scripture and the nature of divine revelation, given that the creation narratives of Genesis could not be literally true. This period of questioning and reflection was ended when, on leaving the office of the Swiss Banking Corporation following a business visit, 'I was taken hold of by a power, or Spirit, which filled me with joy and peace and courage. My doubts about God were transcended. He needed me and called me.'[10]

Matthews enrolled at King's College, London, certain that he wished to probe religion more deeply, but not at all sure that he could become a candidate for

---

[6] Ibid., 24.
[7] Ibid., 32.
[8] For Thomas Percy Nunn (1870–1944) see ODNB.
[9] MM, 35.
[10] Ibid., 42–3.

Holy Orders. The Principal and Professor of Dogmatics was A. C. Headlam, who appeared formidable and High Church: 'The first impression was abundantly verified, the second turned out to be an illusion based on Headlam's nervous tick of bending his knees at intervals when speaking in public. Careful observation soon convinced me that his genuflexions had no relation with the words he was uttering.'[11] He valued the teaching of Alexander Nairne, Professor of Old Testament, and was grateful to the Professor of Church History, E. W. Watson, for prompting him to think about the nature of historical evidence, Watson's satirical tongue notwithstanding. The New Testament Professor, H. J. White, though a good scholar, adopted conservative positions, and mentioned German biblical criticism only to rebut it.[12] Matthews's greatest debt was to the Professor of Philosophy, Alfred Caldecott. As his major work testifies,[13] Caldecott delighted to present the systems of others, and to comment upon them, but he never developed a system of his own; his students were left to guess what his opinions might be. Matthews dedicated his Boyle Lectures, *Studies in Christian Philosophy* (1921) to Caldecott, to whom he owed his 'deepest and most abiding obligation'.[14]

With the passage of time, and by now in possession of his BD, Matthews felt an increasingly irresistible call to ministry, though he entertained less than wholehearted commitment to the Church of England's Thirty-Nine Articles of Religion. He overcame his scruples and was ordained in 1907: 'Perhaps', he later reflected, 'I was wrong, but I can at least claim that I have missed no opportunity of trying to get the Articles either abolished or changed.'[15]

Matthews's first post was that of lecturer in philosophy at King's College. With this he coupled part-time service as assistant curate, first at St Mary Abbots, Kensington, where his radical politics and 'modernist' theology were not well received, and then, together with his college friend, R. Neville Pyke, at St Peter's, Regent Square. In 1911 he married Margaret Bryan, a schools inspector's daughter, whom he had met while she was a science student at Royal Holloway College. Of her he wrote, 'She was never, I think, an orthodox churchwoman, but she was deeply religious. She helped me in ways that a more docile believer would not have found possible.'[16] Their first child, Michael Harrington, was baptized by Alfred Caldecott, who had succeeded Headlam as Dean of King's College.

---

[11] Ibid., 46.

[12] For Arthur Cayley Headlam (1862–1947), Alexander Nairne (1863–1936) and Henry Julian White (1859–1934) see ODNB.

[13] *The Philosophy of Religion in England and America*, London: Methuen, 1901.

[14] W. R. Matthews, *Studies in Christian Philosophy* (hereinafter SCP), London: Macmillan, 1928, xii. The book was first published in 1921, but I use the second edition because of the new material it contains. For Caldecott (1850–1936) see DNCBP.

[15] MM, 62.

[16] Ibid., 77. During their courtship Matthews invited her to read T. B. Strong's *A Manual of Theology*. She never reached the end of it, and was not persuaded by what she did read.

Michael, who became a Sub-Lieutenant RNVR, 'was killed on HMS Greyhound, the destroyer which was the first to reach Dunkirk, on May 28th, 1940'.[17] Their second son, Walter Bryan, became Professor of Clinical Neurology at Oxford;[18] and their daughter, Barbara, an Oxford graduate in Modern Languages, served with the Women's Auxiliary Air Force (WAAF) during the Second World War, and married Captain Martin Hebb, who was wounded in Italy, but survived. Margaret died on 11 October 1963.

Student numbers were depleted at King's College following the outbreak of the First World War, and the financial position of the College became precarious. The Dean and senior staff held the fort, but Matthews, as a junior lecturer, undertook parochial duties, notably at Christ Church, Crouch End, where he found his sermons compared with those of George Ernest Darlaston at the local Congregational Church. Unlike Matthews, who held that 'No man has a right to accept the protection and the amenities of civilised life unless he is prepared to uphold and defend the State and its institutions when they are attacked by an enemy,'[19] Darlaston, an able scholar, was a convinced pacifist, on which account some of his members defected to Christ Church, though most who disagreed with him did not.[20]

In 1918 Matthews succeeded Caldecott as Dean and Professor of the Philosophy of Religion at King's College. He accepted the unsought post with some trepidation. Professor H. J. White 'deplored and protested against my election as Dean',[21] and Matthews 'knew that the story of my election "over the heads" ... of far better and more orthodox candidates was current in episcopal circles'.[22] The fears of the orthodox were somewhat allayed when, at Matthews's invitation, Charles Gore joined the staff following his retirement from the bishopric of Oxford.[23] Reflecting later upon his Deanship, Matthews wished that he been more drastic in his criticism of the curriculum under which ordinands were trained, and that he had paid more

---

[17] MM, 248.

[18] For whom see *Who Was Who 2001–2005*, London: A. & C. Black, 2006.

[19] MM, 87.

[20] MM, 86, 95. For Darlaston (1876–1931) see *Congregational Year Book 1932*, London: Congregational Union of England and Wales, 219. Born in Birmingham and educated first at Mason College, he graduated BA (London) with first class honours, and was immediately appointed lecturer in Anglo-Saxon and English Literature. He proceeded to the London MA, and after one year, having won a scholarship, he resigned his post and trained for the ministry at Mansfield College, gaining his BA in the Honour School of Theology. He proceeded to Germany, where he studied under Harnack in Marburg and Pfleiderer in Berlin. He ministered at the Church-in-the-Grove, Sydenham (1903–11) and thence at Crouch End until his death. His obituary mentions his chaplaincy of summer camps for public schoolboys, but not his pacifism.

[21] MM, 100.

[22] Ibid., 103–4.

[23] For Gore (1853–1932) see ODNB.

attention to their spiritual development. On the other hand, 'In the theological colleges, as they had developed since the Oxford Movement, [the policy was] that of isolating theological students from worldly studies. In my opinion the isolated theological colleges, though often wonderful schools of spiritual life, had, on the whole, been mistakenly aloof from the world.'[24] He also thought that the average Scottish minister was more thoroughly trained than the average Church of England priest;[25] and when in the United States he was astounded to encounter BDs who knew no Greek – 'a kind of contradiction in terms, ... I had to admit that there was a case for substituting psychological, sociological and philosophical study for linguistic scholarship.'[26] The effort to keep King's afloat and to maintain his teaching commitments consumed his time and energies.

Matthews developed good relations with the political theorist and newly-appointed Principal of King's College, Ernest Barker.[27] Barker was by now an Anglican, but he had been raised under the thoughtful Congregationalism of F. J. Powicke at Hatherlow, Cheshire.[28] In the wider University Faculty of Theology, which embraced a number of denominational colleges, Matthews was on cordial terms with such colleagues as the Congregationalists P. T. Forsyth, Principal of Hackney College, and A. E. Garvie, Principal of New College; and H. Wheeler Robinson, Principal of Regent's Park College, the Baptist. Forsyth's thought 'did not move on lines that were easy for me to accept', said Matthews, but he recognized Forsyth as a theologian of importance, and once dogmatically declared that 'everything of value in the writings of Karl Barth had been said earlier and more clearly by Forsyth'.[29] Garvie had taught the student Matthews Comparative Religions, and Matthews recalled him with affection as a brilliant linguist and pioneer ecumenist.[30] For his part Garvie expressed his pleasure

---

[24] MM, 115.

[25] Ibid., 116.

[26] Ibid., 120.

[27] For Barker (1874–1960) see ODNB.

[28] For Powicke (1854–1935) see Alan P. F. Sell, *Enlightenment, Ecumenism, Evangel. Theological Themes and Thinkers 1550-2000*, Milton Keynes: Paternoster, 2005, ch. 1.

[29] MM, 123. A slightly exaggerated judgement, perhaps, and one that should not tempt us into thinking that Forsyth was, as has frequently been said without qualification, 'a Barthian before Barth'. See Alan P. F. Sell, *Testimony and Tradition*, Aldershot: Ashgate, 2005, 221. The Forsyth bibliography is considerable. A start may be made with ODNB; John Taylor and Clyde Binfield, eds, *Who They Were in the Reformed Churches of England and Wales 1901-2000*, Donington: Shaun Tyas, 2007; Alan P. F. Sell, *Testimony and Tradition*, chs. 7, 8; idem, *Nonconformist Theology in the Twentieth Century*, Milton Keynes: Paternoster, 2006; Leslie McCurdy, *Attributes and Atonement: The Holy Love of God in the Theology of P. T. Forsyth* (includes a substantial bibliography), Carlisle: Paternoster, 1999.

[30] Ibid., 124. For Garvie (1861–1945) see ODNB; *Who Was Who 1941–1950*; J. Taylor and C. Binfield, eds, *Who They Were*; Alan P. F. Sell, *Nonconformist Theology*, *passim*.

at attending Matthews's installation as Dean of Exeter and then of St Paul's, and declared that 'I set a high value on his contributions to theological and philosophical thought.'[31] Matthews's closest friend in the Faculty was Wheeler Robinson, with whom he also cooperated as joint editor of Nisbet's *Library of Constructive Theology*, the objective of which was to elevate experience and to expound theological subjects 'on the basis of the religious consciousness'.[32] He found it somewhat incongruous that the Baptists, with their Puritan inheritance, should be occupying a magnificent mansion in Regent's Park, and on a visit there he said to the students, 'Having in mind your traditions and the purpose of this College, I must assume that the charming young creatures depicted on the ceiling and walls of this sumptuous apartment are cherubs, but I must own that to my Anglican eyes they look uncommonly like cupids.'[33] Among Matthews's Baptist students was the historian and ecumenist Earnest A. Payne who, after teaching at Regent's Park College, Oxford, became General Secretary of the Baptist Union of Great Britain and Ireland.[34]

In 1920 Matthews was appointed chaplain to Gray's Inn, and preacher in 1929. From 1923 to 1931 he was chaplain to the King. Meanwhile, on 20 November 1926, at a meeting of the electors to the Ely Professorship of Divinity at Cambridge, W. R. Inge, Dean of St Paul's, expressed the hope that Matthews, although he was not a candidate, would be elected to the vacant Chair. Inge's objective was 'to bring a philosopher to Cambridge, where they are rather overloaded with commentators'.[35] In the event J. M. Creed of St John's College was elected – 'a very good man, and of my own way of thinking',[36] said Inge.

By the time he left King's College for the Deanship of Exeter Cathedral in 1931, Matthews had published his major philosophical works, *Studies in Christian Philosophy* (1921), for which he was awarded the degree of Doctor of Divinity (London); and *God in Christian Thought and Experience* (1930), which he dedicated to his wife. In addition, three courses of Lectures given under the auspices of the Liverpool Diocesan Board of Divinity had appeared: *The Idea of Revelation* (1923), *The Psychological Approach to Religion* (1925); and *God and Evolution* (1926); while in *The Gospel and the Modern Mind* (1930) he

---

[31] A. E. Garvie, *Memories and Meanings of My Life*, London: Allen & Unwin, 1938, 213.

[32] So the Introduction to Matthews's own contribution to the series: *God in Christian Thought and Experience* (hereinafter GCTE) London: Nisbet, 1930, viii. Cf. MM, 125. For Robinson (1872–1945) see ODNB; Ernest A. Payne, *Henry Wheeler Robinson: Scholar, Teacher, Principal. A Memoir*, London: Nisbet, 1946.

[33] MM, 125. The Baptist College removed to Oxford in 1927.

[34] MM, 125. For Payne see ODNB; W. M. S. West, *To be a Pilgrim. A Memoir of Ernest A. Payne*, Guildford: Lutterworth, 1983.

[35] W. R. Inge, *Diary of a Dean. St. Paul's 1911-34*, London: Hutchinson, 1941, 116. For Inge (1860-1954) see ODNB.

[36] Ibid.

revealed his considerable ability in taking the deep questions posed by the person in the street with the utmost seriousness and addressing them fluently and with integrity. This latter ability was to stand him in good stead when he occupied cathedral pulpits; gave broadcast talks of which examples are to be found in *The Hope of Immortality* (1936) and *Signposts to God* (1938); and over the 24 years in which he contributed religious articles to *The Daily Telegraph*, some of which are reprinted in *The Search for Perfection* (1957) and *The Year Through Christian Eyes* (1970). In similar vein are the earlier volumes, *Essays in Construction* (1933), a series of papers, dedicated to his mother, based on articles published in *The Guardian*; and *Our Faith in God* (1936), his contribution to the London Diocesan series of study books. As editor, he gathered an ecumenical group of authors for *The Christian Faith. Essays in Explanation and Defence* (1936), and among his smaller works are *The Moral Issues of the War* (1940), his Myers Memorial Lecture to the Society for Psychical Research, 'Psychical research and theology', his Essex Hall Lecture, *Reason in Religion* (1950), and his Presidential Address to The English Association, *The British Philosopher as Writer* (1955). As he was about to leave Exeter to assume the Deanship of St Paul's in succession to Dr W. R. Inge,[37] Matthews dedicated his now expanded Holy Week meditations, *Seven Words* (1933) – originally delivered in the Cathedral on Good Friday, 1931 – to the Cathedral Chapter 'with gratitude for much friendship'. Among his last publications is a booklet with a self-explanatory title which takes us back to his pre-ordination questionings: *The Thirty-Nine Articles. A Plea for a New Statement of the Christian Faith as Understood by the Church of England* (1961).

What is noticeable is the dearth of more philosophico-theological tomes in Matthews's post-King's period. We have his Alexander Lectures, *The Purpose of God* (1936), which were delivered in the University of Glasgow in 1935; and his F. D. Maurice Lectures of 1949, *The Problem of Christ in the Twentieth Century* (1950, 1951).[38] The obvious explanation is that his official work first at Exeter and then at St Paul's gave him a wider platform than he had enjoyed previously, and of this he took advantage to great effect. His lot became ever more stressful following the bombing of St Paul's on 29 December 1940. The repair and renovation of the Cathedral drained his energies, but he lived to see it fully restored, and published his account of *Saint Paul's Cathedral in Wartime, 1939–1945* (1946). As William Wand, Bishop of London, wrote on Matthews's retirement from St Paul's in 1967, 'To have led the team which preserved [the Cathedral] during the ravages of war, to have cleaned and restored it when the conflict was over, to have built

---

[37] Matthews was Inge's 'first choice' for the post, and he informed Archbishop Cosmo Gordon Lang of his opinion. The Archbishop concurred. See Inge's *Diary of a Dean*, 171, 177. Matthews's' appointment 'is a great pleasure and relief to me', wrote Inge, ibid., 179. In turn, Matthews wrote a memoir of Inge: 'William Ralph Inge 1860–1954,' *Proceedings of the British Academy*, XL, 1954, 263–73. For Lang (1864–1945) see ODNB.

[38] Matthews himself had instituted the Maurice Lectures when he was Dean of King's. See MM, 318.

its new choir school, and to have set the whole, vast enterprise fully equipped on a new stage in its age-long witness to eternal truth: what more could a man wish to take with him into his retirement?'[39] I am quite prepared to believe that these are sufficient grounds for his relative scholarly inactivity. But there is also a suggestion that he, who had held so many visiting lectureships at home and abroad, was peeved, or wounded, or both, because he had not received an invitation to deliver the prestigious Gifford Lectures and, consequently, he had withdrawn from philosophical publication. He refers to F. R. Tennant and himself thus:

> neither of us was invited to give the Gifford Lectures which are supposed to be devoted to the defence and exposition of 'natural religion' or 'rational belief'. I say nothing about my own eligibility for the lectureship, except that I have written quite a lot on the subject; of Tennant, any critic of sufficient learning to have a right to an opinion would say he was the outstanding author of the day in the field of English philosophical theology. At least both Tennant and I would claim that we wrote about the subject of which Lord Gifford founded his lecture to advance the study, while some of the Gifford Lectures were almost irrelevant and at least one Gifford lecturer explicitly denied that there was such a subject and held that the time spent lecturing on it was not only wasted but promoted a dangerous illusion.[40]

These words might be taken as suggesting either a certain arrogance, or an honest conviction that he had been unjustly overlooked. I incline to the latter view on the ground that in other aspects of his life Mathews did not appear as a proud man,[41] but as one who was not slow to point to his failings. We have already heard him lament his slothfulness regarding the revision of the theological curriculum and the spiritual life of his students, and he could also confess, 'I fear that my ministry has often been less useful than it might have been, because I did not feel deeply in my spirit the need of a sinner for the assurance of forgiveness. When I ought to have been answering his question, What must I do to be saved? I have been offering him reasons for believing in the existence of God.'[42] It is also the case that Matthews could be forgiven for feeling somewhat of an outsider: he had been made to feel that on more than one occasion. Just as some had stood aghast at his appointment to the King's Deanship, which many would have regarded as 'naturally' an Oxbridge

---

[39] W. Wand, 'Salute to Dean Matthews'. *The Church Times*, 12 July 1967, 10. For John William Charles Wand (1885–1977) see ODNB.

[40] MM, 161–2. Why, one wonders, did he not name Karl Barth?

[41] Cf. MM, 388, 406. Though he did enjoy his membership of the Athanaeum, and the numerous society dinners he was invited to attend.

[42] Wand wrote of Matthews that 'He never preaches either the Evangelical "expository" sermon or the Catholic "teaching" sermon. He always likes to be overheard trying to work something out. In other words, he is still the philosopher even in the pulpit.' See 'Salute to Dean Matthews'.

bailiwick, so when he went to St Paul's the Oxbridge 'prejudice was powerful enough to be an "accepted" principle in many quarters'. Indeed, 'The installation in St. Paul's had been protested against by the senior canon, Alexander, on the ground that my London degrees did not qualify me to hold the office of Dean of St. Paul's, even though I had Letters Patent from the Crown appointing me "for the term of my natural life".'[43] It should also be noted that Matthews was not alone in thinking that he would have done justice to the Gifford Lectureship. When he retired from St Paul's in 1967, William Wand, noting that Matthews had held the Wilde Lectureship in the Philosophy of Religion from 1929 to 1932, continued, 'If only someone had had the sense to make him Gifford Lecturer after that, we might have had some more outstanding volumes in the philosophy of religion.'[44] Perhaps, but, to repeat, when we recall the work he undertook at home and abroad, and the challenges he faced, during his post-King's ministry, there are explanations of his philosophical silence which seem more cogent than disappointment at not being invited to deliver the Giffords.[45]

Not, indeed, that Matthews was deprived of honours. He was appointed KCVO in 1935 and CH in 1962 – 'a most fitting honour for a man who has graced the Deanery of St. Paul's for many years with a quality of scholarship and preaching which loses nothing by its unpolemical tone', opined an editorial writer in *The Times*.[46] In 1947 Matthews was admitted to national orders in Norway and Czechoslovakia; he held seven honorary doctorates, and was a Fellow of the Royal Society of Literature. He died on 5 December 1973, and among the tributes paid to him was one by Marcus Knight, a successor in the Deanery of Exeter:

> Hundreds of Anglican clergymen who were at King's College between 1918 and 1931 recall his gifts as a teacher with gratitude. He ruled the Theological Department with kindness and firmness, and as Dean of the College was a fine administrator. As a colleague later, one realized that his witty style concealed a considerable talent for business and financial affairs.[47]

In the course of the 1952 session of the General Synod of the Anglican Church of Canada, Matthews delivered a sermon in the course of which he said,

---

[43] MM, 183–4.

[44] W. Wand, 'Salute to Dean Matthews'.

[45] Cf. H. P. Owen, *W. R. Matthews*, 70. Owen correctly states that after GCTE Matthews 'did not write another work of comparable scope. This was due chiefly to the duties involved in his ecclesiastical offices, but partly to the fact that (to his disappointment) he was not invited to deliver the Gifford Lectures.' Did Matthews speak to Owen in these terms? Is this hearsay? I have found no published evidence that disappointment was the reason why Matthews wrote no more substantial philosophical works, and Owen cites no manuscript source(s).

[46] *The Times*, 1 January 1962, 11.

[47] M. Knight, 'Dr. W. R. Matthews'. *The Times*, 7 December 1973, 21.

We shall be judged indeed by our faithfulness and our loyalty to Christ, but included in that faithfulness is the question whether we have served Our Lord fully with our minds, and thought courageously enough, and deeply enough, at this time of opportunity. Have we been sufficiently careful to show our generation that Christ is the truth – the answer not only to the needs of their hearts but to the questions of their minds?[48]

In his own case the answer must surely be, 'Yes.'

I

Before turning to Matthews's specific philosophical, doctrinal and ethical positions it will be helpful to delineate four general themes which underlie all his writing. They are the experiential basis of religion; the psychological interest; the relations between religion and science; and the need of a viable apologetic.

As already hinted, the authors engaged to contribute to *The Library of Constructive Theology* edited by Matthews and Robinson wished 'to lay stress upon the value and validity of religious experience and to develop their theology on the basis of the religious consciousness'.[49] This approach, they felt, accorded with that modern emphasis upon observation and experiment which had overtaken abstract *a priori* reasoning. For his part, Matthews expresses his indebtedness to Schleiermacher and Otto. Of the latter he writes, 'I would put Rudolf Otto very high among the teachers who by their thought and personal character have helped me.'[50] Schleiermacher had made religious experience the foundation of his theology, and Matthews endorses his attempt 'to treat the religious impulse as an inherent and necessary quality of human consciousness which normally develops along with the mind itself.'[51] Schleiermacher does not, however, emerge entirely unscathed from Matthews's scrutiny: he does not sufficiently clearly distinguish between 'feeling' in the sense of emotion and 'feeling' in the sense of perception, yet his theory is intelligible only if the latter is given due weight. I would add that there is an objective, cognitive, dimension in the eighteenth-century connotation of 'feeling' which is sometimes extruded from the term as used in the present day, and is as far as possible from emotion *qua* 'cosy glows'. As Matthews himself puts the point: 'the feeling of dependence in which many, following Schleiermacher, would find the germ of religion, involves the conception, however dim and confused, of some power or person of a supernatural kind'.[52]

---

[48] MM, 363.
[49] W. R. Matthews, *God in Christian Thought and Experience* (hereinafter GCTE), London: Nisbet, 1930, viii.
[50] MM, 218.
[51] GCTE, 7.
[52] SCP, 25.

Matthews further suggests, first, that Schleiermacher might have devoted more attention to the place of reason and conscience in religious development. I, in turn, feel that Matthews might have allowed more to Schleiermacher's motive in seeking a firmer foundation for religion than that supplied by those rational theistic arguments propounded down the centuries by Christians and attacked with some justification by religion's cultured despisers. Secondly, he complains that Schleiermacher's 'feeling of absolute dependence, taken by itself, seems to rule out the sense of co-operation with God which has been an element in some at least of the most highly evolved religious experience'.[53] Thirdly, Matthews prefers Otto's understanding of the 'numinous' – that distinctive emotion which at its highest is the apprehension of the transcendent 'Other' – to the 'feeling of dependence' because there are feelings of dependence that have no religious tone. But (a) we note the quiet dropping of the adjective 'absolute'; and (b) Matthews both questions 'the real existence of this special and distinctive "numinous feeling"' and four lines later affirms that it is indeed distinguishable from all other feelings.[54] With his general conclusion, however, it is possible to agree, namely, that both Schleiermacher and Otto 'have been too eager to delimit religion as a specific form of experience, and have distinguished it too sharply from other activities of spirit'.[55] With Otto still in his sights he bluntly declares that

> there are many points in Otto's theory which are open to grave dispute. In particular the persistence with which the object of religious reverence is described as the non-rational must cause anyone who cherishes a belief in the unity of the life of the spirit serious disquiet. It is curious that so many defenders of orthodoxy have welcomed Otto's numinous reality who would flee in horror from Spencer's 'Unknowable'.[56]

Again, 'No amount of talk about the "feeling of reality" will deliver us from the task of reaching some rational criterion by which we may distinguish the kind of God who can really be held to exist from the conceptions of deity which must be denied reality'.[57] For all his criticisms of some of Otto's conclusions, Matthews nevertheless feels that 'he has elucidated an essential, even the fundamental, element in religion. In its nature this element is pre-rational, and if he is right, anyone who has no experience of the numinous has no experience of religion'.[58]

Matthews's own broad characterization of the religious state of mind is as follows:

---

[53] GCTE, 7.
[54] Ibid, 8.
[55] Ibid., 9; cf. 11.
[56] Idem, *The Psychological Approach to Religion*, London: Longmans, Green, 1925, 15.
[57] Ibid., 16.
[58] Idem, *Reason in Religion*, London: The Lindsey Press, 1950, 14.

Religious states of mind contrast with those which are scientific or simply practical or moral in this respect, that whereas the scientific and moral are attempts at mastery over the not-self, to bring the objective material within the categories of the understanding or to bend it to the purpose of the will, in religion the self seeks rather to be mastered, to bend itself to that 'other' with which it is continuous. This is because, for religion, the 'other' is the realization of its values. In this respect the religious attitude is more closely akin to that of aesthetic enjoyment, which wishes not to alter the object but to remain in its presence. There is, however, an important difference from the aesthetic attitude. The religious attitude, though self-abnegating, is not passive, for it includes the possibility of co-operation. This difference ... is connected with a difference in the interpretation of the object. For the religious state of mind the object is not passive but active, not dead but alive.[59]

Religion, epistemology, morality or aesthetics, he continues, 'all have their fundamental problems which arise from the central situation – that of the self in contact with an object with which it can neither be wholly identical not from which it can be wholly different'.[60] Thus, for example, where religion is concerned, a purely immanent deity would finally be indistinguishable from ourselves, while with a purely transcendent one we could have no possibility of communion. Later, reverting to Schleiermacher, Matthews declares that 'Our first preoccupation as Christian thinkers is to maintain the reasonableness of what Christian experience has found God to be. Religion, as such, is concerned with maintaining the ultimate dependence of all things upon God ...'[61]

Since the experience of God has a basis in history and (*pace* Spinoza[62]) does not originate in general ideas or rely upon on the rationalistic deduction of consequents from self-evident principles, 'the modern scientific temper' has no grounds for complaint, for its phenomena, like those of theology, 'are known by observation, record and narration. The researcher must depend on human testimony.'[63] In the case of Christianity, 'we begin with the conviction that our religion rests upon an experience of God which was enjoyed by historical persons and, in a supreme degree, by one historical Person ...'[64] Against Bultmann's view that we have no access to Jesus' experience, but only to what he willed, Matthews retorts,

> Even Professor Bultmann holds that we have ample material for a knowledge of what Jesus willed. The theory that we can know this yet be wholly in the dark concerning Jesus' consciousness of God rests upon a psychology which is surely

---

[59] GCTE, 21.
[60] Ibid., 25.
[61] Ibid., 236.
[62] Matthews quotes *Tractatus Theologico-politicus*, IV, GCTE, 44.
[63] GCTE, 46.
[64] Ibid., 47.

one of the strangest. Obviously we cannot separate the will from the personality in this arbitrary manner.[65]

In fact, says Matthews, the experience of Jesus shows both that absolute dependence upon God which Schleiermacher brought to the fore, and also the element of cooperation with God, which Schleiermacher omitted from due consideration.

But if Matthews finds his starting point in the religious consciousness, he is by no means persuaded by some writers who also elevated experience. Whilst welcoming Ritschl's protest against the 'idol' of the Hegelian Absolute and a narrow intellectualism which does not give due place to the moral consciousness, he cannot not, for example, agree with Ritschl, that 'the question of the existence of God is outside the purview of rational enquiry, and belongs to the religious consciousness, which is taken to be a distinct and separate activity of spirit'.[66] At this point John Baillie regretted Matthews's

> tendency ... to suppose that Ritschl places his reliance on *uncriticised* religious experience. ... Ritschl's whole work consisted in bold and even revolutionary criticism of religious experience ... What he was desirous of excluding was not criticism, but criticism by the application of standards foreign to the essential nature of religion. He is never willing to dismiss a false or defective religious belief by showing that it is out of accord with the current conclusions of natural science or with the views of any school of metaphysicians. He never feels that he has really dealt it a serious blow until he has been able to show that it is inadequate and unsatisfying from a *religious* point of view. And this he can only do by criticising it in the light of some religious principle, some higher insight into spiritual value.[67]

As we shall shortly see, Matthews would nevertheless maintain that, what might be called Ritschl's 'in-house' criticism was inadequate because the elevation of any one of the varieties of religious experience to normative status implies a view of the nature of reality, and any such view is susceptible to rational interpretation and critique.

Matthews finds a *prima facie* unlikely similarity between Ritschl and those who referred religious experience to a mystical grasp of the super-rational gained through a special faculty enabling the intuition of the Divine. Over against undue confidence in mystic union with the divine,[68] Matthews emphasizes the importance

---

[65] Ibid., 50.
[66] W. R. Matthews, SCP, 10–11.
[67] J. Baillie, review of SCP in *The Philosophical Review*, XXXI no. 2, March 1922, 194.
[68] Elsewhere, in his review of W. F. Cobb, *Mysticism and the Creed*, in the *International Journal of Ethics*, XXV no. 3, April 1915, Matthews agreed with the author that 'the merely historical is not yet religion', denied that the transcendence of the historical is possible for Christianity, and pointed out that the very creed on which Cobb was reflecting contained

of the doctrine of creation, and especially of the Creator-creature distinction; and he appeals to Paul's injunction that we 'try the spirits to see whether they be of God' because he is 'inclined to think that there are mystical states which are morally and spiritually either indifferent or evil'.[69] Again, on the one hand, he opposes those who contend that religious experience is the sole ground of religious belief, for any experience is open to adverse criticism, and if, from the many varieties of religious experience, one species is taken as normative, this selection 'can only be made by the help of a criterion which is not religious experience';[70] and any such criterion will involve, 'explicitly or implicitly, a view of the nature of Reality. ... From the beginning, religious experience is indissolubly connected with affirmations about the universe which are capable of philosophical criticism and interpretation.'[71] On the other hand, if some unduly elevated experience, Matthews laments the way in which records, books, or doctrines deemed to enshrine a revelation could be elevated by others to such a degree as to 'usurp the authority of the personal experience, which lies at the root of the religion, and ... take its place;'[72] and he repudiates the idea that those who appeal to experience necessarily seek to bypass reason, 'for reasoning is itself a part of experience'.[73] In the last resort, it is through religious experience that we discover the efficacy of religion. To say this is not to make the pragmatist's claim that that is true which works, for where religion is concerned, 'It's "working" does not constitute its truth but is part of the evidence that it is true.'[74]

---

strong historical assertions and was 'not only a collection of maxims for mystics.' See ibid., 415, 414.

[69] Idem, 'Psychical research and theology,' 4.

[70] W. R. Matthews, SCP, 7. It must be granted that Matthews is not in all places as explicit at this. In what is an admittedly a brief paper on 'The Christian belief in God' he does not dwell on the 'trying of the spirits', and is thus rebuked by Kathleen Walker MacArthur who notes that intuitional knowledge is liable to error. But while Matthews might have done well to guard his flank as regards the testing of experience, Walker may be accused of unjust selectivity; for she refers to Matthews's assertion that 'belief in God depends, in the last resort, on experience, on what has been called "revelation"', but she omits the latter half of his sentence: 'but it is, in this respect, in the same position as the other beliefs [such as that 'our fellows exist in the same way as we do'] on which we act with complete confidence every day'. Nor does she take the measure of his claim that 'Though belief in God does not originate from philosophical or scientific reasoning, it can be both defended and clarified by thought.' It goes without saying that Matthews knows better than to attempt an *argument* from religious experience. See K. W. MacArthur, review of W. R. Matthews, ed., *The Christian Faith*, in *The Journal of Religion*, XVIII no. 3, July 1938, 327, and W. R. Matthews's paper in the same book, 75, 77.

[71] SCP, 8, 9.

[72] Idem, *The Idea of Revelation*, London: Longmans, Green, 1927, 7.

[73] Idem, *Essays in Construction*, London: Nisbet, 1933, 33. I use the second edition of 1934 in order to take note of its new Preface.

[74] Ibid., 34.

II

Turning now to Matthews's psychological interests, we find that when his book, *God in Christian Thought and Experience*, appeared some readers construed 'experience' in purely psychological terms after the manner of William James. Matthews was, after all, writing in the heyday of psychological accounts of, and in some cases dismissals of, religion. But in relation to their *Library of Constructive Theology*, 'Wheeler Robinson and I, though deeply interested in psychology, thought we were writing theology.'[75] Taking this assertion as a cautionary word, we must nevertheless say something of the psychological ingredient (I do not say 'thrust') in Matthews's thought, not least because it typifies his openness to new ideas and his desire to elucidate Christian thought in relation to them. That he was also in part motivated by an irrepressible tendency to cock a snook at Christians of the stuffily traditionalist sort need not be doubted. In this connection, William Wand referred to 'his interest in such unlikely subjects as spiritualism, eugenics, and what not. He enjoys them all the more if they are looked at askance by the unco'guid.'[76]

Matthews was a member of the Society for Psychical Research, and in 1940 he delivered the sixth Frederic Myers Memorial Lecture.[77] He sets out by acknowledging that the Church's attitude to psychical research has been one of suspicion if not of antagonism. To some the spectre of communication with 'familiar spirits' was raised; others were opposed to what they regarded as dangerous meddling with psychic phenomena; and the scientific community at large was sceptical. But recently the Archbishops had set up a commission to investigate the relations of psychical research, spiritualism and the Christian faith – on which Matthews drily remarks, 'This Commission reported sometime ago and the delay in the publication of its findings suggests that they may have found their final resting place in the archiepiscopal pigeon holes, if not in the archiepiscopal mind.'[78] It is characteristic of his own openness of mind that while spiritualism may testify 'to the persistent needs of the human mind and its readiness to be deceived' there may also be 'some basis in genuine experience for these ancient beliefs'.[79] He further points out that while there cannot be a purely empirical argument for theism, and that God cannot be 'the conclusion of an investigation by scientific methods', empirical data are nevertheless the starting-point of the cosmological and teleological proofs, and 'The most which we can expect from psychical research is some significant addition to the data.'[80]

---

[75] MM, 127.

[76] W. Wand, 'Salute to Dean Matthews'.

[77] For Myers (1843–1901), a founder with Henry Sidgwick and others of the Society for Psychical Research (1882), see ODNB.

[78] W. R. Matthews, 'Psychical research and theology', 2.

[79] Ibid., 5.

[80] Ibid., 7.

Such research may also support the theologian by reason of its anti-materialistic thrust. It will not disprove materialism, 'the great enemy of theistic belief', but it 'makes the hypothesis not more plausible but less'.[81] Again, 'there are indications that the purely empirical investigation renders [the persistence of the personality after the dissolution of the physical organism] more plausible that it was when these super-normal phenomena were regarded as nothing but illusion'.[82] He repeats, however, that 'I do not think for a moment that any direct support for belief in God can be gained from' a survey of well-authenticated psychic phenomena.[83] He does nevertheless think that the Society for Psychical Research is a 'standing refutation' of Hume's argument against miracles, namely, that it is more probable that testimony in favour of a miracle *qua* 'event contrary to common experience ... should be false or mistaken than that a miracle should happen', since 'all the phenomena which our Society investigates are contrary to common experience, yet we are persuaded that some at least of them occur'.[84] As to the question of survival after death,

> In my opinion, the only arguments for personal immortality which have any value depend upon the belief in the existence of God; and further no accumulation of evidence could prove the reality of everlasting life. Plainly the evidence could, at the most, show that some persons survived bodily death, but it could not show that all persons did, nor could it show that any persons triumphed over death so that it had no more dominion over them. The possibility would remain that extinction took them in the end.[85]

Ten years after his lecture to the Society for Psychical Research Matthews drew on more recent developments in that field when discoursing upon the person and work of Christ. He now regards the case for telepathy as strong and, in relation to the claim that Jesus 'knew what was in man', he suggests that 'We could conceive an experience in which the telepathic content was, so to speak, raised to a vastly higher power than any known to us. Would that not mean that the thoughts and emotions of many other persons would be present to the consciousness, though neither willed nor voluntarily accepted by it?'[86] This leads him to speculate that by Christ's bearing of our sins we could understand that all the thoughts, emotions and desires of the world might flow into Christ, who would know them all from within, and gain mastery over those that were evil or foolish: 'Would not such an experience be bearing the sins of many and the victory over them?'[87] Again, from Extra-Sensory Perception we might learn that 'there is an aspect of

---

[81] Ibid.
[82] Ibid., 9.
[83] Ibid.
[84] Ibid., 10.
[85] Ibid., 12.
[86] Idem, *The Problem of Christ in the Twentieth Century*, London: OUP, 1950, 53.
[87] Ibid., 55.

human personality which is not chained to the present moment and may possibly transcend time'.[88] But for all its hints and suggestions, we cannot establish doctrine upon psychological results: 'Psychology cannot give the final answer to any of the fundamental questions, though it may help us to put them more clearly and indicate fruitful fields for thought. In the end ... the meaning of personality raises questions which only philosophy can deal with ...'[89] I must in justice add that 20 years on Matthews wrote with respect to these suggestions, 'I still think that in the main I was right, but I have to admit that I was too optimistic about the actual state of knowledge.'[90] He cautioned against credulity in this region, for he had come to see that concentration on 'spiritual' beings could be dangerous, and he thought that the confusion of the psychical with the spiritual was an error to be avoided in psychical research.[91]

Matthews ended his Myers Memorial Lecture by tentatively suggesting that 'It may have been worthwhile to try to map out the country which, as I think, waits for theologians to explore.'[92] Seventy years on, the country still waits for most theologians to venture into it, though whether this fact witnesses to the inhospitable nature of the country or the failure of nerve or plain lack of interest of theologians, or both, I do not presume to judge. At the risk of appearing myopic, I can but testify that I seem to have managed quite well thus far without venturing into psychic realms. It also seems clear that while Matthews was open to, and interested in, empirical evidence yielded by psychic research, he did not regard such evidence as demonstrative of Christian claims, still less as necessary to the support of Christian faith claims, though it might tend to confirm them, or at least make the denial of them somewhat more difficult. Underlying his discussion is his commitment to the criterion of rationality. To this he appeals in connection with the evidence of psychic research no less than when he discusses Schleiermacher's emphasis upon feeling, or Otto's upon experience.

But there is more to a psychological interest than the glamour or the hazards of psychic research. In one of his most positive assertions concerning psychology Matthews avers, 'it is idle and misleading to fall back upon the religious experience of mankind as a basis for theology unless we are prepared to consider attentively what the psychologist has to say'.[93] Not, indeed, that he believes that the theology of the future must be based on psychology, for in 'many quarters the psychology of religion threatens to take the place not only of theology but of religious belief'.[94] But this need not prevent our acknowledging the assistance which psychology can afford the theologian.

---

[88] Ibid., 57.
[89] Ibid., 60.
[90] MM, 345.
[91] Ibid., 345–7.
[92] Idem, 'Psychical research and theology', 15.
[93] Idem, *The Psychological Approach to Religion*, 1.
[94] Ibid., 3–4.

In the first place, over against undue intellectualism, or the idea that in dogma we find the essence of the religious attitude, he is persuaded by the psychological theory which 'finds the matrix of the religious consciousness in a state of mind which is not yet explicitly cognitive'. This leads him to define religion as 'a felt continuity with a Reality which is beyond yet not wholly other than ourselves'.[95] But, in keeping with the holistic approach which we have already encountered, he does not think that the continuity is 'felt' alone. Rather, it 'affects the whole personality, and by an inherent necessity expresses itself in act and thought.'[96] In other words,

> in the centre of personality, in the knowing subject and the creative core of the self, we encounter a new and higher order of being, one which can never be, in the full sense, an object of our knowledge or a part of nature, but which, nevertheless, like all other orders, interpenetrates those below it and produces effects in them.[97]

The self, then, is 'the whole which is formed by the super-temporal subject and its successive experiences'.[98]

As already hinted, Matthews was well aware that not all aspects of psychology, and not all psychologists, are kindly disposed towards religion. First, he sets his face against those who deny the real 'self'. Some psychologists, he argues, fail to distinguish 'between the concept of self or personality and the intuition of selfhood'. They consider the origin of the idea of self, but they do not admit 'a subject of experience as the essential datum'.[99] His own view is that 'There is always "given" in experience the central, organizing and active ego.'[100] The exclusive route to the making of this affirmation of the activist view of the self is that of introspection. The results of such introspection, however, can never yield adequate knowledge of the self's nature because 'In so far as our activity is determined by the environment we are debarred from a complete knowledge of ourselves.'[101]

Secondly, Matthews rebuts the arguments of behaviourists, whom he regards as near relations of materialists. He concedes that in some instances it may be appropriate to regard bodily processes as the sole causal agent, but taken as a comprehensive theory behaviourism 'involves the conclusion that the world would be precisely the same as it is had there been no consciousness at all; that, for

---

[95] Idem, 'The nature and basis of dogma', in W. R. Matthews, ed., *Dogma in History and Thought. Studies by Various Writers*, London: Nisbet, 1929, 9.

[96] Ibid., 10.

[97] Idem, *The Idea of Revelation*, London: Longmans, Green, 1923, 45.

[98] GCTE, 260.

[99] Ibid., 168. He refers approvingly to James Ward's *Psychological Principles* (though wrongly naming it *Principles of Psychology*), Cambridge: CUP, 1918, 34–41.

[100] Ibid., 169. He here follows Francis Aveling, *The Psychological Approach to Reality*, London: University of London Press, 1929, 192–3.

[101] GCTE, 172.

example, the written works of Shakespeare would have come into existence just as they did even if there had been no thought in the mind of Shakespeare'. It further implies that consciousness, the product of organic evolution, is of no use to those animals which possess it, since 'their actions would have been no different had the quality been entirely absent'. He scornfully concludes that 'It is really difficult to retain an adequately courteous demeanour towards people who can believe that such nonsense is the solution of the problem of body and mind.'[102]

Thirdly, Matthews counters the view of some psychologists that religious experience is illusory or the product of projection. This assumes that the self has an ability in its own right which enables it 'to project its independent imaginings'[103] and this Matthews denies, for the self 'has being and it develops only through its relation with that "other" with which it is continuous'.[104] Moreover, if it were the case that the self had this abstract character, scientific concepts, ideas of reason and value judgements would all share this psychical origin and 'no mental or spiritual activity of ours' would have 'any objective validity'.[105] Elsewhere Matthews appears to concede more to the idea of projection. He grants that 'the origin and retention of the idea of God have mental causes' and in this sense the idea may be said to be a projection; but the idea is not a projection and nothing more. The idea of God, 'no less than the idea of nature, has value for life and has helped man to gain command of the circumstances in which his existence is cast'.[106] His homeliest expression of the point is as follows: 'The real question at issue is not, Is the idea of God a projection, but is it *only* a projection. If the phrase may be allowed, Does the projection *hit* anything?'[107] Finally, as for Freud's argument that religion is illusory because it is a way of escaping from the real world: this view begs the question for it 'assumes that we know what Reality is. It assumes that the world is known to be exactly as it was conceived by nineteenth-century materialism; and the religious consciousness is dismissed as the source of illusion, because it finds Reality to be something quite different. But clearly the nature of the real world is the whole question at issue.'[108] For his part Matthews concurs with John Oman that 'man is in contact with an invisible environment, the Holy or the Sacred'.[109]

---

[102] Idem, *The Psychological Approach to Religion*, 64.

[103] GCTE, 22.

[104] Ibid., 23.

[105] Ibid.

[106] Idem, *The Psychological Approach to Religion*, 20, 21; cf. idem, *The Gospel and the Modern Mind*, London: Macmillan, 1930, 94.

[107] Idem, 90.

[108] Idem, *Essays in Construction*, 23. He refers to Freud's *The Future of an Illusion*, trans. W. D. Robson-Scott, London: L. and Virginia Woolf at The Hogarth Press, 1928.

[109] Ibid., 31. He refers to Oman's *The Natural and the Supernatural*, Cambridge: CUP, 1931. For Oman see Alan P. F. Sell, 'Living in the half lights: John Oman in Context', forthcoming.

III

To one willing to take psychic research seriously, albeit not uncritically, more conventional approaches in science held no terrors. Far from wishing to embark upon a futile attempt to protect Christianity by holding science at bay, Matthews regrets that 'at the present time much Christian teaching has an appearance of standing in opposition to scientific conclusions, which is as unnecessary as it is unfortunate'.[110] In his opinion there are some grounds of optimism that the days of hostility between science and religion are drawing to a close, and this owing to changes of attitude on both sides: 'On the one hand, thoughtful Christians have come to recognise that many Biblical narratives which conflict with the results of natural science are no part of the essential Christian belief, while, on the other hand, a much more accurate notion of the function and limitations of the scientific method has been reached.'[111] Thus it is now more generally understood that science offers but one way of interpreting objects, and that its method is that of analysis, simplification and abstraction.[112] That is to say, 'the scientific method can never give a complete account of Nature. It concentrates upon that aspect of nature which lends itself to mathematical treatment – to what can be counted and measured. As the phrase goes, it abstracts from the other aspects.' The consequence is that 'We never get an answer to the question, why? but only a partial answer to the question, how?'[113] It is precisely because science has to do with what is measurable and quantifiable that its results can seem more definite: its method of experimental verification is attuned to the abstracted elements with which it deals. If anything this makes it less, not more, complete than knowledge derived from art, morality or religion, subjects which, though less measurable, may be no less concerned with the truth.[114] In the last resort, however, both science and religion are brought to the bar of experience: 'A theory which conflicts with experience cannot stand. But in neither science nor religion do we appeal to the general experience of the ordinary man. We depend upon the consentient experience of those who are in a position to observe the relevant facts.'[115]

The above points were reiterated in the sermon that Matthews delivered in St Paul's on 24 July 1960 to the Fellows and guests of the Royal Society, which body was celebrating its tercentenary. The text was Psalm 43: 3, 'O send out thy light and thy truth; let them lead me; let them bring me unto thy holy hill and to thy tabernacles.' As well as reminding the congregation that 'The original members of the Royal Society were not ... opposed to religion ... they were Christian believers of liberal views and they were convinced that, in the end, their investigations would

---

[110] W. R. Matthews, *God and Evolution*, London: Longmans, Green, 1926, 51.
[111] SCP, 3.
[112] W. R. Matthews, *Essays in Construction*, 13.
[113] Idem, *Signposts to God*, London: SCM Press, 1938, 15.
[114] See GCTE, 14–16.
[115] Idem, 'The nature and basis of dogma', 21.

lend support to the belief in God and the chief Christian doctrines,'[116] Matthews made his methodological point in the following terms at a time when scientific humanism was increasingly vocal:

> No doubt there are scientific humanists who do not hold that there is no truth but scientific truth, but when we are exhorted to accept a view of existence and of the place of man in it based solely on scientific results we may ask whether the foundation will sustain the structure. For surely it cannot be accepted that there is no significant knowledge except scientific knowledge. There are things of great moment of which we are certain, but not in the sense that they can be scientifically proved. That is it better to be merciful than cruel; that it is better to be a victim of injustice than to be unjust; that truth is always to be preferred to error and illusion [a delightful *tu quoque* claim when almost certainly confronted by some in the congregation who urged this very point against Christianity]; all these propositions, and others of like kind, seem to be more certain than, let us say, the second law of thermodynamics, and to be of more enduring value to the human race, and yet, if I were challenged to give any scientific reason for believing them, I should not know where to begin. ... [S]cience, by its method, abstracts from values and can therefore not judge them. We may use the results of science for any purpose we choose, but science cannot tell us whether our purpose is good or evil.[117]

Matthews draws further encouragement from the fact that 'Scientific research itself is finding mechanism and mechanical causality insufficient for the understanding of life and mind, and proclaiming that when we pass to the higher levels of existence we require new principles of explanation.'[118] This implies that one of religion's old enemies, materialism, which 'was always absurd' has become even more difficult to formulate, for 'When no one even professes to know what is meant by matter, it is difficult to start an argument about materialism.'[119] Again, whereas in the past many scientists were content to interpret higher and more complex systems of life in terms of the lower, now, through the writings of Whitehead and others, the idea of organism is being expounded; that is, 'a conception derived from the study of living beings, is used for the interpretation of the non-living'.[120]

---

[116] Idem, Sermon in the report 'Service at St. Paul's Cathedral', *Notes and Records of the Royal Society of London*, XVI no. 1, April 1961, 96.

[117] Ibid., 97–8.

[118] Idem, *The Idea of Revelation*, 43–4.

[119] Idem, *Essays in Construction*, 57.

[120] Ibid., 59. Though Matthews cannot resist the observation that 'Unfortunately, Professor Whitehead has chosen to write in a manner which makes reading his more recent books like the attempt to discover the meaning of the most exasperating oracle', ibid., 58. Susan L. Stebbing's devastating remarks in her review of Whitehead's *Religion in the*

Well aware that the term 'evolution' may become 'one of those "blessed words" which have so often earned the gratitude of weak humanity by their capacity to save us from the trouble of thinking'; and regretful of the fact that 'religious people have often confused the fact of evolution with theories about its causes',[121] Matthews nevertheless thinks that, properly conceived, the idea is a genuinely creative one – not least in that he detects a convergence between the idea of emergent evolution as propounded in their different ways by the realists Samuel Alexander, C. Lloyd Morgan, Whitehead and others,[122] and the Italian idealists Croce and Gentile, for whom Reality is no longer thought, but thinking: 'Mind is not substance but activity.'[123] The implication of the newer 'activist' idealism for science is that 'The "nature" which science postulates as the sphere of its inquiries is not an independent order of being having a real existence independent of mind; on the contrary, it is an abstraction made for practical ends from the concrete reality of history, it is in fact a creation of thought.'[124]

But for all the encouragement he is able to draw from recent approaches in science and idealistic philosophy, Matthews fully understands that the accord between these and theology is by no means complete. Proponents of emergent evolution and its variants in process philosophies, though contributing to fresh thought on the teleological argument for the existence of God, stumble at the bar of history, will not allow that not organism, but 'Mind is the only possible, or at least the most probable, Source of the order of the world'[125] and leave us with 'a description [emergence], not an explanation';[126] while the newer idealists end by 'swallowing up the many thinkers in the one Thinking', and this because they lack a doctrine of creation which accommodates 'the finite self's otherness with respect to God'.[127] Matthews concludes that 'The Christian view of the world cannot

---

Making come to mind at this point. See *Mind*, NS XXXIX, 1930, 475. Thirty-six years later Matthews doubted whether Whitehead's influence would be lasting. See MM, 299.

[121] W. R. Matthews, *Essays in Construction*, 61, 64.

[122] Matthews doffs his cap to Herbert Spencer as a fountainhead of emergent evolutionary thought, but says that with the passage of time the problems which confront it 'have stood out more clearly than they ever did in the comprehensive but somewhat woolly intelligence of the nineteenth-century sage'. See *God and Evolution*, 15.

[123] GCTE, 128.

[124] Ibid., 129.

[125] Idem, *The Purpose of God*, London: Nisbet, 1935, 90; cf. idem, *Signposts to God*, 22.

[126] Idem, *God and Evolution*, 39. Matthews welcomes Bergson's vitalism for its critique of materialism, and because, in holding that the creative urge's end is freedom, it goes some way towards a teleological understanding of the universe. But 'it is not a thorough-going teleological conception, since it is opposed to the belief that development is the working out of a transcendent purpose. That view, which Bergson described as "Radical Finalism", would in his opinion be as fatal to the possibility of freedom as the blankest materialism'. See *God and Evolution*, 19.

[127] GCTE, 129, 130.

hold that evolution is ultimately true in the sense that the universe as a whole is evolving, or that God is within the time process. Evolution is true in the sense that process is going on within the whole.'[128]

IV

As to Matthews's fourth general concern, the need of a viable apologetic, I may be brief. The evidence supplied in my biographical sketch regarding his preaching, his journalism, his broadcasts and many of his books is more than sufficient to warrant the claim that the adjustment of Christian thought to the needs of the age was among his primary concerns. It is therefore at first sight odd that in introducing the *Library of Constructive Theology* he should declare that 'The time has gone by when "apologetics" could be of any great value.'[129] But the inverted commas around 'apologetics' are significant; for what he has in mind are defences of propositions already accepted on authority. The scene, he argues, has shifted in such a way that the authorities, both biblical and ecclesiastical are no longer deferred to as once they were and hence, 'Nothing less is required than a candid, courageous and well-informed effort to think our anew, in the light of modern knowledge, the foundation affirmations of our common Christianity.'[130] Only if we place 'the Christian consciousness of God within the larger frame of religious history ... can we hope to arrive at an effective defence of the Christian faith for our modern world'.[131] The context of this endeavour is a society which 'appears to be emerging having no necessary connection with religious faith, and this is a completely new fact'.[132] He attributes this 'decay of religion' to 'the weakening of what we may call the "metaphysical impulse"', by which he means 'not the presence of the modern mind but the modern absence of mind in the full sense'.[133] His diagnosis is that 'The Gospel does not appeal to people often because it answers a question which they have forgotten to ask.'[134] The twin facts remain, namely, that moral values are permanent, and the modern person needs salvation. To these factors we must appeal as we translate 'the good news out of language which has grown archaic into words which speak directly to the man of to-day'.[135] I need only remark that for all that Matthews says concerning the need to engage in the apologetic 'defence' of the faith, albeit in a new key, his deepest motive is to *commend* Christianity to the people of his time. It is my own understanding

---

[128] Idem, *God and Evolution*, 57–8.
[129] GCTE, vii.
[130] Ibid.
[131] Ibid., 4.
[132] Idem, *The Gospel and the Modern Mind*, 82–3.
[133] Ibid., 35.
[134] Ibid.
[135] Ibid., 38.

that the intellectual defence of the faith is best conceived within the context of commendation; but that requires that we first ask, What is it that we wish to commend?[136] As we turn to Matthews's approach to questions philosophical and doctrinal we shall need to keep in mind the questions of the content of the Gospel and the viability or otherwise of his experiential-starting point.

V

We shall do well to begin by considering Matthews's understanding of the relation between philosophy and religion. 'Every philosophy,' he declares, 'which is more than a criticism of others, claims to be a presentation of absolute truth.'[137] He does not claim that all, or any, attempts to achieve this lofty goal succeed, but, he says, 'philosophical activity proceeds on the assumption that absolute truth is possible of attainment'.[138] Philosophy and religion are akin in that both 'have as their motive force the desire to pierce behind the appearances to Reality'.[139] Furthermore, he follows Croce in contending that 'All religion ... has implicit within it a view of the world and cannot therefore be radically distinct from philosophy.'[140] His continuing debt to philosophical idealism emerges no more clearly than when he writes of goodness, beauty and truth, that 'Religion ... is the completion of other forms of the life of the spirit, the climax towards which they tend, so that each of them, when intense and full, passes over into religion.'[141] But that time is not yet, as Matthews makes clear in an important paragraph that I must quote in full:

> It will conduce to clearness if I state at once the position which I desire to defend. In the first place, it seems to me obvious that in their present stages of development religion and philosophy are distinct from one another, and that there is a true sense in which the philosophical attitude of mind differs from the religious. Further, so far as can be seen, this distinction will persist for an indefinite period, since there is no philosophy which can really substantiate the claim to include all that religion has of value, nor, on the other hand, has religion succeeded in formulating its concepts in so definite and coherent a manner that it may venture to demand the absorption of philosophy in itself. But it appears to me that Croce is right in holding that there is no inherent and necessary distinction between them. The divergence which actually exists arises, not from

---

[136] See Alan P. F. Sell, *Confessing and Commending the Faith. Historic Witness and Apologetic Method*, Cardiff: University of Wales Press, 2002; Eugene, OR: Wipf & Stock, 2006.
[137] W. R. Matthews, *The Idea of Revelation*, 38.
[138] Ibid., 38–9.
[139] Idem, *The Gospel and the Modern Mind*, 129.
[140] GCTE, 90; cf. SCP, 4.
[141] Ibid., 24.

the essential natures of the two activities, but from their imperfect development and from historical causes. In so far as they approach their ideal completion they will converge and become united. They are therefore to be regarded as different aspects of one movement of the human spirit, and the question whether religion is to be absorbed in philosophy or philosophy in religion ceases to have any importance, and may be left to the lexicographers of a remote future to decide.[142]

In the light of this we must assume that when Matthews declares that 'philosophy and religion are distinct' in that 'philosophy seeks [an abstract] synthesis in terms of the idea', religion looks for 'a wider and richer synthesis, one which will embrace conduct, emotion and imagination and be, not a well-articulated skeleton, but a living reality by which we ourselves may live',[143] he means that they rightly are *pro tem* distinct in the manner described.[144] The implication that Matthews does not desire any premature harmony is reinforced by the evident peril he perceives in the intellectualist position of Spinoza which, in his view, was as much the inspiration of later idealism as was the philosophy of Kant, and which threatened to vanquish religion by absorption within philosophy. 'Spinoza', he writes,

> is really the figure of crucial importance in the history of modern thought on religion. He poses the fundamental problem with which the philosophy of religion must grapple. Is there any independent status to be vindicated for religion? Is it a necessary 'moment' in the life of Spirit? Or is religion only philosophy speaking in parables, mythological metaphysics, and faith merely a stop-gap for the true system of logic?[145]

As I reflect upon the foregoing statements a number of points occur to me. In the first place, it is clear that even in the earlier days of Matthews's career there were

---

[142] SCP, 23–4. John Baillie thought that Matthews stated his view of the religion-philosophy relation 'with almost unusual baldness'. See his review of SCP, 193; cf. D. C. Macintosh's review of the same book in *The Journal of Religion*, III no. 2, March 1923, 214. Forty-eight years on, in MM, 163, Matthews seems more tentative: 'Philosophy and religion have more to reveal of their content and *perhaps* when that process is nearer its end they will be seen to be one.' My italics.

[143] Idem, *Reason in Religion*, 23.

[144] In his discussion of Matthews's position on the philosophy-religion relation, Sydney G. Dimond concludes that 'unless philosophy is subservient to religion or religion is lost in philosophy there is no possible identification of the two'. See *Heart and Mind. Studies in the Philosophy of Christian Experience*, London: Epworth Press, 1945, 35. But if philosophy were subservient to religion there would be no identity of status between the two, and if religion were lost in philosophy talk of identification would be redundant.

[145] W. R. Matthews, 'Three philosophers on religion', *The Church Quarterly Review*, C, April 1925, 126.

philosophers who would have denied that it was any part of their purpose to 'pierce behind the appearances to Reality' or 'seek a synthesis in terms of the idea', still less to give 'an interpretation of the whole of experience';[146] and certainly from the 1950s onwards there was an army of philosophers who repudiated metaphysics, contented themselves with the analysis of discourse, and would have regarded the articulation of world views – even if a possibility – as being quite beyond their purview. In this last connection Matthews is unquestionably correct in thinking that, however it may be in principle, the realization of the complete harmony of philosophy and religion is a long way off – it may even be an eschatological hope. Certainly the principles upon which Matthews's Christian world view are based, namely, that 'To believe in God means that we assume the universe to be rational [and that] it exists for the production and the preservation of values'[147] would not have commanded the assent of those of his secular philosophical colleagues to whom I have just referred. It is therefore a pity that he does not address the methods and presuppositions, often undisclosed, of his antagonists, but rather adopts a dismissive attitude towards them, as when he affirms that 'professional philosophers have so largely retired into the twilight of Semantics',[148] which he finds 'deadly dull'.[149] In more plaintive mood, he deems it 'a grave misfortune that ... so many philosophers have given up the attempt to grapple with the great problems which centre upon [sic] the nature of man and his place in the universe'.[150] With reference to current philosophico-semantic pursuits he says, 'I was too old to start a new game.'[151] This is the more to be regretted since he had the kernel of a possible reply to those philosophical sceptics who shelved the adumbration of world views in favour of more linguistically technical pursuits. Conscious of those who might repudiate his view that religion and philosophy are ideally in harmony, he grants that 'it would be ridiculous to argue that Materialism or Naturalism has a religious aspect', but they do 'aim at a species of deliverance, even though it be merely the escape from superstition and illusion, and the peace which comes from the abandonment of baseless hopes. In every case the motive is to set the individual in right relation with the universe.'[152]

If some philosophers are reluctant to admit that a worldview underlies their methods and practice, some religious persons may be tempted to overlook, or deny, the fact that religion 'rests upon a few simple affirmations of a philosophical

---

[146] Ibid., 22.
[147] Idem, *The Hope of Immortality*, London: SCM Press, 1936, 40.
[148] Idem, 'The British philosopher as writer', 5; cf. 13.
[149] MM, 300.
[150] Idem, 'The aims and scope of the philosophy of religion', *Journal of the Transactions of the Victoria Institute*, LXXXIV, 1952, 123.
[151] MM, 300. Though G. E. Moore's *Principia Ethica* appeared when Matthews was 22, and Ayer's *Language, Truth and Logic* when he was 55. In between came Wittgenstein's *Tractatus*, when Matthews was 41.
[152] SCP, 29.

character'.¹⁵³ Were it otherwise, it would not be possible to counter materialism, which denies the place of mind;¹⁵⁴ naturalism, which denies transcendence;¹⁵⁵ absolute idealism, which loses the individual in Mind and plays down the moral consciousness;¹⁵⁶ mysticism and process thought which, in their different ways, blur or obliterate the Creator-creature distinction; vitalism which issues in an impersonalist intuitionism;¹⁵⁷ and radical pluralism, which reduces to the belief that 'finite individuals are the sole reality'¹⁵⁸ and cannot justify 'the objectivity of the moral ideal'¹⁵⁹ or easily give any account of the common good;¹⁶⁰ nor would it be possible to defend the view that 'the Christian view of the world is deeply concerned to maintain the personal nature of God and the real freedom of finite spirits'.¹⁶¹

Although Christianity has its own world view, Matthews agrees that 'it has nevertheless made use of pre-existing philosophies for the expression of its belief'.¹⁶² It was, he says, 'unavoidable that the new wine should be poured into old bottles – for there were no others'.¹⁶³ But the enterprise has not been entirely successful. Thus, for example, Aquinas turned to Aristotelianism because 'it seemed to offer a more secure ground for an ethical conception of God than the immanence which was implied in Platonism', but 'it was a desperate and hopeless project to substitute the God who "so loved the world"' for the impassible Aristotelian God.¹⁶⁴ Matthews recognizes that the scholastic project in general adheres to the biblical revelation, albeit uncritically, and also to the Church, the conciliar dogmas of which it likewise accepts at face value; it is 'magnificently insistent upon the divine transcendence',¹⁶⁵ and it rightly affirms the Creator-creature distinction. But it wrongly presupposes that 'the nature of Deity is given to us, in principle, through the analysis of concepts which are in the end abstractions. God is in essence the infinite First Cause, the Pure Activity of Aristotelian metaphysics.'¹⁶⁶ The terminus of this line of thought is that a wedge is driven between the knowledge and will of the unlimited being, and knowledge and will as we know them in our experience. In his own words: 'A thought of God ... which has expunged all tincture of anthropomorphism must decline into a concept

---

153   Ibid., xi.
154   Idem, *Essays in Construction*, 57.
155   SCP, 91–2; *The Idea of Revelation*, 25.
156   Ibid., 86–7; cf. GCTE, 130.
157   SCP., 97.
158   Ibid.
159   Ibid., 146.
160   Ibid., 153.
161   Ibid., 204.
162   Ibid., 68.
163   Ibid., 68–9.
164   Ibid., 69–70; cf. GCTE, 102–3, 227.
165   GCTE, 101.
166   Ibid.

of a being for whom no human values are real, into an unknowable ground of the universe or an order of nature.'[167] Matthews finds the stance of Berdyaev troubling in a different way. Berdyaev is learned in philosophy, he adumbrates a vision of reality in relation to alternative world views; and while his method evinces the engagement of his whole personality and not simply of his intellect, the problem is that 'there is scarcely any argument and no chain of reasoning which could compel our assent'.[168]

Matthews thinks it a matter of regret that 'In general, Christian theology suffers at the present time from two opposite defects; it either ignores philosophy completely or treats the utterances of philosophers with exaggerated respect.'[169] His own view is that since abstractive natural science neither solves ultimate problems nor propounds a world view, 'Theology must still seek for some philosophical ally, though it will be a philosophy which has absorbed the results of science.'[170] He later qualifies this assertion by remarking that 'Theology ... should, like other sciences, get along without metaphysics as long as it can, even though in the end it must try to come to terms with ultimate philosophical concepts.'[171] On the other hand, he later suggests that the prevailing confusion of voices in philosophy amounts to 'a challenge and an opportunity to develop for the first time a philosophy from within Christianity itself'.[172] I shall return to this possibility at the end of this chapter.

This brings us to the threshold of the philosophy of religion. We must ask how Matthews understands that discipline, and then introduce his contributions to it. In his address, 'The aims and scope of the philosophy of religion', delivered at the Victoria Institute on 18 February 1952, Matthews begins by observing that simply from the vast quantity of books written on his subject it cannot be inferred that the problems with which the philosophy of religion deals are genuine problems, since numerous books have also been published on astrology, and 'any contribution which they have made to human knowledge has been fortuitous, the by-product of a futile quest'.[173] Whereas a generation ago the philosophy of religion 'threatened to push theology itself into the background',[174] nowadays theology repudiates philosophy's assistance, while philosophy deems religion a non-philosophical topic. This, he surmises, is a passing phase, as is indicated by the fluctuating relations between philosophy and religion throughout the history of Christian thought. Matthews finds that Barth stands in the line of Tertullian and Luther (though I must interject that it depends upon which portions of Luther's writings one reads) in isolating theology from philosophy, while the logical

---

[167] Ibid., 38.
[168] Idem, *The British Philosopher as Writer*, 6.
[169] SCP, xii.
[170] GTCE, 119.
[171] Ibid., 250.
[172] Idem, *The Problem of Christ in the Twentieth Century*, London: OUP, 1950, 62.
[173] Idem, 'The aims and scope of the philosophy of religion,' 109–10.
[174] Ibid., 109.

positivists have gone further than Hume, who, unlike the positivists, did not deny the meaningfulness of such propositions as 'God exists.' By both sides the province of reason is severely restricted, and the efforts of mind to know reality are scoffed at. Matthews turns from the 'long and difficult task' of countering the unwelcome views, and instead sets out the terms of reference of the philosophy of religion as he understands them.

He proposes that the philosophy of religion set out from a phenomenological account of religion as such – a study the objective of which is so to interpret comparative and psychological insights as to 'enable us to relate the phenomena to the rest of our experience'.[175] He recognizes that not the least of the problems of the philosophy of religion is that of defining religion itself. It is not an unimportant question, since religion needs to be distinguished from magic, and for this to be done a defining criterion is required. In fact, however, multiple definitions of religion have been proposed, none of which has met with universal approval. Accordingly, 'We must be content ... with the reflection that, in a general way, we know a religion when we see it and recognise a religious experience when we have it, just as we know when a man is trying to talk philosophy.'[176]

When seeking for coherence or significance in a diverse group of phenomena, he continues, 'we are looking for some kind of dialectical development in them'. By this he means, 'a process that exhibits some intelligible internal principle which enables us to grasp the purpose as one whole'.[177] This is not to say that one expression of religion can be shown to be as good or as true in its way as all the others, for in the world as it is contingent forces have overwhelmed, distorted or arrested the dialectical process. The second question raised by phenomenological investigation is whether the dialectical process will result in the absorption of religion in something else, or whether 'religion is a permanent and distinctive form of the Spirit'.[178] Croce and Collingwood (albeit with many reservations) thought that religion would be superseded as humanity became more self-conscious, whereas A. E. Taylor and W. G. de Burgh regarded religion as an independent Form. Matthews's own position is that 'admitting for the sake of argument, that the three Forms of Spirit are Art, Religion and Philosophy, I should maintain that Religion, in its ideal development, could be conceived as including the other two far more easily than either of them could be conceived as including religion'.[179]

The second group of problems with which the philosophy of religion is concerned are epistemological in character. The phenomenological enquiry itself prompts the question whether religion and philosophy seek different kinds of knowledge. Certainly religion does not claim apodeictic knowledge as some philosophers have done; religion is concerned with belief, but belief is 'a kind

---

[175] Ibid., 113.
[176] Ibid., 114.
[177] Ibid.
[178] Ibid., 116.
[179] Ibid.

of knowing'.[180] When believers say that they know God, they are saying more than that they know something about God, and religious experience is experience shared within a community of faith with common heritage, a community which manifests 'continuity, though not identity, from generation to generation'.[181] The community has its symbolic expressions, and we have therefore to ask 'are there aspects of reality, or apprehensions of reality, which can be formulated, presented and expressed only in the language of poetry, or on the contrary must we hold that truth can be conveyed and presented only in concepts and logical propositions?'[182] This question, he feels merits closer attention than philosophers have thus far given it.

Metaphysics supplies the third group of topics to which the philosopher of religion must devote attention, and cosmology supplies the fourth. At this point I begin to supplement Matthews's necessarily brief lecture with observations from his other works, because to the theistic arguments and cosmology he devoted considerable attention. I simply mention in passing my regret that he did not deal more directly with religion's opponents as specified under his heading of phenomenology, and that he did not pursue the symbolic element of religious discourse at greater length. Moreover when he declares that 'belief is a kind of knowing' a whole range of issues is opened up, of which the first is, 'Of what kind of knowing is belief?' This is a pressing question, given that in traditional epistemological discourse knowledge is generally contrasted with belief where the latter concerns propositional content and not the mental state of believing as such; and also the question whether the beliefs are mediated or unmediated – another issue. Knowledge is generally regarded as being more secure in the sense of demonstrable; and as having to do with truth rather than even probable opinion; whereas claims to believe may prompt calls for the justification of the beliefs held which, if successfully accomplished, admits the claim to knowledge.

Matthews doubts that a copper-bottomed demonstration of God's existence can ever be offered, for 'The God of religion is never the conclusion of a deductive argument';[183] and he is certain that thus far such a demonstration has eluded us. He therefore regards the traditional theistic arguments as several ways of verifying the God hypothesis. He at once concedes that this 'hypothesis' is not on all fours with scientific hypotheses because it concerns not a limited set of phenomena or a definite problem, but represents an attempt 'to explain the whole of phenomena'.[184] Furthermore, the God hypothesis is not conjured up by ourselves, it comes to us with centuries of thought and emotion behind it; and, moreover, our choice whether or not to entertain it is not simply an intellectual, but

---

[180] Ibid., 117.
[181] Ibid.
[182] Ibid., 118.
[183] Idem, *Essays in Construction*, 45; cf. idem, *The Search for Perfection*, London: SPCK, 1957, 19.
[184] Idem, 'The aims and scope of the philosophy of religion', 120.

an existential matter. It seems to me that a little unpacking is required at this point. First, we might say that, psychologically, the believer's psychological attitude is not that of one who goes through life entertaining the possibility that new evidence may require the abandonment of the God hypothesis, whereas scientists ought always to be open to the possibility that new discoveries may require the modification or even the abandonment of their hypotheses. One might, crudely, say that whereas a scientist might, on evidential grounds, be persuaded to change his or her mind, a believer would need to be converted out of his or her religion. This is because, as Matthews suggests, scientific hypotheses concern the part, the God hypothesis concerns the whole: the believer makes what has been described by some philosophers as a 'total assertion'; or, to put it otherwise, a world view, and not simply a single theory, is at issue, with all that that entails concerning a way of life and habits of thought. In Matthews's own words, when pondering the reality of God believers 'start from a movement of the whole personality – from an experience which is given.'[185] Secondly, I think it misleading when Matthews says that the God hypothesis represents an attempt to 'explain' all phenomena. I should prefer to say that it 'accounts for' in the sense of '*testifying to* the origin of' all phenomena, and this precisely because the God hypothesis is not on all fours with any scientific explanatory hypothesis. All of this granted, in certain contexts, notably the apologetic, believers may well propound their beliefs as if they were hypotheses analogous with scientific ones. They are then reflecting upon what they hold in a second-order way, and they are inviting those whose views differ from their own to consider the grounds of their beliefs, and what would follow if their 'hypothesis' were justified.[186] Matthews puts it well: 'When we worship God He is to us certainly not a mere hypothesis. But we must sometimes, as Bishop Butler says, "sit down in a cool hour" and reflect upon the logical basis of our faith and worship. When we do this, we cannot avoid recognizing that our belief in God is one possible way of thinking of the universe and can be compares with other possible ways.'[187]

Matthews regards the particular theistic arguments as severally taking aspects of our existence with a view to showing that if we think out their implications to the end 'we are brought to the conception of Deity'.[188] Thus, for example, when Bertrand Russell reproaches Leibniz for devising a theory of Monads which will not make sense unless there is a Supreme Monad, Matthews accuses him of injustice, for 'what more impressive argument could there be than the discovery that, at the end of every research into the universal characters of our experience,

---

[185] Idem, *The Search for Perfection*, 19.

[186] For further discussion of world-views see Alan P. F. Sell, *Confessing and Commending the Faith*, 355–61, and ch. 5 below.

[187] W. R. Matthews, *Essays in Construction*, 49.

[188] Idem., 'The aims and scope of the philosophy of religion', 121.

we find the hypothesis of universal mind forced upon us?'[189] Matthews finds that in their several ways all of the traditional theistic arguments prompt us in that direction. Anselm's ontological reflections led him to conclude that the idea of God implies the reality of God. Descartes, Spinoza and Leibniz cashed their ontological reflections in terms of God's necessary being, to which the latter added the thought that the idea of God is that of 'a "possible" being, i.e. of a being the conception of which involves no contradiction'.[190] Reverting to Anselm's mode of expression, Matthews observes that in the phrase used of God, namely, that he is 'that than which no greater can be conceived', 'greater' is ambiguous, for it can be construed ontologically or morally: it can refer to reality (largest) or value (most perfect). The significance of this for Matthews is that when Anselm, whose faith was seeking understanding, reflected upon God's reality he was thinking out his religious experience, and was not concerned with an Absolute which was not at the same time holy and supremely good. To Bonaventure, the idea of God was 'direct and immediate evidence for the reality of God'.[191]

By contrast, Aquinas denied that we could form an adequate idea of God and hence the existence of God was not self-evident. Thus whereas those in sympathy with the ontological argument presupposed that we could not entertain the idea of God unless it has been imparted to us by God, Aquinas and those in his train concluded that all human knowledge comes *via* the senses. Kant, on the basis of his epistemology according to which we can have knowledge of phenomena only, and not of things in themselves, rejected the ontological argument on the ground that it turned on the mistaken belief that existence is a predicate, to which a rationalist such as Spinoza might reply that he was not concerned with such empirical considerations but with God as a transcendent reality. The ontological argument could not arise in the absence of the conviction that 'the end of the intellect is truth and that truth is not an illusory value'.[192] In other words, 'every claim to possess real knowledge rests upon an ontological argument, or perhaps more accurately upon an ontological assumption'[193] namely, that there is a knowable reality beyond my own experience. At this point Matthews signals his own general view, namely, that all of the theistic arguments 'are attempts to substantiate a belief which is already held, or at least to support an hypothesis which already exists [or, better,

---

[189] Ibid. Matthews was not, however, so content when George Galloway, confronted by the difficulty of relating individual monads to the Supreme Monad, postulated a created psychical medium in which the monads exist. 'I have an uneasy feeling,' wrote Matthews, 'that if we grant Dr. Galloway his monads and his medium we might find that we could do very well without his God.' See Matthews's review of Galloway's *The Philosophy of Religion*, in *International Journal of Ethics*, XXV no. 1, October 1914, 118.

[190] W. R. Matthews, *The Purpose of God*, London: Nisbet, 1935, 16.

[191] Ibid., 17.

[192] Idem, 'The aims and scope of the philosophy of religion', 121.

[193] Idem, *The Purpose of God*, 21.

is already entertained]. In this sense it is undoubtedly true that arguments for the existence of God start from the idea of God in the human mind.'[194]

Matthews proceeds to rehearse the cosmological arguments, four of which are found among Aquinas's 'Five Ways'; he thinks that causality is integral to the constitution of the external world, and therefore that Hume's understanding of it as constant conjunction will not suffice; and he dissents from Kant's view to the effect that the category of cause, though serviceable in relation to sense data, has no purchase where supersensible reality is concerned. Despite its inconclusiveness, the argument does suggest, says Matthews, that the phenomenal order is not self-explanatory and that 'The mind in its search for coherence and understanding pushes of necessity beyond phenomena in order to account for them.[195] The problem is that while 'Every constructive philosophy is based upon a cosmological argument ... not every constructive philosophy is Theistic'; thus in concluding to an infinite and perfect being the cosmological argument 'goes beyond the premises'.[196] As with the ontological, so with the cosmological argument: the absolute reality from which the former sets out and to which the latter purports to lead, is not the God whom religious persons worship.

If we were to stop at the cosmological argument, Matthews continues, we should risk a one-sided view of the divine nature. It is the teleological argument which elevates the facts of time and change, and 'if we find signs of the action of purposive intelligence in the confused spheres of nature and history, we have the confirmation both of our religious faith and of our theological speculations'.[197] Matthews is thus led into a full account of the teleological argument – an account which occupies the bulk of his Alexander Lectures on *The Purpose of God*. A blow-by-blow account of his case being precluded, I shall simply announce the salient positions towards which he argues. First, an adequate teleological argument will show that God is not only the efficient, but also the final cause of all that is: 'not only the Source of All but the Goal of All'.[198] Matthews is impressed by Leibniz's 'thoroughgoing attempt to do justice to the multiplicity and variety of the world, which is treated as illusion by all forms of pantheism'.[199] Integral to his case is the conviction that there is an unavoidable *a priori* element in the teleological argument, for it turns upon 'the necessary but undemonstrable assumption that we have true and objective judgments of value', and upon 'the [equally undemonstrable] presupposition that the world is rational'.[200] The argument also proceeds by analogy in that we 'explain by assimilating the facts to

---

[194] Ibid.
[195] Ibid., 30–31.
[196] Ibid., 35–6.
[197] Ibid., 43.
[198] Ibid., 50. We note that as late as 1935 Matthews is still found using some very Victorian capital letters.
[199] Ibid., 50.
[200] Ibid., 66.

our own experience'.[201] As indicated earlier in another connection, a teleological argument requires the justification of the assertion that 'Mind is the only possible, or at least the most probable, Source of the order of the world',[202] or as Matthews elsewhere puts it, 'immanent teleology implies transcendent teleology, and that, in its turn, implies transcendent thought'.[203] Furthermore, 'The approach to the teleological argument through the door of the emergence of mind offers us a way of escape from some of the difficulties which arise when we think of the Creator under the analogy of a contriver or craftsman.'[204] It is, moreover, inconceivable that the evolution of life and mind are 'mere resultants of the non-living or the non-mental, produced by causes which are at work in the inorganic world' (shades of his critique of naturalism and materialism).[205] This is confirmed by our intellectual, moral and aesthetic experience. Finally, the cosmic purpose which is implied in the teleological argument, if it is not to be a mirror image of deterministic materialism, must give due place to the development of freedom. From the fact that the fulfilment of this purpose is thus far deferred, even partially frustrated, we are led towards the theological consideration that what is disordered requires redemption and that divine provision has been made for this.

Standing to one side of the ontological, cosmological and teleological arguments is the moral argument, elevated by Kant, though in terms of one of three postulates (that is, conditions) of thought: God, freedom and immortality. Matthews welcomes the fact that, by undermining the metaphysical basis of the 'rational theology' which had been regarded as the bulwark of Christian life and faith, Kant 'left the way clear for a doctrine of God based upon the moral and religious consciousness'[206] – a doctrine whose herald was Schleiermacher. It is therefore not surprising that, given his experiential starting-point and his concern for ultimate value, Matthews finds the moral argument, together with the teleological argument, the most persuasive of all the theistic arguments. He reflects upon the 'moral evolution of mankind' and asks what it implies concerning the nature of the universe; he discusses the conscience and asks, 'On what grounds can we justify that sense of obligation which is the characteristic property of moral experience?'[207] He ponders the nature of the good, and asks, 'What is the place of the Good in

---

[201] Ibid., 68.
[202] Ibid., 90.
[203] Idem, *God and Evolution*, 49.
[204] Idem, *The Purpose of God*, 96.
[205] Ibid., 104.
[206] GCTE, 109.
[207] SCP, 120. Matthews's emphasis upon the character of moral values as obligatory makes one wonder why, when H. P. Owen writes 'Rather, I should say that the divine ground of moral values becomes apparent only when their obligatory character is taken into account', he thinks he is correcting Matthews. See *W. R. Matthews: Philosopher and Theologian*, London: Athlone Press, 1946, 41.

the general structure of the universe?'[208] He finds that in each case he is led to the theistic hypothesis. Consistently with his caution regarding the other arguments, he declares 'It would be too much to maintain that the facts of morality furnish us with premisses from which we can, by a necessary argument, deduce the existence of God; but we may reasonably hold that they afford a cumulative argument by which His existence may be established with a high degree of probability.'[209] (I should prefer to say that we may hold that it is *not irrational* to *testify* to God's existence – the phrase '*established* with a *high degree* of probability' being a question-begging hostage to fortune. Furthermore, I recommend caution where cumulative arguments are concerned since six broken signposts point the direction no more clearly than one.)

On the ground that 'minds form ideals and acknowledge themselves to be under moral obligation',[210] Matthews rebukes Bertrand Russell for failing to include moral phenomena within his understanding of 'fact',[211] and then argues that in the moral life we proceed on the assumption of the objectivity of the moral ideal. He admits that in one sense moral duties are relative: particular actions and ends are 'determined by the conditions of our lives and vary with infinite complexity', but this does not imply incompatibility with an objective moral ideal, for 'without particular occasions there would be no moral *action*, but without an objective ideal there would be no *moral* action'.[212] If we conceive of the moral ideal as having, at one and the same time, objectivity and as an ideal, 'we shall be compelled to think of it as a completely conceived but as yet unrealised purpose ... In other words, we are led to postulate a transcendent teleology.'[213] This, Matthews suggests, would take us only as far as deism; but the objective and independent moral law must find some purchase in human nature if it is to have any authority. This necessity is met by theism, which

> holds that the Deity transcends the temporal order, and therefore that the moral ideal is objective, and objective as an ideal. But at the same time, with its doctrine of the immanent Word or Reason, it enjoins us to hold that the apprehension whereby we discern the Good is the reflection of the Divine knowledge, and that the will whereby we attempt to realise the Good is not unrelated with the will whereby God seeks to realise His own end.[214]

---

[208] Ibid.
[209] Ibid.
[210] Ibid., 122.
[211] He refers to B. Russell, *Mysticism and Logic, and Other Essays*, New York: Longmans, Green, 1918, 30, 31.
[212] Ibid., 139.
[213] Ibid., 141.
[214] Ibid., 142.

But with talk of the immanent Word or Reason, the Good as the reflection of the Divine knowledge, and the consummation of God's purpose, we stand at the threshold of revelation. What guidance can Matthews offer us on this topic? He first casts his eye over 'the whole range of religious development among men' with a view to showing either that 'the Christian idea of revelation ... is the culmination of the conception of revelation which is found in other religions', or that it 'represents a complete break and a new beginning'.[215] He passes swiftly through magic, with a nod to James Frazer, and then considers the major historical religions. He notes two characteristics common to them all: each turns upon an alleged revelation given through inspired persons; and each is marked by a tendency for the revelation to become depersonalized. That is to say, 'The record, the book, or the set of doctrines which are believed to enshrine the original revelation, seem, almost inevitably, to usurp the authority of the personal experience, which lies at the root of the religion, and to take its place.'[216] When the extreme is reached of holding that 'the actual words of a book or a law are divine', we have 'the pathology of religion, which is another name for magic'.[217]

Ever keen to 'test the spirits, to see whether they are from God',[218] Matthews thinks that while a wise religion will apply this rubric to what purports to be revelation, no less than to any other religious or moral experience, it remains the case that 'what the religious consciousness fundamentally means by revelation is a fact of experience as indubitable as the existence of the world of perception'.[219] At the same time, he recognizes that 'we never come across the "given" ... in an undiluted form. ... All experience is in some degree also interpretation.'[220] Hence, 'Revelation is interpretation, but it is also datum to be interpreted: the Logos immanent in human minds, and the Word made flesh in Christ.'[221] To this he adds the gloss that the interpretation is more than an individual matter; it is 'the outcome of the corporate thinking of the community which has grown out of the original experience'.[222] He then declares that whereas Protestants have emphasized revelation as being not a matter of the communication of truths about God, but the self-disclosure of God in personal life, Catholics have rightly seen that the Church requires its doctrines and traditions, 'for it is normally through the community and its institutions that the revelation can become available for the mass of mankind'.[223] At this point I demur. On the one hand, none have been more eager to specify their beliefs in confessions and declarations of faith that the

---

[215] Idem, *The Idea of Revelation*, 4.
[216] Ibid., 7.
[217] Ibid., 22.
[218] I John 4: 1.
[219] SCP, 33.
[220] W. R. Matthews, 'The nature and basis of dogma', 12.
[221] Idem, *The Idea of Revelation*, 23.
[222] Ibid., 51.
[223] Ibid.

Lutherans, Reformed and (at least classical) Baptists; on the other hand, nowhere have mysticism and manifold 'devotions' flourished so profusely as in the Catholic tradition. Again, Matthews's point concerning the importance of the Christian community is well taken, but he is incautious when he says that the communal interpretation of revelation is 'an extension of the Revelation',[224] for this might be understood to mean that the community somehow adds to, or increases, the revelation, whereas what it should do is to receive, testify to, and live by it. It is notorious that problems have arisen which continue to plague the *oikumene* when it has done the former. Matthews is, however, as accurate as he is brief when he says that 'Revelation is always the self-disclosure of God and not the supernatural announcement of theology.'[225] But the idea of revelation implies a recipient of it. In this connection Matthews holds that the revelation of God 'must proceed *pari passu* with man's discovery of his own nature. ... The two fundamental maxims of Greek and Hebrew aspiration respectively "Know thyself" and "Know God", are not contradictory but complementary, for man knows God in so far as he truly knows himself and he knows himself through knowing God.'[226] Since revelation, like all data of experience, needs to be understood and related to the rest of our experience if it is to have more than transitory significance, 'the work of theology is ... a permanent need of religion itself'.[227]

In a word, revelation is the foundation upon which reasoned doctrinal exposition may be built. Revelation is not a bolt from the blue which somehow bypasses human reason; rather, as issuing from the divine Word it appeals to the whole person, not least to the mind, and it requires the reasoned as well as the emotional response of the whole person. Indeed, 'an intellectual element enters into all religious experience, ... [and] Our first preoccupation as Christian thinkers is to maintain the reasonableness of what Christian experience has found God to be.'[228] Matthews testifies that '"Rational faith" to me is a meaningful expression and not a contradiction in terms.'[229] He further informs us that during the 1920s, 'the conviction grew steadily that a rational doctrine of Revelation, and of Incarnation as the culmination of Revelation, was needed and that the lack of them

---

[224] Ibid.

[225] Idem, *Signposts to God*, 91. Cf. idem, *The Gospel and the Modern Mind*, 131–2: '[I]t is a profound mistake to think that the Christian Revelation is a body of infallible truths about God or a supernaturally guaranteed system of doctrine. The Christian faith is not that God disclosed interesting philosophical propositions about Himself, but that He revealed Himself in the person of Jesus Christ.'

[226] GCTE, 34.

[227] Ibid., 92.

[228] Ibid., 90, 236. This dimension of Matthews's thought is overlooked by Edwin Ewart Aubrey in his review of GCTE in *The Journal of Religion*, XII no. 1, January 1932, 142, in which he dismissively concludes that Matthews's case will 'probably be "acceptable to the reason of modern men" who have already accepted it'.

[229] MM, 5.

constituted a threat to the future of the Church'.[230] Observing that 'Much earnest preaching of the gospel rests upon no respectable theological or philosophical basis', he is convinced that the decline of religion is chiefly owing to the fact that 'large numbers of people do not find Christianity as presented by the Church a credible or even an intelligible doctrine',[231] and this in a society marked by social, intellectual and moral incoherence.[232]

It will be noted that this conviction regarding the need of a rational faith grew contemporaneously with the bursting onto the theological scene of Karl Barth, whose theological method caused concern to Matthews for a number of reasons. He laments Barth's rejection of natural theology and his refusal to give reasons for believing that revelation is true;[233] he considers that Barth's method entails the dissociation of Christianity from all other religions, and this he regrets;[234] and he cannot agree that the kingdom of God has no connection with the values of civilization.[235] For his part, 'I like, if possible, to see the Christian revelation confirming and enlarging beliefs which we had some good ground for accepting already. Revelation crowns reason but does not supersede it.'[236] To which I should add: where the noetic effects of sin are concerned, revelation also redeems and reorientates human reasoning.

Although he was open to the possibility that there was, perhaps, 'a remnant of old-fashioned Victorian rationalism in me',[237] Matthews cannot seriously be described as a rationalist. Thus, for example, he opposes the systems of Augustine and Calvin because, in his (somewhat uncritical) view, they comprise rationalistic deductions from a Bible deemed infallible.[238] Positively, he wishes to give due place to both reason and experience, and he is in full accord with that non-rationalistic broadening of the scope of reason which I have already endorsed in the writings of W. G. de Burgh, whom Matthews quotes with approval, thus:

---

[230] Ibid., 165.

[231] Idem, *Essays in Construction*, viii.

[232] Ibid., ch. 1.

[233] MM, 148; cf., 296; idem, *Reason in Religion*, 9. Cf. Matthews's strictures upon Mansel's method, SCP, 81; MM, 295–6; *Reason in Religion*, 10. At the end of his favourable review of Matthews's *God in Christian Thought and Experience*, the reviewer in *The Expository Times*, XLII, 1930-31, 67, declared that 'The Barthian reaction from the theology of experience will have to reckon, in this country at least, with such a work as this.' In the event, 'lofty disdain' – even in some cases 'hostility', rather than a genuine 'reckoning', would seem more aptly to characterize the attitude of some Barthians towards the method proposed by Matthews and others of his ilk.

[234] Idem, 'Psychical research and theology', 3.

[235] Idem, *Essays in Construction*, 19.

[236] Idem, *The Hope of Immortality*, 15; cf. ibid., 33.

[237] MM, 298.

[238] GCTE, 226.

My contention is, that whenever in our experience there is conscious unification of diverse elements, be the unity discovered in the real, or constructed by human agency; wherever we discern or produce form in a given material, be it in sense-perception, in a work of art, in moral or economic action, in scientific, philosophical, or religious thinking – there intellect or reason (I use these terms synonymously) is at work. In a word, the essential feature of reason is as Shelley said of the imagination, that of synthesis. It is in relation to this synthetic activity that analysis and logical inference have their secondary, though vitally important, place.[239]

What, then, is the shape of the doctrinal edifice that Matthews erects upon the foundation of experience as interpreted by faithful reason?

VI

In view of Matthews's openness to new ideas, and his less than hide-bound attitude towards creeds which derives from his conviction that revelation is 'not the supernatural disclosure of philosophical propositions, but the experience of God in human life',[240] it is no surprise that he was happy to regard himself as a theological liberal – even as a modernist. In partial evidence of this we may note his membership of The Modern Churchmen's Union. But labels such as 'liberal' and 'modernist' are notoriously slippery,[241] and should not be taken at face value. If William Wand is to be believed, there is a temperamental aspect to the matter: 'In theology [Matthews] has enjoyed identifying himself as a modernist. But he is the most orthodox modernist one ever met.'[242] This judgement will be substantiated in what follows. It is certainly not the case that Matthews was the kind of liberal who sentimentalized God's love; who reduced the Gospel to what right-minded people had always thought – that, he thought, would lead to 'the complete ruin of Christianity as a religion';[243] or who merited the criticism of P. T. Forsyth: 'Too many are occupied in throwing over precious cargo; they are lightening the ship even of its fuel.'[244] He did, however, feel that many theologians were unduly

---

[239] Idem, *Reason in Religion*, 21–2, slightly misquoting W. G. de Burgh, *The Life of Reason*, London: Macdonald & Evans, 1949, 19–20. I give de Burgh's actual words.

[240] Idem, 'The nature and basis of dogma', 23.

[241] See Alan P. F. Sell, *Theology in Turmoil* (1986), Eugene, OR: Wipf & Stock, 1998, chs 5, 6. On 20 January 1937 Matthews resigned as President of the MCU over tensions between liberal evangelicals and Anglo-Catholic modernists. See A. M. G. Stephenson, *The Rise and Decline of English Modernism*, London: SPCK, 1984, 150–53.

[242] W. Wand, 'Salute to Dean Matthews'.

[243] W. R. Matthews, *Essays in Construction*, 137.

[244] P. T. Forsyth, *Positive Preaching and the Modern Mind*, (1907), London: Independent Press, 1964, 84.

conservative in their concern with 'what Christianity had been in the past and too little [concerned] with what it would have to be in the future'.[245] But he was also critical of some liberal theological endeavours, as when they entailed the deprecating of 'the theological and dogmatic strain in the Gospels, and still more in the Epistles'.[246] Indeed, 'Liberal Protestants have too often taken for granted that the Gospels are the text and the Epistles only comment. The truth is that both text and comment are inextricably intermingled – the person and words of Jesus are mediated through the experience of the first Christian generation.'[247]

Again, 'While valuing the modernist's 'witness to the claims of the intellect and the duty of seeking truth', Matthews half suspected that by allying themselves so closely with immanentist and evolutionary thought the modernists were in danger of repudiating supernatural religion and with it the essential gospel.[248] Yet again, he refers to the *pro tem* prominent liberal, R. J. Campbell, sometime minister of the City Temple, London, thus:

> Campbell ... was working up towards his 'New Theology',[249] which he later abandoned, and, while attracting large congregations, was not in favour either with Anglicans like Bishop Gore or with Protestant divines like P. T. Forsyth, who remarked acidly that the New Theology was like a bad photograph, over-exposed and under-developed. The stricture had some truth, as Campbell later acknowledged; but the work of alerting the intelligent laymen to the crisis of faith was necessary and, as the then Bishop of Woolwich has shown, still needs to be carried on. Indeed, when I read Bishop Robinson's book [*Honest to God*], I thought, 'I have read all this before.' The differences between then and now are that Robinson is a first-rate New Testament scholar and Campbell was not, and Campbell was an idealist in philosophy with a tendency to Pantheism, while Robinson, writing at a time when philosophy in England is confused, has no metaphysical foundation.[250]

A summary statement of this 'liberal's' 'conservatism' is not hard to find:

> Though we may prefer to regard the Christian idea of God as the culmination of all the conceptions which men's minds have entertained ... we cannot let go the ancient claim that the Christian God is the only true God, the Father of the Lord Jesus Christ the only true object of worship, and that every declension from this

---

[245] MM, 135.

[246] GCTE, 82.

[247] Idem, *The Gospel and the Modern Mind*, 46–7.

[248] Idem, *Essays in Construction*, 41.

[249] The allusion is to R. J. Campbell, *The New Theology*, London: Chapman and Hall, 1907.

[250] MM, 56.

thought of the Divine Being is to be resisted and condemned as a falling back into superstition and error.[251]

But none of this prevented his urgent and consistent plea for the revision of the *Thirty-Nine Articles* of the Church of England. Matthews is not opposed to creeds as such. While he thinks that religion is possible without conscious intellectual formulation, *a* religion is not.[252] His principal complaint against the *Articles* is that the mind of the Church has moved on since they were first promulgated, and they do not address the questions of contemporary society. While granting that 'The fundamental reactions of the soul in redemption, loving trust, spiritual power, worship, are constantly renewed' as the 'living power of the words and story of the Man of Galilee ... vibrate again in the souls of men from generation to generation', 'the Christian idea of God is scarcely likely to be the creed of the future if its defenders feel obliged to ignore or minimize every acquisition of fresh knowledge'.[253] He takes what was in his day fashionable exception to the Calvinism of the *Articles*, making a meal of double predestination, and in conclusion reiterates his concern that if we shirk the task of credal revision, 'I see little hope for the evangelisation of England.'[254] It is interesting to note that in the matter of credal revision, Matthews was in advance of the 'modern churchmen' of the first three decades of the twentieth century: 'I do not remember one who was in favour of disestablishment, nor one who wanted to abolish or revise the Thirty-Nine Articles. Why these radicals in theology were so conservative in theology,

---

[251] GCTE, 2–3.

[252] Idem, 'The nature and basis of dogma', 8.

[253] GCTE, 111, 112.

[254] Idem, *The Thirty-Nine Articles. A Plea for a New Statement of the Christian Faith as Understood by the Church of England*, London: Hodder & Stoughton, 1961. Cf. idem, *God and Evolution*, 1; MM, 144, 211–16. My phrase 'fashionable exception to Calvinism' refers to the widespread sigh of relief emitted by more liberal theologians of many Christian denominations when they concluded that modern biblical criticism and the evolutionary *theme* had rescued them from the scholasticism of Calvinism. See, for example, Alan P. F. Sell, *Enlightenment, Ecumenism, Evangel*, ch. 5; *Hinterland Theology. A Stimulus to Theological Construction*, Milton Keynes: Paternoster, 2008, ch. 9. I think, however, that the time has now passed when a scholar could escape unscathed after writing such an undiscriminating sentence as the following: 'By abstracting the concept of sovereignty or power and making God practically equivalent to this idea, Calvin really destroyed the validity of moral distinctions.' See Matthews, GCTE, 106. To take exception to these words is not to defend double predestination, or to deny that predestination needs to be rescued from the clutches of philosophical necessity (see Alan P. F. Sell, *Enlightenment, Ecumenism, Evangel*, 325–38); but it is to acknowledge that Calvin may justly be called the theologian of the Holy Spirit; that, *contra* Matthews's assertion that 'Calvinism is built up round the idea of sovereignty as a logical notion' (ibid.), there is nothing especially terrifying about sovereign *grace*; and that it is not good practice to elevate a doctrine which, to the theologian concerned was not central, to the prime position.

I cannot say. I think most of them had been low churchmen and feared the Catholic type of modernism as a version of "popery".'[255] Nothing shook his conviction that 'A fixed dogmatic system which has no place for revision is a dogma not of life but of stagnation.'[256] As to the problem of subscription to the Articles, Matthews's rueful conclusion was that this 'will not be solved so long as the Church is "by law established"'.[257]

Having rehearsed Matthews's general stance in relation to Christian doctrine, I shall now indicate his position on some particular doctrines. Matthews surmises that if we wished to offer a philosophical definition of belief in God 'we might say that it is the faith that reality and value coincide ... that the supremely real Being is the supremely Good';[258] or, to put it otherwise, the idea of God implies 'an objective standard and an objective judge'.[259] But there is much more to be said, for Christianity proclaims a living God, and such a God must be a personal God, 'for to be a person is the most adequate way of being alive'.[260] Furthermore, since in our experience aesthetic and moral values concern personal imaginations and wills, we infer that such values have their ground in the divine personality (which is not to say that God is necessarily *a* person: for Christians the Godhead is triune[261]), and this personality is 'manifested in the Incarnation through the life of a perfect human Person'.[262] Indeed, 'The Christian view of the nature of God is determined by the belief that Jesus Christ is the unique Son of God and the Incarnate Word or Thought [and action] of God.'[263] Unlike our limited and imperfect personalities, the personality of God knows no limitations. Since Matthews's assertions strike the ear as being both definite and bold, I must hasten to point out that he is more cautious than might at first sight appear. He declines to define 'personality' because 'I believe personality to be indefinable. ... [It is] that which for us is ultimately real, that from which we derive all our conceptions of reality and being, and at the same time is incapable of being an object of knowledge in the ordinary sense.'[264] The fact remains that the typical Christian experience is not of union with or

---

[255] MM, 309.
[256] Idem, 'The nature and basis of dogma', 23.
[257] MM, 387–8.
[258] Idem, *The Search for Perfection*, 7.
[259] Idem, *The Year Through Christian Eyes*, London: Epworth Press, 1970, 54.
[260] GCTE, 161.
[261] SCP, 173–5. Cf. idem, *The Gospel and the Modern Mind*, 106–7.
[262] GCTE, 163. Cf. *The Gospel and the Modern Mind*, 115, 116: 'Values ... exist for persons and are realised only in personal life. ... [M]oral values have their basis in the nature of Reality; they are grounded in the central core of Being.'
[263] Idem, 'The Christian belief in God', in W. R. Matthews, ed., *The Christian Faith. Essays in Exploration and Defence*, London: Eyre and Spottiswoode, 1936, 86. My insertion is intended to capture a further significant aspect of the connotation of *Logos*.
[264] GCTE, 164. Cf. SCP, 184; idem, *The Gospel and the Modern Mind*, 110–11.

absorption by God, but of communion with him, and 'Intercourse can subsist only between persons and has no meaning apart from them.'[265]

We have already seen that in his philosophical prolegomena to theology Matthews is concerned to hold the correlative terms, transcendence and the immanence, in balance,[266] but in more theological contexts he emphasizes God's transcendent character as holy love, a claim that is made on the ground of God's self-revelation, but one which does not imply that we can fully grasp its significance. On the contrary, God's transcendence means that he is ultimately incomprehensible to us: God alone knows himself as he truly is; our knowledge of God is 'that knowledge which is possible to man',[267] and by reason of his self-revelation he is not altogether unknowable by us. The believer is assured of his immanent presence by the Holy Spirit: 'The divine presence is within all creation, but in fullness and in power with those who, responding to the divine initiative, have become joined with Christ in affection and will.'[268] In short, a supernatural religion 'finds the Eternal to be, not a mere Absolute or Infinite Being or Moral order of the world, but a living, personal Spirit who draws near to man with creative and redemptive purpose'.[269] Of such a kind is the Christian religion.

Now the idea of God's purpose recalls the teleological thrust which, as we have seen, is central to Matthews's thinking. In his view, if God is a purposive God we cannot subscribe to the ancient but abstract view that God is self-sufficient in and for himself. In other words, God cannot be impassible and incapable of change. At this point he parts company with William Temple, who 'adhered to this venerable theological tradition, with the consequence that his views on purpose and freedom seem to me to be obscure.'[270] As to impassibility, Matthews's objection to the doctrine underlies his adverse comments upon scholastic philosophy, to which I have already referred. He agrees with Clement Webb that Aquinas turned to Aristotelianism in the expectation of finding a firmer basis for an ethical conception of God than was supplied by Platonic immanentism, 'But it was a desperate and hopeless project to substitute the God "who so loved the world" for the Aristotelian God who ... is Himself moved by no impulse of love, without transforming the whole structure of the philosophy.'[271] While being cautioned by Robert Mackintosh that 'An unhappy God would mean a bankrupt universe, a

---

[265] SCP, 172.
[266] GCTE, 132.
[267] Idem, 'The nature and basis of dogma', 19.
[268] GCTE, 85.
[269] Idem, *Essays in Construction*, 40.
[270] Idem, *The Purpose of God*, 173. Though he described himself as not a fan of Temple (MM, 145), Matthews contributed a gracious and perceptive paper on his thought to *William Temple: An Estimate and an Appreciation*, London: James Clarke, 1946, ch. 1. He did, however, regret that Temple paid no heed to the evidence of psychical research, and took little account of developments in psychology. See ibid., 20, 23.
[271] SCP, 70. Cf. GCTE, 96–7.

demonstrated pessimism, a doomed faith',[272] he nevertheless argues that to say that God suffers is not to say that pain is the predominant note in God's experience:

> The faith that God suffers in and with the creation, and is without ceasing bearing the labour of redemption, is not faith in an 'unhappy God'. For the power is adequate to the emergency. There can be no evil which, in the end, will frustrate the divine redeeming Will. The suffering of God is transfigured by the vision of the travail of His soul in which is His satisfaction.[273]

In a striking statement Matthews declares that '[God] alone perhaps sums up in His experience the sufferings of "the world". The only being who has the right to be a pessimist in God.'[274] He later testified that during the Second World War the doctrine 'that suffering is a part of God's experience – became to me an indispensable conviction'.[275]

---

[272] GCTE, 247, quoting R. Mackintosh, *Historic Theories of Atonement with Comments*, London: Hodder and Stoughton, 1920, 254. Matthews takes the quotation from J. K. Mozley, *The Impassibility of God. A Survey of Christian Thought*, Cambridge: CUP, 1926, 171. It would, however, be wrong to present Mackintosh as being opposed to passibility without qualification. In his book he avers that God is love, and that he would not have been true to his name 'had He contented Himself with constitutional excuses for inaction' (23); and he asserts that 'A deity of stoical apathy is not the God whom Christ reveals' (253). But he also affirms that 'A God who fluctuates with changing circumstances, physical or human, is a Pagan god; and in the end that turns out to mean No God at all' (255). But if for 'fluctuates with' we read 'responds morally to', we seem to be in accord with Mackintosh's following sentence: 'Difficult as it is to construe Christology in better terms than those of the now anachronous creeds, may we not trace part of the significance of the incarnation of God in Christ just here, that Divine love now knew suffering as suffering? And so the love that emptied itself in the act of redemption is the greatest and divinest of all' (255–6). This is not to deny that there was divine suffering before the incarnation, or that God agonized over the sins of Israel. The underlying problem is that if, partly by way of excluding tritheism, we claim that the work of one person of the Trinity is the work of all, it is difficult to see how there could be a genuine revelation through the 'economic' God if there were also an impassible God somewhere else (to use strictly inappropriate spatial language) in eternity, or an aspect of the divine which was not concerned with matters economic – a schizophrenic god, perhaps? My view is that the one God cannot change in the sense of acting out of accordance with his nature, but his holy, loving nature is such that he cannot but act responsively according to the diverse moral and existential situations of persons created in his image and the fluctuating condition of the created order. See further on impassibility, Alan P. F. Sell, *Hinterland Theology*, 606–10. For Mackintosh (1858–1933) see DNCBP; DTCBP; ODNB; Alan P. F. Sell, *Robert Mackintosh: Theologian of Integrity*, Bern: Peter Lang, 1977.

[273] Ibid., 248.

[274] Idem, *Essays in Construction*, 162.

[275] MM, 263.

As one might expect of a Christian theologian, Matthews upholds God's nature as love. This makes his assertion, 'If I were asked why I believed in God, I should put this experience of a greater than ourselves in the forefront'[276] appear inadequate. However that may be, he is careful to insist upon the fact that God's love is holy love.[277] 'The holiness of God,' he explains, 'is His love, viewed from the angle of the good which He wills for His creatures.'[278] He does not shrink from also associating the holiness of God with the wrath of God. The New Testament writers posit a dualism between God and all that opposes him. They are not, of course, thinking in terms of a metaphysical doctrine of dualism, but a spiritual one. This is not, however, an absolute and final dualism; it might be called an 'interim dualism';[279] and it is one which is finally overcome by holy love. 'It is only safe,' Matthews declares, 'to approach the doctrine of the divine Love through the doctrine of the divine Holiness.'[280] We shall resume this theme in connection with the doctrines of humanity, sin and atonement. But if we would fully understand Matthews it is of crucial importance that we do not think of redemption only in connection with humanity. He is concerned with the whole created order, and the doctrine of creation is central to his thought, notably, as being that which guarantees the Creator-creature distinction and precludes all pantheisms and process thought excesses.

Matthews's exposition of creation is inspired by the following convictions:

> The religious experience is that of communion with God. For Christian piety the highest good is not absorption into the Divine life, still less is it devotion to a baffled leader of the hard-pressed forces of the Ideal; it is an unbroken fellowship with a personal God who is the source of the soul's life, but never identical with the soul. Thus the Christian view of the world is deeply concerned to maintain the personal nature of God and the real freedom of human spirits. ... It would hardly be too much to say that the conception of creation in some form is a vital element in Christian Theism. If we should be compelled to abandon it under the pressure of criticism we should be left to a melancholy choice between a Pantheism for which there is no world and a Pluralism for which there is no God.[281]

Matthews does not find the explicit affirmation of an absolute creation in the Old Testament. Such an idea is implicit, he thinks, in the highest thought of the Hebrew

---

[276] Idem, *Signposts to God*, 12.

[277] One is tempted, rather cheekily, to surmise that, in view of the considerable emphasis placed upon this point by his former colleague, P. T. Forsyth, Matthews would hardly have dared to do otherwise.

[278] GCTE, 233.

[279] W. R. Matthews, *The Year Through Christian Eyes*, 41.

[280] GCTE, 80.

[281] SCP, 204, 205.

prophets, but the Genesis creation narratives suggest the divine Spirit's bringing to order of pre-existing chaos. The latter, however, is a dualistic notion, and the Christian doctrine of creation *ex nihilo*, which 'appears to have been a peculiarity of Christian thought',[282] runs counter to it. Moreover, unlike emanation theories, which are compatible with pantheism, or Aristotle's view that creation occurs in the process of the divine self-contemplation, the Christian doctrine 'conceives the created world as depending upon an activity which is at least analogous to will, it exists [not necessarily but] by reason of the choice of its Creator'.[283] Indeed, 'The God of St. John and of St. Paul is first of all the Creator. We might almost say without being untrue to the Apostolic thought that it is in virtue of His creativeness that God is God.'[284] Moreover, commitment to the view that God is personal entails commitment to the view that he creates, 'for otherwise we should be denying to Him the possession of that quality which is pre-eminently a mark of the highest personality.'[285] 'The problem of creation,' he declares, 'is a special form of the old puzzle of the one and the many', and 'We have to reconcile belief in God and the thorough-going dependence of the temporal order with genuine though limited freedom and being-for-self of the higher elements in that order.'[286]

As to human beings, it is in the doctrine of the *imago dei* that both the reality of the image and the individual's otherness *vis-à-vis* God are asserted. With this we come to Matthews's account of the divine objective in creation:

> the created order exists that it may be the sphere in which free moral personalities arise and develop, attaining through struggle and aspiration, the Kingdom of God, of which the essential character is the communion in unrestricted intercourse of the created persons with the supreme Father of Spirits. ... In so far as the creation is the necessary condition of the fulfilment of the Kingdom of God, it has its *raison d'être*. ... Those spiritual values which we sum up under the term the Kingdom of God, are part at least of the purpose of creation; but we have no sufficient ground for believing that they are the whole purpose. ... [T]here are doubtless purposes which are in no immediate relation to us, and the stone and the star must have value for God which we cannot understand. In ways beyond our fathoming the Lord rejoices in all His works.[287]

When Matthews was discussing the teleological argument for the existence of God he asserted that 'the problem of evil has no bearing on our argument', because the argument 'does not depend upon the assertion that the universe is wholly good, but

---

[282] Ibid., 208.
[283] Ibid., 211; cf. idem, GCTE, 109.
[284] GCTE, 72. Matthews cites Romans 1: 20.
[285] SCP, 228; cf. idem, GCTE, 173–4.
[286] Ibid., 218.
[287] GCTE, 220, 222.

simply upon the plain fact that within it knowledge of good and of truth occur'.[288] He did concede, however, that a full teleological account of the meaning of the universe could not be achieved unless evil and suffering were confronted. The problem arises because, as Schleiermacher correctly saw, we cannot separate the idea of creation from the idea of preservation, since these are 'one-sided representations of the ultimate religious truth – the absolute dependence of all things on God'.[289] How, if at all, are we to accommodate belief in the good and loving God with the manifest facts of evil, sin and suffering? In a *prima facie* problematic sentence Matthews writes, 'The problem of evil may furnish a theoretical difficulty for belief in God and offer a standing problem for Theism, but the fact of evil, at least in the sense of imperfection, is the starting point of religion.'[290] But (a) what, now, of the experience of dependence as the starting point of religion? (b) Can we truly take the measure of evil and suffering unless we first hear the Gospel? Matthews returns a negative answer to this question on the ground that where individual sin is concerned persons of all religions and of none may feel guilt and express remorse. No doubt; but when sin is understood as the flouting of God's holiness and the disobeying of his law, Sydney Cave's assertion is correct: 'It is because of Calvary, not because of Eden, that we are compelled to judge gravely of sin.'[291] We shall do well to bear these questions in mind as we proceed.

Matthews regrets that discussions of evil occur in the absence of reference to the good, whereas 'There is a problem of good.'[292] I do not think he is on firm ground at this point, for while the origin or attribution of good are intriguing questions, they are hardly problems for the unbeliever in the sense in which evil is for the believer. Sceptics cannot be defeated by the *tu quoque* argument: 'You ask me how I can believe in a good and loving God given all the evil in the word – but how do you account for the good in the world?' – because sceptics are not obliged to do any such thing; they can simply accept the good and enjoy it. It is the believer who has the problem. When, further, Matthews avers, in good 'liberal' fashion, that 'values ... have their life by a constant overcoming of their opposites. Without the element of negation there would be no movement in the sense of growth of value',[293] the personification of values is less than helpful; and the sceptic might suppose that a world in which only positive values were found would be preferable to the world we see, and more in compatible with the idea of a God deemed to

---

[288] Idem, *The Purpose of God*, 122.

[289] Idem, *God and Evolution*, 54.

[290] Idem, *The Gospel and the Modern World*, 128.

[291] S. Cave, *The Christian Estimate of Man*, London: Duckworth, 1844, 228. Cf. his *The Doctrine of the Work of Christ*, London: University of London Press, 1937, 234. For Cave (1883–1953) see ODNB; Trevor A. Hart, ed., *The Dictionary of Historical Theology*, Carlisle: Paternoster, 2000; C. Binfield and J. Taylor, *Who They Were*. Cave succeeded Garvie as Principal of New College, London, in 1933.

[292] Idem, *Essays in Construction*, 164.

[293] Idem, 166. Cf. ibid., 168.

be loving and good. Matthews, on the contrary, says that 'a teleological argument which succeeded in showing that the whole creation was perfectly adapted to the production of the maximum good, though it might demonstrate the existence of God, would have destroyed the basis not only of Christianity, but of all religion, for it would have, so to speak, in proving God to have proved, at the same time, that we needed Him not'.[294] Yes and no; it would have proved that religion as we know it is redundant, but it would also have proved that that perfect communion with God which humans need to be truly fulfilled were the reality on earth; that the Kingdom, for which Christians currently pray, had come.

But, as everybody knows, it is not so. As Matthews knew only too well, the facts of experience in nature and history lead us to the assertion that 'God's in His heaven but something has gone wrong with the world.'[295] In a number of places he refers to the doctrine of original sin as witnessing to the pervasiveness of sin but, not surprisingly, he will not countenance the transmission of guilt from one person to another or from one generation to another on account of the transgression of an allegedly historical Adam. This is not to deny that contributory to what I have sometimes called the world's out-of-sorts-ness is human sin; and Matthews does well to bring creation and redemption into close relation.[296] Reflecting upon Jesus' word from the Cross, 'They know not what they do',[297] he observes that 'Most things of importance are done in our world by collections of people, and most evil is done in this way. The most appalling feature of modern sin is its dreadful anonymity.'[298] This seems to me to be undeniable, but caution is needed lest we vitiate morality by supposing that individuals are objectively morally responsible for the actions of others of which they know nothing, and even for the consequences of their own actions which they could not have foreseen. Moreover, language concerning 'structural sin', which has come to prominence in some circles since Matthews's day, though his words are a harbinger of it, should not encourage any to seek to evade moral responsibility by lamenting, 'What could I do – I am embroiled in sinful structures?' The crux is that sinful structures cannot repent.[299]

As for the sins against God's holy love of which we are aware and fully responsible, Matthews says on his own account that 'I have to ... "remake" myself through the power of the Eternal Spirit.'[300] As it stands this is an incautious remark, for it suggests that the remaking, albeit through the power of the Eternal Spirit, is predominantly a 'work' undertaken on his own initiative. That this is not, however, what Matthews really believes is clear from the concluding sentence of a prayer

---

[294] Idem, *The Purpose of God*, 130.
[295] Idem, *Signposts to God*, 81. Cf. ibid., 14.
[296] See, for example, idem, *The Purpose of God*, 145.
[297] Luke 23: 34.
[298] W. R. Matthews, *Seven Words*, 35.
[299] See further, Alan P. F. Sell, *Aspects of Christian Integrity* (1990), Eugene, OR: Wipf & Stock, 1998, 65–8.
[300] Idem, *Seven Words*, 133.

which follows two pages later: 'Thou hast given me a soul to make; make Thou it for me, and build me into Thy spiritual temple, for Jesus' sake.'[301] This seems more akin to the 'I, yet not I but Christ' experience which is at the heart of all Christian moral endeavour. As Matthews later writes in relation to the Cross, 'The offering which satisfies God is made by God. Though completely and absolutely human, it is also a Divine act.'[302] So, analogously, it must be with all our lesser strivings and sufferings. The gracious assistance of the Holy One is indispensable, for 'The Christian view of man does not authorize us to entertain any sanguine hopes of man as he naturally stands. Its hope is in a redeemed humanity, and it holds that man's highest quality is that he is capable of redemption.'[303] 'The natural man,' he avers, 'is a potential child of God';[304] though I should prefer to say that while human beings are by nature children of God – created in his image – they may by the grace of adoption become sons and daughters of God. As Matthews elsewhere says, 'God's strategy in the face of the rebellion of His creatures is not to reduce them to slaves or puppets who are incapable of rejecting His laws, but to make them sons who are in harmony with His will';[305] 'we become dead unto sin by becoming alive unto God'.[306] This is consistent with what he wrote of conversion: 'It is a change in the whole orientation of the self, and the dominant note of the experience is the feeling that some power, the grace of God, which was not within the resources of the previously existing personality, has caused the transformation.'[307] It is, he declares, greatly to the credit of Kierkegaard and those in his train to have 'emphasised a mode of religious consciousness which is of fundamental importance'.[308]

The good news is that God 'has taken the initiative to rescue and redeem. The Incarnation and the Passion of the Son of God are the sign that God, with a cost to himself which we cannot understand, has taken the burden of evil and is overcoming evil with good.'[309] What is more, the God who so acts is, to resume the point briefly indicated earlier, the God of holy love. In fact, 'The central insight in which the Gospel is founded is that the Holy One who laid down His life for His friends is not only the supreme example of heroic human goodness, but the most complete revelation of the character of God.'[310] In order to put flesh on these doctrinal bones we must now investigate more closely Matthews's understanding of who Jesus Christ is, and what he has done.

---

[301] Ibid., 135.
[302] Ibid., 168.
[303] Idem, *Essays in Construction*, 10.
[304] Idem, *The Search for Perfection*, 21.
[305] Idem, *The Year Through Christian Eyes*, 45.
[306] Idem, *The Search for Perfection*, 11.
[307] Idem, *Reason in Religion*, 15.
[308] Ibid., 16.
[309] Idem, 'The Christian belief in God', 89.
[310] GCTE, 224.

As he looked back across the years, Matthews recalled that 'In the twenties the conviction grew steadily that a rational doctrine of Revelation, and of Incarnation as the culmination of Revelation, was needed and that the lack of them constituted a threat to the future of the Church.'[311] At one and the same time this proposition manifests his starting-point and his distance from Karl Barth. In a word, Matthews proceeds to incarnation as a culminating point, whereas Barth sets out from revelation.[312] More basically, and in terms which remind us of his apologetic interest: 'My modest suggestion is that, if we are to think at all, we shall have to start from where we are and with the material which is ready to our hand, and moreover, it is only by starting there that we can hope to think out a doctrine which will be intelligible to the educated persons of our day.'[313]

Amongst the material to hand we find the benefits of modern biblical criticism and the important emphasis upon the Jesus of history. Indeed, while Matthews considered that the Ritschlians were unduly suspicious of metaphysics and mysticism, he felt that with their grasp upon the truth that 'The only starting-point for any Christian doctrine is the historical Jesus and his impact upon our spirits and minds'[314] they had found the pearl of price. By contrast, Matthews felt that those New Idealists who followed in the train of Hegel, had, in their theory of history, lost something of great importance. They had sacrificed 'the last vestiges of the scandal of transcendence which remains in Hegel under the form of the universal Mind' for an immanentism which, in holding that 'every attempt to write history is a revival of the past in the present consciousness of the historian, and the past has no existence outside the present consciousness', left no criteria for judging the truth of competing interpretations of history: 'One man's re-living of the past is as good as another's.'[315] In Matthews's opinion this view of Croce's condemns us to 'complete historical scepticism'.[316] This criticism is the more telling because Matthews had been philosophically raised in the climate of idealism, and he never reneged on the idealistic position that 'there is no existence apart from mind'.[317] What is more, he insists, a radical immanentism cannot give due place to persons, who are the actors in history: 'when once we have admitted the reality of persons and personal activity we have broken the chain of immanence. Something transcendent to the process has been found, for if the historical process is itself, in some degree at least, the creation of persons, we cannot dissolve those persons

---

[311] MM, 165.

[312] See idem, *The Problem of Christ in the Twentieth Century*, 3–4.

[313] Ibid., 41.

[314] Ibid., 39–40. Cf. GCTE, 255.

[315] GCTE, 151. As he elsewhere drily remarks, 'Some very bad histories are very good autobiographies.' See *Essays in Construction*, 102.

[316] GCTE, 151. Cf. idem, *The Purpose of God*, 134.

[317] Ibid. For this reason, among others, H. P. Owen is correct in saying that Matthews's 'account of religion and its relation to philosophy owes scarcely anything to Hegelianism'. See *W. R. Matthews: Philosopher and Theologian*, 45.

into the historical process without remainder.'[318] Again, whereas Croce's view would prohibit the judgement of the past, the writing of history in fact implies the possession of, or at least the acknowledgement of, an absolute standard which transcends the temporal, and to which appeal is made. Matthews testifies that the historical process 'gets its significance from eternal Reality, which is more or less adequately reflected or incarnate within the time process'.[319]

Where, in all of this, is Jesus? Matthews goes so far as to speculate that a profoundly modified Christianity of ideas might survive the loss of the historical Jesus (and there were absolute idealists before, and existentialist theologians after, who came close to holding this view, if, indeed some of them did not positively assert it); but Matthews does not think that this extreme case 'has any plausible appearance of being true.'[320] On the contrary, 'Christianity is rooted in history because it has been created by a belief in the historical person Jesus of Nazareth.'[321] Indeed, 'To me it seems evident that the coming of Jesus Christ was the turning-point of history; it was, even from the point of view of the unbeliever, the most important event which ever happened.'[322] More particularly,

> For the Christian, the central fact of history is the life, death, and resurrection of Christ, which is, moreover, that which gives all other history its true meaning and enables us to see it in proper proportion. In the Incarnation we have the supreme instance of God's providential guidance and a revelation of His providential Purpose. The advent of the Redeemer is 'in the fullness of time' ...[323]

This entails that Matthews's strong advocacy of divine transcendence must be balanced by the idea of 'thoroughgoing immanence. ... Though God is not exhausted in the world, He is manifested in it all.'[324] Matthews is well aware that a deep philosophical problem is hereby raised: how can the absolute and final appear 'within the process of time and under the conditions of space'?[325] Yet this is what Christians proclaim: 'In Christ we are invited to see the absolute Personality.'[326] and 'There is no higher revelation of God'[327] than that found in him. The way in which Christians articulated what they thought was revealed in Christ deeply interested Matthews, and he wrote at some length, for example, on the Virgin Birth,[328] and

---

[318] GCTE, 154.
[319] Idem, *Essays in Construction*, 105.
[320] Ibid., 108.
[321] Ibid.
[322] Idem, *Signposts to God*, 31.
[323] GCTE, 273.
[324] Idem, *The Gospel and the Modern Mind*, 145.
[325] Idem, *Essays in Construction*, 91.
[326] Ibid., 94.
[327] Idem, *The Gospel and the Modern Mind*, 147.
[328] See *Essays in Construction*, chs 12, 13.

on the Christological problems which the Council of Chalcedon was intended to solve. I do not think he was at his most successful in the area of patristics, though I grant that his adverse criticisms of the Chalcedonian Formula were advanced by others whose primary field that was; and I decline to probe his psycho-analytical speculation concerning the Libido which, 'very tentatively', he holds was a reality for Jesus.[329] I shall simply say that the complaint that the Formula leaves us with two natures and two wills side by side is mitigated to some extent by the fact that, against dualism, the fifth-century theologians affirmed unity of the person of Christ as well; and also by the fact that they understood that if, albeit mysteriously, Jesus did not have a human nature and will he was not like us in all things, sin excepted, and therefore could not save *us*; and if he had not a divine nature and will he could not *save* us, since salvation is God's work alone.[330] That Matthews would not disagree with this is clear from his exhortation that we must never 'separate the work of Jesus from His Person', and that Christ 'is what he is because he does what he does and he can do what he does because he is what he is'.[331] Furthermore, 'we have no good news of God on the Cross unless the Cross was not only an act of man but also an act of God'.[332] I am in entire accord with Matthews's judgement that the conciliar Christological definitions 'whatever their defects, had the merit of negating speculations which would have compromised the essential faith'.[333]

As if to clip the wings of those theologians whose incarnational theology was unduly inspired by post-Hegelian immanentism,[334] Matthews adverts to the 'commonplace' that without faith in the resurrection of Jesus 'there would have been no Christian religion and no doctrine of Incarnation. ... The Resurrection

---

[329] Idem, *The Problem of Christ in the Twentieth Century*, 46. I concur with Daniel Day Williams: 'The mystery of the inner self-consciousness of [Christ's] life we can never in this life penetrate, nor is it essential to Christian faith to do so.' See his review of *The Problem of Christ in the Twentieth Century*, in *The Journal of Religion*, XXXII no. 2, April 1952, 135.

[330] For an attempt to discuss the Formula in a devotional context see Alan P. F. Sell, *Christ Our Saviour*, Shippensburg, PA: Ragged Edge Press, 2000, 75–8.

[331] W. R. Matthews, *The Problem of Christ in the Twentieth Century*, 54. The statement in 'The nature and basis of dogma', 14, is thus one-sided: 'It is because He was what He was and His consciousness was what it was, that the whole array of Christian doctrines came into existence.' But do we not know who he is through what he has done, supremely at the Cross? Matthews, as we have seen, does not deny this, but in this instance he lets his guard down. For reflections upon the approach to Christology through soteriology see Alan P. F. Sell, *Aspects of Christian Integrity*, ch. 2; and for the centrality of the Cross (construed as an umbrella term) see idem, *Enlightenment, Ecumenism, Evangel*, ch. 13.

[332] W. R. Matthews, *Seven Words*, 126, 165. Cf. ibid., 168.

[333] Idem, *The Problem of Christ in the Twentieth Century*, 28.

[334] For some of whom see Alan P. F. Sell, *Theology in Turmoil*, ch. 1; idem, *Philosophical Idealism and Christian Belief*, Cardiff: University of Wales Press, and New York: St. Martin's Press, 1995; Eugene, OR: Wipf & Stock, 1998.

must be the starting point of any doctrine of the Incarnation.'[335] Certainly there would have been no Gospel apart from the resurrection, but there would have been no resurrection had there been no Cross. Matthews does not, of course, deny this. On the contrary, he declares that 'the Resurrection is the completion of Calvary',[336] and that 'It is the Cross which has made Christianity a world religion.'[337] In the Cross, he continues, 'we find the supreme act of God's love, reconciling the world to Himself, manifesting His hatred of sin and His love for the sinner'.[338] The importance of this claim is that for Matthews God in Christ is active at the Cross: it is not that the Cross is simply a visual aid designed to show us the lengths to which God will go to redeem us. That it does manifest his love is clear, and as for the manifestation of God's hatred of sin, Matthews pulled no punches: 'to imagine that God must "let everyone off", because He is love, is to forget His Holiness'.[339] But does not the Cross do more that manifest God's hatred of sin: does it not vanquish it? Have we not an attenuated Gospel unless we affirm this? How else could Matthews's own prayer be answered: 'May the Cross of Jesus be to me the assurance of pardon and the fountain of refreshment for every day; for the sake of Him who died for us, even Jesus Christ'?[340] Matthews restores the balance when he affirms that 'The Cross stands for the ultimate problem of evil and negation faced and conquered',[341] and assures us that Christ's 'victory ... can be ours, in some measure, if we truly want to share his life'.[342]

While both the incarnation and the resurrection can be shown to be not unreasonable – we may, for example, allude to the Church's experience of the risen Christ's presence through history, and to the change of the disciples from scattered terrified individuals into heroic ambassadors of the Gospel – they cannot be demonstrated to the satisfaction of the sceptic. They are spiritually-discerned matters of faith.[343] As for the resurrected Jesus' tomb, its emptiness cannot be demonstrated to anyone, and belief in it is not necessary to belief in the resurrection.[344]

Matthews says that 'The Cross is not a spectacle to be gazed upon but a human experience which reveals God, and, because a human experience, a revelation which we can understand.'[345] Properly distinguishing the experience of God's saving grace from the multiple theories about it – indeed, he confesses that 'I have

---

[335] Ibid., 18. Cf. idem, *Essays in Construction*, 223.
[336] Idem, *Seven Words*, 14.
[337] Ibid., 11.
[338] Ibid., 15.
[339] Idem, *The Year Through Christian Eyes*, 68.
[340] Idem, *Seven Words*, 39.
[341] Idem, *Essays in Construction*, 156.
[342] Idem, *The Search for Perfection*, 35.
[343] See idem, *Essays in Construction*, 224.
[344] Ibid., 229.
[345] Idem, *Seven Words*, 17.

never been able to arrive at any satisfactory doctrine of the Atonement'[346] – he declares, 'The Cross is to us the tree of life, not in so far as we believe rightly about the Atonement, but in so far as we are one in spirit with Him who died upon it.'[347] In fact, 'no doctrine of the Atonement is part of the Christian faith and ... many different views are possible concerning the manner of the Divine forgiveness'.[348] Related to his failure to arrive at a doctrine of the atonement which satisfied him (and it is noticeable that he nowhere subjects traditional accounts of the matter to close examination) is Matthews's regret that the doctrine has fallen into the background – not least because 'The older doctrines of sacrifice, satisfaction for sin, vicarious suffering, seem to us to be crude or unintelligible, and we have nothing to put in their place.'[349] The way forward, he thinks, is along the line of seeing in the Cross 'the sacrament of God's eternal life. In other words, there must be in the divine experience a suffering for sin'[350] – with which we come full circle to divine passibility. 'Such a conception of God', he concludes, 'would lead us to believe that there is no evil which is not "atoned" and overcome in the divine experience, and no error or suffering which is not both shared and transcended.'[351]

How, then, shall we sum up Matthews's Gospel? He may answer for himself: 'It is precisely because God loved us when we did not deserve it, because while we were yet sinners Christ died for us, that there is any good news to proclaim.'[352] Not, indeed, that Christ's saving work has an individual reference only. On the contrary, 'The coming of Christ as Saviour has meaning because He comes to a human world which needs redemption, that is, to one which is in rebellion and alienation, to one in which the Will of God is not done.'[353] Putting both aspects together, he says, 'Jesus died for the Kingdom of God, to bring in the rule of God in the world and in the hearts of men.'[354] Yet he can also say that 'The preaching of the Gospel is the presentation of Christ to the soul as the highest ideal, the one centre round which the self may securely build its life.'[355] This seems to represent an attenuation: suppose that I need a Saviour, not an ideal (an ideal is simply profoundly irritating to the enslaved will); and suppose I need help to build, or rebuild, my life?

Elsewhere Matthews speaks of preaching in terms that are less problematic, and more hopeful for the sinner: 'The preaching of the Gospel is the presentation of the grace of God in Jesus Christ, the holding up of the ideal of life that it may form the

---

[346] Idem, *Essays in Construction*, 132.
[347] Idem, *Seven Words*, 169.
[348] Ibid., 29.
[349] Idem, *Essays in Construction*, 177. Cf. idem, *Reason in Religion*, 19.
[350] Ibid., 186.
[351] Ibid., 191.
[352] GCTE, 228.
[353] Ibid., 275.
[354] Idem, *Seven Words*, 14.
[355] Idem, *The Gospel and the Modern Mind*, 167.

centre round which the personality of the struggling sinner may grow.'[356] Again, the following 'liberal-sounding' nouns that Matthews uses of Jesus represent an attenuation of the Gospel: 'The chief source of the abiding power of Christianity lies in the belief and experience that Jesus may be our example, companion, and leader in our lives.'[357] I wonder whether this is attributable to something that Matthews, with great honesty, recognized in himself? We recall his already quoted words, 'Salvation to me has always been a kind of enlightenment. I fear that my ministry has often been less useful than it might have been, because I did not feel deeply in my spirit the need of a sinner for the assurance of forgiveness. When I ought to have been answering the question, What must I do to be saved? I have been offering to him reasons for believing in the existence of God.'[358] On the other hand, he can write tenderly, 'For us the gospel of forgiveness is the door by which we enter, and the divine love which seeks the sinner is the charter of our worship.'[359] Perhaps, then, it is better to think in terms of occasional temperamental fluctuations, rather than of attenuations of the Gospel. However that may be, nothing could be more positive than this concerning the earliest Christians: 'The risen life of the Lord who had been crucified had taken them up into itself, so that they were immortal, not, so to speak, in their own right, but by grace, because they had been adopted into that victorious life which had already triumphed over death and would, in the end, destroy it. That is still the Christian belief.'[360] In a very important statement, and one which has implications for ecclesiology, he declares that 'it is the Gospel which invests both Church and Bible with their authority'.[361] It would be surprising if Matthews had not heard this cardinal principle expressed by his Congregational colleague, P. T. Forsyth.[362]

Matthews, primarily a philosophical theologian, did not dwell equally on all Christian doctrines. For example, there are passing references only to the Holy Spirit in his many writings; and, just as his exploration of classical patristic Christology was cursory, so his refusal to engage in a depth exploration of the traditional doctrines of the atonement on the ground that we are not saved by doctrinal theories could be construed as evincing a lack of interest in the witness of the Christian ages. Similarly, he does not offer a full-scale treatment of the Trinity or of ecclesiology, though he believed the former and was deeply, if sometimes critically, attached to the Church. On immortality he has a little more to say, no doubt because this was a subject which, in his manner of treatment, accorded with his psychological interests. I shall close this doctrinal section of

---

[356] Idem, *The Psychological Approach to Religion*, 42.
[357] Idem, *Seven Words*, 84.
[358] MM, 163.
[359] Idem, *The Search for Perfection*, 8.
[360] Idem, *The Hope of Immortality*, London: SCM Press, 1936, 52.
[361] Idem, *The Gospel and the Modern Mind*, 46.
[362] See P. T. Forsyth, *The Principle of Authority* (1913), London: Independent Press, 1952.

my chapter by gathering a few of his scattered thoughts on the Trinity, the Church and immortality.

Although it is not found in so many words in the New Testament, the dogma of the Trinity is, says Matthews, 'not an addition to Scripture, but an explanation of what Scripture implied'.[363] He is well aware that throughout Christian history trinitarian discussion has sought to uphold the divine unity on the one hand, and to maintain personal distinctions within that unity on the other. He is equally aware of the pitfalls of unitarianism on the one side and tritheism on the other.[364] His own approach, not surprisingly, is along the line of a view of personality according to which, while it would be misleading to refer to God as 'a person', the Godhead is personal. 'We are concerned,' he writes, 'to maintain the validity of creative Personality, the God on whom all things depends, not the idea of the Absolute in whom all things are. The Divine Unity, moreover, must be ... a concrete unity, which means a unity of multiplicity and not a bare unitary self. ... [O]ur conception of God leads us to think of the Divine Nature as a unity of Persons in mutual responsiveness and fellowship.'[365] It is equally unsurprising that Matthews reaches this conception by the pathway of experience: 'Father, Son and Holy Spirit,' he declares, 'can be discerned in every complete religious experience.'[366] Through the Son we come to the Father, and within the fellowship of the Church we partake of the Spirit, the life of the Christian community.[367] 'The Spirit,' he says, 'moves the will of personal beings by presenting to them the Son in whom they see the truth of their nature, its ideal perfection. And when they perceive Him, they desire to move towards Him.'[368]

It is perhaps surprising that one who builds so firmly upon Christian experience should proceed to argue against the view that the doctrine of the Trinity is merely economic and not ontological. To Matthews the economic Trinity implies a distinction between a God in himself and a God as revealed in human experience, and asserts that the former is unknowable. This, he thinks, leaves us with an ultimate agnosticism. I am not sure that this is necessarily so. Why may we not say that as God has made himself known to us (economic), so he is (ontological)? If it were otherwise we should not have received a revelation of God, and that might suggest that there were a God-beyond-God about whom we could know nothing; and this is what Matthews wishes to deny. To say that we have received a revelation of God is not to say that we have been made aware of everything there is to be known about God; it is simply to say that the one who has granted

---

[363] W. R. Matthews, 'The Christian belief in God', 90. The page reference is incorrect in H. P. Owen, *W. R. Matthews: Philosopher and Theologian*, 77 n. 33.

[364] See SCP, 174–6.

[365] GCTE, 176, 177.

[366] Idem, *The Gospel and the Modern Mind*, 134. Cf. idem, *Our Faith in God*, London: SCM Press, 1936, 90.

[367] See GCTE, 184–7.

[368] Ibid., 201.

us such knowledge as we have of God is God and no other, and that he does not set out to misinform us as to his nature and purposes. It is to rehearse the theme so popular among Puritan writers, namely, that while we may truly apprehend God, we cannot fully comprehend him.

Matthews's trinitarian reflections include a discussion of the two analogies – the individual and the social – under which the Trinity has historically been conceived. The former is associated especially with Augustine, the latter with the Cappadocian Fathers, and with F. R. Tennant. Matthews recognizes that if pressed too hard 'the one would issue in the crudest Unitarian anthropomorphism, the other in a kind of polytheism. ... [Nevertheless], 'If the human personality shows a multiplicity in unity ... then it is not absurd to hold that there is a triune nature in God.'[369] He therefore suggests that the two analogies converge. In one of his most comprehensive and concise statements, Matthews sums up his view of the Trinity, cautions against thinking of the three persons as three distinct individuals, and leads us into ecclesiology:

> The doctrine of the Trinity ... must not be understood to imply that each Person of the Trinity acts independently of the others. Though we are justified in thinking that there is a special activity or function of each Person, we must also add that in all Divine action the whole of the Godhead takes part. When we speak of the Father we think of the transcendent and ultimate Source, 'the Fount of Deity', as the Greek Fathers called Him. When we speak of the Son we think of the self-knowledge of God, His blessed contemplation of His own Being, and also of the activity of God in creation and redemption. When we think of the Holy Spirit we think of the perfect unity of the Divine Persons and of the Divine element and impulse in creation, and particularly in man, to seek after God, and the power by which men are enabled to transcend their lower selves and become members of Christ,. And in particular we think of the activity of God as manifested in the Church, residing in it and constituting it, in spite of all its human imperfections, a Divine society, the instrument of the Son for the setting up of God's Kingdom. But in all these various activities the whole of the Godhead is acting and revealed.[370]

---

[369] Ibid., 192. A. M. Ramsey refers to this passage in a valuable survey of 'The doctrine of the Trinity in Anglican theology'. See his *From Gore to Temple. The Development of Anglican Theology between* Lux Mundi *and the Second World War 1889–1939*, London: Longmans, 1960, Appendix C, 179–84. In the course of his remarks Ramsey refers in passing to Barth, 'who writes in total unawareness that there is such a thing as Anglican theology', ibid., 183. *A fortiori*, one might add, Nonconformist theology, for which, on the social Trinity, see Alan P. F. Sell, *Hinterland Theology*, 587–90; and more generally on the Trinity see idem, *Nonconformist Theology in the Twentieth Century*, 71–84, 176–8.

[370] Idem, *Our Faith in God*, 97.

At this point I enter two caveats: first, it is important, especially in relation to present-day discussions of 'Father' language, to emphasize that when Christians 'speak of the Father' they speak first of the one who is the God and Father of our Lord Jesus Christ.[371] Secondly, I do not think it can be said that the Church 'sets up' the Kingdom; it witnesses to it, and is called to be a foretaste of it, but it is not, as might be inferred from Matthews's words, coterminous with it – a claim which Matthews himself denies elsewhere: 'It would be absurd to identify the actual Church ... [or] even an ideal Church with the Kingdom. At best the Church is the symbol and the foretaste of that Heavenly City, in which the full meaning of individuality and the full possibilities of fellowship are realised.'[372]

In a statement summarizing texts from Ephesians and I Corinthians, Matthews declares that the

> Church was created by the Resurrection, and it differs from all merely human organizations in that it is the fellowship in which Christ is present, through the Spirit, His instrument and body for producing effects in the world, so that every individual can regard himself as a member of Christ's body having his appointed function in the redemptive work of God.[373]

So far, so good; but what is interesting is what is omitted: Romans 1: 7, for example, where believers, Christians, are referred to as 'saints by calling'. I do not say that Matthews nowhere mentions Romans 1: 7, but when, elsewhere, he does refer to it he construes Paul as meaning that Christians are to be 'useful persons in society.'[374] A more drastic dilution of the apostle's meaning it is scarcely possible to imagine. Paul means that the Church is that into which people are called by grace. Or, to invoke Johannine thought, it is the fellowship of the 'twice born'. By not adverting to this aspect of the matter, Matthews makes it easier than it should be to hold the Augustinian and subsequently the Anglican-parochial view that the Church comprises wheat and tares and, by not understanding church members to be enrolled saints, to blur the distinction between the local church and the congregation (both of which no doubt contain wheat and tares, though it is beyond our remit and competence to label them). As I understand it, the Church is distinguishable from 'all merely human organizations' not only because the risen Christ is present in its fellowship, but because entry to it is by divine calling. The Church is not a club for the promotion of the interests of the like-minded. On the contrary, the Church comprises people who may have very little in common, except that by grace they have been called together and they have been enabled to

---

[371] See further, Alan P. F. Sell, *Enlightenment, Ecumenism, Evangel*, 365–75.
[372] W. R. Matthews, 'The Christian ideal for human society', in George A. Yates, ed., *In Spirit and in Truth. Aspects of Judaism and Christianity*, London: Hodder and Stoughton, 1934, 129.
[373] GCTE, 70.
[374] Idem, *The Year Through Christian Eyes*, 184.

respond.³⁷⁵ The doctrine of vocation is at stake in this issue. I grant that Matthews elsewhere declares that 'The Church, in idea and ideal is the fellowship of the redeemed',³⁷⁶ but there is nothing like the empirical reality of the visible saints, the professed and enrolled believers, for challenging Christians as to the calibre of their fellowship and the practice of their calling. Nor should the ecumenical implications of visible sainthood be overlooked, for one cannot be a 'Christian in general', and to be a member of the Church catholic is to be a member of the Church local, and all who are called by grace and grafted as branches into the Vine are of that company.

All of the foregoing notwithstanding, Matthews holds the Christian fellowship in high esteem:

> To be in the fellowship and to partake of its traditions of worship and faith should mean much to us. But not all. We shall be imperfect Christians if we do not feel that the Church at its best, and our own religion as members of the Church, are but an anticlimax when compared with the beginning in the Cross and Resurrection.³⁷⁷

But Christians must not be content with the backward glance; they must look forward, for 'The Christian Church ... is scarcely out of the nursery.'³⁷⁸ They must pray for a renewal of the Church's life and, not least for the unity and fellowship of all Christian people, 'so that the power of the Spirit of Jesus may work unhindered for the healing of the nations'.³⁷⁹

With this we come to Matthews's ecumenical concerns. It is his conviction that the major division among Christians cuts across denominational lines. It is between those who shun modern thought and knowledge, and those who believe that the Gospel must be related to the thought of the age. As we have clearly seen, he stands with those in the latter group. But he also understands that in moving forward some of the traditionally neuralgic points will have to be dealt with, among them the status and role of bishops. He cannot believe that bishops are of the *esse* of the Church, and he surmises that 'Even the most intransigent upholder of the episcopacy would ... if pressed, agree that it is more important to believe in God than in bishops.'³⁸⁰ Bishops are, however, 'the *bene esse* of the Church and "fathers in God"'.³⁸¹ As to the current contingent of bishops, Matthews

---

³⁷⁵ See further, Alan P. F. Sell, *The Spirit Our Life*, Shippensburg, PA: Ragged Edge Press, 49–52.
³⁷⁶ W. R. Matthews, 'The Christian ideal for human society', 129.
³⁷⁷ Idem, *Essays in Construction*, 235.
³⁷⁸ Ibid., 236.
³⁷⁹ Ibid.
³⁸⁰ Ibid., xi.
³⁸¹ MM, 150.

was somewhat less than sanguine: 'our contemporary bishops carry little weight. This is partly because they have nothing worth hearing to say'.[382]

On the related question of authority in the Church I resume Matthews's view, briefly noted earlier, that the Gospel takes precedence over the Bible and the Church, both of which are its creations. 'We must not identify the Gospel with Christian institutions. ... [While] the Gospel requires both Church and sacraments for its expression ... they are the instruments of the Gospel, not part of it. They are the creations of the message, not the message itself.'[383] Moreover, 'when, as Dr. Forsyth has said, "faith has really meant faith in the Church and acceptance of its absolute authority", then we have the beginning of intellectual tyranny which the human spirit must always rise and overthrow'.[384] 'I have no sympathy', he thunders in good liberal fashion, 'with any appeal to authority, whether it be Church or Bible, which would place fetters on the mind.'[385] This is not to say that the Church has no authority whatsoever. Belief in the Holy Spirit 'would seem to preclude us from holding that the Church can have been wholly mistaken, or that its persistent spiritual life is nourished on mere illusions. Any self-confident disregard of the authority of the Church must therefore appear as both sinful and silly.'[386] But the Gospel comes first, for 'The essence of the Church, what it is for and what keeps it alive, is the proclamation of the revelation of God in Christ and the propagation of that experience of God as Father and Redeemer which came into the world with Jesus.'[387] But he characteristically adds that 'The growth of knowledge and the enrichment of spiritual life, which may go along with intellectual progress, demand that we should be prepared to revise the doctrine of the Church and find new and better statements of what she stands for.'[388] As we saw earlier, the accomplishment of credal revision remained for Matthews a forlorn hope.

I need only add that Matthews, who was deeply conscious of the fact that 'The Church with its politics and policies obscures as well as proclaims the Gospel',[389] was, unlike many of his Anglican colleagues, in favour of the disestablishment of the Church of England, and he recognized that if ever the Articles were to be revised, or abandoned, this issue would have to be faced.[390] Indeed, in old age he felt that the Articles would never be revised until the Church of England were disestablished. From my perspective the problem here is a pragmatism which is characteristic of many clergy and laypersons of the Church of England where the establishment issue is concerned. 'We ought to retain it because it gives us a voice

---

[382] Ibid., 306; cf. 353.
[383] Idem, *The Gospel and the Modern Mind*, 45.
[384] Idem, *The Idea of Revelation*, 53.
[385] Idem, *Signposts to God*, 46.
[386] Idem, 'The nature and basis of dogma', 24.
[387] Idem, *Signposts to God*, 55.
[388] Ibid., 56.
[389] Idem, *The Gospel and the Modern Mind*, 74–5.
[390] Idem, *The Thirty-Nine Articles*, 25.

in high places'; or, 'We should dispense with it (so Matthews) because then the revision of the Articles in the interests of communicating the Gospel would be more easily accomplished.' These attitudes completely bypass establishment as a theological question concerning the sole Lordship of Christ in his Church – a view which it has been the privilege of the English, and formerly of the Welsh,[391] Dissenters and their heirs to articulate, sometimes at great personal cost, for more than four centuries past.[392]

Matthews has one more thing to say about the nature of churchly fellowship, and it brings us to his account of immortality. The Church, he writes, 'is to be a fellowship of men and women who are trying to live as citizens of the world to come'.[393] They can make this attempt only because 'Christ is the mediator of the life of God to men, so that those who are joined to him by faith are the partakers of the eternal life of God.'[394] It is noteworthy in this connection that for all his interest in things psychical, Matthews came increasingly to see that 'There is a trap in psychical research: to confuse the psychical with the spiritual. The "gift of God is eternal life", not an extension of our temporal lives, but a quality of life which transcends time.'[395] Yet at the same time he envisages individual progress in the afterlife, whereby, 'the soul which is orientated aright but immature may reach the full stature of the child of God'.[396] Further, if we believe this, 'we must surely also believe that prayer for the departed is legitimate, and indeed a duty'.[397] Matthews here sets his face against the Protestant antipathy to prayers for the dead, but it must be said that he does so by speculative assertion rather than by detailed argument. In so far as there is an argument for personal immortality as such, Matthews thinks it must be based upon ultimate values, but these need belief in God to sustain them, since 'a value divorced from a personal consciousness is an abstraction'.[398] But the hope of immortality also turns upon the dualism of mind and body, construed, after Plato, in such a way that 'the mind is a higher kind of existence than matter and body, and that there is no good reason for supposing that mind depends for its existence on the organism with which it is associated'.[399] This dualism is, in Matthews' opinion, given in human experience.

---

[391] The Church in Wales has been disestablished since the Act of Parliament of 1914 took effect in 1920, albeit to judge by the attitudes of a few, the news may not as yet have percolated to all of its members.
[392] See further, Alan P. F. Sell, *Testimony and Tradition*, ch. 11.
[393] W. R. Matthews, *The Search for Perfection*, 61.
[394] Ibid., 94.
[395] MM, 347.
[396] Idem, *Seven Words*, 55. Cf. idem, *The Hope of Immortality*, 64–5.
[397] Idem, *Seven Words*, 55. Cf. idem, *The Hope of Immortality*, 85.
[398] Idem, *Essays in Construction*, 221.
[399] Idem, *The Hope of Immortality*, 30.

Specifically Christian teaching on immortality 'is different from other teachings by reason of its basis in the resurrection of Christ'.[400] He draws a distinction between what he calls natural immortality and personal immortality on the one hand, and eternal life on the other. The latter is God's gracious gift.

As to other eschatological themes, Matthews is interesting, but brief. He has a reply to Christians who fear that 'the message of salvation must lose its appeal when men can no longer be frightened by the terrors of a material hell. They need not be anxious. The city of destruction is within, and the craving for deliverance is based in the profoundest depths of [man's] psychical being.'[401] He exhorts us to think of the divine judgement as the judgement of love, which

> can be more shattering than the judgment of impersonal authority. Many a sinner, who faced a court and public opinion with comparative indifference, has been pierced to the heart by the thought of the agony of some one person who loved him and, while judging him, loves him still. This judgment of love can have a healing and restoring virtue which impersonal justice cannot have.[402]

But will all be saved? Matthews, though appreciating the attractiveness of the possibility, cannot return an affirmative answer to this question – 'I cannot think it is the Christian doctrine. ... It is a fundamental doctrine of the New Testament that eternal issues depend upon our choice and that we dare not say, "All will in the end be well whatever I do and whatever choice I make".'[403] He invokes Jesus' parable of the sheep and the goats in support of his opinion, and then makes this striking affirmation:

> If we are free and not puppets, if we are created to be moral and spiritual beings who can enter into communion with God, we must be able to cast ourselves away. The dignity of man demands that he should be capable of being damned. ... The essence of Hell is complete separation from God. And that is the ultimate disaster.[404]

By contrast, 'The blessedness for which the Christian hopes consists in a closer communion with God, and a more adequate vision of Him.'[405]

---

[400] Ibid., 54.
[401] Idem, *The Gospel and the Modern World*, 164.
[402] Idem, *The Year Through Christian Eyes*, 12.
[403] Idem, *The Hope of Immortality*, 59.
[404] Ibid., 60.
[405] Ibid., 63.

VII

I come finally to Matthews's contribution to ethics. In his helpful account of Matthews's thought, Huw Parri Owen includes a chapter entitled, 'Christology and ethics'. He discusses the former topic at some length and then, in the concluding paragraph and his chapter title notwithstanding, says, 'I do not propose to dwell on Matthews's ethics. ... [H]e was primarily a philosophical and doctrinal theologian.'[406]

No doubt he was; and I have presumed to hint that in the technical sense he was more the former than the latter, but let that pass. My point now is that although Matthews did not devote a large-scale tome to ethics, his theology, strongly rooted as it is in an ethical theism, is pervaded by the ethical interest – his attention to the moral argument for the existence of God is a prominent example of this; while his excursions into Christian social ethics reveal him to have been as open-minded and forward-looking in morals as he was in apologetics, doctrine and psychology.

I shall set the ethical scene by referring to Matthews's lucid and concise introduction to his edition of Butler's *Fifteen Sermons Preached at the Rolls Chapel and A Dissertation upon the Nature of Virtue*. He presents Butler as one who distrusts speculation for its own sake, who has a strong practical bent, and whose writings are imbued with a proper agnosticism, as when he writes, 'Other orders of creatures may perhaps be led into the secret counsels of heaven; and have the designs and methods of Providence, in the creation and government of the world, communicated to them: but this does not belong to our condition.'[407] Butler addresses pressing moral questions, with a view to presenting, not his own opinions of them, but the conclusions of rational enquiry. The materialism of Thomas Hobbes is in Butler's sights, as is Hobbes's egoism, according to which human beings are not by nature social beings, but beings who are motivated by pleasure, preservation and power. Genuinely disinterested affections are not foolish, they are impossible. This leads to the view that there cannot be a transcendent all-embracing Good, there are only the goods as perceived by individuals. Hence inter-human strife and discord, which require the state enforcement of natural laws by a strong state-appointed Governor. Only so will society be preserved.

The rational intuitionism of the Cambridge Platonists constitutes one line of opposition to Hobbes. To the Platonists 'moral ideas are as universal and unalterable as the ideas of the intellect ... morality is rooted in the nature of the universe'.[408] Cudworth, for example, repudiated Hobbes's view that morality 'depends on the

---

[406] H. P. Owen, *W. R. Matthews, Philosopher and Theologian*, 69.

[407] J. Butler, *Fifteen Sermons*, XV para. 16. A sentiment which might well be placarded in the studies of those theologians who know too much about God's inscrutable will, or about the inner workings of the persons of the Trinity.

[408] W. R. Matthews, 'Introduction' to Butler's *Fifteen Sermons* (1914), London: Bell, 1953, xvii.

arbitrary law or convention of the state'.⁴⁰⁹ Rational intuitionism almost certainly flowed down to Butler through his friend Samuel Clarke, who goes further than Cudworth in specifying the self-evident moral intuitions: Reverence, Equity, Benevolence, Self-preservation. As Matthews correctly perceives, 'it is clear, when we have the alleged first principles of morals before us, that they are not really analogous to the axioms of speculative reason; and it is also evident, not only that they require definition, but that they may conflict with one another'.⁴¹⁰ Perhaps this is why Butler, although he speaks of rational intuitionism with respect, 'prefers to meet Hobbes on his own ground ... the nature of man as revealed by experience.⁴¹¹

A different line of argument against Hobbes was pursued by Shaftesbury, who appealed to conscience, the moral sense of mankind. The theory is not concerned with general principles of morality, but with 'the immediate judgement of particulars. The Conscience is not a rational function which applies universal laws to the regulation of conduct; it is rather a species of tact, or a system of instinctive reactions, which causes us to feel rightly in the presence of virtuous or vicious actions.'⁴¹² Shaftesbury also held that actions are good or bad independently of our judgement of their quality. In this connection Shaftesbury introduces the idea of a system: 'Anything is good which is in harmonious relations with the system of which it is a part. Hence it follows that human goodness consists in being in harmony with the species of which the individual is a member, and virtuous conduct is that which conduces to the good of the species as a whole.'⁴¹³ The virtuous person thus balances out self-interest and altruism. By this approach Butler was considerably impressed.

Butler agrees with Hobbes in setting out from human nature as it is, but he thinks teleologically in terms of 'final causes'. This leads him to ask what is humanity's true end. Against Hobbes's view that social life is artificially constructed Butler argues that it is natural. Above all, against Hobbes's psychological egoism Butler makes his case that 'all desires for particular objects are ... disinterested, since they seek their external object as their end'.⁴¹⁴ It is not the case that 'all desire is necessarily for the pleasure and power of the agent'.⁴¹⁵

Matthews correctly notes that Butler's view of conscience falls between that of the rational and the aesthetical intuitionists: 'He seems to agree with Shaftesbury that there is a special moral faculty, but for him it is more than feeling or instinct. It is a "principle of reflection", it partakes of the nature of reason',⁴¹⁶ but it is not

---

⁴⁰⁹ Ibid., xviii.
⁴¹⁰ Ibid., xix.
⁴¹¹ Ibid.
⁴¹² Ibid., xx.
⁴¹³ Ibid., xx–xxi.
⁴¹⁴ Ibid., xxii.
⁴¹⁵ Ibid., xxiii.
⁴¹⁶ Ibid.

the theoretical or pure reason of rational intuitionism. At this point Matthews finds Kant's distinction between the pure and practical reason latent in Butler's thought. Where Butler is most akin to the rational intuitionists (and, as we have seen, to W. R. Matthews) is in his presupposition that 'Ethics run up into philosophy, and depend on some general theory of the nature of reality as a whole.'[417] From his belief in a divine Creator and Governor Butler infers a teleological interpretation of the world and human nature. Were there no supreme Intelligence we could not decipher man's true end. The voice of conscience is the voice of God, he declares, but he is not as persuaded as Shaftesbury was that virtue and self-interest always coincide in this life. In the future life earthly discrepancies will be corrected and 'in the long run, the path of duty will be seen to have been the path of true self-interest'.[418]

Having expounded Butler's position, Matthews raises two difficulties with it. First, although Butler normally regards conscience as supreme in discerning the right and the good, there are occasions when he seems to elevate self-love to equal, or even superior status.[419] Secondly, Butler 'takes for granted too lightly that, apart from the influence of "superstition", the pronouncements of Conscience are always clear and identical'.[420] For all that, Matthews finds Butler's method instructive in the way it looks back to Aristotle and forward to modern idealism and, above all, he thinks that Butler can make a contribution to current ethical discussion by virtue of

> his clear recognition of the two sides to the study of morals, the scientific and the philosophical, or, as he might have said, the natural and the supernatural. ... [H]e realizes the inadequacy of a merely abstract or deductive treatment and the importance of a study of the actual phenomena of the moral life, but he holds, at the same time, that morals have a super-phenomenal basis. This general truth is important and necessary at the present day. No study of the mere phenomena of morals, whether psychological or historical, can give us a true moral imperative. Only when we adopt a teleological point of view is it possible to reach a conception of a Good which man ought to pursue. In other words, Ethics, if it is to be a complete account of moral obligation, requires some doctrine of the nature of the universe and man. Morality is intimately connected with religion, and Ethics needs some form of Theology as its completion and support.[421]

---

[417] Ibid.

[418] Ibid., xxiv.

[419] Matthews quotes *Fifteen Sermons*, XI para. 20, xxv.

[420] Ibid. For a stimulating collection of more recent studies of Butler's thought see Christopher Cunliffe, ed., *Joseph Butler's Moral and Religious Thought. Tercentenary Essays*, Oxford: Clarendon Press, 1992. See also Terence Penelhum, *Butler*, London: Routledge & Kegan Paul, 1985.

[421] Ibid., xxvi–xxvii.

It was to the attempt to do justice to both the phenomena of the moral life and its philosophico-theological underpinnings that Matthews returned time and again in his writings. For example, he faults G. E. Moore for neglecting the metaphysical significance of ethical judgements that he agrees that we make. In response to this, Matthews says that the question, 'On what conditions can the sense of obligation be justified?' is a legitimate one. He continues, 'Admitting that I believe myself to have true judgments on the nature of the Good and that I believe myself to be under an obligation to pursue the Good, in what kind of universe would these beliefs of mine be justified?'[422] More generally, he affirms that 'an ethical theory which is not contented to assassinate moral action must preserve the distinction between ideality and actuality, while refraining from exhibiting this distinction as an absolute opposition'.[423] Again, 'When we are morally awake, we recognize that we are confronted with a hierachy of values which we did not create and which we cannot alter. ... The ordinary good man does not feel first of all that he is legislating for himself, but that there are principles which legislate for him, themselves being grounded in the structure of the universe.'[424] Most directly of all, he writes, 'we believe that moral values have their basis in the nature of Reality; they are grounded in the central core of Being'.[425] But to Matthews this Being is God, and with this we come to the theological considerations which he thinks complete and support ethics. He builds upon the idea of the personal God, and on his view that personality is shown nowhere more clearly than in creativity. This granted, 'The creation which depends on a holy Creator must be a moral order, and this involves that, in the end, the evil will always be defeated.'[426]

The fact that 'Jesus has little or nothing to say concerning most of the great practical problems of life'[427] causes Matthews no concern whatsoever; it is simply what we should expect, given that Jesus was a child of his time. But if he did not address our current ethical issues, he has undoubtedly 'shown us the attitude of mind and will in which these and all our problems can be faced, He has given us the principles in which their solution can be found', and hence 'He is able to be the Guide of all generations.'[428] Of these principles, that of love is supreme. This, at least, is Matthews's general position. He says that 'for Jesus, and for the New Testament as a whole [love is] more than the first principle of ethics. It is the clue to the meaning of the universe. God is love.'[429] However, in a later book he argues that there are some virtues and duties 'which cannot be regarded as special cases

---

[422] SCP, 136.
[423] Ibid., 229.
[424] Idem, *Essays in Construction*, 84.
[425] Idem, *The Gospel and the Modern Mind*, 116.
[426] Idem, *The Year Through Christian Eyes*, 59.
[427] Idem, *Seven Words*, 18.
[428] Ibid., 19–20. Cf. idem, 'The Christian ideal for human society,' 124–5.
[429] Idem, *The Gospel and the Modern Mind*, 182.

as special cases of love and must be brought under the heading of "justice"'.[430] He continues:

> I find it difficult to dispense with justice as a principle distinct from love, because it seems to me that occasions often arise when we have to choose between trying to be just and trying to act lovingly. Those who tell us that to be just is really to be loving, or contrarywise that to be loving is really to be just, may be right, but the formula, though probably orthodoxly Christian, is not helpful in practice.[431]

On the contrary, it seems to me that it is helpful in practice to be challenged by the God of holy love to hold love and justice, righteousness and mercy, in balance, lest love degenerate into sentiment or antinomianism, and justice into malice or vindictiveness.

Be that as it may, when Matthews considers the making of moral judgements he, like Butler before him, gives a high place to conscience. He grants that 'only a being who both thinks and feels would be capable of moral choice', but, leaning in the same direction as Butler, he contends that 'thinking, intellectual activity, judgment is the core of the experience which we call "acting conscientiously"'.[432] He further explains that 'To be good does not mean to obey a set of rules imposed from outside, but to follow the dictates of our own highest and most rational self.' Hence the feeling of remorse when we have been 'traitors to our true personality'.[433] Well aware that moral judgements may be distorted by those who have a preconceived notion of what God has willed, Matthews cautions that 'An ethical theology is the best kind of theology, but a theological ethic may be the worst kind of ethic.'[434]

Turning now to applied ethics we find that Matthews fully understands that Christian ethics has to do with more than the individual. It has an inescapable social dimension, for Christians are members of a community, the Church, and are called to bear witness to, and to serve, the wider society of which they are a part. However, Christianity understands the social order in the context of the eternal order. It teaches that 'society exists, in the end, for the promotion of man's true good, which is no temporal well-being, but the attainment of "salvation" or the vision of God'.[435] It follows that 'The Christian social ethic is essentially opposed to all worship of the State, and to every social idealism, whether it be Fascist or State Socialist, which exalts the nation or the community at the expense of the individual. The State exists for man, not man for the State.'[436] The reason for this

---

[430] Idem, *The Year Through Christian Eyes*, 118–19.
[431] Ibid., 119.
[432] Ibid., 114.
[433] Idem, *Signposts to God*, 40, 41.
[434] Idem, *Essays in Construction*, 85.
[435] Idem, 'The Christian ideal for human society', 121.
[436] Ibid., 127.

is not that the individual has, or may acquire particular qualities. It is because the individual 'is one of those for whom Christ died; one who was the object of divine compassion when God Himself came to seek and to save those who were lost.'[437] Indeed, 'the fundamental faith in the value of persons because of their relation with God is a motive of social progress far more potent than any purely secular ideal' such as J. S. Mill's utilitarian quest of 'the greatest happiness of the greatest number'.[438] Secular 'Utopias are dead ends; the Kingdom of God is a pillar of fire.'[439]

Like many other theologians, Matthews could not remain silent on the outbreak of the Second World War.[440] As early as 1940 we find him reflecting on *The Moral Issues of the War*. He sketches the circumstances which led to war, and then adduces two arguments to show that Britain was both justified and morally obliged to oppose the Nazis. The first is the need of self-preservation. He admits that some Christians regard this as a less than respectable, even almost an immoral, motive, but 'to preserve life and health is a moral duty',[441] and while a nation or a state is not precisely analogous to an individual (a state can enforce taxation upon its citizens, an individual who extorted money by force from others would be a criminal) but, *qua* organism, the state may preserve its being and affirm its will to live. While the nation has much to repent of, it must also be grateful for its heritage and seek its preservation. Secondly, however, there is the higher motive of the securing and preserving of freedom in the world: freedom for nations as well as for individuals. Indeed, 'Perhaps the most horrible of all the manifestations of Nazi tyranny is the continued and largely successful attempt to force the minds of children into the totalitarian mould.'[442] Such totalitarianism must be countered in the interests of law, freedom and truth: 'We must meet the organized will for destruction and evil with a more determined will for construction and good. ... Though we are not righteous our cause is righteous. We should be adding to sin if, because of our sense of unworthiness, we failed to defend the right.'[443] Matthews agrees with Christian pacifists that war is contrary to the mind of Christ, but he pulls no punches:

---

[437] Ibid., 128.
[438] Ibid., 130.
[439] Ibid., 131.
[440] During the First World War Matthews reviewed a collection of papers entitled, *International Relationships in the Light of Christianity*, in *International Journal of Ethics*, XXVII no. 1, October 1916, 107–9. He was impressed by J. M. Lloyd Thomas's argument for the non-pacifist position, but felt that the case for pacifism had not been well made by J. W. Graham.
[441] Idem, *The Moral Issues of the War*, London: Eyre and Spottiswoode, 1940, 13.
[442] Ibid., 27.
[443] Ibid., 32, 33.

To anyone who understands the type of man with whom we have to deal it is ludicrous to suggest that they could be deterred by the spectacle of the Peace Pledge Union gravely disapproving of their action. The Jews could offer nothing but passive resistance to their persecutors, and we know what has happened to them ... When it was too late our pacifist friends would realize that they had been standing idly by while the soul of their people was being murdered. ... One who has taken the gifts of civilization cannot honourably refuse to defend it.[444]

While Matthews does not address pacifist arguments, he does consider the requirements of post-War peace: 'The primary condition of peace ... is that there should be enough of the spirit of Christ in those who will make the settlement to frustrate the impulses of vindictiveness and revenge. ... It would be a Pyrrhic victory if we defeated Hitler only to become a people with a Hitlerian outlook.'[445] He concludes that 'There are two duties laid upon us: to give the best service in our power to the nation in its hour of crisis, and to preserve clear and firm those values which alone make the nation and its cause worthy of our sacrifice.'[446] It remains only to add that 30 years on, as Matthews reflected autobiographically upon the War, he posed two questions which troubled him:

Does not the New Testament teaching about sin and forgiveness and about the Atonement imply collective responsibility? Can St. Paul's 'As in Adam all die, even so in Christ shall all be made alive', be understood at all without bringing in some idea like corporate guilt and corporate redemption?[447]

Would that he had addressed these intriguing questions in detail.[448]

In 1961 Matthews became an Honorary Fellow of the Eugenics Society, and in his autobiography he refers to a number of committees on which he sat, and papers which he wrote, which were concerned with issues of sex, marriage and the family. I simply select a few of his conclusions on these matters by way of showing the adventurous character of his practical ethical thought. He could not sign the report of the Archbishop's Commission, *Artificial Human Insemination*, because of the conclusion that A.I.D involved a breach of marriage. Matthews could not agree that A.I.D was always inherently evil, or that it was a kind of adultery. In fact, he thought, 'women who resorted to A.I.D. were often childless married women who

---

[444] Ibid., 34, 35.
[445] Ibid., 38–9; 40–41.
[446] Ibid., 41.
[447] MM, 287; cf. 88.
[448] For a brief discussion of two of Matthews's younger contemporaries who did discuss collective responsibility – H. D. Lewis and N. H. G. Robinson – see Alan P. F. Sell, 'Clarity, precision, and on towards comprehension: the intellectual legacy of N. H. G. Robinson (1912-1978),' 283–5. See also Alan P. F. Sell, *Aspects of Christian Integrity*, 65–8.

refused to take the adulterous way out'.[449] In his 1961 Herbert Gray Lecture on *Eugenics and the Family* he addressed the 'population explosion' and the threat it posed to the welfare state, in a context in which some eugenists were advocating the widespread use of A.I.D. 'One suspects', he 'cautiously' said, 'that many parents who ought to have many children have only one or two; while very many whose contribution to the upgrading of the human race is likely to be negative have all too many.'[450] I cannot but interject that this is Matthews at his most chilling. The chill is somewhat reduced by his disagreement with Julian Huxley that all children might be born by A.I.D. 'To imagine a community of families in which no child knew his father is too much',[451] he retorted. He also pointed out that 'it is a dangerous fallacy to suppose that we are completely determined by heredity and environment or that we are and can be nothing but what they make us. ... we may make something good and valuable out of the given material or something worthless and mean'.[452]

That Matthews did not restrict his practical ethical interests to the beginning of human life is clear from his advocacy of voluntary euthanasia, a matter on which he went public on 2 May 1950, in an address to the Society for the Legalisation of Voluntary Euthanasia.[453] The crux of his argument was that since the Creator has given us reason, freedom of choice and conscience, we are to apply these to evils that have no remedy, and hence 'we are required by our belief in God to give the most earnest consideration to the proposal to legalise voluntary euthanasia'.[454]

Matthews surmizes that moralists wrongly suppose that the religious problem is not their business, and therefore they pay no heed to religion. It surprises Matthews that since the problem is how to become good, moralists fail to pose the question, 'How is the good man produced? Here religion claims to be heard ... "Not that we are sufficient of ourselves to think anything as of ourselves; but our sufficiency is of God" (2 Corinthians 3: 3).'[455] Religion contributes 'a new dimension, insisting that the Good is that which fulfils man's spiritual nature', and this requires that by the grace of God our incompleteness be overcome and we are 'made whole in God'.[456] Since our primary obligation is to God and not to human beings, 'For a religious ethic the cry must always be, "Repent, for the time is short."'[457]

---

[449] MM, 349.
[450] Ibid., 350.
[451] Ibid., 351.
[452] Ibid., 352.
[453] Ibid., 253–5.
[454] Ibid., 355. For the paper, 'Voluntary euthanasia', see *The Modern Churchman*, XL no. 2, June 1950, 115–18.
[455] Idem, *The Year Through Christian Eyes*, 123.
[456] Ibid., 127.
[457] Idem, *Essays in Construction*, 124.

VIII

Matthews was something of a poet – humorous and otherwise, and his published prayers are elegantly phrased and nicely balanced. He even turned his hand to satire in response to the attack on Christianity launched by George Bernard Shaw in his, *The Adventures of the Black Girl and her Search for God* (1932). Matthews's reply of the following year was entitled, *The Adventures of Gabriel in his search for Mr. Shaw, a Modest Companion for the Black Girl*. Matthews, in reflecting upon this skirmish, writes, 'Mr. Shaw is reported to have said, "It's a pity the Dean is so frivolous when I am so serious." Since then, I have kept my essays in satire for private circulation only.'[458] His self-discipline in this particular style of writing notwithstanding, Matthews's writing is almost invariably clear, rarely technical, and his memoirs are littered throughout with trenchant observations, thought-provoking epigrams and occasional *bon mots*, among them the following: 'Every victory of cynicism is a defeat of humanity'; '[T]he standard of preaching has declined and that is partly due to a decline in the intelligence of congregations'; 'The plain fact is that theology is in sad straits because so many theologians do not believe in God'; '[I]f there is no such thing as eternal truth, there cannot be any sense in "contemporary truth"'; '[I]t is unlikely that the good news about God will attract much attention from persons who think He is a myth.'[459]

As to his self-assessment, Matthews did not think that as a person he was 'specially remarkable'; 'My failing as a student has always been lack of concentration. I have read too much – or rather too indiscriminately'; 'I am glad that there never was a serious proposal that I should be a bishop for more than one reason; but chief among them is the consciousness that, though I have persevered in prayer, I have never advanced far in the art';[460] 'For me, the ambition of my life was that I should be a professor and perhaps be mentioned in learned works on theology and philosophy. I thought that this was a possible achievement if I worked hard'; '[T]here was a touch or irony in the fact that, when I was a boy, I had been distressed ... about the meaning of "saving faith" and now, when a doctor of divinity several times over and a former professor of theology I was as perplexed as ever'; 'I have sometimes suspected that I was rather clever in some respects, though stupid in others, and I have, I think, a certain obstinacy beneath a gentle and conciliatory manner which sometimes surprised people who are misled in the belief that I am easily over-ridden when principles are involved; but the epithet "great" is not for me.'[461]

So much for Matthews's opinion of himself. I have offered some observations on his views *en passant*, but how shall we sum him up? Without question his

---

[458] MM, 180.

[459] Ibid., 17, 96, 147, 162, 294.

[460] On his appointment to St Paul's, 'I remember thinking ... that no one would expect me to be a bishop now, which I thought a piece of good fortune.' MM, 180–81.

[461] MM, 13, 38, 64, 79, 364, 380, 388.

teaching was well received and his Deanships were outstanding; but my particular concern is with his thought, and in this I seem to detect a certain ambivalence. I can best show this by placing side by side two of Matthews's concise statements as to his method:

> It is worth while to get some clear idea of the true order of thought in any reasonable presentation of Christianity. First comes the belief in God. In order to establish this we shall have to make use of the moral and religious experience of mankind, and in this will be included the consciousness of Jesus. From that we may go on to show the uniqueness and centrality of Jesus as the supreme revelation of God. When we have done this, we shall undoubtedly find a new and deeper meaning in the idea of God.[462]

Here Matthews in 1925 seems to be a child of the philosophical age of his mentors. Twenty-five years later he comments upon the current 'confusion of minds' in philosophy, regarding this as 'plainly a challenge and an opportunity to develop for the first time a philosophy from within Christianity itself'.[463] That this was not an afterthought is clear from the fact that in 1930 Matthews had criticized scholastic divines for being so in thrall to a philosophy which derived from a non-Christian milieu that 'the heart of the Christian Gospel was not taken up into'[464] their own philosophy.

In a word, it would appear that there is a tension which runs throughout Matthews's writings between the older apologetic starting-point and a more thoroughly Christocentric (though not a Barthian) one. We have seen, for example, that on the one hand, Matthews paid considerable attention to the theistic arguments, notably to the teleological and moral ones, and this despite the fact that he did not regard the arguments, even when taken all together, as demonstrable proofs of God's existence, or as yielding the God whom Christian actually worship. On the other hand, although he had much to say concerning the Cross as the heart of the Gospel, he almost completely bypassed traditional theories of the atonement on the ground that we are not saved by theories but by the Gospel. One wonders why, given that he saw a need to supplement scholastic philosophy, or even to launch out from a different starting point, he did not pay greater attention to the heritage of witness concerning the Cross. The puzzlement increases when we recall his insistence that the Gospel originates in the Cross-resurrection event, and that, where authority is concerned, the Gospel must be accorded priority over Bible and Church alike for they derive from it. Why was he 'antiquarian' in theism but not in soteriology? Was it just, as he confessed, that he had never, personally or intellectually, come to grips with saving faith, and that, as he also said, he had found himself answering the question 'What must I

---

[462] Idem, *The Gospel and the Modern Mind*, 55.
[463] Idem, *The Problem of Christ in the Twentieth Century*, 62.
[464] GCTE, 110.

do to be saved?' with an account of the grounds for believing in the existence of God? Are we to suppose that the one who made so much of experientially-rooted theology had a lacuna in his own religious experience that disabled any attempt at developing a philosophy from within Christianity itself? I think that the most charitable way of reading the situation, and I suspect that it is the true way, is to say that Matthews increasingly felt that the older apologetic would no longer suffice, and that the Barthian alternative was too disjunctive in temper; but that in the event, world-shattering events and multifarious ecclesiastical duties precluded further intensive reflection on his part on what is involved in the adumbration of a Christian view of the world.

There are the germs of a theory in his later, shorter and more devotional books; would that he had been able to develop the insight that, when viewed from the perspective of the Gospel, both the theistic arguments and the heritage of thought on the atonement, and well as other aspects of doctrine, morals and aesthetics, may be invoked as providing reasonable grounds, or at least helpful analogies, to those who would adumbrate a Christian view of the world; but that if we set out from any other starting-point than the Gospel we may not, as Matthews thought the scholastics did not, be able to work in all that we wish, as Christians, to say. Such an approach would, as it seems to me, bring together Matthews's interest in both the Gospel and experience:

> The theology of the incarnation is necessary to explain our Christian experience and not our rational nature, nor our religious psychology. It is not a philosophical necessity, nor a metaphysical, but an evangelical. ... We begin with facts of experience, not with forms of thought. ... The mighty thing in Christ is His grace and not His constitution – that fact that it is God's grace that we have in Him ... That is our Christian faith. And that certainty of the saved experience is the one foundation of all theology in such Churches as are not stifled in mediaeval methods or burdened by their unconscious survival.[465]

Matthews was well aware that he was a theologian between the times – as all theologians to some degree are. But his were unusually tumultuous times, both intellectually and in terms of world events. It was, perhaps, not the time for an 'English', non-totalitarian settlement of theology – one which thinks more in terms of 'both ... and' than of 'either ... or', and the judicious balancing of 'on the one hand', with 'on the other hand'. It was certainly the time for adventurous, questing, Christian thought, and from that challenge Matthews never flinched, speaking out as he did from his rostrum and his pulpits, and engaging through his books, broadcasts and journalism with a diverse and numerous audience. There is much to be learned from him – especially, perhaps, concerning the place of reason as construed by de Burgh and himself, the analysis of 'conscience' in the wake of

---

[465] P. T. Forsyth, *The Person and Place of Jesus Christ* (1909), London: Independent Press, 1961, 9, 10.

Butler, the importance of the Creator-creature distinction, the relativity of credal and confessional statements, and much more besides. Furthermore, theologians, if they were to return to him, would be reminded of the fact that attempts to articulate the Gospel will raise metaphysical and ethical questions which are too routinely shunned by some. The Gospel is in no way harmed by reasonable (not rationalist) presentation. Above all, we may learn something from Matthews's attitude and sense of vocation. As to his attitude: at the end of his book, *The Problem of Christ in the Twentieth Century*, he refers to the lectures that it contains and says, 'If there is anything in them which offends against the deepest reverence and love for the Lord Jesus, may it be forgiven and obliterated, and if there is any glimpse of truth in them, may it commend itself to the judgment of his Church.'[466] His sense of vocation is best encapsulated in the anthem, 'Thou hast a work for me to do'[467] – a setting of his own words to music by R. Walker Robson:

> Thou hast a work for me to do;
>   O Lord show it to me;
> Thou hast a place for me to fill;
>   Give me grace to fill it to Thy glory.
> Thou hast given me a soul to make;
>   Make Thou it for me;
> And build me into Thy spiritual temple
>   For Jesu's sake.
> Amen

---

[466] W. R. Matthews, *The Problem of Christ in the Twentieth Century*, 85.

[467] Idem, 'Thou hast a work for me to do'. London: Novello, 1936, reprinted in *The Musical Times*, LXXVII, September 1936, 817–19.

Chapter 4
Oliver Chase Quick (1885–1944): Philosophy, Theology, Ecumenism

> Breadth of mind is not the attitude of thought which seeks to acquiesce in anarchy, but the attitude which seeks to find room for the greatest possible variety of opinions as all contributive to a common truth.[1]

Oliver Chase Quick was born in the vicarage at Sedbergh – then in the West Riding of Yorkshire, now in Cumbria – on 21 June 1885.[2] His father was Robert Hebert Quick (1831–91),[3] trained in mathematics and the classics, who became an educationist with special interests in the training of secondary school teachers and the practical application of educational ideas. R. H. Quick served two brief curacies and taught in a number of schools, including Harrow and Cranleigh.[4] He was not of robust health, hence his acceptance of the living at Sedbergh in 1883. Sadly, the duties of the ministry drained him and he resigned in January 1887. In 1876 he had married Harriet Bertha, daughter of General Chase Parr of the Indian army. As well as Oliver, they had a daughter, Dora.

The death of his father when he was only five did not prevent Oliver's progression to Harrow School as an Anderson scholar. There he attained the position of head boy, demonstrating his integrity by burning the collection of cribs which head boys had traditionally guarded – an action which did not commend itself to other pupils. From Harrow he proceeded to Corpus Christi College, Oxford. He was placed in the first class in Honour Moderations, but achieved only a third in *Literae humaniores* (Greats). Lucas speculates that he did not fare well in examination

---

[1] O. C. Quick, *Modern Philosophy and the Incarnation*, London: SPCK, 1915, 18.

[2] Although it is of no relevance, it is pleasant to recall that I enjoyed a first pastorate at Sedbergh and Dent. For Quick see DTCBP; ODNB; William Temple, 'Memoir' prefixed to O. C. Quick, *The Gospel of the New World. A Study in the Christian Doctrine of Atonement*, London: Nisbet, 1944; J. K. Mozley, *Oliver Quick as a Theologian*', reprinted from *Theology*, January–February 1945, London: SPCK, [1945]; Paul Lucas, 'Oliver Quick', *Theology*, XCVI, January–February 1993, 4–17; D. M. Mackinnon, 'Oliver Chase Quick as a theologian', ibid., 101–17.

[3] For whom see ODNB. A memorial plaque may be seen in the Parish Church of St Andrew, Sedbergh.

[4] Where I spent most of my childhood – a further irrelevance.

conditions,[5] though his earlier success would seem to belie this suggestion. The alternative suggestion, that he was intellectually at odds with his philosophy tutor, the pragmatist F. C. S. Schiller (1864–1937),[6] who taught at Corpus Christi College from 1887 to 1926, is true; but it does not follow that Schiller was unjust to Quick or that, even if he were, the opinion of one hostile tutor would suffice to 'down' an able student. Whatever the reason, Quick himself was deeply disappointed by the result. He did, however, win the Ellerton essay prize, and the substance of this became his first major article, 'The value of mysticism in religious faith and practice'[7] – a most un-Schiller-like topic.

Quick was ordained in the Church of England in 1911. He held a succession of brief appointments, including a curacy at St Martin-in-the-Fields, where he found a likeminded colleague in H. R. L. (Dick) Sheppard; and the post of domestic chaplain to Randall Davidson, Archbishop of Canterbury, whose secretary, Frances Winifred, daughter of Hugh William Pearson of Malton, Yorkshire, he married. She had been educated at Cheltenham Ladies College, and had stayed on there in order to gain the London external BA in French and English.[8] The Quicks had two daughters and two sons.

In 1920 Quick became a canon of Newcastle and, in 1923, of Carlisle. His next appointment was a further canonry, this time at St Paul's Cathedral, London. He found life at the rather conservative St Paul's somewhat constricting. It would seem that his dean, W. R. Inge, was not altogether happy with his younger colleague, for Inge wrote to the Dean of Durham under whom Quick had served in these terms: 'I too suffered under Oliver Quick – prickly is the *mot juste* – and a conscience without elasticity.'[9] None of which prevented his appointment to the Chair of Theology at the University of Durham in 1934, or to the Regius Chair of Divinity and the associated canonry of Christ Church, Oxford, in 1939.

In 1922 Quick was appointed to the archbishops' commission on doctrine, the chairman of which, William Temple, became his close friend and eventual memoirist. A thoughtful and discriminating enthusiast for the modern ecumenical movement, Quick participated in two early Faith and Order conferences: Lausanne (1927), where the objective was to determine the degree of common ground and the points of theological difference among the numerous participating traditions, and where Quick spoke on the sacraments, as we shall see; and Edinburgh (1937), where the decision was taken to unite with the Life and Work movement to form a council of churches – something realized in 1948 when the World Council of Churches was constituted. Quick also attended the Jerusalem meeting of the

---

[5]   P. Lucas, 'Oliver Quick', 4.

[6]   For whom see ODNB.

[7]   O. C. Quick, 'The value of mysticism in religious faith and practice', *Journal of Theological Studies*, XIII, January 1912, 161–200.

[8]   For life at Lambeth Palace, and for the Quicks' home life, see P. Lucas, 'Oliver Quick', 8–10.

[9]   Quoted by P. Lucas, 'Oliver Quick', 13.

International Missionary Council (1928), at which the themes pursued included religious education, and mission *vis-à-vis* race, industrialization, and rural affairs.[10] His Jerusalem address of 26 March 1928 was highly regarded by William Temple, who was among the delegates.[11]

The training of the ministry was a subject in which Quick took a keen interest. Among his friends was J. K. Mozley, principal of the Leeds Clergy Training School, where Quick himself had served as vice-principal from 1913 to 1915. He was deeply disquieted by the provision made for ordination training in the Church of England. Indeed, he thought that the most immediate reform required across the entire community of the Church was 'more adequate and comprehensive instruction in theology. And the instruction must begin with those who are to be commissioned to instruct others. ... The strategic point of the Church's whole position is the theological college.'[12] He lamented the fact that a course of eight months only was prescribed for intending ordinands. While such candidates were normally expected to be university graduates, they were not necessarily graduates in theology. How, Quick wondered, could adequate attention be paid to theology in that limited period of time, having regard to the pressure of all the liturgical, pastoral and other subjects which required to be taught? On returning to the theme three years later, he was even more trenchant:

> The Church of England really bears no sufficient public witness to the principles on which she exercises her stewardship of the Christian faith.
>
> Among other disastrous consequences of this omission is the fact that there is no modern dogmatic basis for the instruction of Ordinands. The text for that instruction is still the primitive Creeds and the Elizabethan Articles, the form of which has no reference and no immediate relevance to the problems and heresies which perplex the modern mind. Can we wonder if clergy so trained betray very little consciousness of modern issues, and seem to speak to the people either in an alien tongue of medieval piety or with the stammering lips of doubt?[13]

---

[10] For the Faith and Order conferences see *Dictionary of the Ecumenical Movement*, eds Nicholas Lossky, José Míguez Bonino, John Pobee, Tom F. Stransky, Geoffrey Wainwright and Pauline Webb, Geneva: World Council of Churches, 2nd edn, 2002; Ruth Rouse and Stephen Charles Neill, *A History of the Ecumenical Movement 1517–1948*, London: SPCK, 1954, 420–25, 431–5. For the Jerusalem meeting see the *Dictionary*, and *A History*, 368–9. The International Missionary Council merged with the World Council of Churches in 1961.

[11] See F. A. Iremonger, *William Temple, Archbishop of Canterbury: His Life and Letters*, London: OUP, 1948, 395.

[12] O. C. Quick, *Essays in Orthodoxy*, London: Macmillan, 1916, 306.

[13] Idem, *The Testing of Church Principles*, London: John Murray, 1919, 38–9.

Wide though his philosophical and theological interests were (I speak advisedly: he was less secure in history, and confessed that he was no Hebraist), there were some spheres in which Quick found it hard to muster any enthusiasm at all:

> He was not good at 'getting on with the troops' or with parishioners with strong prejudices or troublesome problems, nor at teaching in the local school, nor at organizing his own possessions or timetable, nor at presiding over meetings which took their time – and his – deciding about such practical problems such as whether sandwiches should be closed or open. Practicalities, personal or parochial, worried and distracted him when there were deeper matters which he must attend to.[14]

Lucas has suggested that on one matter of great moment Quick might have shown more interest than he did. When the proposals which led to the formation of the Church of South India were in the air, a sizeable number of Anglo-Catholics, urged on by Kenneth Kirk, Quick's bishop in Oxford, 'threw itself into a campaign, vigorous to the point of bigotry, against the proposals. ... Quick could have provided a saner version of the Catholic vision of the Church and saved Anglo-Catholicism by his sympathetic criticism from a shameful chapter which soured its life for a generation. But he did not.'[15] Lucas speculates that the reasons were that Quick found the battle too distasteful; or that his strength was undermined by illness or by the battle against Nazism; or that 'there was a touch of Olympian detachment' prompting 'almost a disdain for ecclesiastical politics'.[16] To me it seems more likely that Quick's reticence was attributable to his method of constructive criticism leading to legitimate compromise. He held that 'The real values within opposed systems of thought, belief and practice are often themselves apparently opposed and antithetical to one another. But it is the faith of reason that such real values can nevertheless be rationally reconciled and combined; and it is the ultimate aim of all legitimate controversy to advance towards that reconciliation.'[17] I suspect that Quick concluded that the more intransigent Anglo-Catholics had too little of the 'faith of reason' to be in any mood to embark upon such a constructive enterprise. Accordingly, he refrained from entering the fray.

Quick was awarded the honorary Degree of Doctor of Divinity by the Universities of St Andrews (1928), Oxford (1939) and Durham (1941). He was appointed a chaplain to the King in 1933. His final years were marked by ill health. In August 1943 he collapsed while reading the lesson in Christ Church Cathedral. He resigned his Chair and canonry in December of that year, and died at his home, Larch Hill,

---

[14] P. Lucas, 'Oliver Quick', 7.

[15] Ibid., 13.

[16] Ibid. D. M. Mackinnon concurs: '[O]ne could even say that questions relating to the structure of the Church bored him.' See 'Oliver Chase Quick as a theologian', 107–8.

[17] O. C. Quick, *Catholic and Protestant Elements in Christianity*, London: Longmans, Green, 1924, 2.

Longborough, Gloucester, on 21 January 1944. Four days later he was buried in the churchyard at Longborough, his wife living on until her death in 1978.

Quick's character was marked by moderation and modesty – qualities which, as we shall see, mark all his writings, to which we now turn. I shall first introduce some of the intellectual and ecclesiastical trends to which Quick had to adjust himself; I shall then discuss the philosophical underpinnings of his thought, the doctrinal core of his message, and his ecclesiological views, so germane to ecumenical discussion. I shall conclude with a brief assessment of this too quickly forgotten philosophical Anglican theologian and ecumenist.

I

The low level of theological attainment on the part of many Church of England clergymen was not the only theological deficiency noted by Quick. He accused some of the then fashionable authors, and, for good measure, Anglo-Saxons at large, of an anti-intellectualism which swept theology off the stage:

> It is so obvious that we need a gospel, so obvious that that gospel must tell us about God, so obvious that what we are told about God must have an intellectual aspect and an authoritative expression, that we are staggered indeed when we find even professed philosophers, from Ritschl to James, at one with the plain man in disparaging theology as a useless excrescence upon faith. ... If faith is to have an intellectual expression, that expression must either be laboriously thought out, or else trustfully accepted. This alternative constitutes the horns of a dilemma to the Anglo-Saxon, whose reluctance to think for himself is only surpassed by his even greater reluctance to let anyone else think for him. The only resource left him is to try to get on without theology at all.[18]

As if to qualify this rather extreme judgement, Quick proceeds to discuss those who do think about theology, but do so in unfortunate ways. He regards the narrow-minded specialist as 'one of the great dangers of our modern civilisation', who 'continues to dig his own several pit, and to sink down into it until he is apt to take for a horizon what is in reality only the edge of his grave.'[19] Then there are those who are so tolerant that they cannot pronounce one way or the other on theological issues, and whose fundamental principle is non-interference with the opinions of others. Nor will sincerity alone suffice, 'For unluckily, the most glaring sincerity belongs, as a rule, to the fanatic. ... Hence the assailants of dogma who believe in pure sincerity are driven to bestow their highest admiration on those very people whose beliefs they are most desirous to attack.'[20] Quick concludes that dogma and

---

[18] O. C. Quick, *Modern Philosophy and the Incarnation*, 8.
[19] Ibid., 13.
[20] Ibid., 16.

freedom of thought must go hand in hand for, to repeat the 'text' at the head of this chapter, 'Breadth of mind is not the attitude of thought which seeks to acquiesce in anarchy, but the attitude which seeks to find room for the greatest possible variety of opinions as all contributive to a common truth.'[21]

There could be no more apt description of Quick's own method than this. In general terms he sought to balance traditonalism against the claims and benefits of modern thought. Thus, for example, he argues that the former has the edge over the latter because of its 'uncompromising emphasis on the objective transcendent reality of God'; whereas the latter has an anthropomorphic God, who 'is not inscrutable only because he is not really above man's level'.[22] Not, indeed, that orthodoxy is without fault: it 'has been constantly haunted and intimidated by the spectre of an unknowable and impassible God, which has long survived the death of Greek religion'.[23] Such blemishes notwithstanding, 'Christianity is supremely the religion of tradition ... But Christianity is supremely also the religion of modern thought.'[24] That there is a certain tension in trying to hold together 'the truth of the historic Incarnation and the truth of the living presence of the Spirit'[25] is undeniable, but it is in principle possible to eradicate the tension. Indeed, 'one great evidence that the Church has indeed been guided by His Spirit is the fact that the Incarnation and the Atonement, the reality of God's love suffering in manhood for man's salvation, taking upon itself manhood to deliver it, are still the centre of her faith'.[26] It follows that 'To weaken the doctrine of the historic Incarnation is to confuse the doctrine of the Spirit. The result is a vague theory of divine immanence which simply mocks the spiritual need of man.'[27] While some of his readers might have been misled into thinking that with his talk of tensions in principle harmonized Quick was placing himself in the line of post-Hegelian idealists, in this last statement we have that radical appeal to God's historic *act* in Christ which runs through all his work, banishing pantheizing temptations and elevating Christianity as a religion of salvation, not simply as a theory allegedly *quasi*-automatic progress which bypasses humanity's greatest need.

Quick brought his general stance as thus described to bear upon the variety of ecclesial-*cum*-theological options which passed across his field of vision. Thus, for example, in his Bishop Paddock Lectures (1922) he weighs the then prevalent liberalism and modernism against the orthodox dogmatic tradition as represented in the historic creeds of the Church. He finds that in the wake of modern biblical

---

[21] Ibid., 18.
[22] Idem, *Liberalism, Modernism and Tradition* (the Bishop Paddock Lectures, 1922), London: Longmans, Green, 1922, 69.
[23] Ibid., 71.
[24] Idem, *Christian Beliefs and Modern Questions*, London: SCM Press (1923), 4th edn 1936, 118, 119.
[25] Ibid., 120.
[26] Ibid., 125.
[27] Ibid., 126.

criticism, modern theology seeks to introduce scientific method into its enquiries. In particular it seeks 'to analyse human experience into facts and beliefs, and to avoid confusion between these two elements of our knowledge'.[28] But, Quick points out, this is really to distinguish between two classes of facts: the actual events which originated Christianity, and the 'progressive interpretation of valuation of those facts, which has determined the subsequent development of the Christian Church'.[29] Two courses of action are open to those who conclude that the original facts no longer justify the beliefs allegedly grounded in them. They may revert to the original facts concerning the 'historical Jesus' as enshrining the essence of Christianity, or they may deem the ideas of Christianity valid even if the alleged facts which prompted them are suspect. On the whole, the Liberal Protestants took the first route, the Catholic Modernists, the second.

Where Plato held that we know appearances only and that the thing-in-itself, the only reality, is for ever unavailable to us; and where Kant maintained that the appearances are all that can be known by us; Ritschl, initially embracing Lotze's doctrine that we do know the real from its effects upon us in ordinary experience, is the fountain-head of Liberal Protestantism. Whereas the Ritschlians charge Catholic mysticism with bypassing Christ's real humanity, they themselves insist that in the historic Jesus we have the reality of the Godhead. In order not to neglect the divinity of Christ altogether, the Ritschlians then either argue, like Hastings Rashdall,[30] that Jesus uniquely embodied his own teaching concerning the Fatherhood of God and the brotherhood of man, or, like the Baptist T. R. Glover, they argue on the basis of his goodness and teaching that Christian experience shows him to have been more than a man.[31] Quick's objection to these approaches is that they make Christ's divinity an effect of his manhood upon us. Accordingly, his sombre assessment is that 'Ritschlian Christology inevitably tends either towards Unitarianism or to ... Jesuolatry. ... No process of dialectic can conjure Godhead out of a mere man.'[32]

Despite its deficiencies, Ritschlianism performed a valuable service in shunning abstruse mysticism; in reminding us that any Christology 'must in the end be tested

---

[28] Idem, *Liberalism, Modernism and Tradition*, London: Longmans, Green, 1922, 1. This book is dedicated to Hugh Richard Lawrie Sheppard, 'in grateful remembrance of fourteen years of friendship and one year of association in his work at St. Martin's-in-the-Fields'.

[29] Ibid., 2.

[30] Quick contributed an article entitled, 'Orthodoxy and Dr. Rashdall' to *The Commonwealth* in November 1921, in which he concluded that Rashdall presented an attenuated version of the Christian gospel. This did not preclude Quick's appointment to Carlisle in 1923, where Rashdall had been Dean since 1917. See further, P. Lucas, 'Oliver Quick', 5–6.

[31] Cf. idem, *The Ground of Faith and the Chaos of Thought*, London: Nisbet, 1931, 90; idem, *The Gospel of Divine Action*, London: Nisbet, 1933, 103.

[32] Idem, *Liberalism, Modernism and Tradition*, 18, 19.

by its power to account for, to stimulate, and to direct the spiritual experience of the Christian soul'; and in recovering 'one vital truth of the Incarnation, which orthodox tradition had almost lost, viz. the truth that our Lord was never more characteristically God than when He suffered on the Cross, that the Cross is in the heart of God, or is the expression of God's own nature to men'.[33] For too long Western orthodoxy had tended to place manhood and Godhood side by side in Christ's person, so that God suffered in his manhood only, for, in the line of Greek thought, suffering could not truly belong to the divine nature. Here, in a nutshell, is Quick's repudiation of the doctrine of the divine impassibility.

If the Liberal Protestants, in their recourse to the historical Jesus, underplayed the development of Christian doctrine through the ages, and tended to deify a man, the Catholic Modernists capitalized upon the presumed progress of Christian thought and found the essence of Christianity in it. Here the fountainhead is John Henry Newman, whose position may be summed up thus:

> (1) Idea is opposed to fact as the basis of Christianity. ... (2) Development is opposed to origin as the essence of Christianity. ... (3) The community is opposed to the individual as the organ of Christianity.[34]

Hence, 'just as the realism of the Liberal Protestant, with its emphasis on the original facts, tended in the long run to a theology abstract, negative, doctrinaire, so the essential idealism of the Catholic Modernist tended to a theology too indiscriminately affirmative, over-ready to accept existing facts'.[35] By dissociating the Church's doctrine of the divine-human Word from the particular man, Jesus, the Catholic Modernists – Tyrrell especially – fostered 'an extraordinary recrudescence of Gnosticism in a modern form ... the living heresy which has now to be faced by the Church of Christ'.[36]

It thus transpires that both the Liberal Protestant and the Catholic Modernist tend to deify humanity in general or in ideal. 'Very roughly and generally speaking', the situation is that

> The Liberal Protestant realist has isolated the facts concerning Jesus and has tried to find just in these facts, as scientifically and impartially established, the law and norm for all religion. The modernist-idealist has fastened on the doctrines of Incarnation and Atonement as representing great human ideas, in the development of which the mental reality of religion is seen and interpreted. Yet somehow the orthodox Christian feels that the Being Whom he calls God

---

[33] Ibid., 20–22.
[34] Ibid., 33. For some reflections upon the development of doctrine see Alan P. F. Sell, *Enlightenment, Ecumenism, Evangel. Theological Themes and Thinkers 1550–2000*, Milton Keynes: Paternoster, 2005, ch. 6.
[35] Ibid., 36.
[36] Idem, *The Testing of Church Principles*, 88, 89.

has been left out of the intellectual construction of both parties, or at last is only brought back and retained inconsistently by an effort of faith or emotion which does not fit into either system as a whole.[37]

Quick tries to do justice to the evolutionary Modernist emphasis upon the divine Christ 'as standing for the genius of man's history or mankind in ideal' by means of a logos Christology in which the logos 'is essentially the true Unity and Unifier of all human souls', whilst at the same time insisting that 'the life of Jesus is not to be isolated from its historic antecedents and consequences'.[38] The fact that the latter can and does happen prompts his verdict, 'Modernism, where it is unorthodox, is not unorthodox because it restates Christianity, but because it states something which is not Christian.'[39]

Eager as he is to find a *via media* between traditional orthodoxy and Liberal Protestantism and Modernism, Quick is by no means blind to the failings of traditionalists: 'Our conservatism has been too much the blind clinging to a formula, our liberalism too much an opposition to external authority as such ... A party zealous to reform dogma, so that it may do its work effectively in modern conditions, has hardly yet arisen.'[40] He urges a return to the creeds, not in order to restate them, but to explain them. There is no need to reaffirm 'every word that the fathers of the Church thought to be true', but we should elevate their fundamental principle:

> For them theology was not primarily the result of any reflection upon their own experience. It was the revelation of God which created both their experience and their theology, and the theology was designed quite as much to guide experience as to interpret it. For them intellect was not a tin-kettle tied to the tail of feelings, urging them to wilder extravagance as it clattered helplessly in their wake. Rather they thought of intellect as a divinely inspired faculty of vision.[41]

Passing reference has already been made to mysticism, and to this topic Quick devoted a good deal of attention. His interest in mysticism is not surprising, given the intellectual context of his day, in which the claims of the new psychology as adumbrated by William James in his *Varieties of Religious Experience*, and the defence of mysticism in Evelyn Underhill's book of that title were receiving considerable attention,[42] and given also Quick's own concern that there should be no skirting of the historical foundations of the Christian faith. In the published

---

[37] Idem, *Liberalism, Modernism and Tradition*, 53.
[38] Ibid., 144, 145.
[39] Ibid., vi.
[40] Idem, *The Testing of Church Principles*, London: John Murray, 1919, 35, 41.
[41] Idem, *Essays in Orthodoxy*, London: Macmillan, 1916, xxxvi.
[42] See W. James, *The Varieties of Religious Experience*, London: Longmans, Green, 1903; E. Underhill, *Mysticism. A Study in the Nature and Development of Man's Spiritual Consciousness*, London: Methuen, 1911. From the same period come many works by the

version of his Ellerton prize essay Quick states the philosophical difficulty at the outset: mysticism 'claims to give the mind a certain knowledge of reality', while at the same time it 'has often claimed to transcend the intellect and to dispense with logic altogether'. This leads rationalists to exclude *ab initio* the possibility of mystical knowledge, while 'transcendental philosophers from Plato to Hegel and his modern followers have used an intellectualist logic as a means to proving a metaphysic which is almost undisguisedly mystical in its conclusions'.[43] The assumption of all of the foregoing, namely, that the intellect is supreme in the acquisition of knowledge, has now been attacked by the pragmatists, who 'draw full attention to the part played by the will and the emotions in the attainment and testing of knowledge ... and create a widespread and consistent doubt as to the infallibility, or rather the possibility, of a purely intellectual criterion'.[44]

In the widest sense, 'the claim of all mystical experience is to tell us of some wider reality beyond ourselves which is not directly apprehensible by or through the senses'.[45] From this, however, we must inevitably infer, in agreement with James, that 'mystical knowledge carries with it no objective criterion of its own validity'.[46] It is Quick's conviction that 'the doctrine of the Trinity expresses both the immanence and transcendence of God, and the teaching of the *via negativa* is always complementary to "the Spirit of adoption whereby we cry Abba, Father"'.[47] The mystic's internal criterion of truth having failed, we have recourse to the religion of the Incarnation, the essence of which is that 'we may see and know God, not only immediately in our inmost selves, but also mediately and externally, first in the record of our Lord's life, and then in whatsoever things on earth are pure, lovely, and of good report'.[48] In this way theology can rescue mysticism from its less desirable excesses – among them the tendency to absorb the individual personality in the divine, while at the same time speaking of 'an ecstacy of love, which must mean in some sense the eternity of personal distinction'.[49] The world-denying aspect of mysticism is also to be regretted. For some mystics, 'God seems so entirely to fill the whole horizon of eternity as to exclude all the human joys for which alone the natural man in his weakness postulates his immortality. ... [T]he general religious consciousness of mankind refuses to be satisfied with a unification of eternal life which excludes rather than includes the elements of variety and differentiation.'[50] Above all, 'the mystics never realized the full significance of the

---

Quaker scholar, Rufus M. Jones, notably, *Studies in Mystical Religion*, London: Macmillan, 1909, though Quick does not refer to these.

[43] O. C. Quick, 'The value of mysticism in religious faith and practice', 161.
[44] Ibid., 162.
[45] Ibid., 164.
[46] Ibid., 166.
[47] Ibid., 172.
[48] Ibid., 173.
[49] Ibid., 181.
[50] Ibid., 192, 193.

fact that God's supreme revelation of Himself took the form of an ordinary human and temporal life in the world'.[51] On the other hand, the Christian mystics have understood that 'side by side with the Incarnation which is the guarantee of self-realization, [Christianity] sets the Cross, the symbol of self-denial. If Christianity teaches anything clearly, it teaches that all human visions and aspirations are clogged and marred by sin. Hence, whatever we may ultimately keep in eternity, we must abandon all to possess it.' The upshot is that both renunciation and the 'divine normality of the ordinary religious life' are integral to a true religion.[52] Hence both unadulterated mysticism and anti-mysticism are to be repudiated, and reconciliation is to be found in the theology of the Cross and the Incarnation, for 'The Cross represents the negative side of the Christian call, the aspects of renunciation and suffering. The Incarnation and the Resurrection convey its positive gospel of consecration and life. To all Christian lives both elements are essential.'[53] Finally, Quick declares, 'in religious matters it must always be borne in mind that sometimes it is the mouth, not of the expert, but of the babe, which is uttering the deepest truth'.[54]

In *The Journal of Theological Studies* of July 1912, Father H. Kelly responded to Quick's article. In his reply to Kelly, Quick conceded that he had been 'too much inclined to take a conventional and uncritical view of the merits of an experience which claims to make possible an immediate approach of the soul to God', and he agreed with Kelly 'in regarding the pursuance of the *via negativa* as at least an essential characteristic of mystical religion'.[55] But he felt that Kelly's definition of mysticism was too wide, and he refined his own definition as follows: 'Mysticism ... is the claim made by the soul to the apprehension of a wider reality in no sense mediated by the data of sense-perception. ... [It is] an immediate inner experience of reality as opposed to a meditation upon abstract ideas which have their concrete source in the external world.'[56] He therefore reiterated his general position, observing against James and Underhill that

> where the inner certainty of a specific experience is made the one authoritative channel of religious truth, the external evidence of historic fact becomes secondary and even logically superfluous. ... As long as the actual events of Christ's Life, death, and Resurrection are recognized as the essential basis of all faith, those who occupy their business in other than directly religious matters, the van-boy in the East End, the commercial churchwarden in the suburbs, have

---

[51] Ibid., 197.

[52] Ibid., 198.

[53] Ibid., 199.

[54] Ibid., 200.

[55] Idem, 'Mysticism: its meaning and danger', *The Journal of Theological Studies*, XIV, October 1912, 1.

[56] Ibid., 2.

a definite assurance that they too may possess a firm grasp of all that is really needful in religious knowledge.[57]

Quick will not allow that 'a specific form of inward experience is ... made the test of religiousness'; he cautions, 'If religion has felt the whips of metaphysic let her beware the scorpions of psychology';[58] and his instinct to harmonize the historic with the inward causes him to resent the imperialism of mysticism's claims which 'seem to exclude it from all positions except the chief'.[59] In this way mysticism, instead of being 'the invaluable handmaid of Christianity' becomes 'its most evil mistress'.[60] Among the unfortunate results of one-sided or extreme mysticism is the apparent denial of the universal compresence of God. By this is meant that 'all things are in direct relation to God, and are what they are because of that relation, though, of course, it does not follow that God is to be identified with all things. Thus evil is evil, and error is error, because they are in direct relation to God's omnipresent goodness, though the direct relation is here one of opposition. ... All knowledge of reality therefore is implicitly direct knowledge of God.'[61]

It remains only to add that if Quick thought Kelly's definition of 'mysticism' too broad, H. M. Waddams thought Quick's definition too narrow. Waddams quotes Quick thus: 'The mystic who penetrates to the direct vision, necessarily ineffable, of eternal reality can have no need of a revelation mediated by particular historical events.' On this the reviewer comments, 'As far as Christian mysticism is concerned this seems quite inaccurate. The whole basis of Christian mysticism surely rests on the knowledge of the grace of God which is given through Jesus Christ. And apart from that, the experience of God which the mystic is granted is not by any means the same as knowledge of God.'[62] But this is precisely the mediating position for which Quick argues, and Waddams adduces no evidence to show that there are no mystics of the kind Quick challenges: indeed, he could not do this because they exist.

A further polarity which Quick explored in mediating style is that between Catholicism and Protestantism. It will become apparent that his lack of deep immersion in Reformation history, and his tendency to describe some of the traditions he discusses in terms of their aberrations, renders his walk through this thicket less than sure-footed. Be that as it may, his objective is 'to elicit and to define some of the different values for which Catholicism and Protestantism

---

[57] Ibid., 7.
[58] Ibid., 8.
[59] Ibid., 9.
[60] Ibid.
[61] Idem, *Catholic and Protestant Elements in Christianity*, London: Longmans, Green, 1924, 61.
[62] H. M. Waddams, review of O. C. Quick, *The Doctrines of the Creed*, in *Church Quarterly Review*, October–December 1938, 149. Waddams's quotation is on p. 104 of the Fontana edition, 1963.

have stood, to set them first in opposition and antithesis to one another, and then to suggest that reconciliation is both a need and a possibility.'[63] He defines the 'convenient, but otherwise unsatisfactory' term 'Protestant' thus: it is 'that type of Christianity which, reacting strongly against ecclesiastical formalism, has relied on the spiritual experience of the individual in such a manner as to discredit the authority of ecclesiastical forms and institutions'.[64]

The first comment to be made on this definition concerns its glaring lacuna. Any reaction against ecclesiastical formalism (and that was not all – there were unwelcome doctrinal accretions and sundry scandals too) was prompted by the prior decision to heed the Word of God in Scripture and to judge matters ecclesiastical in the light of it. This is the source of the critique, not the individual's experience. It would be more accurate to say that individualism flows from the Renaissance rather than from the Reformation. Yet Quick can repeat that 'In opposition to the outward authority of priest and Sacraments, Protestantism has set up the spiritual experience of the individual.'[65] Again there is no reference to the authoritative Word. Elsewhere, as if Calvin were not a strong churchman, Quick declares that 'typical Protestants' alleged that 'The Church ... should not be regarded as belonging to the primary essence of the Christian Gospel at all. Christianity is essentially constituted by an individual relation between the soul and God wrought through the Atonement of Christ and maintained by the presence of His Spirit.'[66] In a footnote he explains (following Troeltsch) that 'This argument belongs originally to Non-conformity rather than to the Church-Protestantism either of Luther or Calvin. Nevertheless, Lutheranism and Calvinism were from the first individualistic in the sense that they found the individual's assurance of salvation, not in obedience to the official hierarchy and sacramental system, but in a simple and personal decision to believe ...'[67] This simply compounds the error, for far from being individualistic, the earliest Nonconformists proposed an alternative idea of the Church *catholic* as being comprised of those who were 'saints by calling'[68] (God's prevenient grace preceding and enabling their decision to believe), who, being severally grafted into the Vine, were necessarily related to all of the branches.[69]

---

[63] O. C. Quick, *Catholic and Protestant Elements in Christianity*, 2.
[64] Idem, *The Testing of Church Principles*, 28 n.
[65] Ibid., 57.
[66] Idem, *Catholic and Protestant Elements in Christianity*, 7.
[67] Ibid., n.
[68] Romans 1: 7.
[69] I cannot deny that Protestantism has spawned individualistic attitudes and isolationist groups; but, to repeat, no Christian tradition deserves to be defined in terms of its aberrations. See further, Alan P. F. Sell, *Saints: Visible, Orderly and Catholic. The Congregational Idea of the Church*, Geneva: World Alliance of Reformed Churches and Allison Park, PA: Pickwick Publications, 1986. Available from Wipf & Stock, Eugene, Oregon.

Time would fail to rehearse all the points at which Quick misses his target. But for a sample, consider first the way in which he contrasts Lutheranism with Calvinism, and the half truths perpetuated by the strong disjunctions in the following sentences: '[Lutheranism] has encouraged other-worldliness but not Pharisaism; it has bred pietists but not Puritans'[70] – as if there were no legalistic Lutherans or pietistic Reformed, notably in the Netherlands. Again, Quick asserts that 'from the Reformation onwards, strong Protestants have found in "conversion", rather than in infant-baptism, the true starting-point of the individual Christian's life', whereas 'Catholicism ... marks the beginning of Christian life by the baptism of infants at an age when no Christian consciousness can exist'.[71] The truth would seem to be that, those of believer baptist traditions apart, the majority of Protestants have maintained paedobaptism, though they have not normally understood the gift of regeneration – *the* operative factor in the translation to new life – as being necessarily received on the occasion of baptism. It is hard to disagree with Quick's friend, J. K. Mozley's verdict that 'Quick was not on ground that he knew well when he was interpreting Protestant belief and emphasis in their historic or in their Anglican forms'.[72]

Difficulties with Quick's historical emphases notwithstanding, there is much to be said for his way of seeking to harmonize Catholic and Protestant insights:

> On the one hand, a new consciousness of God is in the New Testament clearly seen to be the ground and basis of Christian life and power; and this is confirmed by the experience of centuries. Conscious faith comes first; conduct proceeds from it. On the other hand, the new consciousness can be prepared for and helped to grow by first doing acts which are appropriate to it, even before it comes.

Within his own communion, Quick had to adjust himself to Anglo-Catholic claims and attitudes. We have already noticed his horror at the antics of the Anglo-Catholics in relation to the proposal to constitute a united Church of South India, but he had additional things to say about this tradition which, in his day, was by no means negligible within the Church of England. In *The Gospel of Divine Action*, Quick draws an interesting contrast between the Tractarianism of the Oxford Movement and the then current Anglo-Catholicism. The former was 'in the main a religion of authority and obedience' – and a non-sentimental, cold and austere one at that. The Tractarians were hesitant concerning the position of those outside what they understood to be the true Church, but they were for the most part 'saved from magical notions' by their strong, 'rather Puritan', emphasis on morality.[73] Their successors, Henry Scott Holland among them, were influenced by the Christian Socialism of Maurice and Kingsley; they were more socially

---

[70] Idem, *The Gospel of the New World*, 86.
[71] Idem, *Catholic and Protestant Elements in Christianity*, 59.
[72] J. K. Mozley, *Oliver Quick as a Theologian*, 4.
[73] O. C. Quick, *The Gospel of Divine Action*, 133.

activist, and 'the cultus of the Reserved Sacrament was a practice which they did not feel called upon to demand, and even viewed with distrust'.[74] By contrast, contemporary Anglo-Catholics are much more interested in ceremonial and the life of devotion. They have turned from social reform which 'is often disparaged ... as a merely mundane and secular occupation',[75] and in their sacramental practice they emphasize symbolism rather than instrumentalism where God's relation to outward things is concerned. This has in some churches 'produced a somewhat narrow pietism which satisfies the religious instinct and makes people "keen Catholics" in religious practice, by attaching them to a cultus which is never coherently related to secular living'.[76] The upshot is that Anglo-Catholics have subordinated theology to worship – a circumstance for which some find justification in Rudolf Otto's elevation of the numinous; and while their liturgy approximates to that of Rome, their intellects are far removed from the rationalism of Aquinas, and they are not concerned to provide theological foundations on which to establish their devotional life.[77] Overcome by devotional experientialism, they thus lack what in sacramental theology was most precious to Quick, namely, 'the element in Catholic doctrine represented by the *opus operatum* ...'[78] 'I claim the right to believe,' he declares, 'that, if my mind is set to receive Christ, then in His appointed ordinance He comes to me and acts upon me really and effectively, even though my feelings be dull and cold and my thoughts hard to fix. And I connect this belief with the notion of an active and living God Who is working in and through this world-order towards a glory which shall be revealed when this heaven and earth and mortal consciousness have passed away.'[79]

One more theological trend remains to be briefly reviewed. In the wake of the First World War much of the older theological liberalism was revealed as hollow – not least its optimistic doctrine of progress. A strong reaction against it was, says Quick, 'both healthy and inevitable'.[80] Not, indeed, that Quick was altogether enamoured of the stance taken by the leading reactionary, Karl Barth. He characterizes Barth's objective as being that of breaking free of the Hellenistic tradition in theology in favour of a radical Hebraism. In the quest for God the human being's faculties of apprehension are beside the point; they are, indeed, confounded by God: the Bible's 'whole story is concerned, not with man's search

---

[74] Ibid., 134.
[75] Ibid.
[76] Ibid., 137.
[77] See idem, *The Ground of Faith and the Chaos of Thought*, 94–5. Cf. idem, 'Reason and Christian experience', *Theology*, XV, October 1927, 190.
[78] Idem, *The Gospel of Divine Action*, 138.
[79] Ibid., 138–9. With these criticisms of the Anglo-Catholicism of the 1930s Donald Mackinnon expressed himself in entire sympathy. See his 'Oliver Chase Quick as a theologian', 109–10.
[80] Idem, *The Ground of Faith and the Chaos of Thought*, 91.

for God, but with God's coming to man'.[81] Nor does creation point towards God, for in Barth's view, 'the Biblical doctrine of the Creation is intended precisely to emphasize the impassable gulf between the Creator and the Creature'.[82] It follows that 'Christ's life as the final revelation of God is in no sense the fulfilment of human ideals of goodness,[83] ... Rather it reveals God in being the crowning act of power, which once for all convicts all human ideals and ideal of their impotence and folly.'[84] All is 'wholly dependent on a special act of God, enlightening the hitherto unconverted mind'.[85] The Christological implication of this, as Quick points out in a discussion of Edwyn Hoskyns' views, is that Jesus is not 'the human symbol of a universal Logos operative in all men ...,' at which point Quick demurs:

> If God be really eternal love, and if from the beginning He so loved the world which He made that in the end He became incarnate for its redemption, then somehow the life of Jesus must be the symbol not only of God's constant purpose and universal operation among men, but also of that perfection in act and knowledge, after which man's natural faculties have from his birth been blindly seeking. I do not believe that Barthians really mean to deny it. True, to think of the Incarnate Life merely as a symbol of what is universal tempts us towards a humanitarianism which forgets the living, transcendent God. Equally to think of it merely as divine act breaking in from above at a particular point leads us to imagine an absolute separation between God and His world, which makes any notion of divine love in creation impossible, leaves human nature as such irredeemable, and proves divine grace a self-contradiction.[86]

If this general approach is correct, Quick muses, we should be condemned 'either to a return to the methods of the Inquisition or else a pure quietism content to do nothing and wait for God. For it is ridiculous to preach the Gospel to those who are inherently incapable of recognizing it as good; and if men are not so incapable, it follows that God has already revealed Himself to them in their own ideals.'[87] All of which is to call into question Barth's view of total depravity and the obliteration of the *imago dei* in human beings. But with original sin as thus understood goes the obliteration of human responsibility, leaving irresistible grace as the only remedy for sin. 'But if saving grace be irresistible, there can be no reason why God should

---

[81] Ibid., 100.

[82] Idem, *The Gospel of Divine Action*, 105.

[83] To Barth as interpreted by Quick, all such ideals – and all human hopes – are frustrated by sin. In this he finds 'a striking agreement between Buddhism and modern neo-Calvinism. ... During periods of gloom and agony in the history of the world both are sure to find disciples'. See *The Gospel of the New World*, 25.

[84] O. C. Quick, *The Gospel of Divine Action*, 105.

[85] Ibid., 106.

[86] Ibid., 109–10.

[87] Idem, *The Ground of Faith and the Chaos of Thought*, 104.

not save all men, if he saves any. Hence Barthianism readily passes from absolute condemnations of everything human into a doctrine of universal salvation for all men.'[88] I, however, think that a case can be made for saying that while Barth himself 'veers towards' universalism, he does not land decidedly in it, nor (save the insubordination) does he explain himself as clearly as one might wish.[89]

Be that as it may, Quick diagnoses the philosophical problem underlying Barthianism thus:

> [A] great deal of Barthian theology seems to me to depend upon an implied argument that, because in revelation the revealing act is God's, not man's, therefore the reality revealed cannot become the object of human thought, or be acknowledged as true by the rational or philosophic judgment of the human mind. The reply to this argument must simply be, *Non sequitur*. We must grant indeed that apart from faith the human mind can never recognize Christ as divine or Christianity as true. But to exclude faith from philosophy is either to make faith irrational or else to confine the sphere of philosophy to the sphere of abstract logic. Against such arbitrary limitations reason will rightly protest.[90]

His rueful conclusion is that Barthianism lands us in radical scepticism, for 'Barth, no less than the sceptic, assumes that man's reason and conscience confine him for ever within the circle of a man-made universe of illusion'.[91] In Barth's case this results from his desire for certainty (conceived as unattainable by human powers of reason) rather than truth: 'the intense, passionate objectivity of his theology was really determined from the beginning by the subjectivity of his personal interest. It was the need for assurance that dominated his mind, just as it had dominated his Ritschlian opponents who won religious assurance by an impossible separation between the value-judgments of faith and the truths of science.'[92]

But this reference to reason prompts us to turn to Quick's own philosophical underpinnings.

II

I shall first show how Quick adjusted himself to certain philosophical traditions, and then I shall review a selection of prominent themes which recur in his work. Scattered through his writings are a number of adverse references to Platonism. Of Platonism's identification of the real with the good he declares that such an

---

[88] Idem, *The Gospel of the New World*, 43 n.; cf. ibid., 116.
[89] For further brief observations on this point see Alan P. F Sell, *Enlightenment, Ecumenism, Evangel*, 331.
[90] Idem, *The Ground of Faith and the Chaos of Thought*, 117 n.
[91] Ibid., 105–6.
[92] Ibid., 106–7.

assimilation can be made only by 'dismissing as illusion most of our present experience of things in this world of space and time'. Moreover, it is a self-contradictory position, 'For, of necessity, it must regard illusion as an evil. If, therefore, it extols the perfection of ultimate reality by making an illusion of ordinary experience, it merely increases the amount of real evil, viz. real illusion, in the universe, and can give no reason whatever why this illusion should exist.'[93] Again, reference has already been made to Quick's aversion to the Greek notion that God is impassible. He elaborates upon his criticism in a number of places. Thus he faults Neoplatonists for teaching that the union of humanity with God can occur only by the negation of all that pertains to human life: 'The fundamental attributes of God being immortality and impassibility, it followed that man in order to become one with God must practically cease to be man.'[94] From the point of view of Christian theology Hellenistic thought is deficient in being quite unable to accommodate either the incarnation or the atonement:

a. It supposes that by descent into matter divine or spiritual being is degraded and becomes less truly divine, whereas Christianity teaches that the Incarnate puts off none of his Godhead in entering flesh. [Elsewhere, with reference to the Dean of St. Paul's under whom he would one day serve, Quick wrote, 'I am not sure that even Dr. Inge, when he urges a return to Platonism as the cure for our intellectual unrest, quite realises what an utter hash is made of the whole Platonic system of thought by importing into it the idea of a particular Incarnation on the phenomenal plane.'[95] When 'the immanence of the eternal goodness in temporal phenomena tends to become inconceivable', a prominent casualty is any idea of Christian sacraments.[96]]
b. It interprets the process of salvation as the soul's raising of itself, not as a work of grace on the part of God who descends.
c. In the ascent of the soul towards God matter is not transformed, nor is the natural man or the material world itself recreated or raised; rather these are left behind. ...
d. It is essentially characteristic of Platonism that to it salvation is a matter of saving the individual soul by detaching it from the historical world.[97]

Platonism was, in Quick's eyes, utterly discredited by modern science: 'The whole attempt to argue along Platonic lines to a static, eternal world of pattern-realities behind such a gigantic flux of phenomena as science now affirms to exist,

---

[93] Idem, *Philosophy and the Cross*, London: OUP, 1931, 15.
[94] Idem, *Liberalism, Modernism and Tradition*, 107.
[95] Ibid., 57.
[96] Idem, *The Christian Sacraments* (1927), London: Collins Fontana, 1964, 52.
[97] Idem, *The Gospel of the New World*, 69; cf. ibid., 99; *The Gospel of Divine Action*, 48–54.

seems as much a play of fancy as Homer's fables of Olympus.'[98] The metaphysical crux is that Platonism 'has no answer to the question, how is it conceivable that the spatio-temporal copy or illusory appearance of the eternal should ever have come to be at all?'[99] The upshot is that the Christian doctrines of creation, incarnation, atonement and sacraments are all put at risk where Platonism holds sway. We shall return to the question of impassibility in the doctrinal section of this chapter.

If the Platonic idealism caused Quick concern, the post-Hegelian idealism of his own day was scarcely less troublesome to him. In a discussion of the views of Walter Moberly[100] he finds that the absolute idealists set out from the law of contradiction as being the supreme test of truth; this law is operative when errors are refuted by reference to a wider whole of knowledge, and we are led on to the view that ultimate reality is a coherent system in which contradictions are eliminated; and hence 'the Absolute is expressible only in terms of mental or spiritual experience'.[101] Quick grants that idealism of this kind has never had mass appeal, partly because of the 'abstruse technicalities' in terms of which it has been articulated, and partly because 'The Briton is as quick to be suspicious of dexterity as he is slow to see through it.'[102] He further grants that in so far as religion concerns the quest of the eternal, the absolutists emerge at first sight as allies in the cause. But Bradley, Bosanquet and others make it 'a matter of logical proof that a mind can only know what is in principle already immanent within it' and hence, 'since the whole is always immanent in all its parts, any doctrine of the self-revelation of God above to Man below, becomes as superfluous as it is self-contradictory'.[103] We are thus left with metaphysics, not religion, and with a 'metaphysical absolute for which the name of Godhead cannot appropriately be used'.[104]

In some respects sailing closer to traditional theology, Josiah Royce sits loose to the historic Incarnation, whilst at the same time wishing to uphold the doctrine of the Holy Spirit as indwelling the Church. But the Church he envisions is the ideal society to which loyalty is owed, but which does not outwardly exist as yet. Hence, 'the religion of loyalty to the community is compatible with the practice of the most exclusive individualism. All Royce can really require from his neophytes is to be loyal to the universe from the depths of their arm-chairs.'[105]

More generally, absolute idealists, in sitting loose to Gospel history, convert Jesus into an embodiment of the moral ideal, and construe the atonement as

---

[98] Idem, *Liberalism, Modernism and Tradition*, 66.

[99] Idem, *The Christian Sacraments*, 53; cf. *Liberalism, Modernism and Tradition*, 55.

[100] Quick refers to Moberly's paper, 'God and the Absolute', in *Foundations. A Statement of Christian Belief in Terms of Modern Thought*, London: Macmillan, 1922, 423–524.

[101] O. C. Quick, *Modern Philosophy and the Incarnation*, 61.

[102] Ibid., 62.

[103] Ibid., 65–6.

[104] Idem, *The Ground of Faith and the Chaos of Thought*, 75.

[105] Idem, *Modern Philosophy and the Incarnation*, 41.

'no more than the supreme example of moral perfection'.[106] Edward Caird, for example, elevates 'the ethico-spiritual gospel of dying to live, ... But he makes it quite plain that for him the core of Christianity lies in the idea and not in any historic person.'[107] For Pringle-Pattison, too, 'It is not that the life of Jesus is not essential to the Incarnation of God, but rather that the life of every other man is in principle also essential.'[108] It is this tendency to reduce God to humanity's idea of its own ideal that Quick finds so damaging to the Christian ideas of transcendence and incarnation. Along the immanentist path 'Everything means God ... but nothing *is* God. So God comes to be conceived ... almost as nothing more than a universal meaning, explanation or ideal.'[109]

Of particular concern to Quick in view of the Christian doctrine of atonement is the tendency of modern idealism to skirt the problem of evil and hence to play down the need of a remedy. In this respect the idealists with whom he is concerned are heirs of Kant, whose 'doctrine of the autonomy of the will, though it expresses a profound truth about human nature as originally created, takes no account of the fall'.[110] In relation to sacramental theology, the 'reluctance to exclude anything whatever from being in the last resort an expression of the Godhead gives [one-sided aesthetic sacramentalism] a pantheistic tendency, and makes it constantly prone to offend the moral consciousness which apprehends God as fighting victoriously with the good against an evil wholly alien from Himself'.[111]

Quick's summary judgement is that 'The impossibility of conceiving how real events can ever proceed from pure reason, or how causative happenings can ever be reduced to a mere system of signs, is the brick wall against which idealist philosophy has been running its head from the days of Plato to the days of Hegel and Whitehead.'[112] But he cannot leave it there, for his impulse to harmonize ostensibly polarized views leads him to suggest that while 'The characteristic vice of modern thought seemed to be that, while it brings the Divine Being into necessary union with the human, it tends to make Incarnation impossible by abolishing all real and substantive difference between the Divine and Human natures', may we not propose that the closer the union, the more clearly the distinction

---

[106] Idem, *The Ground of Faith and the Chaos of Thought*, 64; cf. idem, 'Reason and Christian experience', 189.

[107] Idem, *Liberalism, Modernism and Tradition*, 40.

[108] Ibid., 43. For a full discussion of Caird, Pringle-Pattison, and other British idealists who were not in principle opposed to religion, see Alan P. F. Sell, *Philosophical Idealism and Christian Belief* (1995), reprinted Eugene, OR: Wipf & Stock, 2006.

[109] O. C. Quick, *Liberalism, Modernism and Tradition*, 47.

[110] Idem, *The Gospel of the New World*, 42.

[111] Idem, *The Christian Sacraments*, 55.

[112] Idem, *The Gospel of Divine Action*, 25.

is perceived?'[113] All of which turns upon a clear understanding that transcendence and immanence are correlatives. Once this is seen a number of undesirable exits are blocked off: 'The deism and the negative mysticism, which in different ways deny God's immanence in the outward world, make Him not transcendent of the world, but absent from it. And the pantheism, which denies transcendence wholly, makes immanence equally impossible, since it leaves no room for any distinction between the Godhead and the totality of that in which it dwells.'[114]

For all its pitfalls and inadequacies, idealism is preferable to materialism, which is 'deadly and dangerous' because 'It cannot be met by rational argument, for it is by distrust of such argument that it defends itself';[115] to naturalism, which cannot explain whence those 'real and solid' facts of moral and religious experience come;[116] to pragmatism with its doctrine that 'The symbols of language which seem to signify truths are really but instruments which assist practical control';[117] and to reductionist views which would make humanity the sole fount of rational order and knowledge simply 'a function of the biological apparatus which enables [man] to control his environment'.[118] Expanding the last point, Quick declares, 'To say that, because human reason is a biological instrument, it is therefore nothing more, is a bare-faced begging of the whole question.'[119] His adverse criticisms of current philosophical positions notwithstanding, Quick's impulse towards harmonization does not desert him. On the contrary, 'The real need of to-day is for a unification of human thought and life, some vision of a common end which can provide an authoritative standard of value.'[120] Whence will come this vision? 'It is the capacity of the spirit of Christ to unify modern life which needs to be further tested and explored.'[121] We shall see how Quick goes about this testing and exploration as we turn to some topics of importance on which he had a good deal to say, remembering that the context of the bulk of his utterances is one in which 'The fabric of Christian faith has during recent years been shaken to its foundations.'[122]

---

[113] Idem, *Liberalism, Modernism and Tradition*, 119. Two lines of Henry Twells's hymn, 'At even, when the sun was set' come to mind: 'And they who fain would serve Thee best Are conscious most of wrong within'.

[114] Idem, *The Christian Sacraments*, 58–9.

[115] Idem, *The Ground of Faith and the Chaos of Thought*, 25.

[116] See idem, *Christian Beliefs and Modern Questions*, 16–19.

[117] O. C. Quick, *The Ground of Faith and the Chaos of Thought*, 17. Cf. idem, *Modern Philosophy and the Incarnation*, 66–70. Quick then proceeds to find Bergson wanting because his theory of absolute knowledge cannot yield certainty because it is enmeshed in his doctrine that the absolute reality is 'all change and flux'. Ibid., 72.

[118] Ibid., 17.

[119] Idem, *Modern Philosophy and the Incarnation*, 30.

[120] Idem, *The Ground of Faith and the Chaos of Thought*, 35.

[121] Ibid., 36.

[122] Idem, *Essays in Orthodoxy*, xiv.

From the hint just dropped concerning Christ as being the authoritative standard of value we can see at once that Quick has no truck for older infallibilities whether biblicist or ecclesiastical. To embrace either would be to submit to an authority which may not be questioned. We purchase certainty at the cost of any right to question promulgated truth. This is a serious matter:

> We may construe this self-abnegation either as intellectual humility or as a betrayal of reason or conscience. But one thing is clear. The assurance which acceptance of infallibility bestows is of the psychological, not of the logical, order. It requires of us to forsake the precept to test all things and hold fast that which is good.[123]

Quick can understand how, out of a sense of despair at the state of the world, some are tempted to opt for allegedly infallible certainties, but he insists that to adumbrate the psychological causes of this choice is not the same as adducing reasons for their belief.

What might count as good reasons for belief? With this we come to Quick's reflections on natural theology and theism. He first explains that there are 'two distinct types of argument for the truth of a belief. The first relies on the coherence ... of the content of the belief when it is compared with other data. ... The second ... relies on the inexplicability of the fact that the belief exists, unless the content of the belief is true.'[124] He labels the former rational, the latter empirical, while granting that both are rational in that they employ logic, and both are empirical in that they concern the content of experience. The older theistic arguments were for the most part of the rationalist type, but with Kant's critique of those arguments and his elevation of moral values as requiring the postulate of God we are led to a restatement of the rational argument in axiological rather than cosmological form. Quick lists Pringle-Pattison, Sorley, Rashdall, Webb, Taylor, Temple and Matthews as persuasive proponents of this type of argument. By contrast, the oldest type of empirical argument is probably that from miracle. Quick briskly discounts this argument (a) because 'if miracle is defined as an abnormal event due to God's action', we land in circularity; while if the reference to God is omitted 'there is no longer any force in the inference that, because it is unaccountable, it is therefore due to God'. He concludes that 'This whole type of reasoning is bad. It makes the supernatural a mere stop-gap in natural causation.'[125]

---

[123] Idem, *The Ground of Faith and the Chaos of Thought*, 33; cf. idem, *Philosophy and the Cross*, 25–6.

[124] Ibid., 46. Leonard Hodgson endorses Quick's view. See his *The Grace of God in Faith and Philosophy*, London: Longmans, Green, 1936, 6, and *Towards a Christian Philosophy*, London: Nisbet, 1943, 13, the Preface to which book explains that the repetition is owing to the loss through bombing of stocks of the former work.

[125] Ibid., 53.

Quick proceeds to explain that a similar argument has been associated with special revelation, whereby unmediated or direct messages from God are conveyed. This will appear as a rational argument (in Quick's special sense of the term) if a message's content is especially illuminating or explanatory; or it may be seen as empirical if it is so out of the ordinary that to posit a divine origin is the only rational course. Orthodox theologians, he continues, in distinguishing between reason and revelation have often sought to separate the rational from the empirical. Hence the scholastic idea that the truths of natural theology – God, freedom and immortality – are susceptible of proof by reason, whereas the truths of special revelation could come only directly from God. In modern thought there has been a widespread movement from the attempt to show that the truths of religion satisfy rational and moral criteria to that of focusing upon the inexplicability and uniqueness of religious experience. Along the former path, which underscores the connection of religion with the whole of life, we may lose the distinct character of holiness and the unique character of the life of Jesus to which the doctrines of the incarnation and atonement bear witness. Along the empirical way the devotional life is more secure, but so much emphasis may be laid upon the sacred as to lose the secular, thereby forgetting that God made both. Furthermore, there is 'grave danger in supposing, as religious empiricists are often inclined to do, that the test of religious experience can be found altogether within religion itself'.[126] Quick confesses that his bias is towards the rationalist approach, not least because 'A doctrine of God which in effect makes us think of Him only as the cause of certain experiences, events or beliefs among others really will not do. He must also be the ground of the reason which constitutes the order, the coherence and the truth of all things.'[127]

Holding that the traditional theistic proofs, even if formally valid, are afflicted with 'incurable abstractness'[128] Quick's own approach is axiological: 'The main argument is directed to show that the moral and the aesthetic consciousness, more especially the moral, must be taken as a guide to the true meaning of reality, and that, if this be allowed, theism offers the most reasonable interpretation of the universe.'[129] Adequately expressed and understood, this argument is 'unshakeable' for otherwise we are driven to believe in 'a final and ultimate opposition between the true and the good'. The choice is thus between 'some kind of theism ... and a fundamental irrationalism'.[130] Not, indeed, that for Christianity, 'Christ Himself is the supreme revelation only in so far as He supremely fulfils the human ideals of beauty, goodness and truth.'[131] Rather,

---

[126] Ibid., 66.
[127] Ibid., 67.
[128] See idem, *Doctrines of the Creed. Their Basis in Scripture and their Meaning To-day* (1938), London: Collins Fontana, 1971, 20.
[129] Idem, *The Ground of Faith and the Chaos of Thought*, 87.
[130] Ibid.
[131] Ibid., 116.

> Viewed in its uniqueness, in its difference from all other human lives, Christ's life is referred to the Godhead as the efficient cause which wholly makes it what it is; viewed in its universality, as giving the key to the interpretation of man's whole experience of the world in which he moves, Christ's life is the human symbol of a divine order present in all things and fulfilling itself in all.[132]

Should any contend that rational argumentation precludes the possibility of special revelation, Quick retorts that this 'is simply to misunderstand the limitations within which [rational] arguments move'.[133] Christianity's explanatory and interpretative power resides in the fact that 'it is Christ Himself, not only some idea or teaching of Christ, that is the illuminator – it is the course of His whole life and message before death, in death and after death ... which enables St. John to call Him the light of men and the modern Christian to see in that light truths of which the apostles never dreamed'.[134] This does not imply that

> Christian faith goes beyond reason. For we do not mean by reason an activity of thought which demonstrates truths *a priori* before the facts of experience are considered. Reason, as we understand the term, considers the facts and interprets them so as to make them intelligible. ... It would therefore be absurd to proceed as though reason apart from Christianity could prove certain truths about God and man, and then faith in Christ came in to complete a knowledge which reason left incomplete.[135]

Lest any should feel that at this point Quick is veering towards a fideistic – even a Barthian – position, he immediately adds,

> On the other hand, still less can we speak as though all true knowledge of God came through faith in Jesus, and the Christian believer moved in a world of specifically religious truth which the philosophic reason is debarred from entering. On the contrary, faith in Jesus shows itself to be true by illuminating the reason and submitting to its criticism; and the philosophy which is enlightened by that faith is simply a better, truer and fuller philosophy than one which either has not considered the facts concerning Jesus or has rejected their Christian interpretation.[136]

The way is thus left open for apologetics. In this connection Quick carefully discusses the kinds of order which are called rational. He sets out from the law of contradiction, according to which every meaningful affirmation must implicitly

---

[132] Ibid., 130–31.
[133] Ibid., 124.
[134] Ibid., 129.
[135] Idem, *Doctrines of the Creed*, 26.
[136] Ibid., 26–7.

deny everything which would contradict it. But while this is an inescapable requirement it tells us nothing at all about the positive nature of religion, or of reality. Next there are the rational demonstrations of pure mathematics, but these are perfectly realizable only in a world of abstractions. Then there is scientific reasoning which turns upon the observation of sequences of events and their mutual coherence, but this coherence is not understood in the strict sense that no other sequence of events is logically conceivable. But the assumption here is that 'the whole of reality is made up of events occurring in space-time' – in which case 'there is no difference whatever between truth and error, virtue and vice, good and bad. In this respect the rationality of all is equal and identical. All are equally subject to the generalizations of scientific law.'[137] Quick therefore posits the appreciative reason which 'apprehends that principle of order in the world whereby things are so arranged as to manifest or embody positive value or goodness'.[138] This order differs from, but is not in conflict with, that of science. It concerns the aesthetic and the moral reason, 'which are in their essential nature theoretical or directed to the true apprehension of reality, and not purely practical or concerned with devising means or ends'.[139] In fact 'The contemplative or theoretical knowledge is the condition of the practical activity.'[140]

Quick sums the situation up thus:

> The demonstrative or mathematical reason fails to find a principle of universal harmony, because the moral and, to a lesser degree, the aesthetic consciousness inevitably rebel against it when it claims to include all reality under that type of order which satisfies it. Similarly the scientific reason fails. For the principle of its order is equally fulfilled whatever value-judgment is to be passed on the cosmic process as a whole. Its very inclusiveness is its undoing. For by including good and evil events indifferently, it excludes from satisfaction that other type of reason which requires the bringing of all reality under the principle of an order which can definitely be called good.[141]

There remains what Quick names the metaphysical reason:

---

[137] Idem, 'Reason and Christian experience. II. What is reason?' *Theology*, XV, 1927, 248.
[138] Ibid.
[139] Ibid., 249.
[140] Ibid.
[141] Ibid., 251–2; cf. idem, *Philosophy and the Cross*, 6–15. In an earlier paper, 'The humanist theory of value: A Criticism', *Mind*, NS, XIX, April 1910, 218–30, Quick found the theory, and his former tutor F. C. S. Schiller, wanting at certain points. The burden of his case is that 'to define truth as value is to destroy the value of truth', and that there is 'a fundamental confusion between the *nature* of truth and its *criterion* at the root of the humanist theory'. Op. cit., 229.

> The claim of the metaphysical reason is to find room within itself for the departmental work of those special forms of reason which we have termed mathematical, scientific and appreciative, and to exhibit the several orders of logical necessity, natural law, beauty, and moral goodness, as being finally harmonized within a whole order which it judges to be good.[142]

The metaphysical reason cannot, however, demonstrate that the universe as a whole is rational. On the contrary, 'An act of faith alone can give assurance' of this. Ultimately the metaphysical rationalist is obliged to urge his faith in reason as a reason for his faith.'[143] What the rationalist theist must show is that 'his belief really exhibits a fuller and more inclusive harmony', while the religious empiricist must urge that 'the religious fact and experience are unique and inexplicable and manifestly God-given precisely in this, that they shed such wonderful illumination upon the whole plan of reality'.[144] We thus see, once again, why Quick contends that 'the consequences of maintaining the traditional distinction between the truths of natural theology which are proved by reason, and the truths of revealed Christian theology which are beyond reason, appear to us to be incalculably harmful'.[145] For this 'encourages the belief that Christianity is, in James's phrase, a mere over-belief to theism, and that the rational order of the world stands secure, whether Christianity be accepted or not'.[146] He concludes that

> Neither dogma nor particular experience of religion has any authority of truth apart from its power to illuminate the world of experience as a rational whole. And if it would show its power it must not remain in the cloister, but come forth into the market-pace of thought. The Parable of the Talents should remind us that not even the faith itself can be kept whole and undefiled by being kept out of circulation.[147]

Moreover, 'the reconciliation between faith and philosophy is seen to depend on maintaining the distinction between the faith which seeks the unceasing cooperation of rational knowledge, and the blind trust which has resigned itself to doing without it'.[148]

A further weakness of the older apologetic is that by laying so much emphasis upon the 'proofs' its advocates leave God's nature and character vague:

---

[142] Ibid., 252.
[143] Ibid.
[144] Ibid., 253.
[145] Ibid., 254.
[146] Ibid.
[147] Ibid., 255. That I find this position unanswerable is clear from my *Confessing and Commending the Faith. Historic Witness and Apologetic Method* (2002), reprinted Eugene, OR: Wipf & Stock, 2006.
[148] Idem, *Modern Philosophy and the Incarnation*, 90.

They have forgotten that if the Christian conception of God's character can be made clear and credible, then the practical facts of life will inevitably force a decision as to its truth; and it is really not obscure which way the sinner who feels his need, and the saint who strives after goodness, will in the long run decide. ... Perhaps the first task even of an apologetic writer should be ... to prove to man that he is drowning, than to prove that the rope must be strong enough to save him. A man can and will settle this latter point for himself. Possibly all that theory of any kind can ever do towards establishing the Christian faith is to make clear its meaning and its relevance; its verification must be left to experience.[149]

If Quick's elevation of value informs his apologetic method, it no less certainly performs the same function in his ethics. We may approach this matter through his critique of a type of philosophy current in his day to which we have not so far referred, namely, the new realism associated with the names of Samuel Alexander and others. They find the world of space-time to be coherent, and Quick agrees that it is, for continuity is of its essence. But he denies that the new realist's world is rational:

[T]he attitude of this realism towards the world is a curious blend of irrationalism and intellectualism. It is a radical irrationalism, for the world must not be conceived as amenable to the demands of human rationality. It is a radical intellectualism, for the intellect is the only true arbiter of cognition, and to allow it to be influenced by considerations of love or hate, or religious or moral edification, is to pervert judgment.[150]

Quick thinks that while this irrational intellectualism suffices for scientific method, it will not serve as the basis for a metaphysic, for it wrongly assumes that 'value is not a fundamental or ultimate or universal or categorial (to borrow Dr Alexander's term) feature of reality'. Its strictly impartial attitude towards the reception of things both good and evil 'does not really accept those facts both as good and evil, but as neither good nor evil. Consequently, if it claims to give a metaphysical account of the universe, it must assume at the outset that value is not a fundamental determinant of all reality.'[151] The contrary is in fact the case, and

---

[149] Idem, *Essays in Orthodoxy*, xlii–xliii.

[150] Idem, 'Value as a metaphysical principle', *The Hibbert Journal*, October 1923–July 1924, 126.

[151] Ibid., 127. Quick surmises that 'It is at least probable that the almost undisguisedly cynical utterances of some realistic metaphysicians argue not so much scientific detachment as repressed sympathies; and this impression is greatly confirmed when their excessively "tough-minded" theories of the universe are accompanied by an almost sentimental championship of the under-dog in society – a championship which, when dispassionately judged in the light of their own theories, is merely absurd.' Ibid., 135.

'all rational explanation, however cold-blooded, regards value as ultimate, and derives existence from value, not value from existence. Rationality, or intellectual value, is no less a value than moral goodness or beauty. And rationalism makes appreciation, not mere cognition, the key to ultimate truth, no less than the most sentimental of Hymns Ancient and Modern.'[152] For this reason the new realism must be, not rejected, but transcended, and Quick suggests that 'a metaphysic of value does seem to offer some hope of making what is right in practice cohere with what is true in theory'.[153] He finds the key to such a metaphysic in Christianity's 'ethic of creative self-sacrifice'. In this ethic the supreme moral value is the self-denying service of goodness, and it is believed that all true self-sacrifice is creative, its end being 'the realization of a perfectly good and happy world; and it cannot be truly creative, if the very thing which it strives and spends all to create is in the end nothing but a delusive dream'.[154] The activism inherent in this approach to Christian ethics meant much to Quick: 'There is a school of Christian piety which comes perilously near to insinuating that a prolonged and fervent crying of "Lord, Lord" will atone for the absence of any equally prolonged and fervent effort to do what the Lord said.'[155]

Quick's approach in Christian ethics finds clear expression in relation to a particular issue in his short but important study of *Christianity and Justice*, which was published near the beginning of the Second World War. He sets out from the contention that justice is a moral, and not simply a legal, principle, for laws can be unjust and are open to criticism; and he then shows that our conception of justice turns upon our conception of the state. The alternatives are: 'Is the State to be regarded as analogous to an organism in which the members are component cells existing to maintain the whole? Or does the State exist to make possible a fellowship in which each individual member realizes his own good in promoting that of others?'[156] The former is essentially totalitarian; the latter is difficult to justify metaphysically unless 'the individual stands in some direct relation to the eternal'.[157] Indeed, 'It is the new and radical disbelief in eternity, ... which is the real cause of a new and radical totalitarianism.'[158] The true view of the state is that it is neither totalitarian nor irredeemably evil.

Quick proceeds to reflect upon punishment, pacifism and war, but we may drive to the heart of his position with this quotation:

---

[152] Ibid., 128. The title of the hymnal is not italicized in the original.

[153] Ibid., 135.

[154] Idem, 'Goodness and happiness', in *Christianity and the Present Moral Unrest*, London: Allen & Unwin, n.d., 81.

[155] Idem, 'Reason and Christian experience. I. Apologetics rational and empirical', *Theology*, XV, October 1927, 190.

[156] Idem, *Christianity and Justice*, London: The Sheldon Press, 1940, 5.

[157] Ibid., 6.

[158] Ibid., 7.

Christianity is a religion which has made the universal justice of God an article of faith; it has insisted, sometimes passionately, on the natural rights and duties of man and on the authority of the individual conscience. But it has never preached a God of mere justice and judgment, the apotheosis of an impartial law. It has condemned mere moralism as the heresy of Pelagius. To it God has always been primarily the living creator who is the victor over evil and the saviour from sin; God's justice is but one aspect or consequence of his all-creating and all-redeeming love.[159]

In other words, 'Justice is good, but it is not a gospel; and therefore few men will die for it unless they see beyond it.'[160] On the other hand, 'It is justice, not love, which is the ideal of "the social order". The more just the social order, the more clearly the gospel will be able to convict men of personal sin in the deepest and most hopeful sense.'[161]

By now it will be abundantly clear that whether Quick is reflecting upon older theisms, prevailing philosophical stances, apologetic method or ethics, a dogmatic strain runs through all his work. This is another way of saying that while, unlike some of the philosophers of his day, he will not rule metaphysics out of court, he will not allow it the last word. Indeed we might say that for Quick, dogma fulfils metaphysics. Metaphysicians are divided among themselves, he says; the subject is so specialized that it cannot 'inspire all the activities of life with the vision of a common goal. ... The metaphysician fails to sympathise with the grocer.'[162] For this reason 'Theology, just because it is to dogmatise about the ultimate ends of life, must be more inclusive than any system of philosophy has any right to be. ... Theology ... must never become attached to, or identified with, any one system.'[163] We return to history: 'it is precisely because the life of Christ alone enables reason and conscience to see light and order where before there was chaos, that we acknowledge Him to be one with the Eternal Word, by Whom all things were made'.[164] Of course faith is involved here; of course dogma is involved, for the declaration is made on the authority of the Revealer; but, Quick insists, in what must have appeared as fighting talk to the Bertrand Russells of his day, 'The only hope for philosophy is to make terms with dogma.'[165] Faith cannot be avoided, for what is declared is that the supreme external Reality has made himself known in the Incarnation in the terms of common humanity; and that conviction is, to repeat,

---

[159] Ibid., 25.
[160] Ibid., 60.
[161] Ibid., 67.
[162] Idem, *Modern Philosophy and the Incarnation*, 20.
[163] Ibid., 24. Cf. idem, *Essays in Orthodoxy*, 69.
[164] Idem, *The Cross and Moral Philosophy*, 48; cf. idem, *Essays in Orthodoxy*, 236–7.
[165] Idem, *Moral Philosophy and the Incarnation*, 87.

held on the authority of the Revealer: it is a dogma. Nor is this faith blind, 'for it has already seen the goal to which it presses.'[166]

'Doctrine is what the Church teaches,' writes Quick, 'dogma what she authoritatively affirms. But clearly what she affirms she must teach, and what she teaches she must authoritatively affirm.'[167] What, then, does the Church authoritatively teach?

III

Following an account of Quick's understanding of the role of creeds as such, I shall outline his position on some major Christian doctrines, reserving ecclesiological and sacramental matters to the following section.

Lest any should be tempted to think otherwise, Quick forthrightly declares that 'The real and permanent object of Christian faith is, not the Creeds, but Christ and his gospel.'[168] Faith is not to be confused with assent to formulae, yet, sadly, this was the impression conveyed by medieval orthodoxy: 'The formulations of the Creeds were taken as the inerrant statement in philosophical scientific terms of Christian belief, and thereby a spurious infallibility was lent to the philosophy and science the language of which they had borrowed.'[169] When the philosophical shell came to be discredited, the gospel kernel was at risk. Hence the current situation which is that 'the heirs of the Reformation have at length expelled one devil of tyranny only to leave the Church's house swept and garnished for the reception of seven devils of confusion'.[170] In fact, 'A living faith must re-express and reinterpret ancient truths, and make ever-fresh discoveries of their meaning.'[171] In this connection the creeds have a conserving and a safeguarding function. At the heart of the gospel is the mystery of the incarnation; the creeds declare this, they do not explain it, but they are intended to 'preserve it from being explained away'.[172] The creeds are directed against heresy, but it would be anachronistic to suppose that they had modern agnosticism in their sights. Rather, 'They were aimed entirely at confident teachers of a different, easier, and less mysterious faith. And that surely should be their purpose still.'[173] This is doubly the case in an intellectual context of competing philosophies: 'Far better that the eternal youth of [the Church's] revelation should remain venerable in a dress which is confessedly

---

[166] Ibid., 91.
[167] Ibid., 9 n.
[168] Idem, *Doctrines of the Creed*, 18.
[169] Idem, *The Testing of Church Principles*, 19.
[170] Ibid., 23.
[171] Idem, *Doctrines of the Creed*, 18.
[172] Idem, *Essays in Orthodoxy*, 58.
[173] Ibid., 183.

out of date. Perhaps, after all, the dress is not less becoming than some more recent fashions.'[174]

It will be convenient to present the several Christian doctrines in the order in which Quick takes them in *The Doctrines of the Creed*, but I shall draw supplementary material from his other writings as appropriate. In discussing God as Creator, Quick notes the ambiguity of 'first cause'. It may have a temporal reference as denoting the first event in a causal series of events; or it may denote 'the *explanation* of a process or series of events, i.e. that which causes it to exist as its reason or ground'.[175] Religion is especially concerned with the latter. For all the light that science sheds on the Creator's method of working, no answer to the question why the world exists at all is possible from the side of science. On the contrary, 'The efforts made from the scientific point of view to dispute the belief of religion in a Divine Creator, too often resemble an attempt to prove that music is unreal, on the ground that nothing is learned about it by taking a piano to pieces.'[176] But if Quick is concerned to keep science in its place, he is no less concerned to repudiate that 'false supernaturalism which would teach that God's activity in the created world is to be looked for mainly in occasional acts which are to be conceived of as interventions from without into its ordered working'.[177]

Why does God create? Quick answers, 'not to supply his own need out of what is beyond himself, but rather from pure love of creation and out of the riches of his own eternal being. Every human analogy at this point inevitably breaks down.'[178] We may say, however, that God's purpose is that the created order shall be reflective of his love, and that to the extent that it is not, he must deal with it by an incarnation entailing *kenosis*. All of which is to recast the concept of omnipotence:

> Outside the abstractions of metaphysics, omnipotence never meant capacity to do anything and everything, but power to achieve a universal purpose in all things. Its practical meaning is to assure us, not that God can do anything that is not impossible, but that certain things are possible for God, and that His purpose of universal love can really be attained. ... [We must not] consider power apart from the thing, or concrete activity, which is powerful. *Mere* power is mere potentiality, and potentiality by itself is just a long word for nothing.

If, on the other hand, the universe is conceived as fulfilling a single purpose of goodness, it is at once evident that the doctrine of omnipotence and the doctrine of perfect atonement are really saying the same thing, and must stand or fall together. For the world can only fulfil its purpose, if its sin can be taken away, and the evil

---

[174] Idem, *Modern Philosophy and the Incarnation*, 55.
[175] Idem, *Doctrines of the Creed*, 47.
[176] Idem, *Essays in Orthodoxy*, 17.
[177] Idem, *Doctrines of the Creed*, 50.
[178] Ibid., 54.

element in things redeemed, so as to become in its final result contributory to the goodness of the whole. This is exactly what the doctrine of Atonement seeks to assert; and, if the assertion be vindicated, the omnipotence of God is vindicated also.[179]

I have quoted at length here in order to show that Quick properly relates creation and recreation; takes sin with full seriousness; and, unlike some of his Anglican contemporaries, brings the atonement, and not simply the incarnation (whether construed after the fashion of philosophical idealism or not), to the fore in all his theologizing. To put the point otherwise: although on the one hand Quick describes himself as a logos theologian – not least as over against Barthians – he is not of the kind to bypass the historic Cross; and he protests against metaphysicians who take the incarnation 'as signifying merely a general truth of divine immanence'.[180] Nor does he overlook the eschatological dimension: 'In Christ, God's whole work of creation and redemption is complete; yet in Christ's members, still living in this world, it remains to be achieved.'[181] We shall do well to have these considerations in mind as we turn to his understanding of the doctrines of the incarnation and salvation.

Though not primarily a biblical scholar, Quick roots his doctrinal studies in the Bible. In particular he reviews New Testament teaching on God, our knowledge of God, and salvation, drawing a sharper distinction between Hebraic and Hellenic conceptions of these matters than some more recent scholars would accept; but this need not detain us here. Not surprisingly, he pays particular attention to Paul, the Johannine writings and the letter to the Hebrews. He finds that for Paul the stages in God's plan of salvation are

> First, the Christ veiling his glory in the form of a servant crucified for men: next, the word of atonement and forgiveness, and Christ speaking in the half-darkness to the spiritual ears of believers whom he guided: finally, the day broken, and the Christ seen face to face in a wholly transfigured and glorious world.[182]

By contrast with Paul, the Johannine writings are not imbued with eschatology, and the term 'hope' is used only once in them. For John the glory of the Lord is already revealed, and whereas with Paul the opposition is sometimes between spirit and flesh, with John it is between God's Spirit-quickened children and 'the world outside which has no true life at all'.[183] If Paul's characteristic word is grace, John's is truth; where to Paul the earthly life of Jesus is 'the supremely effective

---

[179] Idem, *The Christian Sacraments*, 91–2. See also idem, *The Doctrines of the Creed*, ch. 7.

[180] Ibid., 68.

[181] Idem, *Doctrines of the Creed*, 58. He regrets that 'some classical treatises on the doctrine of the atonement are gravely incomplete, because they do not face the eschatological issues which are raised by the very nature of the doctrine itself'. Ibid., 197.

[182] Ibid., 107.

[183] Ibid., 117.

act of God's love, to St. John it is its uniquely true symbol or expression'.[184] On this Quick remarks, 'When Christian thought has succeeded in doing justice to both aspects of the truth together, Christology will be complete.'[185]

Turning to Hebrews, Quick finds that here, in contrast to the rest of the New Testament, the emphasis is upon humanity's approach to God, not *vice versa*. If, in their different ways, Paul and John speak of God as coming to humanity in Christ, the author of Hebrews sees Christ as the perfect high priest who enables our approach to God. At the same time he knows that God has spoken to us in his Son, and, using the analogy of the veil which obscured the inner shrine of the tabernacle, he declares that Christ has come to us from God, through the veil erected by sin. Moreover, 'the sacrifice of Christ avails for Christians, because his offered life of obedience in all its heavenly and spiritual power is communicated to them from the unseen world in answer to their faith'.[186]

There follows a brief sketch of the history of Christological doctrine. Quick finds that while the Fathers constantly affirmed the incarnation, they could never fully square it with their view of divine immutability not as signifying 'moral steadfastness of will and purpose' but as 'ontological unchangeableness' – impassibility. Some more recent scholars have queried the accuracy of this account of the Fathers' view but, however that may be, Quick is surely correct in asserting of the Chalcedonian Formula that its great lacuna is the lack of any interpretation of 'the saving act of God in the human life of him "who for us men and for our salvation came down from heaven"'.[187] Donald Mackinnon reports a conversation with Quick in which the latter declared that in this Nicene clause was to be found 'the dividing line between permissible and impermissible deviations from the norm of Christian orthodoxy'.[188] Accordingly, when discussing kenotic Christologies Quick argues that 'if we conceive God's changelessness to consist simply in the absolute steadfastness of his perfect will of love, we can at once deny that the self-limitation of the eternal Son in the historical manhood of Jesus involves any real variableness in the deity; since it is the consistency of God's love for man which the very cause and ground of the self-limitation'.[189] It is imperative, he continues, that we 'build our Christology on that fundamental conception of God's nature as eternal *agape*'.[190] That is to say, 'Our guiding idea must be that the historic life of Jesus is the supremely characteristic action of God's love', and

---

[184] Ibid., 119.

[185] Ibid.

[186] Ibid., 128–9.

[187] Ibid., 133. Cf. ibid, 194: 'Neither divine nor human nature, considered *in se*, is changed by incarnation, but a new relation between them is established by divine act.' See also, *The Gospel of Divine Action*, 93–4, 96–7.

[188] D. M. Mackinnon, 'Oliver Chase Quick as a theologian', 103.

[189] Ibid., 144.

[190] O. C. Quick, *Doctrines of the Creed*, 150.

'Such love ... can only be revealed to man in person and in act.'[191] Moreover, this revelation 'is absolutely final, because it is inseparable from the final victory which Christ accomplished'.[192]

Let us pause to take stock of Quick on impassibility. Clearly, he cannot rest content with a God conceived as static, remote, unmoved by human sin and suffering. He will not divorce God's power from his love. On the contrary, 'His almighty power is itself and characteristically the power of the love which suffers and wins, not that weaker and illusory power of force which can only compel.'[193] The underlying question is whether, as many medieval theologians insisted, God, *qua* eternal, is for ever above and beyond time and, *a fortiori*, living in bliss beyond suffering and pain. It seems to me that in face of the *a priori* claim that this is the case a reverent agnosticism is called for. What does seem clear, and what Quick avers, is that the Father suffers in his Son: indeed, that any *kenosis* having redemptive purpose must, given humanity's sin and the world's 'groaning and travailing', necessarily entail suffering. It seems to me that the two pitfalls which need to be avoided are first, that of forgetting that the triune Godhead is not divorced from the actions of any of the three persons; and secondly, that of supposing that there is an impassible 'God beyond God' – a claim which we are too ignorant to make. While it is logically conceivable that there is much *more* to the Godhead than has been revealed to us, it would be a gross slight upon God's integrity to suppose that anything beyond what has been made known to us would contradict, invalidate, or otherwise undermine what he has been pleased to reveal to us. The soundest theology is ever built upon the revelation given, not upon *a priori* speculations – speculations which, oddly enough, are frequently promulgated by those who make most of the appeal to mystery.[194]

It remains to add that in Quick's view

> Christ's victorious and redemptive life not only reveals God's love but also embodies in manhood man's own true ideal of human goodness. That is the truth which Christian humanists from Abélard to the Liberal Protestants have persistently vindicated, and which Augustinians and modern Barthians too often reject. God created man's spirit to mirror his love, and never has the glass been completely darkened by sin.[195]

The viability of Quick's overall position clearly turns upon the acceptability of the two-nature doctrine of the person of Christ. This, for Quick, is a datum: 'We are compelled ... at the outset to declare that our Lord does unite the Divine and

---

[191] Ibid., 150–51.
[192] Ibid., 151.
[193] Idem, *Liberalism, Modernism and Tradition*, 22.
[194] See further Alan P. F. Sell, *Hinterland Theology. A Stimulus to Theological Construction*, Milton Keynes: Paternoster, 2008, 606–10.
[195] O. C. Quick, *Doctrines of the Creed*, 152.

human natures; that He is God and Man.'[196] Neither the Arian demi-god will suffice, nor will the 'intolerable limitation on the gospel' proposed by writers like Evelyn Underhill, who confine 'the Christian character in our Lord Himself and in his followers to one specific and rare psychological type'. In both cases there is imposed a barrier between God and humanity in general, whereas the fact of the incarnation is their union.[197] But although the union of the two natures in Christ is to be clearly asserted, their distinctness must be as clearly noted. For 'even in Christ manhood is not itself deified. To make the distinction between God and man into an insuperable barrier is the sin of idolatry; to seek to remove it altogether is the sin of a perverted mysticism.'[198]

It should also be remembered, says Quick, that 'The original Gospel of the Church consisted in the Inacarnation and the Atonement conceived, not as theological doctrines, but as evangelical facts.'[199] Thus,

> The psychological order in which Christology was reached gives us the following sequence. (1) The new human life of fellowship comes (2) through Jesus Christ (3) from God. The logical order in which Christology is stated inverts the sequence. (1) God (2) through Jesus Christ (3) gives the new life of fellowship to men.[200]

Crucially, the thoughts which led to the two-nature doctrine sprang from the experience of those who rejoiced in the Gospel of resurrection and had experienced new life in the Spirit.[201] Theoretically, 'the notion that Jesus Christ can represent God to man, without being really identical in Godhead with the Father, is just as repugnant to the reason as the notion that he can represent men to God, without their being really identified with Him in the inmost nature of their manhood'.[202] Elsewhere he adds the caution that

> There is ... an ultimate difference between the indwelling of the Godhead in Christ and the indwelling of the Godhead in an ordinary human being, however truly redeemed and perfected. Christ is God from the beginning. In his Incarnation He takes up manhood into Himself and revealed Himself through it, but the Godhead remains His own proper and essential nature. In the ordinary man ... the indwelling of the divine nature is a gift from without bestowed by the grace

---

[196] Idem, *Modern Philosophy and the Incarnation*, 49.
[197] Ibid., 50–51.
[198] Idem, *Essays in Orthodoxy*, 50–51.
[199] Idem, *The Testing of Church Principles*, 16.
[200] Idem, *Liberalism, Modernism and Tradition*, 96. I should add 'by the Spirit' at the end the third point of the psychological sequence, and at the beginning of the first point of the logical sequence, thereby casting the whole in trinitarian terms.
[201] See O. C. Quick, *Christian Beliefs and Modern Questions*, 47–51.
[202] Idem, *The Christian Sacraments*, 72.

of God.²⁰³ ... Sin is the only barrier to that union. But the union only takes place in and through Christ.²⁰⁴

My preferred way of stating this is to say with Paul that Christ is Son of God by right from the beginning, and that we, by grace, may become sons and daughters by adoption. Whatever form of words is used, Quick returns to the notion of Christ's two natures as a datum when he cautions that 'the mode of their union is left, as it must always remain, a mystery'.²⁰⁵

Not reluctant to theorize as far as that is appropriate, Quick's thought is never far from practical considerations. Thus he declares, 'If God through Jesus has accomplished something different in kind from what He has accomplished through any other man, we have a perfect right, nay we are bound, to say that Jesus, though truly man, is yet also truly different in kind from all other men.'²⁰⁶ What, then, has Christ done? We have already noted Quick's strong emphasis upon Jesus as both revealer of God's love and as God's love in action. Indeed, among his criticisms of Platonist constructions of Christology is that it misses the essential point that 'God is not only truly revealed in Jesus, but that he has decisively and finally acted.'²⁰⁷ It must be said that on occasion Quick himself so emphasizes the objective of the divine-human union as to omit reference to what had to be *done* to secure it. Thus, for example, he writes, 'The revelation in Himself of that communion between two distinct natures is the whole meaning of Christ's Person, the fulfilment of that communion in the world is the whole purpose of Christianity. There, in a sentence, is the Christian gospel.'²⁰⁸ I fear not: there is an attenuated gospel. More characteristically,

> The life, death, resurrection and ascension of Jesus taken together are the symbol of the plan and purpose which God is achieving through the spatio-temporal world as a whole. But the Cross which is the redemptive act of surrender is the cardinal point in the symbol; it is only because the act is real in fact that it is truly symbolic.²⁰⁹

This is consistent with Quick's finding that 'In the New Testament the thought that God has acted in Jesus is the foundation of the whole doctrine of Christ's Person.'²¹⁰

---

²⁰³ It is, accordingly, an odd form of words to say that 'In Christ's Manhood humanity *has redeemed itself* (my italics). See O. C. Quick, *Essays in Orthodoxy*, 300.
²⁰⁴ Idem, *Essays in Orthodoxy*, 61–2.
²⁰⁵ Ibid., 68.
²⁰⁶ Idem, *Liberalism, Modernism and Tradition*, 140.
²⁰⁷ Idem, *Doctrines of the Creed*, 140.
²⁰⁸ Idem, *Essays in Orthodoxy*, 45.
²⁰⁹ Idem, *The Gospel of Divine Action*, 114.
²¹⁰ Ibid., 102.

What, then, was the crucial act, and why was it needed? We may set out from Quick's clear grasp of the reality of sin as being that with which the Saviour must deal.[211] In the most general terms Quick declares that 'When all apologists have had their say, it remains true that man's fundamental discontent is God's most universal witness; and discontent implies some sort of effort after some kind of salvation.'[212] Christianity, however, is more specific: 'the radical evil in the world is sin', and this is presupposed by the doctrines of atonement, judgement, heaven and hell, and apart from this presupposition they are unintelligible.[213] Jesus Christ is the Saviour from sin. Accordingly, in face of those rational apologists who lose the historical Cross, those thinkers who present Christ as simply the embodiment of a moral ideal and sin as simply a 'growing pain of man's moral nature',[214] 'Christian devotion cries out that philosophy has taken away its Lord.'[215]

Although Quick takes sin with utter seriousness, he does not endorse exaggerated accounts of original sin and total depravity, for these deny human beings their proper responsibility and posit irresistible grace as the only remedy for sin. 'But,' he continues, 'if saving grace be irresistible, there can be no reason why God should not save all men, if he saves any.'[216] At this point I demur. For 'irresistible grace' need not be construed as sheer force: it can mean that God's grace is so winsome that none who experience it would resist it.

As we might by now expect, Quick is equally opposed to Platonic and Aristotelian views which understand humanity's predicament as requiring the dissipation of error, and hence theophany; and not forgiveness and salvation from sin, and hence atonement.[217] Augustine was inconsistent in deriving the doctrine of evil as a privation of good from the Greeks, whilst also upholding the biblical belief in evil as sin; while Aquinas holds that since God is the efficient cause of all that is, and that what is, is good, evil can have no real being at all, since God cannot be its author.[218] Quick's own view is that 'we may ascribe the origin of all

---

[211] As I leave Quick's Christological views I am conscious that I have not referred to his position regarding the Virgin Birth. Suffice it to say that, no more than the New Testament itself, does he build his account of Christ's person on this doctrine. He notes that the New Testament does not connect belief in the Virgin Birth with belief in saving faith, but when he thinks of what is said in the New Testament, of the tradition of the Church, and of Marian devotion, he does not find it easy to conclude that these things have their origin not in historic fact but in pious myth. See *Doctrines of the Creed*, 166–9. The supremely important question is whether the belief deepens and protects the mystery of God's love as revealed by Christ. See *Essays in Orthodoxy*, 303–4.

[212] O. C. Quick, *The Doctrines of the Creed*, 199.

[213] Ibid., 201.

[214] Idem, *Essays in Orthodoxy*, 131.

[215] Idem, *The Ground of Faith and the Chaos of Thought*, 64.

[216] Idem, *The Gospel of the New World*, 43.

[217] See O. C. Quick, *Doctrines of the Creed*, 201.

[218] See idem, *The Gospel of the New World*, 21–6.

evil to finite free will', and thus 'we can account intelligibly for the fact that evil has entered a world wholly created by God, and as created, wholly good'.[219] The essence of sin is the abuse of God-given freedom in order to disobey God's will. In all of this 'It is sin that blinds the intellect, not ignorance that causes sin.'[220] The consequence of sin is a breach of personal relationship with God and hence to separation from him.[221] As he strikingly puts it, 'Fashioned truly in the image of God, [man] makes himself into an idol, because he will not be a sacrament.'[222] Thus at the heart of sin is not simply the rejection of sovereign law, but the prideful rejection of God's love and hence of eternal life.[223]

From all of this it is clear that in Quick's opinion salvation is not just from suffering and pain, but from moral wrong, and it issues in a restored God-humanity relationship. How is this brought about? By Christ's atoning work at the Cross. If the incarnation is 'the sacrament of God's self-expression',[224] the atonement is 'the sacrament of God's power in act'. Moreover, while 'it is on the reality of the Incarnation that the whole possibility of redemption depends ... the Atonement is the primary aim and purpose of the Incarnation, since it was to save His people from their sins that Jesus was born'.[225] The Cross, the apparent instrument of defeat, becomes the instrument of God's power, 'For it is the instrument of good whereby evil itself is made instrumental to goodness. It is the means of real *conversion.*'[226] Nor is the significance of the Cross merely individual or local; it is cosmic:

> [W]hen it is asserted that the Atonement wrought by the Cross of Christ is universal and all-sufficient, we desire to understand that the Crucified Saviour is in space and time the one perfect sacrament of the power by which in the end, or in the whole, all evil is redeemed, and the rational perfection of the universe vindicated and fulfilled.[227]

In view of all of this, Quick's assertion, when contrasting Catholicism with Protestantism, that Protestantism is like Platonism in that to it '*History does not matter*'[228] is nothing short of staggering, the fact that there have been other-worldly Protestants notwithstanding. However it may be with Platonism, in Protestantism,

---

[219] Ibid., 27.
[220] Ibid., 33. Cf. idem, *Doctrines of the Creed*, 213.
[221] See idem, *Essays in Orthodoxy*, 89, 91.
[222] Idem, *The Realism of Christ's Parables*, London: SCM Press, 1931, 50–51.
[223] See idem, *Doctrines of the Creed*, 209, 214–15. Cf. idem, *The Ground of Faith and the Chaos of Thought*, 138.
[224] Idem, *The Christian Sacraments*, 102.
[225] Idem, *Essays in Orthodoxy*, 77.
[226] Idem, *The Christian Sacraments*, 90; cf. idem, *Christian Beliefs and Modern Questions*, 39–40.
[227] Idem, *The Christian Sacraments*, 94.
[228] Idem, *Catholic and Protestant Elements in Christianity*, 112, his italics.

surely, the Cross is the centre of history, and history is the stage on which the drama of redemption is played out.

Quick reviews ancient and modern atonement doctrines and finds that they all have a contribution to make:

> Abelardian theories are seen to be true to the utmost, as far as they go. The cross and resurrection are indeed the unique demonstration of God's eternal love for man. But they are that demonstration, just because they are something infinitely more than a mere demonstration. They bring into being the manhood of the world to come, the first-fruits of the new creation, the sacrificed and living manhood of Christ, who through that manhood has become the head of his Church. ... Juridical theories again are entirely true as far as they go – provided they avoid the false suggestion that Christ's death propitiated God so as to change his attitude towards man from wrath to love. Christ in his perfect holiness did undergo the shameful death which was the penalty of sin. But the avail of that death is due less to any supposed 'transference of merit' than to the very fact that by thus dying Christ changed penalty into sacrifice and shame into glory, and by his risen life enables his faithful followers to do the same.[229]

The main elements in Quick's constructive doctrine of the atonement may be indicated by three terms: sacrifice, resurrection and new life. Christ's sacrifice at the Cross, his 'willing surrender and expenditure of existing goods ... is the very means whereby that which exists as evil is overcome, and made in the end contributory to goodness'.[230] The perfect sacrifice 'can only be achieved by the divine love which in Jesus has shown itself willing to share the utterly unholy death of the criminal which is the penalty for sin'.[231] But 'The atonement of the cross would not be complete apart from the resurrection.'[232] Indeed, the 'metamorphosis of death is the most essential and enduring miracle of Christ.'[233] It means the 'restoration of life after death and possibly through death', whereas philosophical conceptions of immortality imply 'persistence of life untouched by death'.[234] Moreover, the death and resurrection of Christ 'meant something much more than the liberation of His spiritual self from an outworn vesture of flesh and blood. ... The whole man had died and risen, and risen because He had been content to die.'[235] Nor was this act simply for himself alone: it has cosmic significance, for in Christ humanity is raised to newness of life: 'manhood at once receives its new

---

[229] Idem, *The Gospel of the New World*, 103. Cf. idem, *Christian Beliefs and Modern Questions*, 66–73.
[230] Idem, *The Christian Sacraments*, 93.
[231] Idem, *The Gospel of the New World*, 101.
[232] Idem, *Doctrines of the Creed*, 217.
[233] Idem, *Christianity and Justice*, 39.
[234] Idem, *The Christian Sacraments*, 103.
[235] Ibid., 107.

life, whole, glorious, and eternal, in God and from God. That is the meaning of the resurrection; and bodily resurrection was necessary, if only because the death could not have been thought of as an accepted sacrifice at all, if the body had "seen corruption" in the tomb.'[236] Hence the significance of the empty tomb – for Quick a fact of unparallelled importance. How does this cosmic event bear upon the individual Christian? Quick answers,

> [W]hat the forgiven Christian has received in Christ is admission to the life of sonship in God's new-created world, and this is inconceivable apart from the fact that the new creation has had its beginning through the resurrection of Jesus Christ. Forgiveness loses its full redemptive effect and issue, unless it implies communion with and in the manhood of him who died and rose again not only that we might be forgiven but also that we might be created anew and set in a new relationship with God.[237]

Moreover, this new relationship concerns not merely things spiritual, but entails the transformation of man's whole being.[238] And, as in the thought of Paul, it is a new life marked by the anticipation of 'the next world, of which Christ Himself is the first fruit. The spirit of the Christian is already risen and dwells with Christ in the other world.'[239] The eschatological dimension of the new life is ineradicable.

The new life is in the first place, life eternal, both here and now and to come.[240] It is 'not life *apart from death*, not life merely *after* physical death, but life *through* death, completed both through the death of the body and the self-surrender of the spirit'.[241] It is also life under judgement. Judgement is not a matter for the 'last day' only: 'It is going on now, continuously.'[242] Thus, 'when the word "last" is used in relation to purpose, "the last thing" does not denote simply or mainly the thing which comes after all others in a series, but that which fulfils the purpose of the whole'.[243] As to the Last Day itself, while, as love, God must will that all souls should finally be saved, he must reject any whose final choice is of evil. It would be foreign to the whole tenor of the Gospel as God's free gift of salvation were any to be forced to accept it. Accordingly, 'That all souls will be saved ... is a Christian hope; but it cannot be a Christian dogma.'[244] As to speculations concerning an

---

[236] Idem, *The Gospel of the New World*, 102; cf. ibid., 114.
[237] Idem, 53.
[238] Ibid., 57.
[239] Idem, *The Gospel of Divine Action*, 75.
[240] See idem, *Essays in Orthodoxy*, 148–9.
[241] Idem, *Christian Beliefs and Modern Questions*, 85.
[242] Ibid., 101.
[243] Idem, *Doctrines of the Creed*, 250. For I. T. Ramsey's discussion of Quick's analysis of 'last' see his *Freedom and Immortality*, London: SCM Press, 1960, 127–9.
[244] Idem, *Christian Beliefs and Modern Questions*, 103; cf. idem, *The Doctrines of the Creed*, 259.

intermediate state between death and the final judgement, Quick says that while such an inference may be supportable from scripture and from 'the commonsense of the Christian conscience, ... it is utterly dangerous in our own case to build on the possibilities of an intermediate state which our Lord has left unrevealed, and to neglect His express warning that the Son of Man cometh suddenly, in an hour when we think not'.[245] More legitimate, thinks Quick, is the speculation that beyond the final judgement there must be 'the fulfilment of God's purpose in a universe which in every corner mirrors and expresses the praise of his goodness'.[246]

A further result of the resurrection is that it paves the way for Christ's gift of his Spirit to the Church; and here we come to Quick's understanding of the Holy Spirit. 'In its widest range', Quick writes, 'the doctrine of the Holy Spirit is nothing else than the manner and method of the presence and activity of the living God in his created world.'[247] The Holy Spirit, who proceeds from the Father and the Son, has eternally proceeded from the eternal Word. A person distinct from Christ, his particular role is to bring 'the presence of the Ascended Christ into the souls of men'.[248] He both witnesses to Christ and enables our confession of faith, and is the agent of our sanctification. Once again, the importance of history is noted by Quick, for the historic facts of Christ's life, death and resurrection supply the criteria by which we test the spirits which would claim our allegiance. It will not suffice to be guided by strength of emotional experience, to be satisfied by a principle of immanence, or to go in quest of a-historical mystical communion. As if putting his finger on tendencies which are very much alive at the beginning of the twenty-first century with its amorphous, sometimes self-serving, 'spiritualities', Quick insists that if we do not test the spirits, 'Either we shall be left at the mercy of every cross-current of pious feeling or shifting wind of specious argument, or, still worse, we shall be led to rely on the *form* of spiritual activity as its only trustworthy credential.'[249]

As Sanctifier, the Holy Spirit guides believers in the way of holiness, informing their ethical decision-making, urging them to do the right, and reproving them when they do not. In this connection Quick characterizes the teaching of Jesus as elevating the right spiritual attitude above outward acts: 'our Lord substituted the principle of the sanctification of all life from within for the law which imposes from without certain definite prohibitions and injunctions'.[250] I cannot suppress the feeling that this is an unfortunate mode of expression, suggesting as it does

---

[245] Idem, *Essays in Orthodoxy*, 141, 143.

[246] Idem, *Doctrines of the Creed*, 247.

[247] Ibid., 272.

[248] Idem, *Essays in Orthodoxy*, 208. In this book Quick oscillates between masculine and neuter pronouns when referring to the Spirit. In later works he consistently uses masculine pronouns of the Spirit.

[249] Ibid., 233. Cf. idem, *Doctrines of the Creed*, 297–8. See also Alan P. F. Sell, *Enlightenment, Ecumenism, Evangel*, ch. 8.

[250] Idem, *Essays in Orthodoxy*, 260.

that Jesus drives a wedge between God's law and a believer's inner dispositions, dispensing with the former. I should rather say that those on the way to sanctification are those best placed to fulfil the law, guided and empowered as they are by the Spirit of Jesus, who in his words and actions drove to the law's heart.

It was Quick's intention to write substantially on the Trinity, but his relatively early death prevented this.[251] We do, however, have sufficient clues in his writings as to the direction his thought would have taken. He reminds us that the doctrine of the Trinity was formulated not in order to explain or expound the Christian faith, 'but to prevent unworthy exponents from explaining it away into some fresh form of Western idolatry or Eastern pantheism'.[252] His fundamental conviction on the matter is that 'The Persons of the Trinity are one and inseparable, and it is the self-revelation of the Father thought the Son, witnessed to and interpreted by the Spirit, which gives us our knowledge of the nature and character of God.'[253] As he further explains, 'the Divine Transcendence of the Father, the Divine Mediation of the Word, must be fulfilled by the Divine Immanence of the Spirit. For thus and thus alone is the whole process of earthly life taken up utterly into the Godhead.'[254]

IV

I come finally to Quick's ecclesiological and sacramental views. Since they concern neuralgic issues as between Christians of various traditions, they will remind us of his ecumenical interests. Within a year of the end of the First World War, we find Quick declaring that 'Undoubtedly at the present moment the real centre of religious interest is the possibility of reunion.'[255] The paradoxical situation is, however, that there are two schools of thought, 'equally zealous for religious unity', which 'seek it along diametrically opposite lines, the one through the weakening, the other through the firmer establishment of ecclesiastical authority'.[256] Thus: 'The Protestant tends to say, "Work for unity by inward and spiritual methods only, and then the unity will express itself in union." The Catholic tends to say, "Unite now in external order: that is the very means whereby the full unity of the Spirit is to be brought about."'[257] Quick is well aware that the former can run out into indefiniteness of proclamation, while the danger facing the latter is that 'the living message' is 'hidden and stifled under the machinery which it should control'.[258]

---

[251] See Paul Lucas, 'Oliver Quick', 19.
[252] O. C. Quick, *Essays in Orthodoxy*, 182.
[253] Ibid., 5.
[254] Ibid., 194. The passage of which these words form the conclusion, pp. 192–4, is as concise as it is illuminating on this foundational Christian doctrine.
[255] Idem, *The Testing of Church Principles*, 1.
[256] Ibid.
[257] Idem, *Catholic and Protestant Elements in Christianity*, 36.
[258] Idem, *Essays in Orthodoxy*, xxiii.

Attempting, in his eirenic way, to bring the two schools together, Quick suggests that they need each other, for 'External union cannot produce inward unity of itself. The spirit of unity must flow from a spiritual source.'[259] At this point one could have wished for a more definite exposition of the unity of the Church as being already given by the Father's call through the Spirit to those who, on the ground of the Son's saving work, make an enabled response of faith and live the new life within the renewed covenant body. This being what God in Christ has done by the Spirit, the challenge to manifest (rather than to seek, or otherwise concoct) the given unity is acute.[260] To be in Christ at all is already to be in the one Church. The closest Quick comes to this is when he says that 'The Church is the fellowship of believers who, looking to Jesus the author and end of their faith, understand God's purpose for the world, and carry on his victorious work on earth by the guidance and power of His Spirit. It is the essential nature of the Church to be both holy and catholic.'[261] Two points are required to be made here.

First, what is the analysis of the phrase, 'carry on his victorious work on earth ...'? I suspect that Quick has in mind the idea of the Church as being the continuation of the Incarnation. Elsewhere he writes, '[T]hat which has been redeemed by the atonement of the Cross becomes the body in which Christ Himself is mystically incarnate ...'[262] I in no way deny that the risen and ascended Christ is present with his people (though as to the 'how', 'when' and 'where' of it there have been floods of ecclesiastical debate), but I cannot agree that the empirical Church in some way continues the incarnation, partly because this would seem to reduce the significance of the once-for-all incarnation no less than notions of a repeated sacrificing of Christ at the eucharist threaten the biblical 'once-for-allness' of Christ's atoning work at the Cross; and partly because, as P. T. Forsyth roundly declared, 'It is a regenerated human nature in which Christ dwells. But that cannot be a prolongation of His Incarnation, wherein there was no regeneration. ... The Church is not the continuation of Christ, but His creation and His response.'[263]

Secondly, the emphasis upon the Church as a fellowship of believers leads me to comment upon a certain oscillation in Quick's writings between the Church as a fellowship and the Church of England as a national institution. The former quite regularly recurs in his works:

> The Christian is in love with his brethren because he is in love with God, and in loving his brethren he loves God also.[264]

---

[259] Idem, *Catholic and Protestant Elements in Christianity*, 37.
[260] See further, Alan P. F. Sell, *Enlightenment, Ecumenism, Evangel*, ch. 11.
[261] O. C. Quick, *The Gospel of Divine Action*, 116.
[262] Idem, *The Christian Sacraments*, 108.
[263] P. T. Forsyth, *The Church and the Sacraments* (1917), London: Independent Press, 1953, 82, 83. Cf. Alan P. F. Sell, *Testimony and Tradition. Studies in Reformed and Dissenting Thought*, Aldershot: Ashgate, 2005, 194–6, 201, 207.
[264] O. C. Quick, *Liberalism, Modernism and Tradition*, 130.

> In a sinful world at least the divine love cannot achieve its purpose by distributing itself equally everywhere at once ... it must work through the Cross in a more restricted sense. It must choose out particular vessels to which to commit a special treasure, in order that when the treasure has been protected for a time, the vessel may be broken so that the treasure may be poured out for others.[265]

> [T]he evidence shows that [Jesus] thought of God's true people as made up of believing individuals, and not as a sort of believing organism in which the individual's function was that of a subordinate cell. ... The Church, as the fellowship of the forgiven and redeemed, is commissioned to carry the gospel of new life and hope to all mankind.[266]

If the quoted sentences were all that Quick had to say we should have the basis for the doctrine that the Church comprises Christians, that is, the regenerate. But cutting across this is Quick's unduly sweeping, undiscriminating, judgment upon the position of 'many Nonconformists and Independents', namely, that 'The theory of the purely spiritual Church has failed.'[267] He represents such Christians as saying that 'It is far better ... to allow Christians to join together voluntarily in any form of outward association which suits their various opinions ...'[268] While I cannot deny that some members of the classes referred to may have thought and spoken in this way, no tradition should be judged by its eccentrics. Had Quick had a little more historical sensitivity and accuracy, he would in the first place surely have seen that, at least as far as Old Dissent is concerned, the voluntarism is not that of those who freely choose join a darts club, but that it echoes the position of the Separatist, Robert Browne, who insisted that 'The Lord's people is of the willing sort'[269] – which is to say that people do not become Christians or church members by being legislated into a 'promiscuous', that is, a sacramentally undisciplined, organization in the interests of national cohesion; rather, they respond in faith to the gracious call of the God of the covenant. Secondly, he would have had the grace to appreciate that, often at great cost, they sought not to associate in such a way as to suit their various opinions; they sought to gather in accordance with what they genuinely understood to be scriptural principles. In turn, thirdly, he would have come to an appreciation of the fact that the maligned traditions

---

[265] Idem, *The Ground of Faith and the Chaos of Thought*, 140; cf. ibid., 144.
[266] Idem, *Christianity and Justice*, 46, 57.
[267] Idem, *The Testing of Church Principles*, 139.
[268] Ibid., 139.
[269] R. Browne, *A Treatise of Reformation Without Tarrying for Anie* (1582), in A. Peel and Leland H. Carlson, eds, *The Writings of Robert Harrison and Robert Browne*, London: Allen & Unwin, 1953, 162.

stood not for a spiritual/otherworldly church, but for one comprising gathered, visible, saints.[270]

Another factor which cuts across what Quick has to say about the Church *qua* fellowship of believers, is his swingeing denunciation of Protestantism for the way in which it restricts membership 'to those whose religious experience takes one definite shape – viz. sensible conversion, or the *feeling* of salvation obtained in the atoning blood of Christ'.[271] If such a body wishes to appeal to those outside the fold (and here Quick uncharacteristically verges upon the acid),

> Either the experience of conversion is produced in a spurious form by playing on the emotions, or it is claimed by those quite ignorant of what it means; or else the society is driven to seek some quite different bond of cohesion more or less foreign to the proper nature of religion. It is thus that the distressing phenomena of 'political nonconformity' and the vague sentimentality of Pleasant Sunday Afternoons are to be explained.[272]

The fact cannot have been lost on Quick, however, that in the heyday of Nonconformity in England and Wales the number of those attending the churches always exceeded – sometimes considerably – the number of the enrolled saints. They were the adherents, and their presence gives the lie to Quick's dismissal of the idea of the gathered church as being unable to cater in a variety of ways to non-members.

A final way in which Quick qualifies his understanding of the Church as a fellowship of believers derives from his commitment to the openness of the Church of England to both believers and nominal members. He understands, and regrets, the fact that 'the Church of England has all along been founded on a mere compromise, not on any clear conception of the nature and function of the Christian Church'.[273] He envisages a time when the Church of England will be self-governing: that is, it will no longer be the Church by law established, and he insists that 'The Church stands for a higher principle of association than the group or the race.'[274] Furthermore, he admits that 'Vast numbers of those who at present come to us for marriage, baptism, and burial are by choice and intention not communicants or even believers in Christianity in any sense in which the Church can legitimately accept the term.'[275] Such persons 'have the spirit, not of converts, but of conformists. ... They have become ... inoculated with the germs of a faith ... and they are thereby rendered almost completely immune from the

---

[270] See further, Alan P. F. Sell, *Saints: Visible, Orderly and Catholic. The Congregational Idea of the Church*.
[271] O. C. Quick, *The Testing of Church Principles*, 57.
[272] Ibid., 57–8.
[273] Idem, *The Testing of Church Principles*, 67.
[274] Idem, *Liberalism, Modernism and Tradition*, 124.
[275] Idem, *The Testing of Church Principles*, 107.

infection of a definite Christianity.'[276] Accordingly, he appreciates the strength of the case for restricting the franchise in the coming Church of England to communicant members. But, given that most communicants are drawn from 'the well-to-do classes of society', would not this alienate the masses still further? He therefore envisages a compromise whereby communicant members only would sit on representative councils, but the franchise would be extended to others: 'In this case it will surely be our duty to make it clear to our non-communicant members that their membership is not a full one, and that they have in reality only the status of "adherents".'[277] All of which seems to one friendly (and puzzled) outsider to lead us back to the 'Church within the Church' after all. Moreover his positive recommendations regarding church order are couched in terms of democracy rather than of Christocracy, and this seems to underline his own point in the second sentence of this paragraph, namely, that the Church of England has difficulty in thinking theologically about the nature, composition and order of the Church.[278]

Quick does, however, contribute a particular line of argument which was novel when he propounded it, but which has become more widely accepted as the ecumenical years have advanced: 'Once it is frankly admitted that *every* divided Church, which maintains the Christian faith, is in schism and yet is within the body of the Church Catholic, the hope of a genuinely catholic reunion may be re-born.'[279] A. M. Ramsey correctly remarked that 'Quick's theory had great influence, and various reunion schemes have subconsciously reflected it, but he added that Quick gave 'insufficient weight to the transmission of authority in the Church through history'.[280] With this we come to those ecclesiological and sacramental impediments to the realization of Quick's ecumenical aspiration which turn upon divergent views of authority and orders.

In general terms Quick argues that the authority of the apostolic witness as recorded in the New Testament must be balanced against the guidance of the Holy Spirit which is available to all believers. In particular, 'The Spirit in the Christian laity must not be quenched.'[281] Four pages later, however, he declares that 'The Christian message is that to believe in Jesus Christ, crucified and risen, sets free the soul; and *the freedom depends on the divine authority of those who declare the message*. It is, moreover, a freedom in the communion of the same Spirit who, according to Christ's promise, will always maintain in his Church the authoritative witness to the truth of the gospel, which is Christ himself.'[282] With the assertion

---

[276] Ibid., 53, 68.
[277] Ibid., 113.
[278] See further, Alan P. F. Sell, *Testimony and Tradition*, ch. 13.
[279] O. C. Quick, *Doctrines of the Creed*, 339, his italics.
[280] A. M. Ramsey, *From Gore to Temple. The Development of Anglican Theology between* Lux Mundi *and the Second World War, 1889–1939*, London: Longmans, 1960, 123–4.
[281] O. C. Quick, *Doctrines of the Creed*, 313.
[282] Ibid., 317.

that Christ is the supreme authority in the Church I am, of course, in entire accord. But the words I have italicized seem to me to be problematic. No doubt many of those who 'declare the message' are authorized to do so, but if they forget, as throughout Christian history they have been inclined to do on occasion, that the authority lies in the message – or, rather, the Christ of the message, not in themselves, the freedom of the laity, on which Quick has insisted, is put at risk and even obliterated by heavy-handed ecclesiasticism.

As to church order, or polity, in general, Quick correctly observes that there are many extant varieties, and wisely cautions that 'it is quite wrong to dispute about them as though any one type could represent a sacred principle to which the Church is bound in all circumstances to adhere. For episcopalianism to claim a special divine authority for all time, is merely disastrous.'[283] That this statement of the obvious has not yet been universally endorsed is clear from restorationists whether biblicist or traditionalist who to this day claim that their favoured polity is the only properly sanctioned one. This being the case, and with hindsight, we can conclude only that Quick was being over-optimistic when, in 1927, he wrote, 'If Rome and Canterbury were to agree on the necessary content of Christian faith, it is hard to believe that any questions about Orders and sacraments would create an insuperable barrier'[284] to union between the two communions; for some Anglicans and most Roman Catholics hold that what they believe about orders and sacraments is given in and with the Gospel and is, accordingly, integral to the 'necessary content of Christian faith'. When Quick further surmises that 'Anglicans would doubtless be willing to acknowledge the Pope as primate among all bishops, and, therefore, as in a real sense the head of the visible Church, so long as his claim to jurisdiction were not put forward in such a way as to interfere with what they regard as the legitimate authority of the Catholic diocese or province',[285] the hyper-Protestant obstacle presented by those clergy of the Church of England who today are not convinced that their own Archbishop is a Christian comes into view. I fear that Quick's earlier judgement is the more realistic one. With reference to 'opposed ecclesiastical parties', he lamented that 'Partisans of all sides, "catholic", liberal, and evangelical, have found it easier to brandish flags, to vociferate battle-cries, and to plunge themselves into the business of propaganda, than to think out in their broad theoretic relations the principles which they are so eager to spread.'[286]

Turning to Free Churchmen Quick reflects upon the conversations which led to the Lambeth Appeal for reunion of 1920, and says that as between the Church of England and the Free Churches,

> The gulf which they had no success in bridging was that between the claim of the free Churchmen that their ministries should be recognised as fully valid ministries

---

[283] Ibid., 329.
[284] Idem, *The Christian Sacraments*, 151.
[285] Ibid., 151–2.
[286] Idem, *Essays in Orthodoxy*, xxx.

of the word and sacraments in the universal Church, and the requirement of the Anglicans that Free Church ministers should receive the laying on of hands from a bishop as a condition of inter-communion being established.[287]

Here are raised the issues of apostolic succession and validity. I shall comment briefly on each in turn.

Quick informs us that there are two quite different understandings of apostolic succession. It is construed either as 'a succession in spiritual office and authority', or as signifying 'the transmission of a peculiar gift to the [ordained] individual by means of a particular sign, viz., the act of episcopal consecration ...' For convenience he calls the former view authoritarian, the latter, indelibilist. Of these, the latter 'normally carries with it both the authority of an office in the Church and the grace to exercise it'.[288] What Quick overlooks here is that there is a third interpretation of apostolic succession – one maintained by millions of Christians around the world and not only by the small English Free Churches – namely, that those who proclaim the apostles' Gospel are truly in their succession (the negative implication of which is that, modes of ordination notwithstanding, those who do not so proclaim – heretical bishops come to mind – are not faithful successors of the apostles). From this point of view the concept of 'validity' is deemed to be quite out of place in discussions of ordination. It is not, of course that Free Churchmen are necessarily unconcerned for good order in the Church (though it must be granted that some sit loose to it and think of themselves as 'non-liturgical' when, since 'liturgy' means 'service', they are simply differently – some would say, inadequately – liturgical). I shall return to this understanding of the matter shortly, but first I must express my view that on the question of validity Quick is, uncharacteristically, insufficiently analytical.[289]

'Validity' in Quick's sacramental writings connotes at least the following:

---

[287] Ibid., 152. For twentieth-century ecumenism with special reference to the Free Churches, see Alan P. F. Sell, *Nonconformist Theology in the Twentieth Century*, Milton Keynes: Paternoster, 2006, ch. 3.

[288] O. C. Quick, *Doctrines of the Creed*, 332.

[289] W. R. Matthews, who, with H. Wheeler Robinson commissioned Quick's *The Christian Sacraments* for The Library of Constructive Theology, said of the book that 'I believe I did some good by clearing up a few passages which were obscure.' See his *Memories and Meanings*, London: Hodder and Stoughton, 1969, 126. He might have done a little more on validity. In his review of Quick's book Edwyn C. Hoskyns queried how far it met the editorial criteria of emphasizing the validity of religious experience and developing theology 'on the basis of religious consciousness', for 'Quick's purpose is to straighten out the traditional theological language concerning the Sacraments by presenting its significance in modern philosophical terms; and he makes use of general human experience to aid him'. See *The Journal of Theological Studies*, XXX, October 1928, 86.

1. A sacrament is valid if the divinely appointed signs are present.[290]
2. A sacrament is valid if the 'celebrant' is duly authorized (the authoritarian view).
3. A sacrament is valid if the 'celebrant' has received both authority and power (*potestas*) through approved episcopal ordination (the indelibilist view).

Quick finds the root of (1) in the Bible, of (2) in the writings of Cyprian, and of (3) in (the ecclesiastical rather than the evangelical side of) the writings of Augustine.

Quick endorses points (1) and (2), but cannot subscribe to point (3) principally because it elevates a postbiblical doctrine into the criterion for determining when the Church is truly Catholic, and 'it divorces validity from authorisation'.[291]

On Quick's position as stated the following comments seem to be called for. As to point (1), he grants that in circumstances in which not all of the divinely appointed signs are present God's grace may still be known.[292] I should prefer to think of such a service as liturgically incomplete rather than as invalid, and of such incompleteness as not being of fundamental importance, lest we descend into liturgical legalism or even liturgical fusspottery. (Quick himself held no brief for obtrusive ceremonialism.[293])

What Quick says at point (2) is complicated by the fact that he also argues for 'degrees of validity' as when he declares that 'even in those Christian bodies which have not retained the apostolical succession through bishops, ordinations are not null or void of validity altogether'.[294] In face of Quick's charitable intention it seems churlish to resort to the slang response, 'Big deal!' or to Bernard Lord Manning's expostulation, 'We do not deal in percentages with the grace of God.'[295] More soberly, the weasel word in the quotation is 'altogether'. It prompts the question, How are these degrees of validity to be calibrated – and by whom? It all seems to invite either a 'Lo, here – but not there' investigation of quite intangible data, or the frank acknowledgement that non-episcopally ordained ministers are duly authorized persons. But Quick cannot take the latter route because he persists in saying that 'It need not be questioned that for fully valid Orders the episcopal succession is a necessity'[296] – and with that in the interests, paradoxically, of catholicity he assumes a sectarian stance. On Quick's view I remain 'however defectively', an ordained person who 'celebrates', 'however imperfectly, the real

---

[290] O. C. Quick, 'The Doctrine of the Church of England on Sacraments', in Roderic Dunkerley, ed., *The Ministry and the Sacraments*, London: SCM Press, 1937, 128.

[291] O. C. Quick, *The Christian Sacraments*, 158; cf. ibid., 142.

[292] Idem, 'The Doctrine of the Church of England on Sacraments', 129.

[293] See idem, *The Testing of Church Principles*, 101–2.

[294] Idem, *The Christian Sacraments*, 149.

[295] B. L. Manning, *Essays in Orthodox Dissent* (1931), London: Independent Press, 1952, 116.

[296] Ibid., 149.

sacraments of Christ's appointment'.²⁹⁷ He comes close to rubbing salt into the wound when he continues,

> [W]ho shall say that the solemn confirmation and authorisation of a Free Church minister's Orders by the hands of an apostolic bishop adds nothing to them, or who shall fix the precise limits of what it adds? And who, again shall say that the acceptance by an Anglican bishop or priest of solemn authorisation to exercise his ministry in a Christian body now reuniting with his own does nothing in a similar way to complete the meaning and reality of his own ordination?

But the ways are not 'similar', and Quick elsewhere gives ample evidence that he knew his Anglo-Catholic brethren well enough to perceive that they would not regard the two traditions as similarly extending the scope of their ministry, but rather would suppose that the Free Church ministers were, by episcopal consecration, becoming something which they had not been before. There is a profound distinction between a legitimate compromise and a doctrinal fudge which results from participants' being able, even perhaps encouraged, to believe what they fancy about the process when it is known that what some participants believe about it effectively repudiates the previous ministry of others. What Quick says regarding authorization can all too easily be hijacked by those committed to indelibility, and they are encouraged in this direction when Quick regrettably employs the term 'validity' synonymously with 'authorization'.

The following considerations bear upon point (3) above:

1. I find Quick's case against indelibility unanswerable. Moreover, the indelibilists are mistaken in supposing that a special power (*potestas*) is conveyed to those ordained which validates their sacramental practice, for there was no transmission of apostolic authority of the kind that theory requires.[298]
2. There is no sacrament if God is not acting, and if God is acting – and who can say that he is not when the saints gather and the Holy Spirit is invoked? – there is no invalidity.[299]
3. Those called to the ministry by God and authorized by the Church are truly ordained, and hence 'reordination', like 'rebaptism' and 'unicorn', is a non-instantiated concept.

---

[297] Ibid., 150.
[298] See T. W. Manson, *The Church's Ministry*, London: Hodder and Stoughton, 1948.
[299] Cf. Bernard Lord Manning, *Essays in Orthodox Dissent*, 116, 117, 75.

4. It is the Church which celebrates the sacraments (hence the inverted commas around 'celebrant' above); it is not that the priesthood (forgive the crudity) does sacramental things to or on behalf of the Church.[300]
5. The sectarianism which divides those whom God has already made one in Christ is to be shunned. There are not many Churches, there is one Church in many places.[301]
6. I conclude that the first and second uses of 'validity' are misplaced, while the third as used by indelibilists is abhorrent – even blasphemous.

We may now ask, How does Quick understand the sacraments as such? In an important paragraph he outlines his general position, making clear the place of Jesus Christ and the way in which the doctrines of creation and humanity come together in sacramental theology:

> [A]s Jesus Christ Himself is the perfect sacrament of created being, so in the light of that one sacrament the Church appears as the sacrament of human society, Baptism as the sacrament of man's spiritual birth to God, Holy Communion as the sacrament of human fellowship in Him, holy days as sacraments of time, and holy places as sacraments of space.[302]

To this we might venture to add, 'and natural phenomena as sacraments of truth', for in the lectures on parables which he gave to Sunday School teachers in Colne, Quick says, 'The true mystery of the Kingdom ... consists precisely in the fact that the natural and earthly, faithfully observed and truly understood, do really illustrate the heavenly and spiritual, because the single order of the divine love and reason embraces and is immanent in both.'[303] This is a further implicit repudiation of any Barthian restriction of the sphere of divine revelation, of any mystical obliteration of things natural, and of any 'Protestant' belittling of the temporal process.[304] Quick insists upon the rootedness of the sacraments in the real world, in which connection he verges on the pugilistic in advocating the

> arraying of those who really believe in the sacramental religion which gives to the historic, the outward, and the particular their proper place and value, against

---

[300] Quick himself opposes 'the characteristic feature of Romanism in practice', namely, that it yields 'two distinct standards, degrees, or classes of membership' – that is, the clergy on the one hand and the laity on the other. See *The Testing of Church Principles*, 53.

[301] See further Alan P. F. Sell, *Nonconformist Theology in the Twentieth Century*, 180–82.

[302] O. C. Quick, *The Christian Sacraments*, 113; cf. ibid., 67.

[303] Idem, *The Realism of Christ's Parables*, London: SCM Press, 1931, 15–16.

[304] Idem, *Catholic and Protestant Elements in Christianity*, 109, where the adverse judgement of 'Protestantism' requires qualification.

those who are honestly convinced that this type of theology should now give way to a more purely spiritual, abstract, and immanental faith.[305]

Quick discusses sacraments as both signs of God's presence and gift, and as means whereby the presence is realized and the gift bestowed: '[I]t is not more true to say that the efficacy of a sacrament depends on its significance than that its significance is dependent on its efficacy.'[306] To think of sacraments only as signs may lead us towards a Platonistic view of reality; to think of them only as instruments of God's action may lead us towards answering activism.[307] They are both signs and instruments. It is not the case that the sacraments 'mechanically impart Christian holiness, any more than the Creeds by themselves or mechanically impart Christian truth. ... [Both] show how and where the twin mysteries of truth and holiness may be entered into by those who hunger and thirst after their attainment.'[308] Hence,

> just as it is an irrational limitation of God's love and power to suppose that God does not bestow His spiritual gifts outside sacramental rites, so it seems to me an equally irrational limitation to suppose that He does not bestow gifts in His sacraments except through the causality which these possess *as signs*. In the former case we should limit God by the forms of institutional religion; in the latter case we should limit Him no less really by the feeble flickering light of human consciousness. All I seek to affirm is that, given a faithful humble disposition of the will towards receiving God's gifts, God may and does, both through sacraments and apart from them, bestow much more on the soul than anything of which its consciousness can be aware. Such efficacy remains necessarily mysterious; but I cannot see that it is either irrational or unintelligible or even miraculous, or that to believe in it is superstition.[309]

On 15 August 1927 a reporter to *The Times* summarized Quick's account of widely-accepted sacramental principles which he articulated at the Lausanne Conference on Faith and Order thus:

> [T]hat in every Sacrament the inward reality is a Divine act; that the Sacraments do not limit God's gracious activity; that true faith and penitence are necessary

---

[305] Idem, *The Testing of Church Principles*, 93.
[306] Idem, *The Christian Sacraments*, 13.
[307] See idem, *The Gospel of Divine Action*, 124–6.
[308] Idem, *The Testing of Church Principles*, 51.
[309] Idem, 'Sacramental theory, *Theology*, XX, May 1930, 275. In this article Quick replies to Charles J. Shebbeare's paper, 'The evangelical conception of the sacraments', ibid., XX, April, 1930.

conditions for the effectual receiving of God's gifts in the Sacraments; and that the soul can receive more in the Sacrament than it is capable of realizing.[310]

Against this general background we may turn to the two dominical sacraments. 'Baptism,' declares Quick, 'gives the power to start life as a redeemed child of God.'[311] This seems to imply baptismal regeneration, a doctrine on which, as far as I can discover, Quick nowhere attempts to justify, though he does characterize it, together with washing and resurrection, as part of a process 'which ends only in heaven and cannot therefore be intelligibly thought of as wholly complete in the moment when the Sacrament is performed'.[312] The sacrament turns upon the idea of the divine Fatherhood, but while granting that some New Testament language suggests that sonship and daughterhood are ours by adoption, he does not wish to deny that in some sense all humanity, as created in God's image, are God's children. Furthermore, he observes that the change in the early Church from adult to infant baptism as the normal practice 'involved a shifting of emphasis from the instrumental to the symbolic aspect of the sacrament'.[313]

Traditionally, the instrumentality of infant baptism was concerned with the washing away of original sin, according to which all human beings were born in a fallen state from which they needed to be rescued. To Quick, however, while the doctrines of the Fall and original sin are not incredible, it is impossible to verify empirically the claim that in the case of any infant baptism effects a change resulting from the washing away of original sin. Hence, again, the sacrament is symbolic more than it is instrumental. Quick recognizes that this interpretation 'changes the emphasis of New Testament theology', where 'the central thought is that of the actual change brought about by the initiation of Christian life with which the Sacrament of Baptism is connected'. He attributes this difference to 'the peculiar and necessarily transient conditions under which the New Testament was composed'.[314] To the biblical scholar, Edwyn C. Hoskyns, this was a 'dangerous' move.[315]

Some of Quick's reviewers regretted that he did not devote more space to confirmation in relation to infant baptism.[316] My concern is that, possibly given his ambivalence over the 'Church within the Church', he did not pay more heed to the New Testament language of adoption in relation to entry into God's covenant – baptism being a sign and seal of the covenant of grace; and to paedobaptism as

---

[310] Quoted by H. Wheeler Robinson, *The Christian Experience of the Holy Spirit* (1928), London: Collins Fontana, 1962, 162.

[311] O. C. Quick, *The Testing of Church Principles*, 50.

[312] Idem, *The Christian Sacraments*, 179.

[313] Ibid., 170.

[314] Ibid., 180.

[315] See his review of *The Christian Sacraments* in *The Journal of Theological Studies*, XXX, October 1928, 88.

[316] He has a note on the subject in *The Christian Sacraments*, 181–4.

witnessing to the heart of the Gospel, namely, that when we can do nothing, God does everything.

Turning to the Lord's Supper[317] we find that in Quick's exposition the symbolic and the instrumental run closely together. This emerges above all in what he has to say concerning the eucharistic presence of Christ. Quick argues that when at the Last Supper Jesus says, 'This is my body', he means 'This symbolizes or signifies My Body.'[318] He further explains that significance is either indicative or expressive. Jesus could have meant, indicatively, that the bread pictorially indicates his body; but Quick thinks that the bread is the body 'because it is the expressive symbol and instrument of himself.'[319] In this way he interprets and restates the Catholic doctrine of the real presence, though making it clear that the relationship between Christ and the bread is spiritual, not physical: 'the body is not in or under the consecrated species'.[320] The relationship is none the less real for that. The contrary assumption, namely, that 'the consecrated species must remain continuously identified with the Lord's Body until its material entity is dissolved seems to me to depend implicitly on the assumption that the relation between the consecrated species and the Lord's presence is of a quasi-physical sort. This assumption I do find abhorrent.'[321] Hence his aversion to the devotions offered before the reserved sacrament.[322] The abhorrent assumption flows down from scholastic teaching on transubstantiation. We have seen how Quick tries to derive something positive from this doctrine, and it is worth adding that not the least of his difficulties with the traditional view of it is that it is wedded to an Aristotelian philosophical doctrine regarding substance and accidents which is now discredited; and Quick was, as we saw, averse to tying theology too closely to any particular philosophical position lest if the latter fell the theology would fall with it.[323]

The idea of sacrifice lies at the heart of Quick's understanding of the Lord's Supper, for the sacrament 'is the perpetual externalisation in human ritual of the self-offering of Christ, which was once for all in fact externalised on Calvary, but is ever real in the inward and heavenly sphere.'[324] In the sacrament Christ draws

---

[317] My favoured term for the sacrament (a) because it is biblical; (b) because it suggests the distinction between the Last Supper and the post-resurrection Lord's Supper: not indeed that it is not also a eucharist and a holy communion.

[318] O. C. Quick, *The Christian Sacraments*, 14.

[319] Ibid., 15; cf. ibid., 221–2; 243–8; 'Sacramental theory', 276–7.

[320] Ibid., 16.

[321] Ibid.

[322] See ibid, 216; cf. idem, *The Testing of Church Principles*, 96; 'The Farnham conference on reservation', *Theology*, XIV, March 1927, 167–8. See also the remarks by J. M. Lloyd Thomas in his review of *The Christian Sacraments* in *The Hibbert Journal*, XXVI no. 3, April 1928, 563.

[323] See idem, *The Testing of Church Principles*, 95.

[324] Idem, *The Christian Sacraments*, 197. The concept of sacrifice and the doctrine of the real presence were among matters raised by Will Spens in articles in response to

his people into his own sacrifice so that they may offer themselves for his sake: it is not that Christ's sacrifice renders unnecessary the believer's own self-offering:

> Christ died once in time, but He offers Himself eternally. In the Eucharist we make a memorial of Christ's death; but we make before God an offering which is one with Christ's present and eternal offering of Himself. ... Thus the life of Christ, which truly offers itself by human and earthly hands in the Eucharist, always includes, not excludes, His death on Calvary, and, in so far as it is communicated to souls still in earthly bodies, it is not merely the heavenly offering of life, but the earthly offering through death, of which these must be made partakers.[325]

At one point Quick seems to complicate matters unnecessarily. We have already seen that he regards baptism as more symbolic than instrumental, and that he thinks that that sacrament affords the candidate's 'initial impulse of the divine power to start him on his heavenward way'.[326] But he then proceeds to distinguish the way in which Christ is present in baptism from the way in which he is present in the Lord's Supper. He claims that it has been 'the Church's constant belief that the presence of Christ in the Eucharist is to be accounted something different from His presence in Baptism'.[327] J. E. L. Oulton justifiably took exception to this claim: 'To assert that the grace of Baptism and the grace of Eucharist are different in kind, and to do this on the ground of "the Church's constant belief", is perilous.' He further remarks that when Quick speaks of the '"renewal" in the eucharist of the contact with God made first at Holy Baptism, the very word "renewal" suggests a kinship between the grace of the one Sacrament and that of the other'.[328] Manning's remark concerning the impossibility of thinking in terms of percentages of the grace of God comes to mind once more, and it makes no clear sense to speak of degrees of Christ's presence anywhere.

In the wake of the historical controversies over the biblical texts which had consumed so much energy during the decades leading up to Quick's publishing life he judges that 'we are no longer justified in resting the whole, or even the main, weight of the authority for the doctrine and practice of any sacrament upon the bare fact that the Bible attributes a particular form of words to Christ Himself'.[329] As we might expect, Edwyn Hoskyns objected to this, not on grounds of restorationism, but because he construes Quick as manipulating the biblical text

---

Quick's book. See 'The Christian sacraments', *Theology*, XVIII, January, February and March 1929, 11–18, 78–85, 137–43. For Quick's reply see ibid., May 1929, 279–81.

[325] Ibid., 198.

[326] Ibid., 186.

[327] Ibid.

[328] J. E. L. Oulton, *Holy Communion and Holy Spirit. A Study in Doctrinal Relationship*, London: SPCK, 1951, 161–2.

[329] O. C. Quick, *The Christian Sacraments*, 125; cf. ibid., 188.

in such a way as neatly to show that the life of Jesus exemplifies the philosophical doctrines of beauty, truth and goodness. In the course of doing this he 'obscures the roughness' of the biblical texts and also bypasses detailed consideration of such a fundamental concept as forgiveness.[330] These judgements should be treated with caution. It does not seem to me that Quick squeezed selected biblical material into a pre-determined philosophical framework; on the contrary, while skilled in philosophical analysis, he is, as we have seen, eager to allow theology to converse with philosophy but reluctant to have it dependent on it. Quick is also in order in dealing in sacramental theology not only with the biblical text but with accounts of how Christ has been received through the Christian ages. On the other hand, it would have assisted his exposition of the sacraments had he provided a fuller account of forgiveness. But my principal concern is not that he omitted this or that biblical theme, but that he did not, in *The Christian Sacraments*, elaborate upon the liturgical relation of Word and sacraments. It may fairly be argued that apart from the Word the sacraments are dumb; that both Word and sacraments are intended to witness to the same grace of God in salvation; and that when Quick elsewhere contrasts Word and sacrament by saying that 'When we preach the Word, the efficacy of what we do is wholly dependent upon the intelligibility of what we say. ... When we celebrate the Sacraments, the significance of what we both say and do, vitally important as it is, depends upon the reality of what God is effecting through us,[331] he shows himself to have a deficient understanding of preaching. The efficacy of preaching is by no means *wholly* dependent upon our intelligibility. On the contrary, the sermon is given in the name of the triune God, and its efficacy depends upon the action of God's Spirit in both guiding the preacher's thoughts and words and applying the truth of the declared Gospel to the hearers. In other words, 'the significance of what we say and do' in preaching no less than in the sacraments, 'depends upon the reality of what God is effecting through us.'"[332]

But Quick must have the last word:

> [I]t is the element in Catholic doctrine represented by the *opus operatum*, to which I chiefly cling. It stands for the precious truth that in the Sacraments what is done and what actually happens is more, and matters more, than what my cognitive apprehension can compass in appreciating what their symbolism means. ... In this world the life of Christ remains the most perfect symbol of

---

[330] E. Hoskyns, review of *The Christian Sacraments*, 88.

[331] O. C. Quick, *The Gospel of Divine Action*, 122.

[332] To me it seems as odd to appear to drive a wedge between the Word and the sacraments as it does to drive a wedge between the dominical sacraments – as happens when Anglican indelibilists accept baptism in the name of the Trinity and with water by whomsoever performed (in some cases because of fears – in my view unfounded – for the eternal state of dying infants), while they would not receive the bread and wine from a Free Church minister, I Corinthians 10: 17 notwithstanding. See O. C. Quick, *The Christian Sacraments*, 142.

God which can be given to us ... But this world is essentially not the sphere of perfect vision or revelation; it is the sphere of active practical training where faith is the guide, and the Cross is the final fact. ... And therefore, though all outwards things may give us hints of an eternal presence, what matters most is that as instruments they should mould us in the pattern of service, until God has completed His work in us, and the six days' labour of time is finished and taken up into the Sabbath of eternity.[333]

V

Oliver Chase Quick stood for a reasoned and reasonable theology in which dogma and freedom of thought went in hand in hand. His discussion of natural theology and his openness to the apologetic enterprise are of abiding interest. As he wrote, 'Rational apologetic emphasizes the connection of religion with the rest of life. It tends to break down the distinction between sacred and secular, and to find a religious meaning everywhere.'[334] Consistently with this he could not treat Christianity as a closed system[335] – the peril of Barthianism – nor allow that religious experience was distinguishable from experience of any other kind, or that it betokened a particular class of experiences. Hence 'He sometimes said that he had never had a "religious experience", and in the misleading sense of that phrase popularized by William James this is probably true.'[336] But, as Temple proceeds to point out, Quick's whole experience was religious: for him to think at all was to theologize, for God was in all his thought.'[337] As I have elsewhere suggested, 'The last six words quoted constitute a fitting epitaph to Quick, and one to be coveted.'[338]

Of considerable philosophical acumen, he brought formidable analytical skills to bear upon philosophical and doctrinal questions, and his judicious balancing of opposing trends of thought with a view to drawing from them insights which might lead their proponents towards convergence was frequently exemplary. His ability in this respect has been attributed to the fact that he was not a 'party man'.[339] But that, in turn, is a consequence of his general philosophical demeanour, as Donald Mackinnon properly noted:

---

[333] Ibid., 138–9.

[334] Idem, 'Reason and Christian experience', 188.

[335] See D. M. Mackinnon, 'Oliver Chase Quick as a theologian', 112.

[336] William Temple, 'Memoir' prefixed to O. C. Quick, *The Gospel of the New World*, xiii.

[337] Ibid.

[338] See Alan P. F. Sell, *Confessing and Commending the Faith. Historic Witness and Apologetic Method*, 485.

[339] See, for example, Alec R. Vidler, *20th Century Defenders of the Faith*, London: SCM Press, 1965, 65; A. M. Ramsey, *From Gore to Temple*, 107.

> It was indeed because he was philosopher as well as theologian that he proved himself so strangely awkward to those who would enlist his authority in defence of their own partisan attitudes. To the neo-orthodox of the 1940s he urged the claim of the open mind ... To the liberal his emphasis on the givenness of the Christian reality proved shocking, while manifest discontent with the way in which what to him was fundamental was often presented invested his thinking with an interrogative character which made those eager for a word they would quickly and confidently proclaim, impatient with scruples and hesitations that were at once religious and academic.[340]

Of particular importance was the way in which Quick queried absolute idealist immanentism, ahistorical incarnationalism, and mystical denial of the world.

I have not felt able to agree with Quick on all points but, apart from the analysis of 'validity' in relation to sacraments, his problematic positions were rather the result of inadequate grounding in history than of incompetence in analytical skills.[341] I do not think that he really 'got under the skin' of the historic Free Churches, or gave them sufficient credence for their ecclesiological insights: his ambivalence on the question of membership in his own Church was perhaps partially responsible for this. At the same time, in what was one of his most important single sentences, he declared that

> The union of Catholicism and Protestantism can only be found in the religion of the Resurrection through the Cross, and that again is the religion of Him Who died on Calvary and rose to give His Spirit to His Church. We must be loyal to the sacramental gospel of the resurrection. There is not, nor ever can be, any other hope for mankind.[342]

Doctrinally, Quick's strictures against the divine impassibility in the interests of God's incarnational and atoning acts in history were very much to the point, as was his approach to the two-nature doctrine of Christ and, above all, the way in which he held incarnation and atonement together, upholding the Cross and resurrection as the very heart of the Gospel. In this connection his respect for the Congregational theologians, R. W. Dale and P. T. Forsyth should not go unremarked. Also noteworthy was his custom of drawing out the implications of central doctrines for Christian living. To Vidler, Quick was among those modern

---

[340] D. M. Mackinnon, 'Oliver Chase Quick as a theologian', 115.

[341] Lest it be thought that this is simply the perverse judgement of a disappointed Free Church theologian, I should point out that Quick's fellow Anglicans, J. K. Mozley and Alec R. Vidler concurred, and that Paul Lucas described his subject as 'a professor of immense distinction without being a reader of immense erudition'. See, respectively, *Oliver Quick as a Theologian*, 4; *20th Century Defenders of the Faith*, 65; and 'Oliver Quick', 15.

[342] O. C. Quick, *Liberalism, Modernism and Tradition*, 150–51.

theologians who were 'much more effective in criticism than in construction'.[343] Unquestionably, his critical powers were considerable and they were used to great advantage. But it would be wrong to minimize the constructive sweep of his thought as a whole with its centre in the Cross and resurrection, its honouring of the created order and its eschatological thrust – all of which Quick summed up in his sacramental teaching. J. K. Mozley was not without justification in stating that 'as an exponent of the essentials of Christian orthodoxy [Quick] was second to none'.[344]

In our own time the Church of England scholar, Mark Chapman, has said, truthfully enough, that Quick 'did not display much originality of thought'.[345] However, as one reviews the voyage taken by the good ship Theology through the choppy waters of the twentieth century, the thought occurs that having regard to the forceful admirals of 'originality' who have mustered loyal, even sometimes adulatory, crews; the more independent old salts who have led us through shoals of *angst*; the maverick captains who have encouraged us to drift unanchored on the Sea of Faith; and the ecumenical pirates who have despatched us to plunder the treasures of others without regard to hidden presuppositional rocks, an influx of theologians thoroughly equipped with the analytical skills and the intellectual discrimination of a Quick would be a boon indeed. If such persons carried their analytical powers into their wit, as Quick did, that would be a very welcome bonus:

> I remember [writes William Temple] a day in the great Missionary Conference in Jerusalem in 1928 when one of its leading members thought we stood in need of uplift; he accordingly addressed us in words and tones designed to produce that effect. As we went out through the door I found Oliver close to me, saying in the iciest tones: 'When X speaks like that it becomes important to distinguish between the things which he says *although* they are not true and the things which he says *because* they are not true.'[346]

---

[343] A. R. Vidler, *20th Century Defenders of the Faith*, 69.
[344] J. K. Mozley, *Oliver Quick as a Theologian*, 16.
[345] M. Chapman, 'Oliver Chase Quick', in DTCBP, 830.
[346] W. Temple, 'Memoir', xi.

Chapter 5
Herbert Arthur Hodges (1905–1976): Christian Philosopher, Believing Sceptic

I can think of no twentieth-century English philosopher other than H. A. Hodges whose obituary in *The Times* is headed, 'Philosopher and Christian'.[1] The conjunction is important. Hodges was not a 'Christian philosopher' in the sense of one who in all his work set out from uncriticized Christian assumptions (least of all from an allegedly inerrant Bible) with a view to presenting a tightly-knit scheme, however abstracted from the intellectual and cultural world around him. He was a professional philosopher who was by conviction a Christian, and in the heyday of Oxford positivism and linguistic analysis, that marked him out as being somewhat unusual. But Hodges was his own man, and with that resolve for which Yorkshiremen are noted, he ploughed his own furrow in philosophy and religion alike. As to the former, his intensive studies in German philosophy distinguished him from many of his philosophical contemporaries, and 'He seldom felt himself called to enter into the contemporary philosophical debates which occupied the minds of so many of his colleagues in the university world.'[2] As to the latter, his pilgrimage took him from Methodism through (brief) atheism to the Church of England, and to increasing empathy with Orthodox theology and liturgy.

Of the four Anglican philosophers discussed in this book, Hodges is unique in at least two respects. First, he was not a birthright member of the Church of England. His Christian roots were in that most independently-minded branch of Methodism, the United Methodist Church, and that in its prominent Sheffield expression. This Church was the product of the union in 1907 of the Methodist New Connexion with the United Methodist Free Churches. Among the motivations of those who seceded from Wesleyanism to constitute the former body in 1797 was the conviction that the Wesleyan body was too clerically-minded. The seceders, by contrast, accorded greater responsibility in their churches to laypersons,[3] and

---

[1]   See *The Times*, 8 July 1976, 18.
[2]   Stephen Parsons (son-in-law), Foreword to H. A. Hodges, *God be in my Thinking*, printed for V. J. Hodges, Leominster: Orphans Press, 1981, 3.
[3]   It is, therefore, not without significance that chapter six of Cyril J. Davey's book, *The Methodist Story*, is entitled, 'All men have their rights: the story of the Methodist New Connexion'. Interestingly, Alexander Kilham (1762–1798), for whom see ODNB, the first to lead a breakaway group from Wesleyanism, was, like John Wesley himself, born in Epworth, Lincolnshire. For the Methodist New Connexion see also George Eayrs, in W. J. Townsend, H. B. Workman and George Eayrs, eds, *A New History of Methodism*, London:

the Constitution of the United Methodist church provided for the Church Meeting which enabled the participation of all members in the governance of the local church.[4] Secondly, notwithstanding that his career coincided more directly than those of de Burgh, Matthews and Quick with the outburst of Oxford analytical philosophy (sometimes characterized as 'cold' and 'abstracted', but in my view encouragingly rigorously cerebral and technically useful), we learn from his more popular writings a good deal about his religious experience and religious struggles – matters on which de Burgh, Matthews and Quick are almost entirely silent. This is not to say that Hodges inappropriately wore his heart on his sleeve in the classroom: he was too discreet for that. Like his senior colleague, de Burgh, he 'tended to assume that Christianity was a highly individual matter, to be discussed with, but not imposed on, students'.[5]

Hodges was born in Sheffield on 4 January 1905. His father was a commercial traveller, and his mother had taught elementary school children. Hodges won a scholarship to King Edward VII School, Sheffield, and then became a classical scholar at Balliol College, Oxford, where he was taught by A. D. Lindsay.[6] He was placed in the first class in both Classical Moderations and Literae Humaniores, and in 1932 he gained the Oxford degree of Doctor of Philosophy for his dissertation on Wilhelm Dilthey. Hodges was the John Locke Scholar in 1926, and in the following year he was appointed lecturer in philosophy at New College. After one year, however, he joined de Burgh in the philosophy department at Reading University. In 1934, still only 29, Hodges succeeded to de Burgh's chair. There he remained until retirement in 1969.

J. C. Holt, the historian of Reading's first 50 years rightly judged that 'Hodges, like de Burgh, approached his work in a missionary spirit', and he records a conversation of 9 February 1970, during which Hodges said,

> Having a university here was pioneer work. I was quite clear that I wanted to be a university teacher and I had wanted to be in Oxford, but as soon as I saw this place I felt the difference in atmosphere. We were teaching not the privileged élite, but people. I was quite clear that my vocation lay in Reading or some place like it, and that this was where I belonged.[7]

Hodder and Stoughton, 1909, I, 481–551; Henry Smith, John E. Swallow and William Treffry, *The Story of the United Methodist Church*, London: Henry Hooks, 1932; and the chapters by John T. Wilkinson in vols. 2 and 3 of Rupert Davies, A. Raymond George and Gordon Rupp, eds, *A History of the Methodist Church in Great Britain*, Peterborough: Epworth Press, 1978, 1983.

[4] See Henry Smith *et al.*, op. cit., 14. In this respect the United Methodist Church was closer in polity to the Baptists and Congregationalists of Old Dissent.

[5] J. C. Holt, *The University of Reading: The First Fifty Years*, Reading: University of Reading Press, 1977, 82.

[6] For Lindsay (1879–1952) see ODNB.

[7] J. C. Holt, *The University of Reading*, 88.

In these words we detect something of Hodges' strong social conscience, and as his career progressed this found expression in a variety of ways. Thus, for example, during the Second World War he served with the Home Guard, and greatly enjoyed mingling with men of all types and backgrounds. He lectured for the Services College and the Workers' Educational Association. As far as the latter was concerned, this was consistent with the fact that

> His politics were of the left [as were Lindsay's], though not of the extreme left, and his lively social conscience found a practical expression when he became a member of the Royal Commission on Betting, Lotteries and Gambling [sic][8] (1949–51). His socialism and a long-standing interest in the arts found a common focus in the ideas of John Ruskin,[9] and from 1954 to 1973 he was Master of the Guild of St. George, which Ruskin founded.[10]

Something of the same social passion emerges in Hodges' advocacy of an Honours Degree in Political Economy. 'Our starting point,' he urged, 'should be our social task. Learning pure for its own sake is today an indefensible frivolity [a point of view not universally expressed by former classical scholars]. ... Increasing numbers will be directly employed in the social services. All will have to become actively interested in social affairs if the concentration of powers in the hands of a planning bureaucracy is to be balanced as it should be by an effective public opinion.'[11]

In 1939 Hodges married his former student, Vera Joan Willis, to whose diary entries concerning de Burgh I have already referred. They had two sons and a daughter. Almost 30 years later they jointly wrote a paper in memory of the Reverend Gilbert Shaw, and it is not difficult to detect the Hodges' sympathy with one who 'reached out to the dockers in the East End, to organise rent strikes and carry banners in protest marches to Hyde Park', who was 'at home in the Athenaeum and in the slums', and who 'met and fought the mystery of evil without paying it the compliment of more attention than it deserves'.[12] Nor can we miss Hodges' ability as an Englishman to empathize with the patriotism of the

---

[8] The word should be Gaming.

[9] Hodges later summed up Ruskin's doctrine as being 'based on an ideal of human life and character, and an ideal of human relationships and social patters following from this'. See *Death and Life have Contended*, London: SCM Press, 1964, 23. Ruskin failed to weld his followers into a social force, says Hodges, and his admiration for the man did not prevent his judging that Ruskin was 'dictatorial, self-indulgent, luxurious, domineering'. Ibid., 26.

[10] Anon., *The Times* obituary, 8 July 1976, 18.

[11] Quoted by J. C. Holt, *The University of Reading*, 125–6.

[12] H. A. and V. Hodges, 'The Revd Gilbert Shaw,' *Sobornost*, V no. 6, Winter–Spring 1968, 452, 454.

Welsh-language poet, D. Gwenallt Jones, fuelled as it was by the sense of oppression by Wales' larger neighbour.[13]

A gifted linguist, Hodges could manage Dilthey's difficult German as well as French and Italian, and he later taught himself Welsh. Music, wild flowers, and the history of Berkshire were among his other interests. He was drawn to Dilthey (1833–1911) because of the latter's breadth of vision. A genuine (non-secular) humanist, Hodges was ever interested in the relations between sociology, literature, history and philosophy. In this connection he acknowledged the influence of Lindsay who, on retirement pioneered the unique foundation year of undergraduate study at the newly founded University College of North Staffordshire (1949) – later Keele University. For his part, Hodges, together with his close friend, H. V. D. Dyson of the Department of English Literature, mounted a combined honours course which began in 1930;[14] and Hodges and Dyson regularly gathered for discussions with the Professor of Fine Art, J. A. Betts.[15] Hodges recalled that 'We organized evening meetings of the three departments. We would miss our dinner, meet in the Art School, take potato crisps and things and have an alfresco meal, and then one of us would hold forth on some topic. A student audience from the three departments would join in.'[16]

'As a university lecturer,' his obituarist recalls, Hodges 'preferred teaching to administration, and his lectures – delivered from minute scraps of paper – were models of lucidity.'[17] Consistently with this, Holt declares that 'If de Burgh swept his students along with broad gestures Hodges patiently dissected and analysed, and he was just as effective in a different style.'[18] Vera Willis (later, Mrs. Hodges), who sat under both de Burgh and Hodges, confided to her diary that, unlike de Burgh,

> Hodges was no orator. He did not build up towers of words, deck his thoughts with example or contort it into paradox. He said what he thought important about the subject in hand, and said it in the simplest way possible. I think he would have called his lectures introductory rather than expository, and certainly they had the effect of making us go straight to the works of which he talked and see for ourselves. Sometimes he had his notes open on the desk before him and sometimes he had not – it made no difference to his fluency or systematic utterance. Clarity of thought and sympathy in interpretation were the

---

[13] H. A. Hodges, 'Gwenallt', *Sobornost*, VI no. 1, Summer 1970, 25–32.

[14] J. C. Holt, *The University of Reading*, 49; cf. 132, 226 n.

[15] Betts and Hodges shared an interest in Ruskin and the Pre-Raphaelites, both were members of the Guild of St. George, and the former was instrumental in attracting a collection of Ruskin material to Reading University. See J. C. Holt, *The University of Reading*, 260 n.

[16] Ibid., 87–8.

[17] Anon., *The Times*, 8 July 1976, 18.

[18] J. C. Holt, *The University of Reading*, 91.

characteristics of his style. ... The most superficial of idealists was allowed a hearing before his interpreter stepped aside to criticize. Even in his criticism he was impersonal. Metaphysics is never easy and often we left his room in a whirl, but even then one enjoyed it.[19]

In 1944 Hodges' book, *Wilhelm Dilthey, an Introduction* appeared. It received generally favourable reviews. P. Lejins of the University of Maryland concluded that the book 'should prove to be a good stimulant' to further study of Dilthey; Charles E. Wallraff of the University of Arizona found it 'most helpful ... straightforward, pellucid and succinct'; while to Brown University's Joachim Wach, the book's 'value and importance are in reverse relation to its small size'.[20] James Gutmann of Columbia University, however, took a different view. In a churlish – even a bilious – review he complained of Hodges' method of presenting first his introduction to Dilthey and then selected passages in translation. Either part, he thought, needed much more space, and many of the translated passages were snippets only. He found the work insular, and judged that it would not advance the reader's knowledge of Dilthey.[21] Hodges' much more detailed study, *The Philosophy of Wilhelm Dilthey* followed in 1952. His Riddell Memorial Lecture, *Languages, Standpoints and Attitudes*, was published in 1953, while his other major philosophical work, *God Beyond Knowledge*, based upon his Gifford Lectures, was published posthumously in 1979.

To Hodges' more popular and theological works I shall come in due course. But if his contribution as a whole is to be fully understood we must pay heed to the more personal aspects of his life and experience. There are the questions of his ecclesiastical pilgrimage, his spiritual experience, about which he has a good deal to say, and his reflections upon the Christian's place and role in the modern university.

Hodges recounts his ecclesiastical pilgrimage with characteristic openness. He was received as a communicant member in the United Methodist Church at the age of 17. At the time he was far from fully conversant with Methodist teaching and, 'being of a religious and at the same time a philosophical disposition, I fashioned for myself ... a religion which bore little resemblance to what the United Methodist Church was supposed to teach'.[22] Neither Methodism nor his manufactured religion could survive Oxford, so although during his first months there he served as a lay (or, in Methodist parlance of the time, local) preacher in the surrounding villages, by the beginning of his third year of study his residual Christianity had

---

[19] Diary of Vera Willis, quoted ibid., 92.

[20] P. Lejins, *American Sociological Review*, XI no. 2, April 1946, 244; C. E. Wallraff in *The Philosophical Review*, LV no. 6, November 1946, 704; J. Wach, *The Journal of Religion*, XXVI no. 3, July 1946, 218.

[21] J. Gutmann, *The Journal of Philosophy*, XLIV no. 22, October 1947, 609–12.

[22] H. A. Hodges on himself in D. Morgan, ed., *They Became Anglicans*, London: Mowbray, 1959, 65.

evaporated, and he was overtaken by scepticism. In 1928, however, aged 23, he underwent what he calls a conversion not to Anglicanism, but to Catholicism, and was received into the Church of England.[23] He valued the idea that that Church represented the undivided Church of the ages, yet without the necessity of the Papacy; and he welcomed the freedom to think about all aspects of the faith which the Church of England encouraged. In that Church he found 'the fullness of the sacramental life, and the Catholic tradition of spiritual teaching and discipline'.[24] Hodges was not unaware of the stresses and strains within the Church of England, but he nevertheless felt that the important question was not whether one should remain loyal to one's principles, but rather, how one's principles might be more precisely defined. In the latter connection his self-confessed sceptical mindset rendered him not immune to doubt, and at the same time stimulated a constant struggle for faith.

Hodges' interest in, and experience of, Orthodox theology and worship increased in his middle years, and he felt able more readily to distinguish the genuinely Catholic from the merely western; yet he did not become Orthodox, but preferred to stay on the western side of that tension. He did, however, join the Fellowship of St Alban and St Sergius, a body founded in 1928 with a view to fostering mutual relations between Orthodox Christians and those of western churches. He lectured on behalf of the Fellowship, and his pamphlet, *Anglicanism and Orthodoxy*, is an expanded version of an address he gave first to the Anglican Society in London, and then to the Fellowship. In it he argues that Anglicans who claim to hold 'the faith of the undivided Church' should pay heed to the Orthodox churches, in which 'the mind and temper' of the centuries before the schism between east and west in 1054 'survive substantially unchanged'.[25] Indeed, 'This absence of change, which makes the eastern Church appear to some in the west as lifeless and fossilised, nevertheless guarantees the identity of its faith and order with those of the undivided Church.'[26] There immediately follows the hypothetical question, 'If, then, the Anglican Reformation was an attempt to recover the faith of the undivided Church, is not that equivalent to saying that it was an attempt to return to Orthodoxy?'[27] Hodges clearly thinks that the answer to the question is, 'Yes'; but this is entirely to overlook both the question how far the pre-schism Church was really 'undivided', and the political dimension of the English Reformation. Again, he distinguishes 'the theological works of Cranmer and

---

[23] Hodges records that 'a friend of mine ... on the occasion of my conversion, took a course of reading in Freud in the hope of discovering what was the matter with me'. See his *Christianity and the Modern World View* (1949), 2nd edn London: SPCK, 1962, 3.

[24] Ibid., 66.

[25] Idem, *Anglicanism and Orthodoxy*, London: SCM Press, 1957, 12. The slightest acquaintance with the history of the Church and of doctrine prior to 1054 suffices to show that the phrase 'undivided Church' does not describe the situation with complete accuracy.

[26] Ibid., 12.

[27] Ibid., 12–13.

other Anglican Reformers, filled as they are with references to the Fathers', from the 'clear, stern, exclusively Biblical approach of Calvin'.[28] But (a) Calvin was intensely pastoral as well as 'clear' and 'stern'; (b) Calvin drew widely upon the Greek and Latin Fathers and was therefore not 'exclusively biblical' in approach;[29] and (c) when Hodges explains the affection of theologically diverse Anglicans for Cranmer's *Prayer Book* in terms of its teaching on 'the doctrine of the mystical union of Christ with the believing soul',[30] he has hit upon a doctrine upon which Calvin placed great emphasis, albeit he construed the mystical union not simply individually as Hodges does here: to him it was the cornerstone of catholicity understood as the fellowship of all those who, by grace, have been called by God and united to Christ and therefore to one another as members of the body, branches of the Vine.[31]

Amidst all the diversity within his Church Hodges found unity in the common liturgy (a claim that was easier to make in 1957 than it would be today, given the variety of orders of worship in use, and the advent of things charismatic in some Church of England circles). It is unfortunate that in speaking up for his Church, Hodges allows himself a not entirely justified passing swipe at the Free Churches,[32] 'where there is no real awareness of anything in Christian history or tradition that is earlier than the sixteenth century'.[33] Happily, his description of those churches whose polity is of the gathered sort, is kinder, though when he describes the polity as a theocratic *democracy*[34] we should not be misled into thinking that in Church Meeting the objective is 'one person, one vote' and rule by the majority. On the contrary, Church Meeting is a credal assembly in which the Lordship of Christ

---

[28] Ibid., 14.

[29] See, for example, Anthony N. S. Lane, *John Calvin, Student of the Church Fathers*, Edinburgh: T. & T. Clark, 1999.

[30] H. A. Hodges, *Anglicanism and Orthodoxy*, 18.

[31] See, for example, J. Calvin, *Institutes of the Christian Religion*, trans. Ford Lewis Battles, ed. John T. McNeill, Philadelphia: The Westminster Press, 1960, III. xi. 10: '[T]hat joining together of Head and members, that indwelling of Christ in our hearts – in short, that mystical union – are accorded by us the highest degree of importance, so that Christ, having been made ours, makes us sharers with him in the gifts with which he has been endowed. We do not, therefore, contemplate him outside ourselves from afar in order that his righteousness may be imputed to us but because we put on Christ and are engrafted into his body – in short, because he deigns to make us one with him.'

[32] This ambiguous term means one thing in Scotland, another in North America, and yet another in England and Wales. Hodges has the last in mind: he refers to the mainline Nonconformists who comprise Old Dissent and Methodism.

[33] H. A. Hodges, *Anglicanism and Orthodoxy*, 29.

[34] Ibid., 33, my italics.

over the whole witness and service of the church is confessed; and the objective is to seek his will, and to strive for unanimity.[35]

Hodges finds things to applaud in both the Catholic principle of fullness or comprehensiveness and the Protestant principle of purity, but both, he thinks with some justification, are liable to serious degeneration. 'Meanwhile', he continues, 'the Apostolic Faith has lived on substantially unaffected by either Papal or Protestant innovations. It presents to us the faith and life of the undivided Church, not as a historical memory but as a present fact; it shows us the meaning of a non-Papal Catholicism, not as a theoretical possibility but as an actuality.'[36] His highest praise for Orthodoxy is that 'that Faith to which the Orthodox Fathers bear witness and of which the Orthodox Church is the abiding custodian, is the Christian Faith in its true and essential form, to which we all aspire and by which we are all judged'.[37]

In view of this strong affirmation, it is puzzling that in his mature conviction, Hodges seems to repudiate the idea that the final word was spoken by ancient General Councils, and to come closer to the idea espoused by many Protestants, namely, that growth into God's truth by the leading of the Holy Spirit is a never-ending process:

> To affirm oneself deliberately as an Anglican is to ... identify oneself with a life which will be one long fight for clarity and integrity of mind. It is to affirm that one believes in God, and not in any formulae about God; in a God who stands in judgment on all our formulae about Him [including, presumably, those devised by General Councils]; in a God whose truth, placed by Him in the keeping of the Church, no one generation of the Church's members can ever fully apprehend; and who bids us move through darkness and self-annihilation to a truer understanding of what we already believe.[38]

Hodges was no mere armchair ecumenist. He was deeply committed to the quest of unity among Christians, and was among the Church of England delegates to the first Assembly of the World Council of Churches (Amsterdam, 1948), where 'The universal Church in God's design' was among the themes discussed; and he attended the World Council's Fourth World Conference on Faith and Order (Montreal, 1963). As a member of Archbishop Michael Ramsey's Commission on Intercommunion he was involved in the preparation of the Report on that subject which was presented to the Tenth Lambeth Conference in 1968; and he greatly regretted the breakdown in 1972 of the conversations with a view to union of

---

[35] It must be confessed that this point has been lost on some Baptist, Congregational and (since 1972) United Reformed church members.

[36] H. A. Hodges, *Anglicanism and Orthodoxy*, 39. So, of course, do the Reformation traditions when properly understood.

[37] Ibid., 47.

[38] Idem, *They Became Anglicans*, 70.

the Church of England with the Methodist Church, which was occasioned by the failure of the Synod of the Church of England to secure the requisite majority – a failure all the more poignant because the Methodist Conference had already approved the scheme.

That Hodges was no stranger to 'darkness and self-annihilation' is clear from his accounts of his own spiritual experience. He experienced his first crisis at the age of 15:

> I was a God-seer from boyhood ... but with a strong streak of defensiveness which, when I reached the age of reason, showed itself in sceptical questioning. The tension between the two drives, of acceptance and rejection, has run through my whole life. ... Three times in a dozen years I went down into the depth of negation, not as an intellectual exercise but as a life-experience, an encounter with nothingness. Three times in different ways I escaped into acceptance of reality and found myself an entity and a lodgment in the world.[39]

The first of the 'two contending dragons' was love – not in the sense in which love signifies a relation between persons, but love 'in the sense of openness to reality', which is 'a fundamental principle of epistemology'.[40] The other dragon was not so much hate, as fear, which renders us defensive rather than open, so that we are inhibited from surrendering ourselves to 'the All of Being'. There follows an important reflection in the light of his experience:

> God-denial does not usually come from seeing the God-vision and rejecting it; it comes from failing to see it. Where the God-seer sees God, the God-denier sees either nothing at all, or a distorted picture which he is often fully justified in rejecting. But his own basic attitude, working unconscious and undetected, may be one of the distorting factors, inhibiting the imaginative daring which empowers the soul for the God-vision.[41]

How in the light of his faith and his religious experience did Hodges view the place and role of the Christian in the modern university? First, he sets his face against those Christians who, while granting that the modern world has made particular discoveries of value, nevertheless feel that such trends of thought as humanism, subjectivism and relativism are to be opposed in the interests of 'the age-long philosophy'.[42] Hodges takes a quite different view. Christians, he thinks, have much to learn from current intellectual trends, and hence the appropriate posture is 'not defensiveness, but adventurous exploration, not smothering the awkward

---

[39] Idem, *God be in my Thinking*, 50.

[40] Ibid., 51. One wonders how many of Hodges' philosophical peers would have thought of epistemology in this way.

[41] Ibid., 52–3.

[42] Idem, *The Christian in the Modern University*, 11.

questions which modern enquiry has raised, but going deeper into them than has yet been done. We have not to bury liberalism, but to save it from itself and give it a spiritual stamina which hitherto it has not possessed; for the only workable liberalism is precisely that which springs from Christian roots.'[43]

Hodges proceeds to invoke three aspects of the Christian faith in support of his claims. There is first the Christian understanding of humanity as created by God in order that human beings may have relations with God. We are potential masters of the created order, but before God we are conscious of responsibilities and obligations, and this both gives us a new dignity and places us at risk of alienating ourselves from God, to our own hurt. Writing in wartime, Hodges adds, 'That man is now tearing himself in pieces is a fact which everyone can see.'[44] Secondly, 'We have not to do with an impersonal or self-absorbed Absolute Being, but with the Living God.'[45] A divine strategy is being pursued through history, and God is the shepherd and king of his people, and 'Those who know that the Lord is King, and follow His known will with loyalty and trust, find their faith more and more justified in experience, and face events with a confidence which has nothing to do with human optimism.'[46] Thirdly, Christian personalism derives from the fact that 'Wherever I see a man, I seen one to whom God speaks, and for whose good will God has paid a great price. This gives to every human being an inalienable value, a claim on our reverence and regard.'[47] Moreover, the God who speaks to everyone can also speak through them to others.

In the light of these Christian convictions, three things appear as ultimate aims. First, we must carry out a study of human thinking in the light of Christian faith. Secondly, we must bring our individual apprehensions of Christian truth under judgement. Thirdly, in a spirit of Christian liberalism, and in the interests of society, we must work for the free articulation and the frank critique of Christian ideas.

So much for ultimate aims; but what must Christian students and teachers do now? They must seriously study theology and disabuse themselves of the false belief that the differences between Christians do not matter. They do, because 'forms of statement, as well as forms of worship, condition the apprehension of reality and mould the spiritual life'.[48] Again, they must ponder the possibility of a theology of university work. The question is not whether university work is useful to society, but whether God is glorified by it. Finally, they must penetrate below current ideas to the moving forces which have produced them. Outwardly the Christian must offer radical yet impartial criticism as appropriate,

---

[43] Ibid.
[44] Ibid., 13.
[45] Ibid.
[46] Ibid., 14.
[47] Ibid.
[48] Ibid., 21.

But his real work is done invisibly, in the imagination and the intellect, where he must labour to penetrate to the heart of the conflicting doctrines, to the spiritual attitudes underlying them, to experience in himself the intolerable tension of their mutual antagonism, and in the exercise of Christ's royal priesthood, with which as a member of Christ he is clothed, to present the suffering world to the Father. This is the peculiar liturgy or service of all who live the life of the mind. It is their peculiar share in the Passion of Christ. ... Where this is done, the scholar's or the student's work is transfigured, and its place in the never-ending dialogue between God and man in Christ becomes clear.[49]

So H. A. Hodges believed, and in the light of this faith he lived, taught and wrote, often in face of indifferent health. His release came on 2 July 1976. He was recalled as

a shy man and some people found him taciturn and elusive. He occasionally said – inaccurately – that he had no small talk. Within his family and by close friends, however, he is spoken of as a most devoted individual and those who worked alongside him in the academic world remember him as a courteous and considerate colleague.[50]

I turn now to consider Hodges' philosophy, his theological writings and his devotional works.

I

I have already observed that Hodges ploughed his own furrow in philosophy. This is not to say that he was unconscious of, or uninterested in, the current trends in his chosen discipline. On the contrary, as we shall see, he was deeply disturbed by some of them, and sympathetic towards others. My point is that he was too much his own man to be unduly swayed by current intellectual fashion. Again, unlike his senior colleague de Burgh, and notwithstanding his grounding in Classics, he did not draw upon the heritage of Greek philosophy to any great extent, and he was almost entirely silent on the medievals. He does not major on any of the standard British or European philosophers, but instead devotes considerable attention to Dilthey, the principal characteristic of whose thought was its embrace of a number of humanities disciplines. Since Hodges' two books on Dilthey are almost entirely expository, I shall not, in what follows, describe their contents in detail. Rather, I shall advert to those aspects of Dilthey's thought upon which Hodges himself drew as he developed his own views. For the present it will suffice to say that it was Dilthey's coordinating and methodologically hospitable approach

---

[49] Ibid., 24.
[50] W. D. Hudson, H. A. Hodges (1905–76), prefixed to H. A. Hodges, *God Beyond Knowledge*, ed. W. D. Hudson, London: Macmillan, 1979, x.

which stimulated Hodges' own discussions of world views, and in the light of it he considered what he called the crisis in philosophy and the logic of religious thinking. Deeply interested in the philosophy of history, Hodges did not contribute greatly to the history of philosophy. By way of placing him, however, we may set out from a brief contribution of his to the latter field of enquiry, 'British philosophy, 1689–1830'.[51]

Hodges declares that by contrast with the 'speculative tendencies' of our 'Continental neighbours' the 'ruling temper' of both medieval and modern British philosophy is empirical, and that British speculative thought generally finds its outlet in poetry:

> Instead of a Leibniz to write a *Theodicy* we have Milton justifying the ways of God to man in epic drama. Our Fichte and Schelling and Hegel are Blake and Wordsworth and Shelley, and the English counterpart of Nietzsche is William Morris. Accordingly, when the British mind does give itself up to philosophy, it does so in a more critical spirit, suspicious of metaphysical systems, but closely allied with scientific inquiry into nature, as well as with the study of moral and political questions, in which an obvious practical interest can be found.[52]

It may be suggested that the contrast is too sharply drawn, for Locke is a rationalist in ethics, and Berkeley's philosophy, as Hodges will remind us, terminates in a psychological-idealistic metaphysic.

Hodges devotes four of his 14 pages to Locke, 'The father of the British School of philosophy',[53] whom he presents as the interpreter and apologist of the Glorious Revolution and of the scientific outlook flowing from Newton and others. 'A passion for freedom and toleration runs through [Locke's] writing', he declares – a judgement that requires the qualification that although Locke's view of suitable candidates for toleration broadened over the years, he drew the line at Roman Catholics, whom he regarded as being in thrall to a foreign power, and hence whose loyalty to Britain could not, he felt, be counted upon.[54] Locke, Hodges continues, asserted the individual's right to pursue happiness in ways which did not restrict the right of others to do the same; and he regarded the state as the defender and guardian of the rights of people to life, liberty and property. But it was Locke's *Essay concerning Human Understanding*, which 'laid the foundations of a most significant movement of thought both here and abroad'.[55] Locke compared the situation of philosophy unfavourably with that of mathematics and natural science

---

[51] In H. V. D. Dyson and John Butt, eds, *Augustans and Romantics 1689–1830*, 3rd revised edn, London: Cresset Press, 1961, 100–113.
[52] Ibid., 100.
[53] Ibid., 101.
[54] See further Alan P. F. Sell, *John Locke and the Eighteenth-Century Divines*, Cardiff: University of Wales Press, 1997; Eugene, OR: Wipf & Stock, 2006, ch. 5.
[55] H. A. Hodges, 'British philosophy', 102.

and, with a view to establishing the discipline of a firm basis, he investigated the powers of the mind and the nature and sources of knowledge. He regarded his work as that of an 'under-labourer', rather than of one who adds to the sum of human knowledge. In Hodges' opinion, 'Locke's performance was not equal to the greatness of his task.'[56] Adopting a psychological approach, Locke concluded that 'all thought and knowledge are derived from sensation. Ideas come into the mind through the senses, and are then made the objects of thought, which by various processes of distinguishing, combining, abstracting, inferring and the like, builds up the system of knowledge. Locke undertakes to show in detail how this is done, a task in which by common consent he fails.'[57] Pointing out that Locke holds that we are certain of the truth of mathematical propositions, of our own existence which we know by direct acquaintance, and of God's existence, which we infer with certainty from our own, Hodges finds it paradoxical in view of Locke's intellectual background that he 'denies that we have anything that deserves to be called knowledge in the strict sense about the external world. We have no direct acquaintance with this world, but only with the sensations which we believe it causes us to have.'[58] While 'the qualities of things is accessible to us, their real essence or substance is not. And therefore we cannot be said to have knowledge of them'.[59] We have only sensations which we believe are caused by the natural world, and we conceive of a world of objects which more or less resemble them.

At this point Berkeley demurs. In Locke's view science shows that some qualities regularly co-exist or succeed one another regularly in accordance with the laws of nature, we cannot say why these things happen: they are brute facts. To Berkeley this was no explanation at all, and he therefore argued that events occur because they are necessitated, constrained. But our only evidence for this is that provided by our own mental experience. Hence, as Hodges puts Berkeley's point, 'if natural phenomena are to be explained by reference to substance and cause, this means that they must be explained as manifestations of mind ... the Mind of God'.[60] Berkeley is thus led to his view that 'The *esse* of the natural world is *percipi*, and when we say that a natural object exists we mean, or ought to mean, simply that it is perceived by someone, or that in certain assignable circumstances it would be perceived.'[61] To this point Berkeley is in succession to Locke, but he then proceeds from logic and epistemology to metaphysics, and propounds a

---

[56] Ibid., 103.
[57] Ibid.
[58] Ibid., 104.
[59] Ibid. This was the point at which, in the interests of averting scepticism, Edward Stillingfleet, Bishop of Worcester, plunged in the knife. See his *A Discourse in Vindication of the Doctrine of the Trinity* (1697), reprinted in *The Philosophy of Edward Stillingfleet*, Bristol: Thoemmes Press, 2000, IV, 233–6. Cf. Locke's *Letter to the Bishop of Worcester*, in *The Works of John Locke in Ten Volumes*, London: W. Otridge, et al., 11th edition, 1812, IV, 5.
[60] Ibid., 105.
[61] Ibid., 106.

Neoplatonic doctrine according to which 'The natural world is a manifestation of the character of its Creator, and in His Mind subsist the eternal archetypal Ideas, of which the ideas that He imprints upon our senses are a distant reflection. The perceived world is His message to us about Himself couched in the language of sensible things.'[62]

In Hume, Hodges declares, Locke's logical and epistemological thrust and his moral and political thrust come together in 'a common dependence upon psychology', and this in accordance with Hume's conviction that 'every branch of knowledge is logically dependent upon a prior inquiry into the nature of the mind which knows, so that psychology is the foundation of all the sciences'.[63] In the wake of Locke, Hume holds that all knowledge derives from sensation:

> There is nothing in the mind except impressions (i.e. sensations) and ideas (i.e. mental images), and all ideas are derived from impressions preciously received. Out of these elements the structure of thought is built up, not, as in Locke and Berkeley, by the purposeful activity of the thinking self, but by processes of recall and combination which take place in accordance with the laws of memory and association. Ideas become associated mechanically, by resemblance or by virtue of occurring together in experience.[64]

To Hume, both the idea of causal actions and the idea of the substantial unity of the self are illusions: 'The self' is just 'a group of psychic events; of any deeper-lying unity there is no trace'.[65] Hume recognizes, however, that the beliefs that philosophy undermines are essential for the conduct of life, and therefore he resites human conduct by arguing that it is the human passions, not reason, which guide the moral life towards that happiness which is the only criterion of right and wrong action. In this he is a forerunner of utilitarianism – the product of the combination of associationism with moral philosophy in eudaemonistic mode which we find in Adam Smith, Jeremy Bentham and James Mill.

Against Locke and Hume, Reid and Dugald Stewart contend that 'the explanation of thought in terms of sense is inadequate, and that there is a distinctively intellective element, as well as a sensuous one, in even the lowliest acts of perception'.[66] The Scottish philosophers, according to Hodges, are 'devoid of creative power, and made no first-rate contribution to philosophy'. When he adds that 'The claim sometimes made, that Reid anticipated some of the work of Kant, is so exaggerated as to be absurd'[67] he is unduly dismissive of pre-Kantian

---

[62] Ibid., 107.
[63] Ibid., 107–8.
[64] Ibid., 108.
[65] Ibid., 109.
[66] Ibid., 111.
[67] Ibid.

intellectualist straws in the wind which he might also have found in Richard Price, whom he nowhere mentions.

Hodges' chapter ends with a brief sketch of Coleridge's thought. Coleridge, originally in accord with Hume's follower, Hartley, came, under Neoplatonic and Berekeleian influences, to believe that the philosophy of experience was moribund, as when Hume left us with an group of mutually isolated mental events. Enter the free activity of the mind in perception, imagination and thought. Coleridge finds his view endorsed by Kant and Fichte. He does not repudiate Hume's mechanism of recall and association, but holds that rational interpretation and feeling take precedence over it. From thence he proceeds to speculative metaphysics, and to the claim that the processes of nature are not mechanical, but organic, with God standing over all as 'the supreme rational Will from which [the natural order] is derived'.[68] Coleridge, Hodges concludes, 'stands as a living witness to a certain idealist strain which, though not usually dominant, has rarely been absent altogether from the philosophy of these islands'.[69] This acknowledgement of idealistic strains of British philosophical thought, which Hodges himself observes in Berkeley's position, belatedly tempers the unqualified empiricist and non-speculative description of British philosophy, with which he opened his chapter.

Given his philosophical-*cum*-interdisciplinary interests, it is not surprising that Hodges had a particular interest in psychology in its humanistic guise. In his discussion of Dilthey's position he carefully sets down the two main alternative attitudes towards the subject. On the one hand there is, as we have just seen, the psychological approach of Locke, Hume and Berkeley. Hume believed that psychology underlay logic, moral and political theory, and that 'even natural science and natural theology need a logical and epistemological foundation which only the science of the mind can give'.[70] Dilthey's Berlin colleague, Helmholtz, advanced a similar theory. On the other hand there is the line of philosophers from Plato through the scholastics and Descartes to Kant and the post-Kantians who contend that

> psychology is a positive science, a study of fact, whereas logic and moral and political theory are normative studies. In particular they argue that psychology is an empirical study of states and processes of consciousness and its object, with a view to discriminating between appearance and reality. Psychology regards true and false belief, veridical perception and illusion, all alike as facts of mental history, and studies them all alike from the standpoint of psychological law.

---

[68] Ibid., 113.

[69] Ibid. For evidence in support of this claim see, for example, John H. Muirhead, *The Platonic Tradition in Anglo-Saxon Philosophy*, London: Allen & Unwin, 1931. In his survey, Muirhead hops from Arthur Collier, who died in 1732, to Coleridge and Carlyle, thereby, like Hodges, neglecting Price, whose name does not appear in Muirhead's index.

[70] H. A. Hodges, *Wilhelm Dilthey. An Introduction* (hereinafter WDI), London: Routledge & Kegan Paul, 1944, 36.

The only effect it can have on the theory of knowledge is to cast doubt upon all our beliefs and pave the way to scepticism, because it shows how many non-logical influences enter into the formation of our judgments. It is by a different study, on non-psychological grounds, that the objectivity of thought and the reality of its objects must be vindicated. Such a study Kant and his successors find in transcendental logic or epistemology. Psychology itself, they say, presupposes such a study, for unless the possibility of knowledge is first established, no positive science can move hand or foot.[71]

On this matter Dilthey is in the wake of Locke, Berkeley and Hume. It is not that epistemology convinces us of the possibility of knowledge. On the contrary, 'Epistemology itself presupposes the knowledge that there is such a thing as knowledge, to give it something to talk about, and the fact that we have knowledge is more certain than any epistemological explanation of the fact.'[72] We learn to test claims to knowledge and truth from childhood onwards, and were the real world not a fact of consciousness, epistemology could not discuss it. On all these points Hodges sides with Dilthey, and this empiricist thrust might make him appear more akin to many of his philosophical contemporaries than I have so far suggested. But that we have to do with more than epistemological empiricism *versus* epistemological idealism becomes clear when Hodges discusses Dilthey's criticisms of the psychology current in his day. In the first place, it was too individualistic: 'Dilthey believes that not only psychology, but also economics, political theory and other kindred studies have gone astray ... through taking for granted the self-contained individual as their foundation, and failing to recognize that the life of the individual consists largely in the social relations into which he enters, the historical process of which he is a product and upon which he reacts.'[73] A true psychology must present humans as social beings. With this Hodges is in entire accord. Indeed, he remarks that to Anglo-Saxon philosophers,

> the most novel and striking thing [in Dilthey's writings] will probably be his delicate and detailed analysis of the process of *understanding* (*das Verstehen*) whereby we come to know our own mental life and that of others. This is a side of epistemology which has been steadily neglected since the very earliest times. Philosophers have devoted endless trouble to discussing how we come to be aware of physical objects and how far subjective elements enter into our

---

[71] Ibid., 37.
[72] Ibid. Cf. Idem, *The Philosophy of Wilhelm Dilthey* (hereinafter PWD), London: Routledge & Kegan Paul, 1952, 31. In Dilthey's view epistemology investigates the sense in which, and the degree to which, 'the selves and objects ... appearing in our consciousness are "real" and "objective". ... [I]n his view, lived experience is the very paradigm of "reality". It is the basis on which imagination, memory, and thought arise, and their sole function ... is to clarify and amplify what is ours in lived experience.' PWD. 50, 51; cf. 55.
[73] WDI, 40. Cf. PWD, 170–72.

experience of them. They have talked as if our world consisted entirely of such objects, and as if knowledge of them were our chief intellectual concern. Yet the most significant of our experiences lie in our relations with other people, and the nature and extent of the knowledge which we can have of other people is a question of equal importance with the first. Dilthey is the first philosopher in any country to tackle the question seriously and systematically .[74]

Dilthey's second complaint against psychology is that its results are uncertain. The reason is that, following Hume, it has been supposed that the way to secure psychology's findings is to apply to the subject the method of the physical sciences:

> This meant reducing the variety of mental life to the combinations and interactions of units of sensation and feeling, supposed to be primary, and to be brought and held together by laws of association. It was a picture as unlike ordinary experience as the physicist's picture is unlike the world we perceive, but it was supposed to be verifiable in the same way as his, by being shown to explain the facts. This, however, is just what could not be done. The method of physical science was here being used in a field where it cannot succeed. ... We can form hypotheses about the relations between mental facts and processes, and between mind and body; but we can form too many, and there is no experimental control.[75]

Here, too, Hodges is in agreement, though he subsequently observes that Hume 'knew in his wiser moments that mental life is not to be explained exclusively in terms of impressions, ideas, and laws of association. But in his less wise moments he wrote as if it could be explained just in those terms.'[76] On the general point, as we shall see later, he was, like de Burgh, Matthews and Quick, fully aware of the folly of supposing that the scientific method was applicable to quite different realms of experience. In the particular case of the mental life, and contrary to what Hume had contended in the Preface to his seminal work, *A Treatise of Human Nature*, physics 'was the wrong model of interpretation, and it could only appear to succeed so long as attention was focused mainly on questions of perception and memory. It could not deal with the deeper levels of the instinctive life, nor yet with the higher intellectual and spiritual activities.'[77] Furthermore, he endorses Dilthey's contention that 'The real unit of mental life is not a sensation or a feeling, or even an isolated "intentional act" with its "content", but a total reaction of the whole self to a situation confronting it.'[78] Here we have a stimulus to that strand of existentialism in Hodges' thought which is important in his discussion of world views. Here, too, we have Dilthey's further idea, which Hodges echoes,

---

[74] Ibid., viii.
[75] Ibid., 41, 42. Cf. PWD, 22–3.
[76] Ibid., 17.
[77] Ibid.
[78] WDI, 43.

that we learn who we are not by introspection or psychological experimentation, but from history. This is consistent with Dilthey's view of consciousness, which Hodges construes as being that it is not subjective only, but 'embraces both poles of the subject-object synthesis'.[79] Dilthey's thought was ever in motion, and in later years he developed this last point more fully. Hodges, with reference to the positivism (Comteian,[80] not logical) and Romanticism which permeate Dilthey's thought, explains matters as follows

> It is the positivist Dilthey ... who discusses the function of theories and hypotheses in psychology, and calls for the adoption of a descriptive method. But he is no positivist when he actually describes the structure of mental life. ... The paradigm of intelligibility, for [positivism and scientific realism], was to bring many particular instances under a general formula. Its procedure ... was always to abstract and isolate, to single out a particular process in mental life for special study, and then build up the whole out of the pieces. This is not Dilthey's way. Dilthey is concerned with the whole man rather than with particular aspects of his mental processes and the laws which govern them; and he sees the whole man not from without, like an impersonal observer, but from within, as the man sees and feels himself. This is the view of life which finds expression in lyric poetry, or in autobiography, or in religious meditations, and it is to these and similar sources that Dilthey calls our attention.[81]

In two sentences Hodges diagnoses Dilthey's situation and also tacitly adumbrates the two sides of his own experience which he ever sought to hold in balance:

> The romantic tradition gives [Dilthey] a lively sense of the depth and movement of the mind's life, but does not correlate it satisfactorily with the scientific view of nature, or apply it energetically enough for the betterment of society. The empirical and positivist tradition has a sense of social function, and a proper respect for scientific knowledge, but its view of the mind's life is crude and superficial. Each requires the other, and one main strand in Dilthey's thinking will be his unceasing effort to combine what is good and true in both.[82]

In the event, Dilthey had to concede that

---

[79] H. A. Hodges, in the symposium, *Phenomenology, Goodness and Beauty* (*Proceedings of the Aristotelian Society. Supplementary Volume*, XI), 1932, 87.

[80] See PWD, 18, 187. Dilthey sympathizes with Comte's view that we have no knowledge of the real nature and causes of things, but he is not thereby prevented from regarding the Frenchman's manner of expression as vague and unscientifically dogmatic.

[81] PWD, 201.

[82] Ibid., 23.

the kind of psychology which the human studies require, a psychology based on the understanding of the structural system of mental life, cannot be incorporated in, or developed out of, psychology as commonly perceived and practised; and he dissociated his structure-psychology so far from science, and brought it so close to literature, that he was forced to reconsider its position in the scheme of human studies, though he never formally adopted a new position on that point. ... It means that Hume's programme can be carried out only if the study of human nature ... is carefully distinguished from experimental psychology, not identified with it as he proposes.[83]

It is abundantly clear that the differing approaches to psychology presuppose different attitudes towards metaphysics. Since the latter pursuit was under a cloud in much English philosophy contemporary with Hodges' career, it will be interesting to see how far the somewhat dismissive tone *vis-à-vis* metaphysics that I detected in his brief account of Augustan philosophy is amplified elsewhere in his writings. Was he, for example, in accord with Dilthey, that noted foe of metaphysics, with whose ideas Hodges spent so much time? Dilthey is reported as holding that 'The "philosophical" disciplines [logic, ethics, political theory, aesthetics] have distinguished themselves from others only by chasing the metaphysical will-o'-the wisp of absolute principles, and in so doing they have wasted their labour.'[84] Philosophy, thinks Dilthey, goes in quest of absolute first principles in all aspects of life and thought. This yields numerous first principles, and the metaphysician seeks to weld them into

a systematic unity, embracing the absolute reality, the absolute first principle of knowledge, absolute good, absolute right, and absolute beauty; to reconcile the regularity which he finds to be absolutely presupposes in natural science with the freedom which is equally presupposed in ethics; and in general to bring all departmental truths together in one absolute truth. ... [T]he philosopher undertakes not merely to do all this, but to make a science of it, to present the result as a watertight logical system with precise definitions and demonstrative arguments. The task ... is beyond human capacity.[85]

Dilthey's contrasting view is that our only source of knowledge is experience, and anything outside the range of observation must be conceived on analogy with that which is observable, and must be shown to be implied in experience. Of course, 'We cannot fulfil these conditions where the Absolute is concerned.'[86] It is no surprise that metaphysics has never reached, and could never reach, an agreed definition of 'substance' or 'causality', yet to take the positivist or phenomenalist route leaves

---

[83] Ibid., 223.
[84] WDI, 60.
[85] Ibid., 94.
[86] Ibid., 95; cf. 91.

us with no metaphysic at all, whereas 'To seek escape through idealism, making mind the only reality, is to transfer the imprecisions and ambiguities into the very core of the system.'[87]

It would be wrong to conclude from this somewhat doleful estimate of the viability of metaphysics that Dilthey was an out-and-out empiricist. He was in fact willing to learn from many, frequently competing, strains of thought, and this may be illustrated by reference to his attitude towards Kant. He welcomed Kant's turn from speculative metaphysics to the critique of knowledge; but regretted that Kant's critique concerned only mathematical and scientific knowledge. Dilthey wished to extend the enquiry to cover historical and social studies. Again, when, at the hands of neo-Kantians, Kant's doctrines were transmuted into *a priori* principles Dilthey protested that

> There is no 'timeless world' of meanings, or essences, or rational principles; there is no clear-cut distinction ... between the rational level of experience and the irrational, the 'spirit' and the 'psyche'; there is no 'metaphysical subject' or 'transcendental self' such as is found in orthodox Kantian and post-Kantian theories of knowledge. There is only the human being, the mind-body unit (*psychophysische Einheit*), living his life in interaction with his physical and social environment; and out of this interaction all experience and thought arise.[88]

Hodges' verdict is that 'when it comes to points of detail, [Dilthey] is plainly nor a Kantian at all'.[89]

It follows that in Dilthey's thought, 'The word "reality" ... has no shadow of a Hegelian meaning. Dilthey does not mean that "mind" is a "higher degree of reality" or "a more explicit expression of the Absolute" than matter ... He is merely making the well-known point that our own thoughts and feelings are experience or lived through (*erlebt*) by us immediately and from within, in a sense in which external objects are not.'[90] It does not follow, however, that Dilthey is an extreme empiricist. As Hodges remarks, 'Where our modern positivists treat metaphysical questions as nonsense, Dilthey treats them as significant but unanswerable.'[91] Philosophers may perfectly properly discuss the motives which lead us to ask questions we have no power to answer. Again, Dilthey's is not a behaviourist approach to the minds of others. He thinks that by imaginative reconstruction, followed by intellectual analysis and theorizing, we can understand not only the behaviour, but the experiences of others. His philosophy would fall to pieces if this part of it dropped out.[92] Dilthey's problem with both Kantians and empiricists

---

[87] Ibid., 96.
[88] PWD, xviii–xix.
[89] Ibid., 2.
[90] Ibid., xix.
[91] Ibid.
[92] Ibid., xx.

is that 'they treat the various factors in mental life too much in isolation', and they overlook 'the influence of historical and social conditions'.[93] On neither point is Hegel to be preferred, for the 'great flaw in his theory' viz., is his '*a priori* formalism which makes him treat the movement of life as if it were wholly a movement of ideal principles, and reduce the whole body of historical and social philosophy to one element in a metaphysic of abstract forms'.[94] Again, whereas to Hegel, 'Art. religion, and philosophy ... are not only ways of expressing and developing the metaphysical consciousness, but ways of reaching ultimate truth', to Dilthey 'the essence of religion' lies in 'man's attempt to make contact with the unseen'.[95] Central to Dilthey's distaste for idealistic metaphysics is his conviction that it leaves the individual and the universal side by side but unconnected. His desideratum was an empirical psychology 'which shall make known the laws in accordance with which the universal becomes individuated'.[96]

II

How far was Dilthey able to synthesize the Romantic and natural scientific strains in his thought, and what did Hodges learn from him in this regard? We may approach an answer to this question if we investigate further the distinction drawn by Dilthey between the natural and the human sciences. In a nutshell, the natural sciences are said to be concerned with factual description and explanation in terms of causal laws, whereas, to reproduce a concise dictionary definition, the basis of the human sciences is 'an analytical and descriptive psychology able to facilitate, through its systematic knowledge of consciousness, an understanding both of structural (or organic) unity of individual and social life and of its historical development as manifested in cultural systems of art, science and religion'.[97] On this broad theme a number of variations are played, as I shall now seek to show by setting down (necessarily baldly) some of the ways in which Dilthey (as Hodges expounds his writings) compares and contrasts the natural sciences with the human sciences (or 'human studies', as Hodges calls them).

In some respects both realms of enquiry are the same. For example, both require reflection upon experience, utilize the logical processes of judgement and inference, and pursue experimental and comparative methods.[98] But the contrasts between them remain significant. Thus, whereas the natural sciences are concerned with sensible phenomena which are produced independently of the activity of

---

[93] WDI, 89.
[94] Ibid., 65.
[95] Ibid., 93.
[96] PWD, 211.
[97] G. Duncan Mitchell in his edited work, *A Dictionary of Sociology*, London: Routledge & Kegan Paul, 1968, 57.
[98] See PWD, 230.

mind, in the human sciences the realities of our lived experience in history and society – material, mental and spiritual – are to the fore. To put it otherwise, 'The natural sciences being with sense-data and cannot find any principle of unity in them; the unity of the physical world has to be supplied by hypothesis. But the human studies can rest upon a direct apprehension of their object as a living unity; the enquirer finds it given in himself by inner perception, and rediscovers it from moment to moment in his understanding of others.'[99] In other words, 'the greatest difference of all is due to the fact that we do not know the inner nature of physical things and processes, and have to read causal order into them by hypothesis, whereas in the world of mind we know directly what we are dealing with'.[100] The upshot is that whereas

> The units out of which natural science builds up its works are hypothetical constructions, divested of all sensuous quality, unperceived and imperceptible, and nothing is known or can be conceived of them except the relations in which they stand ... In the human studies it is the other way round. The units here are individual minds, real, concrete, known to us as they are, and the only realities which are so known.[101]

But since no two individuals are absolutely alike, 'the discovery of general laws, which is the greatest triumph of natural science, is hardly possible in human studies ... over the greater part of our field we have only empirical generalizations'.[102] Thus, while Dilthey was impressed by Comte's hierarchical ordering of the natural sciences in terms of their degree of complexity, and his claim that they were properly grouped in accordance with the method of investigating them, he disagreed with Comte's view that the human sciences could be gathered under sociology, and that this compendious subject could be the apex of the scientific disciplinary pyramid. The human sciences, he contended, are various, and their methods are distinct from those of the natural sciences: they rest upon inner experience, not outward observation and experiment.

Among other contrasts is the fact that the natural sciences are not concerned with value judgements as such: impartiality is their goal; whereas in the human sciences, says Dilthey, we evaluate on the basis of emotions and volitions and make corresponding utterances, we do not pass 'judgments';[103] but by 'moral feeling' Dilthey means 'not a chaotic aggregate of passive impressions, but a "purposive system", "not heterogeneous from reason", which springs from the end of our being (*Zweck unseres Wesens*) and expresses to our consciousness in

---

[99] Ibid., 124.
[100] Ibid., 230.
[101] WDI, 76; cf. PWD, 235–6, 259, 270.
[102] Ibid., 79.
[103] PWD, 78.

intuitive form the immanent teleology of our nature'.[104] This must be understood in relation to Dilthey's anti-metaphysical claim that 'There ... are no absolute values or unconditional norms of conduct. ... His principles are not self-luminous, nor are they known to us by rational analysis. They are known by induction from experience, and express what life itself teaches us.'[105] All of which is to say that Dilthey's ethic is grounded in social fact, and is opposed equally to transcendental and empiricist moral theory, both of which he pronounces bankrupt.[106]

Yet another contrast between the natural and the human sciences is found in the fact that the former are not concerned with history as such, whereas the latter consider the relationships between individuals and groups from the point of view of their ability or otherwise to produce value and meaning, and achieve purposes. It should carefully be noted that in what Dilthey calls his Critique of Historical Reason – that project in which he takes up where he thinks Kant left off – he is decidedly not out to propound a philosophy of history designed to disclose the overarching 'meaning' of history.[107] On the contrary, he sets his face against any such metaphysical objective, feeling that in the hands of Hegel above all, 'the philosophy of history became part of a grandiose synthesis, as speculative in its fundamental principles as it was often reckless in its treatment of details'.[108] Instead, he proposes to conduct a philosophical investigation of the methods and conclusions of social and historical research. Among his findings is the fact that while in the natural sciences 'time' is an abstract concept, in the human sciences it is the relation between past and present, the understanding of which involves the use of memory, which yields the historical category of meaning. This meaning is read into history by individuals, and 'to study the meaning of history is to analyse the human value-consciousness'.[109] As Hodges construes Dilthey: 'In coming to grips with an outstanding individual or movement in the past, whatever help we may get from general truths and causal inferences, the most proper and (to be paradoxical) the most objective approach is the most subjective, the reliving in ourselves of what we study.'[110] Hodges further explains that, according to Dilthey,

> The data of history not only are manifestations of mind, but are perceived as such, and this makes an epistemological difference between historical study and natural science. The scientist observes things and processes, but perceives no activity in them, no dynamic relationships. What he learns of their causal connections is learned by hypothesis and experiment and remains in the form of

---

[104] Ibid., 100; cf. xxi–xxii.
[105] Ibid., 81, 82.
[106] Ibid., 183.
[107] See W. Dilthey, *Introduction to the Human Sciences*, eds R. A. Makkreel and F. Rodi, Princeton, NJ: Princeton University Press, 1989, 141.
[108] PWD, xvi; cf. 167, 264–9; 299–303.
[109] PWD, 190.
[110] WDI, 20.

abstract law. But the manifestations of mind are instinct with the life from which they seeing and upon which they continually react. ... We cannot observe them at all without seeing them as parts of a dynamic process, and this is the very thing that is meant by calling them 'historical'.[111]

Moreover, we are selves who live within this process: we shape, and are shaped by, history, but this not in an atomistic way. On the contrary, we come to know our own individuality as we have experience of that of others.

Perhaps the greatest distinction between the natural and the human sciences, according to Dilthey, is that the former is methodologically abstractive while the latter is not: 'whereas natural science abstracts from the perceived world those aspects which can be built up into a regular quantitative system, the human studies treat the world, or rather certain objects in it, as matter for understanding'.[112] The natural sciences are not concerned with what is given in lived experience. This is not to deny that the subject matter of the natural and human sciences may overlap: for example, 'the human organism has to be studied in the light of biology';[113] and the course of history itself is not immune to causal factors. It is also the case that the human sciences may be described as in one (different) sense abstractive; that is, they can be considered severally as well as in relation to one another. On the main point Hodges justifiably opines that 'The paradoxical character of the scientific view of nature and the artificiality of its starting point would be better realized if they were not so familiar.'[114] Moreover, it is precisely because of its delimited terrain that the natural sciences can achieve a degree of objectivity and precision that are denied to the human sciences. 'This', says Hodges, 'is the price they pay for their greater concreteness and nearness to the wealth and colour of human experience.'[115]

It should not be necessary, but it will do no harm, to emphasize that it would have been quite out of character for Dilthey to posit a metaphysical distinction between the natural and the human sciences which might, for example, yield a causality-freedom dualism. Rather, the distinction is one of method and content and, as we have seen, in these connections certain common interests are discernible. Positively, Dilthey showed that 'the two methods, though different, are not antithetic'.[116] Negatively, he showed that it is not the case that where the natural sciences are intellectually rigorous, the human sciences are 'a mere welter of subjective impressions, but have rigorous methods and controls of their own'.[117]

---

[111] Ibid., 21.
[112] PWD, 254.
[113] Ibid., 169.
[114] WDI, 74.
[115] Ibid., 76; cf. PWD, 128.
[116] WDI, 13.
[117] Ibid., viii. He rebukes Bergson and Gentile for not being rigorous enough. See ibid., 12–13.

His reflections on the natural sciences-human sciences debate lead Hodges to make some observations on ethics, education, and Christianity in relation both to the social and the natural sciences. As to ethics, we find that in his symposium paper on 'Things and persons' he argues that

> Philosophy makes a big mistake if it confines its interest in logic, in aesthetics, or in ethics to the processes which go on within the thinking, contemplating or deliberating mind, or to the formal principles by which these processes are or should be guided, and overlooks the interplay between subject and object which is the very meaning of all these spheres of activity. But for ethics it is only the relationships with human beings which are of prime concern.[118]

He proceeds to discuss relationships between strangers, associates and fellows, and finds that our interest in other persons turns upon two factors. The first is cognitive: our understanding of one another. Hodges explains that he uses 'understanding' in Dilthey's sense, but presses the idea further:

> I know what it is to be a man. I know it intimately, from within, because I am a man, and I not only have experiences like other men, but can reflect on them. ... But the understanding which I have of human life like my own is not merely, as Dilthey maintains, the epistemological foundation of the *Geisteswissenschaften*; it is also the cognitive side of the foundation on which morality rests.[119]

But, says Hodges, we might understand others correctly profoundly and yet remain indifferent to what we know of them. Accordingly, 'the love and reverence for other persons, which animates my conduct so far as it is moral, is an appreciative attitude, made up of affective and volitional elements, and not a form of cognition. And therefore there is and can be no reason for it. It is one of those "passions" whose "slave" reason "is and ought only to be".'[120] In the concluding paragraph of his paper Hodges poses the following question: 'How can we prevent the sense of the importance of persons from being overlain and stifled by other motives and interests?' He recognizes that this has been a perennial danger but he thinks that the threat has never been more serious than it now is. He cites 'the power-cult which stands at the centre of many modern movements' as being 'incompatible with ... reverence for human persons';[121] and then, evincing not a little prescience, he considers it probable

---

[118] Idem, 'Things and persons', in the symposium of that title, *Proceedings of the Aristotelian Society. Supplementary Volume*, XXII, 1948, 195.

[119] Ibid., 199.

[120] Ibid., 200.

[121] Ibid., 201.

that the intellectual habits associated with scientific work are, if not incompatible with this reverence [for other persons], at least inimical to it. These forces, relatively new in man's history, are in process of bringing about changes in his ways of thinking and living which we cannot see to their end. Those who do not wish to let morality as hitherto known go by default must ask themselves what forces they can put into the field against those which are making the drift. It seems unlikely that an answer will be found quickly and easily, if it is found at all.[122]

Sixty years on, the search for an answer continues, as ethical committees scrutinize the research proposals of scientists, seeking in some cases to persuade them than in the interests of persons, they might consider that it is not necessarily right to achieve results that it might theoretically be possible to achieve, and even on occasion pressing for legislation against experimentation deemed to be immoral or otherwise harmful in itself and/or in its probable consequences.

Where education is concerned, Hodges detects, and regrets, a chasm which he says has latterly opened up between the humanities and the social sciences. By 'humanities' he means linguistic and literary studies, art history and criticism; and by 'social sciences' he means psychology, anthropology, economics, human geography and sociology. He finds that the humanities have retained 'much of the spirit of scholarship which dominated the Renaissance',[123] while the social sciences have turned in the direction of the natural sciences. As for history, it 'stands in a manner between these two groups, able to ally itself with either'.[124] Rickert is among those who have adduced logical grounds for making the distinction, while Dilthey, on the contrary, insists that 'methods are accidental and subject-matter essential, that as man in all his being is one entity, in his reflexes and his senses and emotions, his thoughts and purposes and creative imagination, his character and outlook, his economic, cultural, social, religious aspirations and achievements, so the study of man must be one study, in spite of all complexities and divergences within it'.[125] From this point of view, says Hodges, 'the question of the architectonic of the human studies is no dry pedantic subtlety, but the expression of a practical need'.[126] But although Dilthey poses the question, 'he does not fully answer it'.[127] He thinks of the humanities and the social sciences as two co-operating parties, the former broadening our horizons, the latter showing how knowledge can work for good in social life; but they remain unharmonized. Where is the common ground which unites them? Hodges argues that the benefits from education are

---

[122] Ibid.
[123] WDI, 84.
[124] Ibid.
[125] Ibid., 85.
[126] Ibid.
[127] Ibid.

knowledge (factual information and technical skills) and wisdom (value-standards and archetypes, social attitudes and adjustments). Now,

> If the humanities at their best make contact with the treasured wisdom of mankind, may it not be said that the social sciences study the soil of life and circumstances from which this wisdom grows? And if they do this, they can surely deepen and enrich this wisdom by making us more fully aware of its context and motives? But of course this depends on how the social sciences are pursued. We shall not get this result if they become a mere register of facts and administrative dodges, but only if they involve understanding and reliving the processes which they study. Social science pursued in this spirit is both a discipline and a humanity, and is rich in wisdom.[128]

To strive towards this goal, he concludes, is in the best interests of both education and society; and the way to proceed is 'to carry further in thought and act Dilthey's conception of the unity of the human studies'.[129]

As to natural science in relation to Christianity, Hodges informs us that 'I have never been one of those who are troubled by a tension between science and religion.'[130] He was, however, deeply concerned by the gulf between the Christian and the general societal mind-set. In medieval times, he explains, 'physics led up to natural theology, which in turn led on to ethics. Knowledge so conceived was closely dovetailed into life.'[131] But from the Renaissance onwards 'The aim of the study of nature ... is to obtain control over it, and science is justified above all by its results in the shape of machinery, medical techniques, and the like.'[132] In this respect the success of science has been brilliant. The problem is that 'it has become in the popular mind the ideal type of knowledge. It is assumed that any branch of thought ... must imitate the methods of physics. Anything which cannot be pressed into this pattern is regarded as inferior, and perhaps not real knowledge at all.'[133] This modern approach to nature does not lead to God as the old way did, and whether or not we believe in God makes no difference to the laws of nature. Thus 'the impression grows that it does not matter' whether God exists or not. 'But it does matter,' Hodges expostulates, 'because the disappearance of our theology affects our ethics. If the meaning of life is not to be determined by reference to God, most people can think of little else in which to find it except the pursuit of pleasure and power, whether for the individual or for the collectivity.

---

[128] Ibid., 86.

[129] Ibid., 87.

[130] Idem, *They Became Anglicans*, 65. This is exactly my own experience. It would, of course, be quite wrong to suggest that the rampant science-religion debate becomes, for some theologians, a refuge from treating the centralities of the Christian faith.

[131] Idem, 'Christianity in an age of science', 46.

[132] Ibid., 46–7.

[133] Ibid., 47.

And that is the unspoken assumption of millions to-day.'[134] The upshot is that 'In a society so minded, the Church can live on only as an anachronism, an unnecessary survival from other days.'[135] But none of this has to do with a fundamental conflict between science and religion. 'The real conflict,' he declares, 'is not between the teachings of science and those of Christianity, but between the spirit and temper of our scientific age and the Christian outlook on life.'[136] This conflict is absolute, and the temptation Christians face is that of conforming to the thought-forms of the age:

> We believe in progress like our fellows, and think that this is the real meaning of what we read in the Bible about the Kingdom of God. We are under a constant temptation to translate our Christian symbols into terms of the modern interpretation of life and history; even God is reduced from the King of the ages to the elected President of the republic of all intelligent beings. I write strongly, but is it not so? And with God thus constitutionalized and brought up to date, the great basic emphases of Christianity, the glory of God, worship, self-abasement, sin and redemption, nature and grace, cease to mean anything of importance, and we are left performing the motions of a religion which has gone dead on us. If this is not the case, whence come our priests who do not preach the Word, and our laity who are offended if it is preached? As if the shadow of God did not lie over them all.[137]

In the light of this the challenge to the Christian is to 'understand the two sides of ourselves, so that the Christian in us may explain himself to the modern man in us in language which then modern man can recognize, without the Christian becoming absorbed into the modern man. Not until we have thus come to terms with ourselves shall we be able to speak as we should to the world about us, or to live out our Christianity with real conviction.'[138]

Hodges may not have preached philosophy in the classroom in the way de Burgh did, but if the quotations I have just offered do not represent impassioned preaching, I do not know what does. They bring us directly to the question of world views, to which matter Hodges, once again in the wake of Dilthey, devoted considerable attention.

---

[134] Ibid.

[135] Ibid.

[136] Ibid., 48.

[137] Ibid., 50. In this connection, I may perhaps refer to my own concern at the reduction, and even the loss, of Christian language in deference to ideological and other factors. See Alan P. F. Sell, *Nonconformist Theology in the Twentieth Century*, Milton Keynes: Paternoster, 2006, 165–70, especially 169.

[138] Ibid., 51.

III

Since I am more concerned with the way in which Dilthey stimulated Hodges' thinking than with Dilthey's own intellectual indebtedness, I have not thus far referred to those by whom the latter was influenced. I cannot, however, proceed without referring to Schleiermacher, to whom he owed much. Dilthey began his university studies at Heidelberg, where he was introduced to idealism by Kuno Fischer. Fischer, however, was required to leave his post under the accusation of pantheism, so Dilthey proceeded to Berlin, where he was taught by Friedrich von Trendelenburg and August Boeckh, themselves former students of Schleiermacher. Dilthey immersed himself in Schleiermacher's thought, he completed the editing of his letters, and he won first prize for an essay on his hermeneutics. This in turn led to a commission to write a biography of Schleiermacher, and this he did. Schleiermacher's ethics was the theme of his doctoral dissertation.

Already Dilthey was intrigued by the ways in which Christians over time had expressed their view of the world, and he resolved to penetrate to the heart of religious experience on which such views were based. Hodges explains that Dilthey's attraction to Schleiermacher was prompted by two considerations: first, Schleiermacher 'represented the religious spirit in the closest alliance with philosophy and with literary and historical studies'; and secondly, he was 'furthest from metaphysical speculation and nearest to the critical position of Kant'.[139] In the event, to Schleiermacher's conviction that at the heart of religion is the feeling of absolute dependence Dilthey in due course added the insight that the feeling of dependence is accompanied by an awareness of things invisible, with the important proviso that these intimations of things invisible are not transcendently sourced, so to speak; rather, while they appear to come to us from without, their actual source is in the depths of our own life. In this latter connection there is a marked breach with Schleiermacher's position, for the latter 'believed that the personalities of individual men flow from the Absolute by a timeless dialectic, and in his historical studies he leaned more on his notion of the Idea embodied in the person than on the historical evidence as to what that person was and did'.[140] This clearly ran counter to Dilthey's convictions concerning our understanding of a person's development by reference to his or her lived historical and social situation.[141] Thus although for both Schleiermacher and Dilthey the individual is

---

[139] PWD, 9.

[140] Ibid., 13–14.

[141] This calls to mind Hodges' comparison of Dilthey with Collingwood. The latter is praised for his interest in history – unusual at that time among English philosophers, but 'Dilthey's ruling conceptions of *understanding* and *life* belong to a different world from the Hegelian conceptions which control Collingwood's thinking'. PWD, 325.

'"the greatest reality" in history', they diverged in their views as to 'the workings of the life-process'.[142]

Dilthey's other great debt to Schleiermacher lies in the realm of hermeneutics. He builds upon his mentor's pioneering work in this field, and is in no way nonplussed by the logical circularity of the hermeneutic enterprise, namely, that 'Interpretation ... must necessarily be a circular process, because every part of a literary work requires the whole to make it intelligible, while the whole in turn can only be understood in terms of the parts.'[143] But if the circle is logically unbreakable, in practice we break it when we understand. We oscillate between part and whole until we have an internally coherent interpretation which 'does violence to none of the parts, and fits into the historical circumstances as known to us. When we have this, we understand.'[144] Moreover, 'the interpretation of a book can widen out until it melts into historical study'.[145] Appreciation and judgement are involved in understanding, and hence 'interpretation passes over insensibly into criticism, and this into the laying down of general principles of criticism, i.e. into aesthetics'.[146]

The process as so far described is not all there is to interpretation: 'There is something in it which cannot be reduced to rule, and which Dilthey, following Schleiermacher, calls an element of "divination". ... To the purely logical mind it is a mystery and an offence, and such a mind can point out that its insights are incapable of proof. ... But if interpretation lacks the dry cogency of logical demonstration, it also escapes its limitations.'[147]

Here, as it seems to me, we have an analogy between natural science and logic, namely, that just as natural science is an abstractive discipline which steps out of line if it presumes to demand that all other facets of intellectual, social, aesthetic and religious life somehow force themselves within its parameters, so, where interpretation is concerned, logic can have a similarly constricting effect. Both sides of the analogy need to be kept in view as we approach the question of world views. We have only to attend to Hodges' summary definition of Dilthey's account of world view to see that this must be so. To Dilthey, a world view is

> a complex of ideas and sentiments comprising (a) beliefs and convictions about the nature of life and the world, (b) emotional habits and tendencies based on these, and (c) a system of purposes, preferences, and principles governing action and giving life unity and meaning. The *Weltanschauung* of a person or a

---

[142] PWD, 14. Hodges quotes W. Dilthey, *Gesammelte Schriften*, Göttingen: Vandenhoeck & Ruprecht, V, 1924, 11.
[143] WDI, 27.
[144] Ibid.
[145] Ibid., 28.
[146] Ibid.
[147] Ibid.

society includes that person's or society's answer to the fundamental questions of destiny which Dilthey calls the *riddle of life*.[148]

World views are prolific because the experiences on the basis of which they are formed are likewise diverse. However, Dilthey maintains that they can be classified, at least approximately, under one of the three systems of relations which pervade all experience: religion, art and philosophy (though these are not, as in Hegel's doctrine, hierarchically arranged ways of reaching absolute truth). The first type of world view is rooted in the animal side of human nature. In religion it appears as a revolt again other-worldliness; in art, as realism; in philosophy, as naturalism or methodological positivism, in which connection Dilthey instances Democritus, Protagoras, Epicurus, Hume and Comte. The second type fastens upon the human experience of free will. In religion human free agency is said to be dependent upon God, the absolute free personal agent; in art the emphasis is upon the world as a theatre of heroic action; in philosophy it has moved from the conception of reason as a formative power (as in Anaxagoras, Plato and Aristotle), *via* the medieval idea of God's personal and providential governance of the world, to Kant and Fichte who think in terms of 'a super-sensible world of values which are real only in and for the infinite will which posits them'.[149] The third type derives from a contemplative and affective attitude to experience. It is found in the panenthism of Indian and Chinese religion, in art in Goethe, and in philosophy in what Dilthey calls objective idealism: the intuitive grasp of the wholeness of things as expounded by the Stoics, Averroes, Bruno, Spinoza, Leibniz, Shaftesbury, Schelling, Hegel, and Schleiermacher.[150]

In reflecting upon Dilthey's position on world views, Hodges observes that 'These, when taken at their face value as descriptions of the real order of things, are not merely different, but irreconcilable. To a believer in metaphysics this fact is an embarrassment; to Dilthey it is merely one of his strongest reasons for not believing in metaphysics. He believes that, if we go behind the *Weltanschauungen* to their respective foundations in experience, we shall once again find ourselves dealing with different but not irreconcilable perspectives.'[151] However, Hodges cites the mutually exclusive positions of Kierkegaard, Marx and Nietzsche as evidence that 'if there is a basic identity of structure in all human minds, it is on a level which allows of deep and irreconcilable conflicts in actual life'.[152] These cannot be removed by historical study or by epistemological analysis, 'for our *Weltanschauungen* affect our theory of knowledge, as well as being affected

---

[148] Ibid., 160; cf. PWD, 85–6, 310.
[149] PWD, 89.
[150] In this paragraph I have summarized PWD, 86–90, reproducing some of the phrases Hodges uses in his fuller account of Dilthey's position. Cf. WDI, 99–101.
[151] PWD, 354.
[152] Ibid., 359.

by it'.[153] In 1883 Dilthey declared that an understanding of the cause and cure of the prevailing social unrest was 'a vital question for our civilisation'.[154] Hodges doubts that his recipe, the human studies, goes deeply enough – 'the refashioning of civilisation calls for more than that. It lays upon us an imperious demand for decision and clear purpose in a changing world, while at the same time it threatens us with a scepticism far deeper than anything that is touched by Dilthey.'[155]

Hodges has one particular criticism of Dilthey which leads us directly into his own position on world views and kindred matters. Dilthey leaves us with a welter of unreconciled and in some case *prima facie* irreconcilable world views. This amounts to relativism. Dilthey says that to recognize this is to free ourselves from illusion, and he also posits that although no world view 'is true in a sense which would make the others untrue, it does not follow that none of them are true in any degree at all'.[156] We can use them all 'and so obtain a richer and more balanced view of life and the world than could be got by accepting any one of them as it stands'.[157] Hodges is blunt:

> This really will not do. It is in conflict with Dilthey's own admissions. For he himself has seen the psychological necessity of a *Weltanschauung* to give unity and direction to a life, and it is obvious that a *Weltanschauung* can only do this if it is not merely toyed with, but definitely held. And that means that its rivals must be definitely not held, i.e. must be rejected. It is possible to play with rival points of view, manipulating them like a juggler, so long only as we have not to live and act in earnest, but in times of stress and danger or in moments of responsibility this is not possible. ... If philosophy, or rather life itself, confronts us with many rival views of things, then we must take one and reject the rest. ... To live is to act, and to act is to choose, and to choose is also to reject.[158]

Hence Hodges' appreciation of Kierkegaard's philosophy, 'which summons us to refuse to drift with the current of events and become ourselves by making a decisive choice'.[159] Hodges cannot envisage a synthesis of world views deemed mutually irreconcilable.

Elsewhere Hodges disdains the vaunted academic neutrality which will not take sides. Writing in wartime he says that 'this very neutrality and objectivity were among the causes which helped to bring about the evil we deplore'.[160] We must, for example, 'show a militant and dogmatic belief in freedom, even if the

---

[153] Ibid.
[154] Ibid.
[155] Ibid.
[156] WDI, 104.
[157] Ibid., 105.
[158] Ibid., 105.
[159] Ibid., 107.
[160] Idem, *Objectivity and Impartiality*, London: SCM Press, 1946.

reasons — dreadful thought — sound like metaphysics'.[161] He agrees that 'Absolute objectivity is beyond our power ... Our business is rather to give utterance to the best views we can form, with due modesty born of the consciousness of relativity, but also with confidence that the vigorous interplay of honestly formed and honestly confessed attachments is the right form, and even the only possible form, for a responsible intellectual life to take.'[162]

In all of this Hodges speaks to himself as well as to others: 'The precondition of sound work in philosophy is the ability and readiness to make a deep self-analysis, to discover what is one's fundamental attitude to life and the world ... The philosopher will be the man who *chooses* to be himself, and goes about it with all the consistency of which he is capable.' It is all the more a pity, therefore that since

> The philosopher's art is both critical and constructive, ... those who would keep it purely critical are robbing it of half its virtue, are untrue to their responsibilities and are a danger to the public. They are actuated in many cases, by a despair ... [at] the now ruined edifice of metaphysics as a demonstrative science, and they have not seen the new vision (which is not new either, but as old as Socrates) of metaphysics as constructive psychotherapy, or rather nootherapy. It is to this that the road through Dilthey leads

— and Hodges recommends that we do go through Dilthey in order to go beyond him.[163] Against his background in Dilthey's thought, and with the verdicts just presented in mind — especially that concerning the necessity of choosing, we may turn to Hodges' Riddell Lectures, in which he presents his own view of *Languages, Standpoints and Attitudes*. He sets out from a discussion of the relations between philosophy and religion. To Hegel, philosophy and religion shared common subject matter, and differed only in their respective ways of treating it. This, says Hodges 'is true when philosophy is geared to metaphysical speculation, and when it is given complete freedom in assessing and interpreting religious ideas'.[164] In patristic and medieval times, he continues, metaphysics, construed as 'a comprehensive science of being, dominated the philosophical scene'.[165] It does so no longer. As he elsewhere wrote, pulling no punches, 'metaphysics, either as a science of being (ontology) or as a science of the real as one intelligible system, is beyond human power'.[166] The centre of interest in modern philosophy is the human being as knower, and the stage was set for the critical method, involving a turn from ontology to epistemology, by Descartes, Hume and Kant. But epistemological questions proved as intractable as their ontological predecessors, and so the

---

[161] Ibid., 11.
[162] Ibid., 22–3.
[163] WDI., 107.
[164] Idem, *Languages, Standpoints and Attitudes*, London: OUP, 1953, 3.
[165] Ibid., 4,
[166] Idem, 'Phenomenology', 94.

movement of philosophy is in the direction of the analysis of the language in which both types of question are formulated. The focus of philosophical interest thus became the human being as speaker. In Hodges' view philosophy cannot rest here, for 'Man the thinker and speaker is only one facet of man the purposeful.'[167] If this be granted, then

> much will depend on whether man the purposeful is conceived as a unit in the prudentially-guided satisfaction-seeking mass of humanity, or as an individual capable of questioning the assumptions of that human mass, and responsible before conscience for what he is and does. ... The deepest question of all is this: granting that man *is* a free and responsible being, capable of choosing his own future self, what are the alternatives before him?[168]

Small wonder, then, that Hodges declares that 'What distinguishes modern philosophy from that of earlier ages is, above all, the seriousness with which the question of first principles and presuppositions is now taken.'[169] When, however, that question leads to the consideration of the degree to which entertained principles and presuppositions may be correlated with pschological types, we can see why 'the modern movement in philosophy is in great part a movement towards a radical subjectivism and relativism'.[170] Hence also the interest in world views.

In building up our knowledge of the world we utilize such principles as the distinction between being and seeming, being and having, and the relation between cause and effect. These are neither tautologies nor generalizations from experience, for 'it is only by applying them that we can obtain a coherent world of experience at all'.[171] Yet 'from a strictly logical point of view our acceptance of them must be regarded as a leap in the dark'.[172] Whereas Kant thought that there was one set of principles which made experience possible, Hodges holds that 'various possible sets of principles ... open up possibilities of experience and inquiry, and that set which is most fertile in this respect is to be preferred. ... [A] set of principles or presuppositions, together with the type of question to which they give rise and the way of looking at things which results from them, is what I call a *standpoint*. At its heart is the assumption that there is an order of existing things, events, or relations whose structure is of a specified kind.'[173] He adds that a standpoint need not be expressible wholly in cognitive statements: 'It may include elements of value-judgment or volitional determination; for these too can be expressed as general

---

[167] Idem, *Languages, Standpoints and Attitudes*, 9.
[168] Ibid., 10.
[169] Idem, 'The crisis in philosophy', in F. W. Camfield, ed., *Reformation Old and New. A Tribute to Karl Barth*, London: Lutterworth, 1947, 185.
[170] Ibid., 186.
[171] Idem, *Languages, Standpoints and Attitudes*, 13.
[172] Ibid.
[173] Ibid., 15.

principles and open up fields of discourse. It is by principles of this type that the field of ethical discourse is constituted.'[174]

At this point Hodges adds a footnote which expresses both his indebtedness to Dilthey and his qualification of the German's position:

> A standpoint as here defined has much in common with a *Weltanschauung* as defined by Dilthey. The differences are two. A *Weltanschauung* is always a standpoint from which one regards the whole of experience, whereas standpoints in my sense can refer to a narrower field than that. Also, a *Weltanschauung* always includes valuational and preceptive elements, whereas a standpoint in my sense may, but need not, include such elements.[175]

Standpoints tend to find expression in characteristic language, and to understand a standpoint it is necessary to learn its language and to enter into its spirit. A given term may function in more than one standpoint and its meaning will be altered according as the standpoints differ. But the standpoint of common sense is universal. However, when such 'ordinary language' terms as 'force', 'power', and 'necessity', became the names of metaphysical entities, and when these were later employed with different meanings by philosophers influenced by new departures in natural science, metaphysical bewilderment resulted:

> Two languages were confronting one another, the language of traditional metaphysics and the language of the new physics, and the two languages had their key words in common. What appeared to the eye, therefore, was not a confrontation of two languages, but an irritating ambiguity in the words of what still seemed to be one language.[176]

As if this were not enough,

> Grammatical forms have been taken as evidence of ontological relations. ... Because common nouns and abstract terms play an indispensable part in speech, it was thought that there are 'universals' among the components of the world. Because the situation confronting one who has to make a decision can be described in a disjunction, it was thought that there are real indeterminacies and open alternatives in nature. Insoluble problems were thus created for metaphysics, merely because linguistic forms were misinterpreted into ontological theories.[177]

---

[174] Ibid.
[175] Ibid., 15–16, n.; cf. ibid., 30.
[176] Ibid., 19.
[177] Ibid.

However, not all philosophical problems arise from 'linguistic mismanagement', and hence they cannot all be resolved by linguistic analysis. Disordered languages results from confused standpoints: 'it is a disorder of intellectual perspectives which sets the use of language wrong'.[178] The question is, 'Is there a normative study of standpoints which can present a reasoned case for preferring one standpoint to another?'[179] If there is, it is not the theory of language as such, for this 'has no authority to set up a standard of its own and judge by that what utterances are meaningful. ... To declare metaphysical sentences to be meaningful, or to be meaningless, is in either case to assert the standpoint from which such a judgment can be made.'[180] Thus, to complain that metaphysical statements 'do not conform to scientific standards of significance and clarity' is beside the point: 'you must learn to judge them as being what they are, not as failing to be what they are not meant to be'.[181] This is not to deny that metaphysical statements may be refurbished. Thus,

> Ontological principles can be taken not as statements of what the world is certainly like, but as statement of the ways in which we do, or could, regard the world. Theories of causality can be taken as statements of what we regard as a satisfactory type of explanation. Even speculative arguments can be taken not as showing that such and such is in fact the case, but as showing that, if we choose to regard the world in the light of certain principles, we shall have to admit the consequences of these principles.[182]

What is happening here is that ontological propositions are being rebaptized as transcendental ones, that is, as propositions which refer not to 'the world' but to 'experience'.[183] Metaphysics can even be transposed 'into the key of language-analysis'.[184] Metaphysical principles will then be seen as verbal conventions, and the objective will be to show that some uses of their terms are not consistent with other uses of them. It will still be a controversial subject, and any who, because they cannot translate metaphysical propositions terms into their own language, brand such talk, 'nonsense', are dogmatists, however much they may regard themselves as empiricists concerned with verification.[185]

Hodges proceeds to argue that philosophy is a normative study which first understands, and then passes judgement upon, standpoints, the judgement being an existential one. Unlike Hegel, who thought that disputes over incompatible

---

[178] Ibid., 21.
[179] Ibid., 23.
[180] Ibid.
[181] Ibid., 27.
[182] Ibid., 30.
[183] Ibid., 40.
[184] Ibid., 31.
[185] Shades of A. J. Ayer.

principles could be resolved in a higher synthesis, Hodges believes that 'there are disputes in philosophy which we only misrepresent if we try to reconcile them; and that their irreconcilability is due to the fact that at their heart lies no mere intellectual disagreement, but a conflict of wills'.[186] Thus, for example, Hodges believes that the view that 'The whole of life is a perpetual confrontation of man by God' is at the heart of the Christian religion. He is fully aware of such problems as the relation between divine omnipotence and human freedom, but he does not think that these are insoluble. His main point is that such difficulties are not the whole of the case against the faith. There is also the 'incompatibility which exists or is thought to exist between Christianity and some other view which a man holds and is not prepared to abandon'[187] – he wills not to abandon it. Not all standpoints can be brought into harmony, and thus 'the acceptance of some standpoints brings with it automatically the rejection of others'.[188]

But do we simply have our standpoints, or do we pass judgement upon them – and if so, in accordance with which criterion? Hodges approaches his answer through a discussion of what he calls basic attitudes. These are the fundamental needs or desires upon which the many-layered structure of the individual's affective and volitional life is based. Basic attitudes shape a person's thought, standpoints, axioms and principles, and they have the power to open up, or to close off, 'whole worlds of experience'.[189] Thus the question whether God exists is an ontological question; the question whether the existence of God is a significant one for a particular individual is a transcendental question which is answered by reference to the person's basis attitudes. Hodges selects from the many available examples of world views, naturalism, positivism, Vedanta and Christianity, and seeks to reveal the basic attitudes on which each rests. Elsewhere he fastens upon pantheism, panpsychism and idealism, all of which 'have an inherent tendency to sink the human individual in the "higher" unity of the Great Mind', and thus reveal themselves to be, together with naturalism, 'non-Christian and anti-Christian doctrines'.[190] Although Hodges does not preclude the possibility that, for example, a dialectical materialist and a Christian may for a limited time and purpose find themselves allies *per accidens*, their world views are mutually incompatible because their basic attitudes differ. The differences have to do with more than contrary opinions on particular points; they concern a total way of viewing the world. Hence to transfer from one system to another requires a change of standpoint, mental structure and basic attitude: in a word, it requires a conversion. As Kierkegaard insisted, 'There are alternative patterns of life and thought, each of which is unintelligible from the standpoint of the others, and there is no *logical*

---

[186] H. A. Hodges, *Languages, Standpoints and Attitudes*, 36; cf. 48.
[187] Ibid., 44.
[188] Ibid.
[189] Ibid., 51.
[190] Idem, 'The crisis in philosophy', 191.

road from one to another. There is a road, but it is the road of choice.'[191] But people make widely differing choices. Is there any way of judging between the choices they make? Hodges proposes his existential test:

> If there is a standpoint which is able to able to make use of, and stimulate purposeful inquiries within, a world of discourse which a rival standpoint can only dismiss as meaningless or at least as mere subjective fantasy, this difference must be recognized as a decisive point in favour of the former standpoint.[192]

This was too much for A. G. N. Flew. In his review of Hodges' lectures he protested, 'This is surely arbitrarily to stack the cards against denial that religious experience or revelation really discloses the Management of the Universe.'[193] A few lines below the offending sentence Hodges, having spoken of Christianity as being concerned with the quest of fullness of life, declares that 'anyone who does question our criterion shows thereby that he is not a whole-hearted life-affirmer'.[194] I fear that Flew would be unimpressed by this *ad hominem* argument, and I agree that, to put it mildly, it is not the most apologetically helpful ploy. It has more the character of unconvincing testimony. Moreover, in view of the fact that many standpoints can 'make use of, and stimulate purposeful inquiries within, a world of discourse',[195] I also feel that more needs to be done to testify to, and commend (I do not say 'prove' or 'demonstrate'), the Christian basic attitude than Hodges here attempts; and this while agreeing with him that there is an inevitable logical gap between the last piece of testimony and that opting in faith in which the existential choice of a world view, or the making of what Dorothy Emmet called a 'total assertion',[196] consists, and that 'It is not possible by dint of *reasons* to turn' the unbeliever into a believer.[197] I do not say that Hodges fails altogether to testify to his faith at the end of his lectures, and I appreciate his methodological objective of writing as a philosopher, not as a theologian. Nevertheless, in his two concluding pages he makes it quite clear that human beings are made for fellowship with God;

---

[191] Idem, *Languages, Standpoints and Attitudes*, 59. Elsewhere he writes, 'Dilthey's philosophy is open in its own way to the criticism which Kierkegaard brought against that of Hegel – viz., that it is full of syntheses where life is full of choices.' See WDI, 105.

[192] Ibid., 64.

[193] A. G. N. Flew, in *Mind*, N.S. LXIII, January 1954, 113.

[194] H. A. Hodges, *Languages, Standpoints and Attitudes*, 64.

[195] I. T. Ramsey also makes this point in his review of Hodges' book in *The Philosophical Quarterly*, IV no. 17, October 1954, 338.

[196] See D. M. Emmet, 'The use of analogy in metaphysics', *Proceedings of the Aristotelian Society*, XLI, 1941, 39; 'Can philosophical theories transcend experience?' *Proceedings of the Aristotelian Society*, XX, 1946, 202–3; *The Nature of Metaphysical Thinking*, London: Macmillan, 1946, 196–201; 'The choice of a world outlook', *Philosophy*, XXIII, 1949, 45–6.

[197] H. A. Hodges, *Languages, Standpoints and Attitudes*, 64.

that they are fallen creatures; and that God has intervened to restore them to their proper status and function. Not the least facet of humanity that needs to be restored is the intellect, which depends upon the will. All of this, he thinks, is pertinent to the desperate situation of the present time. Into that situation 'Christianity is able to bring in a decisive new factor in the enlightening action of God.'[198]

Having moved so far towards theology I could wish that Hodges had made it clearer that in choosing the Christian world view, it is not as if we lay all the possible choices out before us and then pick our favourite; rather, God graciously approaches us in Christ, and we, by grace make our enabled response. As Norman Snaith correctly put it, 'the idea of a human choice is the language of the newly converted, but ... the certainty of the divine choice is the language of the sanctified'.[199] In other words, while Hodges' emphasis *qua* philosopher is upon the choice, or decision, of the one who leaps in faith that person, having landed, may well come to reflect that the graciously pre-donated 'God vision', as Hodges calls it, to which the believer has responded, was the operative factor. Moreover, since the embracing of a world view is the concern of the whole life, and not merely of the intellect, one could wish that Hodges had developed more fully the hints he occasionally drops concerning an ethic of thinking: 'the adoption of one thought-paradigm as against the other', he writes, 'is ... also implicitly a preference for the life-pattern which naturally goes with it'.[200] As he elsewhere put it,

> The determinants of belief lie at least as much in the region of character as in that of intelligence. And from this it follows that belief is a moral act, for which the believer is to be held responsible. ... It is ... in a man's standpoint and the attitudes underlying it, that the ethical character of his thinking properly resides. ... In adopting such and such basic attitudes, he determines what kind of a world can exist for him, what the quality and structure of experience shall be for him, what life itself shall be for him and for those who come under his influence. He determines whether, and in what ways, he is to be a source of enrichment or of impoverishment to human life and experience generally. And because thinking has this ethical character, there is a place in moral theory for a discussion of the ethics of thinking. It is true that moralists in general have neglected to do this part of their work.[201]

At this point the observation of P. T. Forsyth comes to mind:

---

[198] Ibid., 68.

[199] N. Snaith, 'Chosen', in Alan Richardson, ed., *A Theological Word Book of the Bible*, London: SCM Press, 1956, 44.

[200] H. A. Hodges, 'What is to become of philosophical theology?', in H. D. Lewis, ed., *Contemporary British Philosophy. Third Series*, London: Allen & Unwin, 1956, 232; cf. idem, *God Beyond Knowledge*, London: Macmillan, 1979, 141.

[201] Idem, *Languages, Standpoints and Attitudes*, 65–6.

> Logic is rooted in Ethic, for the truth we see depends on the men we are. Ethic is rooted in theology for we are made men by the gift and grace of God. And theology is rooted in living faith – which is the Supreme Gift of God *in* man, because it is the response evoked by His supreme revelation and gift of Himself *to* man as Father, Saviour, and King.[202]

In justice to Hodges I must at once point out that in others of his writings he supplies the deficiency in regard to prevenient grace that I have just noted, but certain attenuations of Christian teaching and experience are also to be found. My way into this part of the discussion is *via* a very brief account of Hodges' book, *Christianity and the Modern World View*. Here, in no uncertain terms he advises us both of the choice he has made, and of what he had rejected in making that choice. He begins by saying that if God 'has graciously allowed us to know something of himself, we cannot help trying to let others know as much'.[203] At once he is well on the way to supplying the deficiency regarding God's gracious approach to us, to which I have referred. But what should we teach and think, he asks, in the prevailing intellectual climate? We must not succumb to the temptation to take the modernist way of attempting to force Christianity into the modern system of ideas; we must not emulate those 'pathetic remnants of the once triumphant liberal host, who still misconceive the trend of the time, and think they can march in step with modern thought to a positive and creative end';[204] neither must we take the path of the nineteenth-century Catholic revival and seek refuge in an earlier age which was thought to be more congenial to the Christian faith. This would amount to 'an implicit atheism, or at least to a heresy which denies God's lordship over history'.[205] What is required is a philosophical inquiry into contending ways of viewing the world with reference to 'their fundamental presuppositions and principles, and the grounds on which these rest'.[206] We need 'a *Logic of Christian Thinking* '.[207] Our non-Christian contemporaries, he declares have not seen Christianity and rejected it; they have not seen it, and we must make it visible, intelligible and desirable. We have to explain that 'the adoption of Christianity represents a total change of mind, intellectual as well as moral, and to present its credentials is to show how this change of mind is justified'.[208]

---

[202] P. T. Forsyth, *The Principle of Authority in relation to Certainty, Sanctity and Society* (1913), London: Independent Press, 1952, 9.

[203] Idem, *Christianity and the Modern World View*, 1.

[204] Idem, 'The crisis in philosophy', 193.

[205] Ibid., 5.

[206] Ibid., 6.

[207] Ibid., 7. The title of Hodges' Gifford Lectures as delivered was 'The logic of religious thinking'; the revised and posthumously-published work is entitled, *God Beyond Knowledge*.

[208] Ibid., 11.

The basic presupposition of Christianity is God. Like all basic presuppositions this one exhibits a peculiar logic:

> It cannot be established either *a priori*, since it is not self-evident, or *a posteriori*, by the evidence of facts, since it is this presupposition itself which gives facts their force as evidence. For the same reason, of course, there can be no evidence against it. ... [A] presupposition is unaffected by the discovering of fresh facts. It is what makes both the theory and its modification by fresh facts possible.[209]

The basic presupposition of both Judaism and Christianity is what Hodges calls the Abrahamic presupposition. Abraham places his life unconditionally into the hands of God whatever God asks of him, and accepts God's promises. This attitude presupposes both God's existence, his purposeful control of all things, and his desire to communicate with human beings, who have a place in his designs. Clearly this presupposition differs from a scientific one, 'but it has the same logical properties and status. It is not a self-evident truth, nor a piece of knowledge gathered from experience, but a presupposition made as a result of a basic acceptance. It is prejustified because it enables us to open up a field of experience which cannot be opened up without it'.[210] The metaphysical presupposition is, to Hodges, the Abrahamic presupposition depersonalized: '*the universe is governed by a purpose to whose nature our own intellectual and moral aspirations provide a clue*'.[211] This presupposition can yield numerous theories including animism, polytheism, pantheism and philosophical idealism. We cannot decide between such rival views directly by observation, or indirectly by the test of consequences. We have only the formal test 'of showing that a theory, while coherent and reasonable in itself, colligates all the known facts in the manner laid down by the governing presupposition'.[212] Hodges proceeds to argue that theism alone, with its commitment to a personal God, succeeds in this. At this point the problem of evil is raised, but against it Hodges pits God's revelation in Christ the redeemer: 'The tragic situation must be accepted and robbed of its sting'[213] – and this has been done at the Cross.

The upshot is that

> The case against God, on the natural man's grounds, is unanswerable ... It is God who must answer the natural man, not by meeting his case, but by leading him to mortify in himself the grounds on which it rested. When we have thus abandoned ourselves and our notions of life, and thrown the whole away as rubbish in the presence of God, and stand naked to receive whatever he gives for

---

[209] Ibid., 15, 16.
[210] Ibid., 17.
[211] Ibid., 18, his italics.
[212] Ibid., 21.
[213] Ibid., 52.

the sake of God who gives it, then we find to our surprise that, besides killing us, he also makes us alive, and that his generosity exceeds what we could ever have dreamed of. But it remains generosity in a strange coin.[214]

It must be admitted that when, in his final, most personal piece of writing, Hodges says that 'we believe not because constrained by evidence, but in order to live meaningfully'[215] we have what seems to be an anthropocentric attenuation of his previously stated belief which might be summarily expressed by the words 'but because by grace we have responded to the approach of God in Christ'. Only so, I think he would wish to say, can the intellect be adequately illumined, the mind be renewed, and the sinful will be freed.

IV

It has already become clear that Hodges' existential commitment to the Christian world view was by no means irrational or groundless. On the contrary he appealed for a logic of Christian thinking. He was a Christian who was a philosopher. We have noted some of his general views concerning the philosopher's vocation: that there is no going back behind the turn to experience to older ontologies; that philosophy should be both critical and constructive; that it is a normative study which first seeks to understand, and then to pass existential judgements upon, standpoints; and that the philosopher should choose to be himself. But what were his mature thoughts on philosophico-theological relations? His appointment as Gifford Lecturer gave him the opportunity to reflect deeply on this question and, in my opinion, the resulting volume, *God Beyond Knowledge* (1979), a reworked version of his lectures as delivered, is as stimulating a work as any I have read with a view to writing this book.

Keeping in mind both his vocation as a philosopher and the terms of the Gifford Trust which require lecturers to discuss natural theology, Hodges provides an illuminating account of that subject with reference both to the history of theism and the present-day role of the philosopher of religion. In the latter connection, for example, he observes that 'natural theology nowadays is not so much about God as about "God"'.[216] It is an examination, not of the question whether or not God exists, but of what prompts people to declare that he does, what might

---

[214] Ibid., 56. The Congregational scholar, Robert Franks, thought that Hodges came to rest too easily in paradox, and wished that he might have considered metaphysics as possessed of objective value as being the most likely healer of 'the open breach with which he leaves us'. See his review of Hodges' book in *The Congregational Quarterly*, XIII no. 2, April 1950, 177. I have presumed to reply to Franks by citing three paradoxes which he cheerfully adumbrated. See Alan P. F. Sell, *Hinterland Theology*, 447.

[215] Idem, *God be in my Thinking*, 24.

[216] Idem, *God Beyond Knowledge*, 5.

be their grounds for so doing, and what they might mean by their claim. As to the underlying existential questions, Hodges feels that the time is not ripe for the full exploration of these. Accordingly, he devotes himself to the preparatory work necessary before such questions can fruitfully be raised, and his book stops where philosophy reaches its limits and the conditions of the Gifford Trust are on the point of being breached.

By 'theism' Hodges means that system of thought which places God first, as the 'wholly unconditioned ... unoriginated origin of all else that is'.[217] The attributes of God, the idea of personal relationships with him and, at the same time the conviction that God is beyond human understanding are further aspects of theism. He proposes to inquire into theism in the spirit of twentieth-century natural theology, that is, he will undertake a logical and epistemological analysis theistic doctrines.

He sets out from a comparison of theistic with scientific claims to knowledge, pointing out that scientific theories, however well supported by evidence, always fall short of logical certitude, and are hence entertained provisionally only. It would, however, 'be pedantic to deny to science the name of "knowledge".'[218] Can theology rank as knowledge? Not if it is expected to meet the logical standards proper to science. Those disquieted by this finding can find no refuge in the appeal to personal knowledge of God analogous to knowledge of other human persons, since God is so unlike humans that the ways we interact with others, and test our responses to them, do not apply in the case of God. Hence, 'assimilating our knowledge of God to our knowledge of other human persons does nothing to strengthen its logical position.'[219] Nor will it do to resort to metaphysical modes of knowledge, for this entails claiming that intuitive apprehensions yield knowledge, whereas in fact they lack the clarity and distinctness that genuine knowledge manifests. Again, as we have already seen, traditional metaphysics is redundant:

> In sum, I agree with the prevailing modern view that any cognitive enterprise deserves to be called knowledge in so far, and only so far, as it approximates to the scientific model. If theology does not meet the requirements of that model, then theology is not to be called knowledge. ... [This] does not entail that it must be dismissed out of hand as a waste of time; but it means that different questions must be asked about theology. If it is not knowledge, what is it?[220]

God is not an object of experience in the standard sense of the term, he continues, and hence, on empiricist criteria theological assertions cannot be known to be true: 'They are speculations which may perhaps have some value as imaginative fiction,

---

[217] Ibid., 8.
[218] Ibid., 11.
[219] Ibid., 13.
[220] Ibid., 14.

but they have no cognitive value at all.'[221] To this general empiricist position the logical positivists added the claim that, as being neither analytic not verifiable by empirical procedures, theological assertions are meaningless. Thus far Hodges is in agreement; but he says that the empiricist account of belief in God cannot explain the experience of God as Absolute, as Being itself – the very features 'which evoke the characteristic response of worship';[222] and it cannot account for the fact that belief in God is not held as an hypothesis liable to falsification which has to be constantly checked and re-checked, but as 'an unquestionable certitude'.[223]

With this we proceed to an account of the classical arguments for the existence of God, to which Hodges adds the argument from religious experience. He does not deny that the classical arguments witness to important insights concerning God, but they are not demonstrable proofs of his existence, and their assumptions fail the tests of logic and empiricism. As for the argument from religious experience, this fails because the experience, though convincing to those who enjoy it, cannot count as evidence because it cannot be unambiguously described and classified, or experimentally controlled. Believers need not be dissuaded by any of this from speaking of God in the personal terms they do, but what they say fails the scientific-empiricist test of knowledge. Neither can religious belief be justified on grounds of metaphysical reasoning, for God is not reached by that route, but by 'an intuitive vision of the world in solidarity with an All-Agent who is also the Absolute'.[224] It is in this life-involving God-vision that religion is rooted. Does this mean, then, that believers assert objective existence on subjective grounds? and 'If we are offered rival reality-pictures in solidarity with rival life-patterns, is there any way of reaching an argued decision between the contestants?'[225]

Hodges argues that it is by existential decision that we come to believe, and 'the acceptance of God is not an ascertainment of existing fact, but a kind of "faith"'.[226] There are, however, rival faiths whose meaning does not centre in God. How are we to judge between these? There is no rational way of doing this, Hodges declares in a manner reminiscent of his view presented earlier, that a person cannot be argued out of his or her world view: conversion would be required. Elsewhere he repeats the point: 'The man who passes from the one state to the other, from faith to unfaith, is neither convinced nor persuaded. He is converted.'[227] It thus appears that at this point Hodges is allowing the maximum to faith, and the maximum to that scepticism which, we recall, had ever haunted him. He is well aware that his indecisive conclusion will not satisfy all, and that some philosophers will continue

---

[221] Ibid., 18.
[222] Ibid., 23.
[223] Ibid.
[224] Ibid., 140.
[225] Ibid., 142.
[226] Ibid., 175.
[227] Idem, 'The crisis in philosophy', 196.

to advance metaphysical cases for or against theism.[228] Those who attempt this, however, 'deviate from the royal road of philosophy'.[229] Philosophy as such can take us no farther than what I might describe as incompatible world views for ever standing apart from one another like book-ends. There is acknowledged scepticism here, and relativism too.

If challenged as to his own life (as distinct from his philosophical) position, Hodges says that he is not obliged to answer the question, but cannot see grounds for refusing. Accordingly he presents himself as one who recites the creed and attends the eucharist, and he recognizes the legitimacy of the questions, 'What does the sceptical philosopher in me thinks of the believer? And what does the believer make of the philosopher's activities?'[230] Having assessed theism philosophically, can he now assess philosophy theistically? He takes some initial steps in that direction. He thinks that the human propensity to fundamental doubt arises from the human dependence upon discursive reasoning. The angels on the one side, and the beasts on the other may be presumed not to have intellectual doubts, or to frame intellectual puzzles and plunge into metaphysics. The believer-philosopher will accept that God has placed us in a situation which forbids our escaping the sceptical predicament. This is not surprising when we recall that the position developed by Anselm, namely, that we believe in order to understand goes back through Philo, Paul and the early Fathers, and it witnesses to the fact that faith comes first. Thus, 'The modern Anselm ... will not be deceived by the ontological argument, but he will be like the original Anselm in that he will begin from the God-vision, and his argument, however it develops, will be essentially an analysis and assessment of that. The conclusion is that modern philosophy does not enable us to decide between the rival standpoints of belief and non-belief, but it 'brings us to the point where the *man* decides. But the man's own integrity requires that, in deciding, he should not disown the philosopher.'[231]

At this point I think we should note what appears to be a development in Hodges' thought towards a more sceptical-relativist *philosophical* position. In his first book, when expounding Dilthey's situation as one caught between natural science and positivism on the one hand and romanticism and idealism on the other he remarks that

> no one who really knows [both sides] can deny that the essential quality of each must find a place in any acceptable scheme of life. Dilthey, attempting in his own mind and life a synthesis which was probably premature, has at least succeeded

---

[228] Robert Franks and, in his own way, Ian Ramsey, among them. See their reviews of *Languages, Standpoints and Attitudes*.
[229] H. A. Hodges, *God Beyond Knowledge*, 176.
[230] Ibid., 176.
[231] Ibid., 181.

in showing that it is not enough to take sides, and that the synthesis is what we ought to work towards.[232]

This is at some remove from the radical choice between one world view and the rejection of others which Hodges later came to advocate. One almost suspects lingering idealism here, his evident distaste for that world view notwithstanding. Between his first book and his last, we recall Flew's objection that Hodges had loaded the dice in favour of his own position by presupposing that his own world view was the most fruitful. That, I suggested at the time, was in the nature of a piece of testimony, and I suspect that the philosopher Hodges of the last book would agree.

Philip E. Devenish of Notre Dame University fastened upon Hodges' conviction that God has placed us in a world in which we cannot escape the sceptical predicament. He writes, 'the serendipitous "fit" between epistemic skepticism and God himself is in its own way a rational warrant which provides sufficient reason for belief in God and makes it more than a preference for one of two equally valid life and thought paradigms. Such a fit means that "thinking everything through" to the end will lead one to see not only that epistemic skepticism is compatible with, but also that it even points to belief in, a God beyond knowledge.'[233] This is not entirely just to Hodges for, according to him, the philosophical scepticism leaves us poised before a choice, but it in no way determines the choice we shall make. The choice can go either way, and there is precisely no 'rational warrant' for the way it goes. There is an existential compulsion, a launching out in faith and, having arrived believers can offer their reasons the choice (they are not irrationalists), but such reasons will not justify the world view as a whole, or conclusively demonstrate God's existence. Reasons will be invoked (if, indeed, they are invoked at all) to commend a way of looking at the world to which the believer has been brought by grace. Hodges contends that the decision to acknowledge God's existence is a responsible act 'In the sense that the believer knows he is liable to be called upon to give an account of his decision, and that he is in principle able and willing to give reasons in explanation and defence of it.'[234] The believer's proffered reasons are part of that testimony, which includes a way of life as well as an intellectual exposition and some doctrinal assertions, which believers are called upon to make (according to their talents) as appropriate.

I say 'according to their talents' because we must not overlook those deeply spiritual people whose experience of God is a strong as their grasp of philosophical techniques or theological niceties is weak. Such people may well take comfort from Hodges' position. 'Why ... ' he asks,

---

[232] WDI, 72.

[233] P. E. Devenish, in *The Journal of Religion*, LXI no. 1, January 1981, 103.

[234] H. A. Hodges, *God Beyond Knowledge*, 134.

should Christians fear in the presence of the crisis in philosophy? Only if they have reason to think that the crisis can touch their own faith: and this it can only do if their faith is somehow dependent on philosophy. ... So long as Christians retain the view, characteristic of Thomism but not confined to it, that Christian truth rests at least in part upon foundations of metaphysical reasoning, so long they will be disturbed by every change of metaphysical fashion. So long as the philosophical reasons which are sometimes urged in defence of Christian theism are treated as if they were the real reasons upon which Christian theism itself is based, so long their Christianity can be threatened by counter-reasons from the same philosophical force. While this is so, there is no escape for the Christian but to try to freeze philosophy at the stage in its development which was most congenial to Christian interests ... [This] is a denial of the Christian doctrine of history.[235]

He elaborates upon this elsewhere by reminding us that 'Theology grows up not out of the speculative ingenuities of metaphysicians, but out of men's commerce with God (or what they believe to be such commerce), just as physics grows up out of men's commerce with the material world.'[236] He rams home the point by boldly asserting that 'Philosophy as we have known it belongs to the period of world history which is going out.'[237] Both the world and the Church, he declares, must be weaned from the pact they have made with 'old [metaphysical] idols ... submit to a purgation of the intellect, [and] enter the active night of the spirit'.[238] In this circumstance, he reminds us, the task of philosophy is 'not to present itself as an additional source of theological information, but to explore the epistemology and logic of religious thinking and to comment on its principles and methods in the light of this exploration'.[239] Those Christian apologists who refuse this way and 'reassert the dogmatic foundations of ancient metaphysics' and 'talk rudely about modern writers whom they have not always understood', may simply reveal 'no more than the natural reluctance of human nature to enter upon the darkness' of the night of the spirit.[240]

It can hardly be denied that Hodges has revealed the point at which philosophy halts on the theistic road; he has made it clear that 'Theology begins only when science has shot its bolt';[241] he has reminded us that those who propounded theistic arguments were not themselves led to faith by assenting to their 'proofs', and he has raised the question of the God-vision as the starting-point for theological reflection. Has he anything further to say? Yes – as a Christian believer. Whereas the believer *qua* natural theologian 'must continually say less than he believes,

---

[235] Idem, 'The crisis in philosophy', 194–5.
[236] Idem, 'What is to become of philosophical theology?', 218.
[237] Idem, 'The crisis in philosophy', 197.
[238] Ibid., 198.
[239] Idem, 'What is to become of philosophical theology?', 218.
[240] Idem, 'The crisis in philosophy, 198.
[241] Idem, *God Beyond Knowledge*, 96.

in order not to say more than he thinks he can prove',[242] when that task is done, the believer can speak as his true self. With this we come to Hodges' religious, devotional and theological writings.

V

On 14 July 1947 Hodges delivered an address to the Chelmsford Diocesan Worship and the Arts Association. In its published form the paper gives as clear an indication as we have of Hodges' view of the relations between art and religion. He takes it for granted that 'if we are going to make a public offering [of worship] to God, we ought to offer the best we can', but his particular starting-point is a consideration of 'that aspect of religion which is not public worship and that aspect of art which is not specifically religious'.[243] He finds a likeness of aim and structure as between the two spheres: 'Art imposes on all who take it seriously a severe discipline of mind and soul, which has no little in common with the religious discipline of mental prayer.'[244] But art and religion are also alike in that 'Both claim to apprehend and express reality, and both are apt to project human fantasies instead of the reality they claim to find. ... When the two activities meet as allies, as they do in the worship of the Church, their combined strength and their combined weakness are alike manifest, and the need for constant vigilance is at its greatest.'[245]

Hodges, following Collingwood, grants that not all art is of the highest type: most popular art is utility art. It is 'produced with a minimum of vision and inspiration, with an eye chiefly to entertainment, or convenience, or edification'.[246] Its inferiority is intrinsic, it is not a consequence of inadequate workmanship. Hodges is not concerned with art of this kind, but with that which Rossetti called 'fundamental brainwork'.[247] Such art is considered on the basis of its merits. It arises from the artist's ability to stand and stare, and such an ability is rare in a society in which both ordinary people and scientists agree that 'the disinterested stare of contemplation is a distraction and a waste of time'.[248] (This universal proposition surely requires qualification in view of the scientific imagination which underlies the formation of hypotheses with a view to experimentation; and in view also of Hodges' general sympathy with the 'ordinary man', who is by no means necessarily devoid of the contemplative spirit. In this paper Hodges is 'laying it on the line'.) Be that as it may, Hodges insists that 'all art-activity finds its centre

---

[242] Ibid., 3.
[243] Idem, 'Art and religion', *Church Quarterly Review*, July–September 1948, 131.
[244] Ibid.
[245] Ibid., 132.
[246] Ibid.
[247] Ibid., 133.
[248] Ibid.

and meaning in just this stare'.[249] It is hard work which requires concentration upon one point and a constant struggle against distractions. To the extent that art is representational the artist must reveal the object as it is and without regard to the feelings of himself or others towards it.[250] To the extent that art is the expression of his ideas or feelings he must express them accurately and with integrity. But the artist's vocation is loftier yet:

> The artist is the human vehicle of the *Benedicite*; it is he who trains human minds to be the channels through which all the world of the Lord may bless the Lord. And further, if opening blind eyes is one of the works of the Messiah, the artist has potentially a place in the work of redemption, whether he knows it or not. All this he has, be it noted, not by virtue of choosing religious themes, nor even by virtue of being personally a religious man, but just by virtue of being an artist at all.[251]

Turning to the religion side of the equation, Hodges defines the central aim of the Christian religion as being the glory of God, 'which we promote by worship and service'.[252] Like the artist, the contemplative Christian may meet with suspicion and hostility, as he lives 'in proximity to the church worker, the institutionalist, and the theological wrangler, who often fail to understand what he is about'.[253] The question arises whether art and religion contemplate the same thing. Art begins with sensible objects, God is not such an object; religion concerns the contemplation of God and 'for it the sensible world is either a ladder to be scaled as quickly as possible, or else a rival attraction to be passed by without heeding'.[254] There may be a middle ground of meeting, or art and religion may

> shoot past each other in opposite directions. The movement upwards from created things to God, if taken alone, can lead only to idolatry, even though it be the magnificent intellectual idolatry of Platonism. It can be redeemed only by being absorbed as a subordinate element into the Cross-centred thought of Christendom, as Platonism is redeemed and transmuted in the Franciscan vision of a St. Bonaventura.[255]

---

[249] Ibid.

[250] In reporting Hodges' views I am conscious of the fact that he was writing before our current, and in my view proper, sensitivity to the use of inclusive language where males and females are together in view. I should turn many of his sentences into the plural, but I retain the masculine form here so that my reporting will not jar with his quotations.

[251] H. A. Hodges, 'Art and religion', 135.

[252] Ibid.

[253] Ibid., 136.

[254] Ibid., 137.

[255] Ibid.

A revealed religion such as Christianity 'moves from the nature of God as we believe it to be made known by God himself to an interpretation of his work and deeds in the light of this'.[256] But to the believer and the artist alike there comes the question whether they are concerned with something that is really there, or whether they are simply projecting something of their own mind into the world. Elsewhere Hodges notes in this connection that there is a modern fashion in aesthetics to major upon the way in which we project symbolic meanings into things, processes and people. On this he remarks that

> Aesthetics conducted in these terms becomes a theory of the way in which the human soul uses nature, and elements of form abstracted from nature, as a medium for self-expression. To me it seems that this modern aesthetic says many true things but misses the truth. Whatever discoveries we may make about the relativity of knowledge to the knower and the constructive powers of the human mind ... we still cannot dissolve away the objectivity of the object, and fundamental to all those basic drives of the soul, which we are told art expresses and satisfies, is the need to establish some kind of relation with the Not-self.[257]

There is a further complication for Christians, for while Coleridge, Collingwood and others have emphasized the creative power of the imagination, both Collingwood and the Bible advert to humanity's corrupt consciousness. The natural faculties of humanity have been rendered unnatural by the Fall. Indeed, according to the biblical witness, the entire 'order of nature is to be understood in the light of [God's] justice and constancy, and not treated as a primary source for the knowledge of him'.[258] For this reason the Church is involved in a perpetual critique of both art and religion: 'Dogmatic reform and liturgical reform together are an expression of the Church's vigilance and the Church's penitence. They are the cleansing of the Temple to make it fit for the offering of the perfect Sacrifice.'[259] We may here note in passing the pre-Vatican II emphasis here upon the eucharist as concerning the repeated offering of Christ's sacrifice, whereas, as we shall see, in his more Protestant and Methodist *personae* Hodges fully understands that the sacrifice has been made by Christ once and for all.

Hodges concludes by declaring that iconoclasm is

> a necessary stage in the life of the individual soul. It is the purgation and reshaping of the soul's attitude to the Church's modes of expression. ... [M]aturity ... means

---

[256] Ibid., 140.

[257] Idem, Review of Hans Urs von Balthasar, *Herrlichkeit: Eine theologische Aesthetik*, vols. I and II, Einsiedeln: Johannes Verlag, 1961–62, in *Journal of Theological Studies*, N.S. XVII, 1966, 528.

[258] Ibid., 144.

[259] Ibid., 148.

fullness of life, and the consecration of every faculty in the act of worship. ... Criticism, iconoclasm, the purgation of the imagination, is a stage on the way to this. But to keep it up permanently and make it the rule for the conduct of public worship is to despair of ever reaching maturity at all.[260]

On the basis of the intimations just recorded, we may now probe a little more deeply into Hodges' own religious convictions. I have already indicated the way in which Hodges regarded himself as a 'Catholic' Anglican, and I have also referred to his growing sympathy with the eastern Orthodox theological and liturgical inheritance. But we recall that he came out of Methodism, and in 1965 he contributed a paper entitled, 'Methodists, Anglicans, and Orthodox' to the collection, *We Belong Together*, edited by A. M. Allchin. As is usual, we know where he stands. He refers to the Epworth, Canterbury, Constantinople axis and declares that 'if this axis does not yet exist as an acknowledged fact, it is something which could and ought to exist'.[261]

Hodges insists that 'there can be no proper basis for union between Churches unless it lies in the possession of a common faith. ... We cannot unite Churches simply in order to save man-power, or funds, or even to present a common front against a supposed secular enemy. We can only do it if we preach the same Lord and the same Gospel; and if we do that then we ought not to be separate.'[262] Certainly we should not unite for the mundane reasons Hodges discounts, but a number of years of ecumenical theological dialogue have persuaded me that determining the content of the 'common faith' is a perilous task, and the longer the list of 'essentials' is the more difficult the task becomes. The practice encourages, and may even seem to sanction, the anthropocentric approach which sets out from the declaration that this is what we believe, this is the shape of our church polity – how far can you measure up? This approach tacitly endorses that sectarian spirit which implies if it does not say, 'Unless and until you affirm precisely what we affirm [as if, in any given tradition, everyone affirms exactly the same things in exactly the same way], or order your churchly life in precisely the way we order ours, we cannot and will not have full fellowship with you.' My proposed remedy is to try some lateral thinking. Instead of regarding our favoured set of doctrines or practices as criteria for the inclusion, or principles of exclusion – in either case, as badges of sectarianism, we might ask, What has God done? It is my conviction that on the ground of the Son's saving work the Father has called out one people by the Holy Spirit, that all thus called comprise the Church catholic; and (church disciplinary cases apart) no member of the Church catholic should be barred from

---

[260] Ibid., 149.
[261] Idem, 'Methodists, Anglicans, and Orthodox', in A. M. Allchin, ed., *We Belong Together*, London: Epworth, 1965, 33.
[262] Ibid.

the Lord's table, or decline the fellowship of, the table – as if some such tables were ecclesiastically 'unclean'. I rest my case.[263]

Hodges finds the basis of union of the Orthodox, Anglican and Methodist traditions in the idea of fullness of the life of the triune God as imparted to the world in the incarnate Son:

> The Incarnation is God taking upon Himself creaturehood and imparting deity to the creature. The whole fullness of God, dwelling in Christ in bodily form, is imparted from Him through the work of the Spirit through the ages to all those who are drawn into His Body; and the whole creation is ultimately to become the setting for the Body of Christ, and so be drawn back to its divine source.[264]

Here, undoubtedly, we have a case where a distinctively, but not exclusively, Orthodox emphasis is invoked by Hodges as a unifying theme. The theme is undoubtedly present in Anglican and (especially) Wesleyan Methodist literature, but it would be an exaggeration to suggest that it is characteristic of the mode of thought of the majority of Methodists and members of the Church of England in Hodges' day or ours.

A similar point may be made in connection with Hodges paper, 'Angels and human knowledge'. In this case, on the basis of the assumption that angels exist because 'their activities are part of the Faith',[265] he discusses angelology in relation to human cognitive powers and imagination. As to human cognitive powers, Hodges sets out from sense-perception, explaining that most of our knowledge is based upon this, or upon inferences drawn from what we perceive. Exceptions to this are the immediate acquaintance we have of our own mental states and processes, and the fact of extra-sensory perception. Logical and mathematical knowledge might also appear to be an exception to the general rule, but it is not so, for it does not concern knowledge of existing things; it is a matter of intellectual insight. The role of imagination as a contributor to knowledge is that it 'fills the gaps between our fragmentary and fleeting perceptions, so that the world appears to us coherent and stable'.[266] An element of intellectual apprehension or understanding is present in perception, imagination and verbal thinking, or ratiocination. He further explains that 'Reasoning is an activity, understanding is an act. ... Reasoning is meditation,

---

[263] I have developed this approach further in *Enlightenment, Ecumenism, Evangel*, ch. 11, and in 'Receiving from other Christian traditions and overcoming the hindrances thereto: some Reformed reflections', forthcoming in Paul D. Murray and Marcus Pound, eds, *Receptive Ecumenism and Ecclesial Learning: Learning to be Church Together*.

[264] H. A. Hodges, 'Methodists, Anglicans and Orthodox', 34.

[265] Idem, 'Angels and human knowledge', (1954), reprinted Crawley: The Community of the Servants of the Will of God, 1982, 1. The pamphlet appears in *The One Tradition Series*, the aim of which is 'to explore and renew the great tradition of the Fathers in spirituality and worship'.

[266] Ibid., 5.

understanding is contemplation.'²⁶⁷ Angels, he confidently advises us, never reason; they are pure intelligences: 'their thinking is all intellectual apprehension (or, in the case of demons, misapprehension)'.²⁶⁸ By imagination we can call to mind 'images of things which are not present to the senses'.²⁶⁹ Angels, clearly, are in this category, and thus they 'present a problem for the theory of knowledge'.²⁷⁰ Hodges admits, in a statement that his secular empiricist colleagues would no doubt regard as a statement of the obvious, that while he can have a perception or direct awareness of his own mental states, 'With regard to angels I am not at all so well placed.'²⁷¹ He grants that 'A large part of our knowledge about angels rests on the authority of revelation.'²⁷² Furthermore, patristic and scholastic philosophy is a form of metaphysics in which angels are placed in a metaphysical order of things. On this Hodges drily remarks, 'Modern philosophers, as is well known, do not do this kind of thing and consider it illegitimate. But the mind of the Church has not changed.'²⁷³

While neither the knowledge of angels gleaned from the Bible nor from metaphysics is experiential, many people do have a psychic experience of angelic presences. Indeed, he continues, 'Angels can of course [note the 'of course' – what could be plainer?] do more than just affect us by their mere presence. They can act upon us deliberately and selectively.'²⁷⁴ He goes further: we can detect the operation of angels 'in the world around us, where they can act upon physical things, on animals, on other human beings, and on the relations between human beings'.²⁷⁵ After these bold claims he does caution us that we must not uncritically accept an event as being angelically produced without pondering the possibility that other causes 'may also' (note the 'also' – he does not say, 'instead of angels') have been at work.²⁷⁶ He further notes the 'minor' difficulty that 'even where we have reason to suppose that angelic agency is at work we have no way of telling how many individual agents may be involved'.²⁷⁷ Not surprisingly, Hodges thinks that even a 'friendly observer' will conclude that 'the empirical evidence for angels is largely ambiguous and inconclusive'.²⁷⁸ Any such evidence always needs to be sifted and tested by revelation, and the task of philosophy is to criticize the forms in which belief in angels is expressed.

---

²⁶⁷ Ibid., 7.
²⁶⁸ Ibid.
²⁶⁹ Ibid., 10.
²⁷⁰ Ibid., 12.
²⁷¹ Ibid., 13.
²⁷² Ibid.
²⁷³ Ibid., 14.
²⁷⁴ Ibid., 15.
²⁷⁵ Ibid., 16.
²⁷⁶ Ibid., 17.
²⁷⁷ Ibid.
²⁷⁸ Ibid., 18.

Hodges contends that a disservice has been done to angels by a deterioration in the imagery used for them on Christmas cards, church windows, tombstones, magazine illustrations, and the like. For example, 'The wings which were [in earlier Christian art and iconography] the symbol of power and aspiration have become too often fluffy and meaningless, anatomically impossible, serving only to make the whole figure incredible and inacceptable [sic].'[279] The concept and image of an evil spirit has likewise suffered: 'A third of the stars of heaven fallen into the abyss – that is an intelligible and a frightening thought. A single "personal devil" floating in the void is a transparent fiction [but is it any less intelligible than the former thought?]'[280] Following this unhappy diagnosis, Hodges' prescription is: 'There can be no recovery of a healthy mind about the angels and demons until their nature is again truly understood; and the bad imagery at present prevailing is both a result of the past adulteration of the Faith and a barrier in the way of our return to the truth.'[281]

At its root the intellectual struggle for the truth about angels is not that between arguments for and against. It concerns the social fact that

> many of our contemporaries ... are simultaneously members of the Church and of cultural groups whose fundamental assumption are incompatible with the Church's faith. ... In short, our ability to open our minds to a true understanding of the angelic world is limited not only by the formal limitations of our cognitive powers, by our dependence on sensation and imagination, but also more subtly and more profoundly by the influence of an alien culture in which we all participate. If one we see this clearly, it is to be hoped that we may be led thereby to make some clear-cut decisions.[282]

We are back, once again, to mutually incompatible standpoints – though the term is not used in the paper just summarized. We are also in the presence of Hodges at his most believing and least sceptical.

But if art and angelology have contributed, and continue to contribute, in distinctive ways to the Orthodox ethos, we should not overlook the importance of other aspects of doctrine to that tradition. Thus, for example, Hodges welcomes the book, *La Vie en Jésus-Christ*, by the fourteenth-century lay theologian, Nicholas Cabasilas. Cabasilas writes of the Christian life as union with Christ. It is a life which begins here and is fulfilled in heaven, and it is a life won for us by Christ's victory over sin. He paid our debt and rendered satisfaction to the Father – and this at the Father's bidding and for his glory. These blessings are conveyed through the Church's sacraments. The initiative in all of this lies with God; our part is 'just to let Him have His way with us. But God in His great courtesy has contrived to leave

---

[279] Ibid., 19.
[280] Ibid., 20.
[281] Ibid.
[282] Ibid., 21.

something for us to do, some kind of merit for us to acquire, which lies in faith, in keeping the commandments, in the use of the Sacraments, and in prayer.'[283] Cabasilas advocates continual meditation on the life and work of Christ: 'Such meditation does not interrupt the daily work of life, and it helps to shape us to the pattern of the Beatitudes.'[284] Hodges thinks that 'There are ideas and phrases in this book which will be displeasing to the children of the Reformation', but wonders whether 'the theological disputes of the sixteenth century might have been less violent and less dreary if a Faith like this had been more widely diffused at that time in the West'.[285]

Turning to a modern Orthodox work, Hodges reviews Vladimir Lossky's book, *The Mystical Theology of the Eastern Church*. Where some might expect to find a work so titled to be concerned with the rise of the soul to God, Hodges notes Lossky's strongly doctrinal thrust. There is Christian experience here, but 'it is the experience of a life lived in the light of the doctrines, the working out of the doctrines in personal experience'.[286] At a number of points in his exposition Lossky contrasts the Western Church unfavourably with the Eastern. For example, he thinks that the Western emphasis upon the imitation of Christ does not capture the closeness and subtlety of the relation. Again, Lossky argues that 'the western doctrine distances us too much from God, and underplays the truth that we are taken up into the divine life and ourselves made divine' – on which Hodges remarks, 'It is undeniable that many in western Christendom are afraid of this doctrine of deification.'[287] As well they might be, say I, if, as the doctrine has sometimes been represented, the idea is that we become God, or gods.[288] Hodges does nothing in his review to allay fears on this score, though elsewhere he does affirm that 'Although created things are in God and he in them, ... yet they are not God; and those of them who are human beings ... are aware of their difference from God as well as their dependence on him, and are able to desire a richer union with God than they enjoy simply by being his creatures.'[289] This remark would seem to land Hodges on the cautious side of deification construed as God-believer identity.

More generally, Lossky contends that 'the western Church is distinguished from the eastern by a greater freedom of philosophical speculation, and that it is this which has unbalanced the doctrines and impoverished the life of the West'. This prompts Hodges' immediate comment: 'This ... will seem strange to

---

[283] Idem, review of N. Cabalisas, *La Vie en Jésus Christ*, in *Sobornost*, IV no. 8, Winter 1963, 469.

[284] Ibid.

[285] Ibid.

[286] Idem, review of V. Lossky, *The Mystical Theology of the Eastern Church*, in *Sobornost*, III no. 24, Spring 1959, 648.

[287] Ibid., 649.

[288] See further, Alan P. F. Sell, *Confessing and Commending the Faith*, 70–79.

[289] H. A. Hodges, *God Be in My Thinking*, 44.

western readers, who have been taught to think of unrestrained speculation as the characteristic vice of the East.'[290] He concedes that

> The case does seem to be made out that there has been an abstractness in our thinking, a licence in our speculation, and a forgetfulness of some parts of Christian truth. Yet we shall want to make sure that in bowing before the divine mystery our intellect does not compromise its rights in its proper sphere, and that the misuse of rational analysis in some instances is not treated as an excuse for ceasing to pursue clarity of thought. The remedy for wrong thinking is to think better, not to conclude that it is wrong to think at all. There is no more crucial issue than this for Christendom.[291]

This is a very important statement, implying as it does that there is something in the Orthodox mind-set with which Hodges is not entirely content. He elsewhere reminds us that the Orthodox have not been faced by a Reformation or by an Enlightenment. We may therefore infer that just as he has reservations concerning Roman and especially papal ways of being 'Catholic', so he wonders whether, in their own way, the Orthodox would welcome the liberty to think that he finds in the Church of England. My way of putting this is to say that it is a characteristic of the Orthodox mind-set to live by and constantly reproduce the doctrinal deliverances of the great Councils of the Church. Thinkers are favoured who do not seek to amend these. Without doubt this policy brings important conservationist benefits, but it can also appear to others as no less stultifying than the *ex cathedra* claims of the Roman pontiff which are deemed to be infallible and hence unalterable.[292] Theologically, the question arises whether these are the most appropriate ways of following the guidance of the Holy Spirit who, no doubt, does not speak discordantly with the Word, but who certainly guides us in understanding it, and may reveal to us hitherto unappreciated facets of divine truth.

But if Hodges was influenced by things Eastern, it is equally the case that when one ponders his own accounts of his religious life there comes to mind the phrase, 'You can take the man out of Methodism, but you cannot take Methodism out of the man.' Indeed, Hodges himself wrote that 'most of what I know about Methodism I have learned since becoming an Anglican'; and, some thirty years after his conversion to (Anglican) Catholicity he could say with reference to Methodism

---

[290] H. A. Hodges, review of *The Mystical Theology of the Eastern Church*, 649–50.

[291] Ibid., 250.

[292] I take leave to introduce an anecdote at this point. During the first round of the international Orthodox-Reformed bilateral dialogue, an Orthodox theologian referred to a point I had made in discussion and said, 'I should very much like to be able to say that myself. But I could only say it if a General Council had first said it. But a General Council can be called only by an emperor, and there is a distinct shortage of emperors at the present time.' There was not a lot I could do about that.

that 'My past has come alive in my present.'[293] Evidence to support this claim may be found in a number of Hodges' writings, but I shall refer to the five in which it is most prominent.

In September 1960 Hodges delivered a paper at the Broadstairs Conference of the Fellowship of St Alban and St Sergius entitled, 'Holiness, righteousness, perfection' – all of them terms characteristic of Methodist literature and hymnody. He begins by saying that although in the English language 'righteousness' has the flavour of a broader, and 'justice' of a more precise, meaning, the terms, etymologically, are synonymous. He observes that it is possible to be both just and non-religious, and that 'the more civilized religions of the world' demand social justice of their members. This, however, is not the core of the religion: 'that lies in some kind of relation with God or the Absolute'.[294] But that is a relation in which God expects things from us, and we find that because of our sinfulness we cannot pay our dues to God. Hence Luther's insight that the righteous God does in Christ what unaided unrighteous humans cannot do for themselves. To underline the point Hodges quotes Thomas Olivers, Calvin, and Zinzendorf. To their words he adds those of Charles Wesley:

> Alive in him, my living Head,
> And clothed in righteousness divine,
> Bold I approach the eternal throne.[295]

Hodges is aware of the controversy over the imputation to the believer of Christ's righteousness, but he wonders whether the doctrine contains the whole truth. In pursuing the point he offers his own testimony:

> Is God content to impute to us a righteousness which we do not possess, without taking steps to see that we come to possess it? For myself I will only say this: to be a Christian is to be in Christ, to be a member of His Body and a sharer in His life. It is to be indwelt by His Spirit and to possess His mind. It is to be a partaker of the divine nature. And if all this does not mean that the Christian is cleansed from the power of sin as well as from its guilt, if it does not mean that Christ's righteousness is really made his and not merely deemed to be his, then words do not mean what I think they do.[296]

---

[293] Idem, 'Herbert Arthur Hodges,' 64, 67.

[294] Idem, *Holiness, Righteousness, Perfection*, London: Fellowship of St Alban and St Sergius [1960], 2.

[295] Ibid., 4. One wonders whether the ranting tune, Sagina, beloved of Methodists, to which these words are frequently sung, would take the Orthodox and some Anglicans out of their comfort zone.

[296] Ibid., 5.

Turning to 'holiness', Hodges invokes Rudolf Otto's understanding of the numinous which arouses awe, and avers that 'God is supremely and incomparably holy.'[297] Holiness in human beings means that they belong to God: 'God in some way takes possession of us, guides and controls us, acts upon us and through us upon others. ... [I]t means that something of God's own power and mystery comes to characterize us [an idea which might have been more fully expounded] ... And ... if God is to act effectively in and through us, we ourselves must be in the appropriate[298] state of mind and will ... we must be conscious of belonging to Him.'

Coming, finally, to 'perfection', Hodges says that the doctrine of perfection as preached by Methodists and others: the idea that Christians can become morally flawless, has been opposed on the ground that it runs counter to humility and flouts experience. He points out, however, that the normal meaning of *teleios* is not flawless, but mature or full-grown. Again, God is said to be perfect, but in his case this cannot mean 'full-grown' because he does not grow at all. In this case 'perfection' is a metaphysical attribute signifying 'pure actuality ... infinite being ... the most real of beings ... the most perfect of beings'.[299] However Christians conceive of their own perfection, he continues, 'it can only come to us from our being drawn into God's perfection, kept faithful by Him who is eternally faithful, raised to the height of our being by Him whose being knows no limit, cleaned from defilement by Him who is goodness itself'.[300] Adding that 'No one has seen or said this more clearly than Charles Wesley', he cites no fewer than six places where Wesley makes the point, among them the request to God to

> Hallow thy great and glorious Name,
> And perfect holiness in me.[301]

As he reflects upon the three terms, 'holiness', 'righteousness' and perfection' in relation to one another, Hodges judges that

> holiness should really be our starting-point. Holiness – in the sense of belonging to God – is the primary thing without which neither of the others can come to us. Our perfection, in whatever sense we take that word, can only be a reflection in us to the perfection of God; and our righteousness is a reflection of God's righteousness, which shines in us precisely because we belong to Him.[302]

---

[297] Ibid., 6.

[298] Ibid. It is interesting that in defining 'holiness' Hodges does not advert to the 'separateness' inherent in *Qadosh*.

[299] Ibid., 7.

[300] Ibid., 8.

[301] Ibid. See idem, 'A neglected page in Anglican theology', *Theology*, XLVIII, May 1945, 104–10.

[302] H. A. Hodges, *Holiness, Righteousness, Perfection*, 9.

In the light of this – perhaps recalling some of the Methodist preaching on which he was reared – Hodges regrets that while Protestant theology begins 'by taking off its hat to the fundamental doctrines about the Trinity and the Incarnation, ... it begins to get really interested when it comes on to talk about the sinful state of man and his helplessness in sin, and to terrify him as to the state in which he is, and then to administer the Gospel of reconciliation'.[303] When this theology is transmuted into homiletics Hodges is repelled: 'There is surely something artificial if not actually unhealthy about this process – deliberately working people up into an acute anxiety state in order then to get them out of it by pointing to Christ on the Cross.'[304] He doubts whether this method was ever appropriate (and we might recall that after announcing the general love of God, John Wesley was not above preaching the law in all its rigours and then, as people became more convicted, mixing in more and more of the Gospel[305]), but he is sure that it is not so now.

The second work in which Methodist themes predominate is *A Rapture of Praise*. This work comprises a selection of the hymns on the Christian Year, the Christian life and the sacraments by John and Charles Wesley, and a substantial Introduction written jointly by Hodges and A. M. Allchin. As with Dilthey, so here: I am concerned not to much with the detail of the Wesleys' theology as with the observations of Hodges and Allchin upon certain aspects of it. In their Introduction they refer briefly to the doctrinal dispute between Calvinists and Arminians (by the latter of whom we should understand the evangelical, not the rationalist, Arminians) The Arminians seemed to suggest that sinners could contribute to their own salvation by accepting God's free offer, whereas the Calvinists wished to maintain that salvation was entirely a matter of God's gracious eternal purpose. One page later, when specifying what Christianity says, the authors in fact resolve the dilemma without saying so: Christianity

> says ... that the right relationship with God ... is not something whose attainment depends on us; for although much effort is indeed required, yet the initiative is not ours, nor the responsibility, nor the power. God gives all, and the chief thing that we have to do is to learn to receive; and this too is something that has to be given by him. But if he gives us this, in so doing he gives us everything.[306]

As I would construe this: in granting that the human response is enabled by God we forsake bald evangelical Arminianism ('God will save you if you let him'); in granting that the response is genuinely ours and that it matters, we leave behind hyper-Calvinism ('If your name is written in the Lamb's book of life you have

---

[303] Ibid.

[304] Ibid.

[305] See his 'Letter on Preaching Christ' of 20 December 1751 in *The Works of the Rev. John Wesley, A.M.*, 3rd edn, London: John Mason, 1830, XI, 480–86.

[306] H. A. Hodges and A. M. Allchin, *A Rapture of Praise. Hymns of John and Charles Wesley*, London: Hodder and Stoughton, 1966, 12.

nothing to do; if it is not, you cannot do anything'). In fact we echo Paul's paradox, 'I, yet not I but Christ',[307] which lies at the heart of the Gospel.

Hodges and Allchin proceed to discuss such themes as conversion and assurance, and they are particularly concerned not to emphasize conversion at the expense of the sacraments or of the Christian life as a life in which one goes on to perfection, by which is meant maturity, as we saw earlier. They note the doctrinal points on which the Wesley brothers differed from one another, and they regret the non-sacramental character of evangelical revivals: 'very often they seem almost totally to ignore the two great Sacraments of the Gospel, by which we are incorporated into Christ.'[308] But, one might reply, (a) how appropriate is it to expect evangelistic activities among the unchurched to include the sacraments of the Church? (b) Is the language of the last quoted clause not misleading (it is certainly a 'Catholic' mode of speech): are Christians not incorporated into Christ by God's free and sovereign grace, to which the sacraments bear witness? Again, they write, 'The union of the Church's offering with Christ's in this Holy Sacrament [the eucharist] is so close that in a sense it can be said both that he offers us, and we offer him.'[309] The precise 'sense' is not specified, but while I can assign meaning to the assertion that Christ offers us to God, and I could agree that we offer ourselves to God, I cannot see that we offer Christ himself to God. This sounds too much like repeating, rather than remembering 'the Lord's *once-for-all* sacrifice upon the Cross', to which Hodges and Allchin refer earlier on the same page.[310]

The following judgement would surely command widespread support: 'we have to recognize that for most people and especially for the less literate, the singing of hymns represents the best way not only of expressing their feelings in worship but also of assimilating doctrine. It is a way by which hearts are moved. It is also a way by which minds are fed.'[311] This simply throws into relief the high calling of the hymn writer, for there is a distinction to be drawn between the 'strangely warmed' heart and heartburn; and between nourishing doctrinal food and hard polemical rusks on the one hand or sentimental blancmange on the other.

As if awarding prizes to both parties in an hoary dispute, there are three publications in which Hodges has some good things to say about the Calvinistic Methodists of Wales, not least that they were in the field of evangelistic advance before the evangelical Arminians. His focus is upon their hymns. He notes the use of imagery – not least that of the Welsh landscape with its rocks and storms; he rightly detects the characteristically Reformed doctrinal emphases upon the

---

[307] Galatians 2: 20. See further, Alan P. F. Sell, *The Great Debate: Calvinism, Arminianism, and Salvation* (1982), Eugene, OR: Wipf and Stock, 1998.

[308] H. A. Hodges and A. M. Allchin, *A Rapture of Praise*, 33.

[309] Ibid., 40.

[310] Ibid. My italics. Cf. H. A. Hodges, 'Art and religion', 148. Matters are not improved when Hodges says that 'the eucharistic sacrifice is offered by the whole body of the faithful who are present at it'. See his *The Pattern of Atonement*, London: SCM Press, 1955, 37.

[311] Ibid., 45.

majesty of God and the eternal covenant. There follow accounts of the contributions of William Williams, Pantycelyn (1717–91), of whom Hodges writes, 'Pantycelyn is not only moving through a world of sin and suffering to the home of perfect holiness and joy; he is also moving through a world of unrealities to the invisible, incomprehensible Reality which is God';[312] of Ann Griffiths (1776–1805), the farmer's daughter and farmer's wife who, following conversion was given to ecstasy, but wrote memorable hymns in which, while the eternal covenant, the incarnation and the atonement all feature, 'in her mind the incarnation seems in a manner to absorb and contain both the others;[313] and H. Elvet Lewis (1860–1953), who has 'none of that vivid experience and inward struggle of which his predecessors sang', but who was in tune with his times in telling us that 'we are God's fellow-workers, engaged in building his house'.[314]

It remains to add that Hodges returned to Ann Griffiths in a short introductory article,[315] and in his Introduction to *A Homage to Ann Griffiths* (1976), a volume which includes his translation of Ann's hymns, all of which were produced within eight years, and which have come down to us only because her friend, Ruth Evans, memorized them all; and his translation of Saunders Lewis's paper, 'Ann Griffiths: a literary survey'. As Hodges remarks, 'what especially strikes [Ann] is how the process of man's salvation redounds to the glory of God. Christ's death saves us precisely because in dying he so honoured God's law, and the wonder is that the transgressors of the law go free without any diminution of the respect due to the law.'[316] Some people have labelled Ann Griffiths a mystic. Hodges agrees that with a 'penetrating vision ... Ann *sees* what so many Christians half-hesitatingly *believe*, the depth of her insight into the sea of wonders, and the intensity of her aspiration to union with Christ. Let the reader think on these things', he recommends, 'and then speak of Ann as he finds appropriate.'[317]

VI

In the course of expounding Hodges' views on art and religion, and having sought to indicate some of the salient features of his spirituality and the factors which fed it, notably Christian hymns, it has proved impossible to keep theology at bay. But there are some scattered opinions and two books which are more obviously and

---

[312] Idem, 'Flame in the mountains. Aspects of Welsh Free Church hymnody', *Religious Studies*, III no. 1, October 1967, 409.
[313] Ibid., 410.
[314] Ibid., 411, 412.
[315] Idem, 'Ann Griffiths: a note of introduction', *Sobornost*, V no. 5, Summer 1967.
[316] Idem, Introduction to *A Homage to Ann Griffiths*, ed. James Coutts, Penarth: Church in Wales Press, 1976, 10.
[317] Ibid., 13.

technically theological, and to these, finally, I turn. I shall refer to God, the person and work of Christ, and eschatology.

In his last book Hodges declares that God is 'the central point in Christianity' because 'he is believed to be central in the world of existence'.[318] Of all creatures, the human being is capable of 'a relation of knowledge and love and conscious life-sharing with God', and 'The central concern of Christian teaching is to tell us how this may be brought about.'[319] The 'God-vision' says Hodges, is 'the experiential foundation of God-belief.'[320] It is 'a peculiar kind of imaginative awareness'.[321] This awareness of God is construed by many Christians in personal terms, notwithstanding that 'the concept of person, or self, or spirit, such as we are able to shape it, is inadequate to characterise the power which energises the universe'.[322] We come to see that God's knowledge and will are beyond human apprehension, and thus we reach a conception of absolute mind or spirit. But God, 'if he is not to be a mere empty shadow, must be the ground of everything ... From this point of view scholasticism, the Christian philosophy of being and of God as Pure Being, has its heart in the right place.'[323] Hodges was never more complimentary to scholastic metaphysics than at this point.

The paradox of Christianity, however, is that the incomprehensible is also the addressable. God does not have personality as we conceive it, yet he deals with us in personal ways. Above all, in Christ God comes to us in personal form. He is God's final revelation. It is a revelation necessarily adapted to human and earthly conditions, and while Jesus was on earth his humanity veiled the full truth of his deity even from his friends. He is not two persons, but one; not a man invested with deity, but 'God who has taken upon himself humanity.'[324] Consistently with his position on the proper sphere of the scientist and the philosopher's sceptical theistic conclusion, Hodges properly cautions that 'You can no more get a God-Man out of the critical historian's study of Jesus than you can get God himself out of the scientist's study of the universe.'[325]

In connection with the inner-trinitarian relations of Father, Son and Spirit, Hodges discusses the *filioque* of the Nicene Creed, namely, the assertion that the Holy Spirit proceeds from the Father *and the Son*. Hodges finds the phrase in the *Book of Common Prayer*, but points out that some Anglicans find this sixth-century addition to the original clause to be unwarranted. In the first place, the Bible nowhere asserts that the Holy Spirit proceeds from the Father as well as from the Son. Certainly Jesus said that he would send the Spirit upon the Church, but

---

[318] Idem, *God Be in My Thinking*, 21.
[319] Ibid.
[320] Ibid.
[321] Ibid.
[322] Ibid., 26.
[323] Ibid., 26–7.
[324] Ibid., 30.
[325] Ibid., 32.

this sending is quite distinct from that referred to in the Creed, where the *filioque* 'refers to the relationships between the Persons [of the Trinity] in eternity'.[326] Hodges notes the suggestion that the clause was admitted to the Creed in order to combat Arianism by making it clear that the Father and the Son were equal in deity. 'If that is the truth of the matter', he drily retorts, 'we have here an instance of the dubious principle of adopting a doctrine which is insecurely founded, not because it is clearly true, but in order to "safeguard" another doctrine.'[327] Hodges recommends the removal of the clause from the Creed. It would then conform to the Creed as used in Orthodox circles. There could then follow open discussion of the reasons why the *filioque* was thought to be important, as well as of other aspects of the doctrine of the Holy Spirit. In reaching this conclusion Hodges was in advance of international ecumenical debate.[328]

But it not enough that Christ should have come. What did he do, and why? Hodges answers that Christ 'comes among us to do the work of man as man for man, to restore human nature in His own person and give us back that nature at once restored and glorified'.[329] Whilst granting that the whole of Christ's work may be encompassed under the term 'atonement', the crucial part of the work is the atoning act at the Cross. In this connection Hodges finds some versions of Catholicism wanting:

> We have known a kind of Catholicism which has talked as if this were the heart of the Gospel; we have been told that Christianity and in particular Catholicism is the religion of the Incarnation. By the mere fact of living among us, God has sanctified our race. By wearing a human body He has declared once and for all the sanctity of matter and put an end to the dreams of the Platonist and the Manichee. He sanctified human labour by participating in it, and on the fact of Christ the carpenter a Christian sociology has been built. These are the beginnings of his ways. The Catholic faith is more than this.

The Apostles did not preach a religion of the Incarnation. They preached the Resurrection.[330]

This important statement places Hodges at odds with a number of Anglicans who, to a greater or lesser degree dressed Christian teaching in the clothes of

---

[326] Idem, 'Filioque?' *Sobornost*, V no. 8, Winter–Spring 1969, 560.

[327] Ibid., 561.

[328] See, for example, Lukas Vischer, ed., *Spirit of God – Spirit of Christ: Ecumenical Reflections on the Filioque Controversy*, Geneva: World Council of Churches, 1981; *An Agreed Statement of the North American Orthodox-Catholic Theological Consultation, St. Paul's College, Washington DC, October 25 2003*, at http://www.usccb.org/seia/filioque.shtml.

[329] Idem, *The Pattern of Atonement*, London: SCM Press, 1965, 26.

[330] Ibid.

philosophical idealism and purveyed an immanentist doctrine of the Incarnation.[331] Hodges (the erstwhile Methodist and admirer of Charles Wesley's hymns) knows that 'The Cross ... has become the symbol of the faith.' He knows, too, that a crucial element of the Christian paradox is 'that the same act by which judgment is brought to a point should also have been the act which brought salvation'.[332]

In *The Pattern of Atonement* Hodges argues that salvation concerns the healing of the breach of personal relationships between God and humanity (though his declaration that man's 'fall is simply his refusal to respond'[333] seems rather tame: it is a wilful determination to do the reverse and say to God, 'We will not have you reign over us'). Human beings are alienated by their sin from God, and at the root of sin is the perverted will. The merit of Christ's death on the Cross 'lies not in the pain, but in the unswerving obedience, of which the willing acceptance of that pain was but the crowning proof'.[334] The Cross is where the victory over sin and death was won. The resurrection is the crown of both the life and the death, and as a result of it the Jesus of history is also 'the indwelling Christ of every day. Christian devotion dwells continually on the mystical union between Christ and the believing soul.'[335]

Turning to the terms 'expiation', 'satisfaction' and 'substitution', Hodges understand the first to mean the purging of the offence and the conciliation of the offended person. He does not find substitutionary theories of the atonement satisfactory, not least because the New Testament has more to say about what Christ does for us, or on our behalf, rather than instead of us; and also because vicarious theories postulate 'a somewhat external ... quasi-legal or even quasi-commercial'[336] relation between Christ and those he saves. Moreover, they are at a far remove from the mystical union of Christ which Hodges finds to be an essential aspect of the atonement:

> substitution doctrine cannot survive without serious modification, for ... the things which Christ is said by this doctrine to do on our behalf are things which we also do in Him. Christ appears before the Father, and we appear in Him; Christ has made the perfect offering, and we as His members join in the making of it; Christ is seated on the Throne and we are seated there with Him.[337]

---

[331] See further Alan P. F. Sell, *Philosophical Idealism and Christian Belief*; idem, *Aspects of Christian Integrity* (1990), Eugene, OR: Wipf & Stock, 1998, ch. 2; idem, *Enlightenment, Ecumenism, Evangel*, 392–5.
[332] H. A. Hodges, *The Pattern of Atonement*, 27.
[333] Ibid., 16.
[334] Ibid., 29.
[335] Ibid., 30.
[336] Ibid., 48.
[337] Ibid., 56.

Does substitutionary language have no place at all? Hodges allows that it underlines the fact that where our redemption is concerned the initiative throughout is with Christ. We have neither the will nor the power to effect our own salvation. Christ alone bore the full burden and he alone won the decisive victory. Again, the true substitution is that of the new creature for the old, for 'to be in Christ is to be a new creature ... It is this new creature ... not the old sinful one, which finds acceptance before God.'[338] God now sees us as we are in Christ. At this point Hodges quotes an eucharistic hymn in which that point is made. He then declares that 'It is in those parts of Christendom where the eucharist has been neglected, or where a minimising doctrine of it has prevailed, that the doctrine of the Atonement too has taken on a meagre and ill-proportioned and often misleading form.' I should like gently to suggest that there are other ways in which the doctrine can take an ill-proportioned form, and that it does so in Hodges' distaste for the concept of satisfaction. He understands that the term denoted 'a salve for wounded honour',[339] but in his discussion he construes it in quasi-commercial terms and in the context of what the atonement does for us. But does it do nothing for God? Is not the Father's holy love, outraged by sin, satisfied, vindicated, by the Son's victory at the Cross, and was it not necessary that this should be done?

Hodges turns next to 'justification'. He presents a careful analysis of the concept, rightly concluding that in Paul's thought God, as judge, pronounces sinners just. It does not mean that sinners are rendered just, yet that meaning has been ascribed to the term from the Fathers onwards – though not in Protestant circles. Can this meaning be found in Paul's writings, and even if it cannot, is it true that sinners are both acquitted and made righteous? Hodges perceives that 'Forgiveness is the main aspect of justification as it is presented in the argument of Romans.'[340] He understands that 'To be in Christ does not mean an immediate end of sinning, but it does mean immediate deliverance from the status of a sinner, from guilt and condemnation.'[341] What leads him to claim that justification is more than acquittal and remission of penalty is the fact that 'the discharged prisoner is drawn back, nay, welcomed back, into the life of the family of God.'[342] In other words, the Christian's righteousness is not merely imputed, but imparted. Hodges emphasizes the latter, not least because he thinks that the former leaves us still in the arena of legal arrangements. 'How,' he asks, 'can I be in Christ, who is all righteousness, and not myself be made righteous?'[343] He seeks support in Paul's teaching on the new birth. At the same time, he fully understands, and endorses, the Reformation protest against any teaching that would state or imply that sinners may earn salvation by their own efforts: salvation is always a gift of God's grace:

---

[338] Ibid., 58.
[339] Ibid., 44.
[340] Ibid., 65.
[341] Ibid., 66.
[342] Ibid., 67.
[343] Ibid., 70.

'To men who had been taught to try to pile up merit, yet with no hope of ever really having enough, the renewed preaching of the doctrine of God's free grace seemed like a deliverance from Egyptian slavery.'[344]

Protestant qualms are raised, however, when Hodges goes on to say that infant baptism 'makes a child a member of Christ and therefore necessarily justifies him'.[345] This is the doctrine of baptismal regeneration, and many would argue that it is flawed because there is no New Testament evidence to suggest that infant baptism and regeneration are necessarily concurrent, or to suggest that God may not regenerate a person at any time – more often than not without the person knowing precisely when the gift was given. Furthermore, God is not bound by his sacraments, and is it his free grace that saves, not the rite as such. It is only fair to add that 17 pages later Hodges does say that infant baptism may be interpreted as follows: 'The child, by being baptised, is not made actually a member of Christ – only faith could make him that – but he has received God's promise, signed with God's seal, that if and when in later life he does believe he shall indeed be a member of Christ, and justified.'[346] But he immediately adds that this interpretation, though 'simple and plausible ... is not the traditional doctrine of the Church. The traditional doctrine, both Orthodox and Catholic, is that baptism actually regenerates, even when administered to infants.'[347]

In his concluding chapter Hodges discusses saving faith. He quotes Calvin's definition: 'Faith is a firm and sure knowledge of God's good will towards us, founded on the free promise given in Jesus Christ, and revealed to our minds and sealed in our hearts by the Holy Ghost.'[348] He finds similar sentiments in the second Anglican Homily on the Passion, and declares of both definitions, 'To talk of saving faith in this way really amounts to saying that one is saved by acquiring a confident belief that one is so.'[349] This really will not do: indeed, it is the weakest sentence in the entire book. The suggestion would seem to turn saving faith into a work, an acquisition, and to suppose that Calvin or the Homily intend this is preposterous. What is being emphasized in the repudiated definitions is faith as trust, *fiducia*, not faith as acquisition or even as assent. Lying behind Calvin's words in particular is the Reformer's foundational doctrine of union with Christ – the very theme that Hodges himself elevates, and of which Thomas Torrance declared that 'It is around this theme of *union* with Christ ... that Calvin builds his

---

[344] Ibid., 79.The doctrine of justification has, like the *filioque*, been the subject of intense ecumenical debate in recent years. For a summary and bibliography see Martien E. Brinkman, 'Justification' in Nicholas Lossky et al., eds, *Dictionary of the Ecumenical Movement*, Geneva: World Council of Churches, 2nd edn, 2002.

[345] H. A. Hodges,*The Pattern of Atonement*, 80.

[346] Ibid., 97.

[347] Ibid., 98.

[348] Ibid., 86. Hodges' source is J. Calvin, *Institutes*, III.ii.7.

[349] Ibid.

doctrine of faith, of the Church as the living Body of Christ, and his doctrines of the Christian life, Baptism, and the Lord's Supper.'[350]

What is Hodges' own understanding of saving faith? It is modelled on Abraham's utter commitment to God; in Christian terms it is a matter of putting oneself 'unconditionally into Christ's hands, and His response to this act of self-surrender is to make us effectively one with Himself.'[351] But, surely, the basis of such an act of self-surrender is precisely trust in the one to whom one gives oneself. For this reason Robert Franks pronounced Hodges' 'rejection of *fiducia* a ... serious matter. Commitment is only possible to the sinner as he trusts in the divine mercy.'[352] I can only concur with Franks's further remark that while Hodges' book is 'a thoughtful and devout study of its great subject ... not everything in it can be accepted by those who stand definitely upon the ground of the Reformation'.[353] My concerns regarding Hodges' positions on infant baptism and saving faith notwithstanding, I think *The Pattern of Atonement* remains a fresh and stimulating study of its theme, and I endorse Cosslett Quin's view of this philosopher's book that 'few professional theologians can produce theology as learned and acute as we get in the text'.[354]

The same may be said of the book, *Death and Life Have Contended*. This work originated in a series of Lenten lectures delivered at two Anglican theological colleges: Cuddesdon in 1960, and St Boniface College, Warminster, in 1961. Unusually in a volume of this kind, Hodges employs a method analogous to that used in his Gifford Lectures, namely, that of seeing how far 'pre-revelation' thought can take us. He begins by asking his hearers (and readers) to place themselves in the position of a 'benevolent unbeliever', who can appreciate much in the character and teaching of Jesus, but who cannot make the theological affirmations of the Christian Creed. Such a person can appreciate that Jesus was a prophet who felt obliged to deliver his message to the world, and who died for the sake of it. But Christians regard the death of Jesus as an event both to be commemorated and celebrated. 'How can it be the latter?' the benevolent unbeliever wonders; and how does the resurrection claim add anything significant to the teaching? It might be said that the manner in which the death was faced, and the memory of the one who faced it, have a continuing influence upon people, but this is far from the Christian claim concerning the resurrection. Hodges intervenes, as it were, to say that the indecisive position reached is the product of the artificial method he has employed,

---

[350] T. F. Torrance, 'Our witness through doctrine', *Proceedings of the 17th General Council of the Alliance of the Reformed Churches throughout the World holding the Presbyterian Order*, Geneva: Office of the Alliance, 1954, 134 (author's italics). See, from many examples, J. Calvin, *Institutes*, III.ii.24, 25.

[351] H. A. Hodges, *The Pattern of Atonement*, 91.

[352] R. S. Franks, review of *The Pattern of Atonement*, in *The Congregational Quarterly*, XXXIII no. 4, October 1955, 367.

[353] Ibid.

[354] C. Quin, review of *The Pattern of Atonement*, in *Theology*, LVIII no. 426, December 1955, 478.

namely, that of studying the Easter custom whilst deliberately omitting everything of religious significance in the festival and in Jesus.

Turning, therefore, to what Christians believe about Easter that a non-believer does not, Hodges speaks of Jesus as both the servant and the Son of God. What he does is ultimately done by the Father in and through him. Moreover, what he does has cosmic significance and is to be consummated in 'a future eschatological event of some magnitude'.[355] At the heart of Jesus's work is his offering of homage to God, and his making a propitiatory sacrifice on the Cross. Hence Christians know him as not merely 'Prophet, Son, Servant and Lover of God; he is also the Saviour of men.'[356] But, still further, Christians believe that Christ is both God and man, and thus we see that there is 'a drama of giving and counter-giving in the very being of God.'[357] By virtue of this Christians, 'Though we are not God's children by direct filiation as [Jesus] is, we are to become children by adoption, being filled with the life of the eternal Son.'[358] All of this turns upon the saving work of God in Christ, and herein lies the uniqueness of Christianity, for 'No other of the great religions offers this atoning sacrifice of an incarnate God. All the rest appear to think that the condition of sincere repentance and amendment is enough.'[359] It might be, Hodges reflects, if the condition could be met by sinners, but this is impossible: we have not the power or the will. We need to be re-made, and it is by our union with Christ that the evil in us dies and the new life in us arises.

Evil, however, is cosmic in scale. All the great religions understand this, and Mazdeism, Judaism, Islam and Christianity all expect a future decisive overthrowing of evil by God. But unlike the other religions, 'Christianity, while still looking forward to the consummation at the End, says that God has already acted in the events of Christ's life and death, and that the decisive victory has already been won there.'[360]

Hodges concludes by reflecting, as a Christian for Christians, upon the double paradox that God dies, and that the death is victorious. The Cross, he argues, makes a threefold impact upon us. It is 'a work wrought *for us*, ... a work to be wrought *in us*, and 'a sign of judgment impending *over us*'.[361] It is for us, for we could not have saved ourselves. It is in us in the sense that once justified the work has hardly begun, for we need to be formed by the Holy Spirit into those who obey, are disciplined, and who deny themselves after Christ's pattern. In further elucidation of this point Hodges shows his high ecclesiastical colours when he

---

[355] H. A. Hodges, *Death and Life Have Contended*, 50.
[356] Ibid., 55.
[357] Ibid., 61.
[358] Ibid., 62. Though I should prefer to substitute the terms 'sons and daughters' for 'children' in this sentence, since all persons, being made in God's image, are his children; Christians are, by grace, God's adopted sons and daughters.
[359] Ibid., 66.
[360] Ibid., 69–70.
[361] Ibid., 77.

specifies purgatory as 'the ante-chamber of heaven, and to find oneself there is to know that one belongs to Christ for ever.'[362] I cannot help but feel that if the knowledge that one belongs to Christ for ever were in some way dependent upon that highly problematic 'location', purgatory, it would be the worse for us. It would also contradict much of what Hodges has said concerning Christ's finished work, which is the ground of the believer's present mystical union with Christ (unless, of course, that union can be broken at a whim, whether human or divine). By contrast with that depressing thought the Calvinistic doctrine of the perseverance of the saints seems positively cheerful. The Cross, thirdly, is over us, for it is 'God's judgment on us and upon the best that we can do, even when we do it for him.'[363] His last word is,

> If the Cross is the sign of judgment over us, let it also be the instrument of execution. We take our place in spirit on our own Cross, the cross of the condemned criminal, praying that it may be also the cross of the penitent thief, and from it we appeal to Christ on his saving Cross: Remember me, Lord, when thou comest into thy Kingdom.[364]

While penitence is never out of place, it is as if, in these last few lines, Hodges has switched off, or at least dimmed, the light of victory. We are at the scene of crucifixion, not of resurrection. There is a line of such Anglican-Catholic spirituality that runs at least from the Puseyites through R. C. Moberly and beyond which returns time and again to the crucifixion rather than to the Cross conceived as the place where sin and death were vanquished once and for all. I do not wish to overstate the case, still less to detract from the many valuable insights in Hodges' exposition of the central themes of Christianity; but his conclusion calls immediately to mind Robert Mackintosh's critique of Moberly:

> One feels as if one were worshipping in some thronged crypt, dark with stained glass, the air heavy with incense, where sacred rites are performed by an emaciated priest, who is bowed with sorrow almost to the ground. The whole scene is exquisitely beautiful, but crushing in its sadness. Then, as we close the High Church volume, and open the New Testament, our eyes light upon such words as these: 'I write unto you, My little children, because your sins are forgiven you for His name's sake.' We are in the fresh air! We are in the sunshine! We are in the presence of a loving God, of a victorious Saviour! How much better God's sunshine is than the Church's crypt![365]

---

[362] Ibid., 85.
[363] Ibid., 92.
[364] Ibid., 94.
[365] R. Mackintosh, *Historic Theories of Atonement*, London: Hodder and Stoughton, 1920, 228–9. Mackintosh quotes R. C. Moberly, *Atonement and Personality*, London: John Murray (1901), 10th reprint, 1932, 322–3.

VII

H. A. Hodges, philosopher and Christian, left writings which encompass philosophy, religious devotion and theology. His particular intellectual contribution, stimulated by his careful studies of Dilthey, was his delineation of the limits of scientific method, his empiricist repudiation of the older metaphysics, and his analysis of world views, standpoints and attitudes. Even as he ended in philosophical scepticism and relativism, theology was, as it were, elbowing its way onto his page, though not in so irrepressible manner as in the case of his older colleague, de Burgh. Moreover, Hodges made more of the logical gap between the last word of philosophy and the first word of faith – with all that that meant in terms of an existential decision – than did de Burgh.

A devout Catholic Anglican, there are emphases in Hodges' ecclesiastical and sacramental writings to which exception may be taken, though his commitment to the ecumenical cause cannot be questioned. Unlike some Anglican theologians he did not elevate an immanentist understanding of the Incarnation above the Cross – Charles Wesley was among those who saw to that; but his doctrine of the atonement lacked the note of *fiducia*, which might have been expected in one so existentially inclined.

Hodges was more forthcoming as to his personal faith and experience than any of the other Anglicans treated in this book. It is fitting, therefore, that I conclude with part of his testimony written one week before he died:

> The God-drenched human experience of the final Consummation will need a different kind of universe from this one, but the Christian myth of the heavenly city has nothing to tell us about it, except that it is suffused with light from a divine source. That, of course, though expressed in a physical image, is really a hint of the kind of God-consciousness that will be normal in the City. Something like it is available intermittently to some of us even here; but then it will be a permanent dimension of awareness. That, and not occasional adventures into states of abstraction, is the real contemplative life to which Christians look forward.[366]

---

[366] H. A. Hodges, *God be in my Thinking*, 66.

Chapter 6
Comparisons, Contrasts and Assessment

Taken all together, the four Anglicans discussed in this book covered a fairly wide range of topics in their writings: classical and modern philosophy, psychology, the history of Christian thought and doctrine, apologetics, ecumenism and spirituality. I have offered comments *en passant* on particular aspects of their thought, but now in conclusion I shall attempt to compare and contrast their approaches to broad philosophical and methodological themes, among them reason, experience, revelation, faith and knowledge, world views and metaphysics.

I

By the time de Burgh, Matthews, Quick and Hodges began their careers the ambiguities of the term 'reason' were widely recognized. Richard Whately, for example, had written of the term that

> This word is liable to many ambiguities ... Sometimes it is used to signify all the intellectual powers collectively. ... Frequently [it is] employed to denote those intellectual powers exclusively in which man *differs* from brutes. ... [It is] often used for the Faculty of carrying on the third operation of the mind; viz. *Reasoning*. [It] is also employed to signify the Premiss or Premises of an Argument; especially the Minor Premiss: and it is from Reason in this sense that the word 'Reasoning' is derived. It is also very frequently used to signify a *Cause*; as when we say, in popular language, that the 'Reason of an eclipse of the sun is, that the moon is interposed between it and the earth.' This should strictly be called the *cause*.[1]

Our four Anglican philosophers unite in according a due place to reason, but they do this in somewhat different ways. They agree that reason is more than ratiocination. DeBurgh put the point as clearly as any: 'The methods of inference are not sovereign, but manifestly instrumental.'[2] He added that 'reason is active in all conscious apprehension of unity in difference or of difference in unity, whether the order apprehended be that of a mathematical formula, of a law of nature, of an historical pattern, of an ethical principle, of an aesthetic harmony, or of God's

---

[1] R. Whately, *Elements of Logic* (1826), London: B. Fellowes, 1829, 312–13.
[2] W. G. de Burgh, *Towards a Religious Philosophy*, London: Macdonald & Evans, 1937, 1.

immanent purposes in the world of his creation'.[3] Aquinas, he explained, held that 'man arrives at the knowledge of intelligible truth by advancing from one thing to another; and therefore he is called rational',[4] – in other words, that reasoning was an inferential process. De Burgh regretted that Descartes, whose scientific-*cum*-mathematical model led him to the same conclusion, relegated 'all thinking that is vague, shadowy and mysterious, to the limbo of irrational feeling and imagination'.[5] To de Burgh, reason had a meaning wider than Aristotle's *nous*, the Scholastics' *intellectus*, and the post-Kantian idealists' *Vernunft*.

In Hodges' opinion,

> Logic by itself is incapable of providing an adequate theory of knowledge. It tells us how, *if* we know one thing, we can pass from it to the knowledge of other things. It shows us how, as a formal exercise, we can work out a deductive system from any set of definitions and axioms we like to take, providing that the definitions are clear and the axioms not mutually inconsistent. As for knowing about reality, or formulating true and well-grounded propositions about the existing world, logic tells us that in order to do this we require both facts of observation and principles by which to interpret and co-ordinate these facts. But logic, so long as it concerns itself with the mechanics of thinking, cannot tell us any way to be certain of our facts or our principles. If there is a dispute between two rival sets of principles, which both enable us to make sense of the world, but not the same sense, logic cannot judge of the dispute. ... For these are questions not of the mechanics of thinking, but of the will to think, and to think in a particular way. The answer to such questions is not a demonstration, but a choice, and if it is supported by argument, the argument must be of the character of a persuasion, an inducement.[6]

Matthews likewise stood for a more-than-inferential, reasoned, method of presenting Christian truth, and for all his emphasis upon religious experience, he was persuaded that that experience was 'indissolubly connected with affirmations about the universe which are capable of philosophical criticism and interpretation'.[7] Accordingly, he appealed to the criterion of rationality when discussing, for example, Schleiermacher, Otto and matters psychical. In Quick's opinion, faith in Jesus was shown to be true because it illuminated reason and was subject to criticism by it. Hodges was concerned that the necessary rational analysis of Christian claims should not be inhibited by the desire to bow before

---

[3] Idem, *Knowledge of the Individual*, London: OUP, 1939, 7.

[4] Aquinas, *Summa Theologica*, Q.79. Art. 8.

[5] W. G. de Burgh, *The Legacy of the Ancient World* (1923), Harmondsworth: Penguin Books, 2 vols., 1955, 555.

[6] H. A. Hodges, *Languages, Standpoints and Attitudes*, London: OUP, 1953, 60–61.

[7] W. R. Matthews, *Studies in Christian Philosophy* (1921), London: Macmillan, 1928, 9.

mystery. On the specific question of natural theology, while all of the four treated the classical theistic arguments with respect, none of them supposed that they yielded demonstrative proof of God's existence. De Burgh did not think that they led to the God worshipped by Christians; Matthews thought that they arose from reflection upon important aspects of human experience; to Quick the distinction between the truths of natural theology and those of revelation was 'incalculably harmful' because it encouraged the view that 'the rational order of the world stands secure, whether Christianity be accepted or not';[8] and to Hodges the point at which theistic reasoning failed was the point at which the existential commitment of faith was required.

Already we begin to see that there are certain differences between de Burgh, Matthews, Quick and Hodges where reason's sway is concerned. Clearly, none of them was an out-and-out rationalist. By this I mean that they did not believe that all of our knowledge is derived from unaided reason, and all gave a place to divine revelation. Thus de Burgh found Spinoza's religion of the intellect inadequate, not least because any system which so determinedly pursues the path of formal logic or pure mathematics cannot inform us as to what exists, or happens, in the world. He also believed in a spiritual realm which lay beyond the realm of sense perception, and that of this world intuitions are given in moral experience – a point to which I shall return. Matthews feared that Spinoza, no less than Kant, inspired the subsequent idealism that threatened to absorb religion within philosophy. Quick, concerned lest it be thought that the test of religious experience was to be found within religion itself, confessed an inclination towards rationalism. At the same time, he argued that faith goes beyond reason, and declared that 'It would ... be absurd to proceed as though reason apart from Christianity could prove certain truths about God and man, and then faith in Christ came in to complete a knowledge which reason left incomplete.'[9] It would therefore seem that de Burgh, Matthews and Quick would have agreed with Clement Webb that, 'Rationalism is not really so much an excess of confidence in reason as a want of confidence in it; since it does not attempt to understand a great part of human experience.'[10] Whereas de Burgh, Matthews and Quick, would not have denied the term 'knowledge' to matters which went beyond, or transcended, experience, Hodges' scepticism, coupled with his commitment to his conviction *qua* philosopher that there was a discontinuity as between the deliverances of reason and those of revelation prevented him from concurring. Indeed, Hodges' contention that we may have knowledge only of matters susceptible to scientific investigation would have been regarded by de Burgh, Quick and Matthews as a damaging concession, and it does seem to sit oddly with Hodges' case against the narrowness of the scientific

---

[8] O. C. Quick, 'Reason and Christian experience. II. What is reason?', *Theology*, XV, 1927, 254.

[9] O. C. Quick, *Doctrines of the Creed* (1938), London: Collins Fontana, 1971, 26.

[10] C. C. J. Webb, *Studies in the History of Natural Theology*, Oxford: Clarendon Press, 1915, 358.

mindset. Moreover, when he declares that the believer *qua* natural theologian 'must continually say less than he believes, in order not to say more that he thinks he can prove',[11] Quick's retort would be 'Then recognize the folly of the alleged reason-revelation divide, and relinquish the role of natural theologian!'

At this juncture I offer three observations. First, when contemplating the limits of our reasoning ability (for reasoning is something we do, it is not a faculty, still less something to be personified by a capital letter), none of the four authors makes an uncritical appeal to mystery which, though no doubt at the heart of Christian experience, is no more a haven from rigorous critique than Spencer's Unknowable or the hyper-Calvinist's inscrutable will of God.

Secondly, none of them majors on the theme of the noetic effects of sin as imposing limits on the efficiency of our reasoning abilities, though Quick's epigram is memorable, 'It is sin that blinds the intellect, not ignorance that causes sin';[12] and his rebuke to Barth on this matter will receive mention shortly. Is not difficult, however, to discover a long line of thought which accords great importance to this notion. At random one might instance the Puritan, Thomas Watson, who declared that 'Sin brings a man low in his intellectual parts. ... Since the Fall, the lamp of reason burns dim.'[13] Again, in the light of Ephesians 4: 18, Titus 1: 15, I Corinthians 2: 19 and Proverbs 3: 5, the celebrated Welsh preacher, John Elias (1774–1841) argued that 'natural reason ... is blinded and confused by sin, and led by imaginations and lusts to choose false principles, to draw erroneous inferences, and to make wrong conclusions from them'.[14] For a final illustration I cite the staunchly Calvinist apologist of the twentieth century, Cornelius Van Til who, on the ground of sin's noetic effects, denied that Christian believers and unbelievers shared common epistemological ground.[15] In all of this there are both epistemological and ethical puzzles, the latter of which recall Hodges' passing remarks concerning the desirability of an ethic of belief and the place of the will in epistemology; and there are also issues regarding the analysis of 'new' in the term 'new life' understood as the gift of God's grace. What are the epistemological and ethical implications of regeneration? The 'new creature' in Christ is clearly not absolutely novel, otherwise we should not be referring to the rebirth of one and the same person, nor would we find Paul confessing that his 'old Adam' continually tries to pull him down, his new life notwithstanding. Furthermore, as Melanchthon recognized centuries ago, the 'renewal of the mind' of which the New Testament

---

[11] H. A. Hodges, *God Beyond Knowledge*, London: Macmillan, 1979, 3.

[12] O. C. Quick, *The Gospel of the New World*, London: Nisbet, 1944, 33.

[13] T. Watson, *The Mischief of Sin* (1671), Morgan, PA: Soli Deo Gloria Publications, 1995, 4.

[14] Edward Morgan, *John Elias. Life, Letters and Essays* (1844; 1847), Edinburgh: The Banner of Truth Trust, 1973, 344.

[15] See further Alan P. F. Sell, *Confessing and Commending the Faith. Historic Witness and Apologetic Method*, Cardiff: University of Wales Press, 2002, Eugene, OR: Wipf & Stock, 2006, 220–22.

speaks does not mean that a person who could not grasp a mathematical concept prior to conversion will be able to do so afterwards simply by reason of his or her conversion.[16] While it is true that Quick did refer in expository vein to the fact of new life as the transformation of a person's whole being, and as having an ineradicable eschatological dimension; and while Hodges referred to character and will in relation to ethics, I should like to have heard more from them and, indeed, from de Burgh and Matthews on these intriguing matters, not least from the point of view of epistemology on the one hand and the apologetic task on the other.

Thirdly, although none of them majored on Karl Barth to the degree that his acolytes might have deemed appropriate, de Burgh, Matthews and Quick were aware of, and perplexed by, what might be called Barthian 'noises off', and this especially in what they perceived to be Barth's dim view of reason. De Burgh thus pronounces that 'Karl Barth glories in proclaiming that religious revelation is not merely supernatural but super-rational. The word of God has no message for the human intellect.'[17] This stance, he felt, was a product of Barth's over-emphasis upon God's transcendence at the expense of his immanence,[18] and he placed Barth in a long line of witnesses:

> We have been told by mystics of an older age, and by not a few among living teachers, that God is above reason ... and that to speak of his reason or of his goodness is to derogate from the infinite majesty of his being. So taught Eckhardt and Boehme; so, in their several ways, Barth and Bedyaev are teaching now. But I am sure they are wrong. Only when, in our arrogance, we take the human mind as the measure, can we plausibly speak of God as super-rational, or of our faith in his revelation as transcending the bounds of reason. It is an old story. For four centuries reason and faith have been drifting apart, on roads that lead logically, the one to a philosophy of mind that negates the claims of the supernatural, the other to a religious supernaturalism that negates the claims of mind and nature.[19]

It was precisely this divide that de Burgh strove to bridge. That the rival claims of faith and reason could be harmonized only in a religious revelation that could be shown to be reasonable, and that faith was a primary condition of all reasonable life, were de Burgh's deeply held convictions.[20] For his part, Matthews regretted the way in which, as he thought, Barth drove a wedge not only between philosophy and theology, but also between Christianity and other world religions; and as to

---

[16] See P. Melanchthon, *The Loci Communes of Philip Melanchthon*, trans. Charles L. Hill, Boston: Meador Publishing Company, 1944, 193ff.

[17] W. G. de Burgh, *Towards a Religious Philosophy*, 245. He repeats the charge in *From Morality to Religion*, 168 n., 293.

[18] See idem, *From Morality to Religion*, London: Macdonald & Evans, 1938, 24 n.

[19] Ibid., 286.

[20] See W. G. de Burgh, *The Legacy of the Ancient World*, 527 n. 1.

method, he and Barth were at opposite poles, with Matthews working his way to the incarnation as the culminating point of philosophical reflection, and Barth setting our from the God's revealed Word. Quick's twofold protest was that 'Barth, no less than the sceptic, assumes that man's reason and conscience confine him for ever within the circle of a man-made universe of illusion';[21] and that Barth denied that 'God created man's spirit to mirror his love, and never has the glass been completely darkened by sin.'[22]

II

What shall we say of the views of the four philosophical Anglicans concerning experience? The slightest acquaintance with the history of thought will suffice to show that, no less than 'reason', 'experience' is a term employed in a variety of contexts: ontological – what is there to be known? Epistemological – how far are experience and truth related to one another? Psychological – how do we come to know? Apologetic – how viable are appeals to experience where the justification of religious claims is at issue? By the time de Burgh, Matthews, Quick and Hodges came upon the scene there was a vast literature on all of these questions. Among the inspirations of this literature in the modern period was Locke, who posed, and answered, his own question:

> Whence has [the Mind] all the materials of Reason and Knowledge? To this I answer, in one word, from *Experience*: In that, all our Knowledge is founded; and from that it ultimately derives it self. Our Observation employ'd either about *external, sensible Objects*; or about the *internal Operations of our Minds, perceived and reflected on by our selves, is that, which supplies our Understandings with all the materials of thinking*. These two are the Fountains of Knowledge, from whence all the *Ideas* we have, or can naturally have, do spring.[23]

Not all felt that Locke's conjunction of sensation and reflection was sufficient. Reid, for example, argued that while from experience we may learn what is or what was, and what may, in similar circumstances, probably be in the future, 'with regard to what must necessarily be, experience is perfectly silent'.[24] For his part, T. H. Green, in whose writings the four Anglican philosophers had been schooled,

---

[21] O. C. Quick, *The Ground of Faith and the Chaos of Thought*, London: Nisbet, 1931, 105–6.

[22] Idem, *Doctrines of the Creed*, 152.

[23] J. Locke, *An Essay Concerning Human Understanding*, ed., Peter H. Nidditch, Oxford: Clarendon Press, 1975, II.i.2.

[24] T. Reid, *The Works of Thomas Reid*, ed. William Hamilton, Edinburgh: MacLachlan & Stewart, 1863, 522.

set his face against the notion that we have in our experience data derived from sensation prior to any intellectual activity:

> For a sensation can only form an object of experience in being determined by an intelligent subject which distinguishes it from itself, and contemplates it in relation to other sensations; so that to suppose a primary datum or matter of the individual's experience, wholly void of intellectual determination, is to suppose such experience to begin with what could not belong to or be an object of, experience at all.[25]

De Burgh, as we saw, would brook no divorce of experience from reason. Indeed, 'Apart from experience,' he averred, 'there is no activity of reason; for the function of reason is to discover what is rational in our experience.'[26] It was equally clear to de Burgh that values could not be severed from experience, for 'man's effort is both to know things as they are and to discharge his moral obligations'.[27] It is, in fact, from experience that we learn that 'Man is an ideal-forming animal, whose thought and conduct alike are guided by standards of truth and goodness.'[28] Values and standards, he insisted, are within experience, not remote from it, but they are never fully realized. But how can the ideal be unrealized and yet real? De Burgh concluded that ethics had no answer to this question, and thus it 'points beyond its own borders to the fields of metaphysics and religion'.[29] In the latter connection he found the importance of the moral argument for God's existence to lie in the principle that 'it is only by the conjunction of religious experience with that drawn from non-religious sources, that the foundation can be secured for a reasonable faith in God'.[30] Although he worked for the synthesis of religion and philosophy, de Burgh was well aware of their different starting-points. He argued that what distinguished the religious *a priori* from those of morality, art and metaphysics, was 'the personal intercourse intrinsic to religious experience'.[31]

Matthews contended that in the absence of an objective moral ideal there would be no moral action, and that since in our experience aesthetic and moral values concern personal imaginations and wills, we may properly infer from them that these values have their ground in the divine personality which, he hastened to add, was not to suppose that God is necessarily *a* person. Quick went so far as to assert that because the aesthetic and moral consciousness – especially the latter –

---

[25] T. H. Green, *Prolegomena to Ethics*, ed., A. C. Bradley, Oxford: Clarendon Press, 1883, 53.
[26] W. G. de Burgh, *Towards a Religious Philosophy*, 139.
[27] Idem, *The Legacy of the Ancient World*, 520.
[28] Idem, *Towards a Religious Philosophy*, 107.
[29] Idem, *From Morality to Religion*, 110.
[30] Ibid., 182.
[31] Idem, *Towards a Religious Philosophy*, 39.

'must be taken as a guide to the true meaning of reality ... theism offers the most reasonable interpretation of the universe'.[32]

In the wake of Schleiermacher, and couching his point in terms of religious experience, Matthews wrote that 'Our first preoccupation as Christian thinkers is to maintain the reasonableness of what Christian experience has found God to be.'[33] When we ask, 'What did the four Anglican philosophers find God to be?' we find that because of his not entirely successful effort to remember that he was a philosopher, not a theologian or an apologist, de Burgh was not concerned to inform us as to his personal religious experience; Matthews's self-estimate was that in his personal experience, inhibited by a certain intellectualism, he had not plumbed the depths of saving faith; and Quick was reticent on the matter. We might have expected that Hodges' existentialist stance would have encouraged him to speak of what he had found and, indeed, he did speak of it: we learn much of his struggle for faith and about his experience of God in times of trial; but he granted that his experience tended towards the intellectual, and this despite the centrality of the Cross in his theology. Perhaps I may make my point by saying that whether because of professional scruples or personal predilection or self-perceived experiential deficiencies, none of the four, whatever they may have 'felt', expressed himself in the almost defiant way that Matthews's older colleague, P. T. Forsyth, did:

> [A]m I really forbidden to make any use of my personal experience of Christ for the purposes of even scientific theology? Should it make no difference to the evidence for Christ's resurrection that I have had personal dealings with the risen Christ as my Saviour ...? There is, and can be, nothing so certain to me as that which is involved in the most crucial and classic experience of my moral self ... [I]f I am not to be an absolute Pyrrhonist, doubt everything, and renounce my own reality, I must find my practical certainty in that which founds my moral life, and especially my new moral life. ... I do not merely feel changed; I am changed. Another becomes my moral life. He has done more than deeply influence me. He has possessed me. I am not his loyal subject, but his absolute property.[34]

There is rather more than a hint here that we may be ill advised to erect a strong disjunction between existential commitment on the one hand and reasoning on the other. Thus, for example, Matthews, for all his emphasis upon religious experience, denied that it could be the sole ground of religious belief, for 'religious experience

---

[32] O. C. Quick, *The Ground of Faith and the Chaos of Thought*, 87.

[33] W. R. Matthews, *God in Christian Thought and Experience*, London: Nisbet, 1930, 236.

[34] P. T. Forsyth, *The Person and Place of Jesus Christ* (1909), London: Independent Press, 1961, 196–7.

is indissolubly connected with affirmations about the universe which are capable of philosophical criticism and interpretation'.[35]

Matthews, Quick and Hodges would have agreed with de Burgh that central to developed religion was the experience of personal intercourse with the divine. Such a relationship, de Burgh declared, could not be supplied by Plato's Form of the Good, by Kant's moral law, or by the absolute of immanent metaphysics. On the contrary, the personal knowledge derived from the approach of the 'other' [albeit not Barth's wholly other] who can enter into personal relations with human beings is a gift of grace which is received by faith.[36] Matthews concurred, adding that the typical Christian experience is not of union with, or absorption by, God, but of communion with him such as can subsist only between persons.[37] How does this square with his further assertion that while God is personal he is not *a* person? It would seem that there is much more to be said concerning the viability or otherwise of 'encounter' language, especially where one party to the relationship is God, as Hodges clearly saw.[38]

III

But already I have strayed into the territory of revelation – not, indeed, that for Christian faith revelation is somehow distinct from experience. On the contrary while 'The seat of revelation is in the cross, and not in the heart',[39] the received revelation is (whether dramatically or, more usually, gradually) transformative of experience. The oscillations between reason and revelation are nicely illustrated by the case of two ministers who served Stand Chapel, Lancashire, in succession. The first, William Harrison, submitted an ordination thesis to the Cheshire Classis entitled, 'On the necessity of Divine revelation', while his successor, William Bond, held that 'The Light of Nature is sufficient for salvation'.[40] As we might expect, the Welsh evangelist, John Elias, was convinced that 'Reason could never, without the Divine revelation, find out that God ever intended to forgive one

---

[35] W. R. Matthews, *Studies in Christian Philosophy*, 9.
[36] See W. G. de Burgh, *Towards a Religious Philosophy*, 46.
[37] See W. R. Matthews, *Studies in Christian Philosophy*, 172, 204–5.
[38] See H. A. Hodges, *God Beyond Knowledge*, 13.
[39] P. T. Forsyth, *The Person and Place of Jesus Christ*, 193.
[40] See Herbert McLachlan, *Essays and Addresses*, Manchester: Manchester University Press, 1950, 121. It is not known whether the saints at Stand Chapel were puzzled by the discrepancy or, indeed, whether they were aware of it, some ministers not being in the habit of sullying the pulpit with disputatious reflections, others, perhaps with an eye to their stipends, being careful not to rock the doctrinal boat. For Harrison and Bond see R. Travers Herford, *Memorials of Stand Chapel*, Prestwich: H. Allen, 1893, 30–32.

transgression ... [or] have any apprehension of the sovereign grace and love of God towards sinners.'[41]

We have seen that the four Anglican philosophers did not agree with Bond, but that they did agree with Harrison and Elias, though with the qualification shared by de Burgh, Matthews and Quick, though not by the philosophically sceptical Hodges, that belief in a religious revelation can be shown to be reasonable. De Burgh made no bones about it: God, he declared, 'is known on the strength of his self-revelation, as the object of a reasonable faith'.[42] Thus it is not simply that in religion knowledge is revealed, for all knowledge is faith in a given revelation. In the case of religion the knowledge of himself is granted by the personal, transcendent-yet-immanent God to human beings, and this is a gift of grace. This is by no means to suggest that human beings can know all there is to know about God; in all apprehension by the mind there are degrees of knowledge and truth, and 'a revelation that was not adjusted to human intelligence would fail to reveal'.[43] Matthews, ever eager to apply the test of reason to putative revelations, nevertheless understood that 'what the religious consciousness fundamentally means by revelation is a fact of experience as indubitable as the existence of the world of perception'.[44] This would seem to echo, albeit in less dramatic language, the sentiments of Forsyth as quoted above. Matthews also did well to remind us that the content of revelation was subject to interpretation, and that in the first place, 'Revelation is always the self-disclosure of God and not the supernatural announcement of theology.'[45] Hodges likewise believed that a revealed religion such as Christianity, 'moves from the nature of God as we believe it to be made known by God himself to an interpretation of his work and deeds in the light of this'.[46] Quick concurred, as is clear from his urging, not that we reaffirm everything the Fathers said, but that we return to the principle upon which they rested, namely, that 'It was the revelation of God which created both their experience and their theology, and the theology was designed quite as much to guide experience as to

---

[41] Edward Morgan, *John Elias*, 348.

[42] W. G. de Burgh, *Towards a Religious Philosophy*, 54.

[43] Idem, 'Intelligence in quest of faith', *The Hibbert Journal*, XL no. 3, April 1942, 225. De Burgh clearly saw that 'transcendence' should be understood in moral rather than in spatial terms. We can then, as I have elsewhere suggested, understand the 'supernatural' not as denoting divine interventions 'from a great height', as it were, but, first, as signifying that the saving *act* does not originate in nature, still less in human beings, but in the holy God of all grace; and, secondly, that the divine objective is to restore nature, especially ours. See *Confessing and Commending the Faith*, 177–82.

[44] W. R. Matthews, *Studies in Christian Philosophy*, 33.

[45] Idem, *Signposts to God*, London: SPCK, 1938, 91.

[46] H. A. Hodges, 'Art and religion', *The Church Quarterly* Review, July–September 1948, 140.

interpret it. For them intellect was not a tin-kettle tied to the tail of feelings, urging them to wilder extravagance as it clattered helplessly in their wake.'[47]

All four of the Anglican philosophers would have endorsed Austin Farrer's gnomic utterance, 'Revelation is what God manifestly does, and is shown to be possible by His doing it';[48] and they clearly understood that what God does is done in history, though whereas de Burgh emphasized the incarnation and Hodges, the Cross, Matthews and Quick gave more or less equal weight to both. On the general point, and against the Neoplatonist predilection for a timeless world of values, de Burgh thundered that 'A Christianity cut adrift from the course of history is no longer a gospel of salvation to all mankind.'[49] The world could not be redeemed by noble abstractions, he declared, and it is in the incarnation of Christ that 'the ghost of the two-world philosophy that was the stumbling-block of Platonism was finally laid, when the invisible things of God were declared to be made manifest for faith in the visible processes of nature and history, and the spiritual order to be immanent in the temporal'.[50] To Quick it was the historic incarnation that excluded a bland, spiritualized, doctrine of divine immanence, and also clipped the wings of any kind of aristocratic mysticism beyond the reach of the generality of people: 'As long as the actual events of Christ's Life, death, and Resurrection are recognized as the essential basis of all faith, those who occupy their business in other than directly religious matters, the van-boy in the East End, the commercial churchwarden in the suburbs, have a definite assurance that they too may possess a firm grasp of all that is really needful in religious knowledge.'[51] To declare that God had made himself known in the incarnation, he said, is a dogma proclaimed on the authority of the revealer. As if to qualify the position of his senior colleague, de Burgh, Hodges warned against a kind of Catholicism which spoke as if the incarnation were the heart of the Gospel; as if 'by the mere fact of living among us, God has sanctified our race. By wearing a human body He has declared once and for all the sanctity of matter and put an end to the dreams of the Platonist and the Manichee. ... The Catholic faith is more than this. The Apostles did not preach a religion of the Incarnation. They preached the Resurrection.'[52]

---

[47] O. C. Quick, *Essays in Orthodoxy*, London: Macmillan, 1916, xxxvi.

[48] A. Farrer, 'Revelation', in Basil Mitchell, ed., *Faith and Logic*, London: Allen & Unwin, 1957, 99.

[49] W. G. de Burgh, *The Legacy of the Ancient World*, 526.

[50] Ibid., 373.

[51] O. C. Quick, 'Mysticism: its meaning and danger', *The Journal of Theological Studies*, XIV, October 1912, 7.

[52] H. A. Hodges, *The Pattern of Atonement*, London: SCM Press, 1965, 26.

IV

De Burgh, Matthews, Quick and Hodges agreed that God's revelation is appropriated by a response of faith. To de Burgh it was 'on the strength of his self-revelation' that God is known 'as the object of a reasonable faith'.[53] He argued that while faith seeks understanding, it is also true that reason calls upon faith as it seeks understanding.[54] In one sense 'faith' is 'a primary condition of all reasonable life',[55] while in another it is trust, commitment, response (*fiducia*). It is experiential and inferential and, above all, it is faith in a person. 'Faith' in this sense does not outrun reason into irrationality. It is faith determined by its object, God, of whom the believer has personal knowledge which is 'distinct in form and content from the inferential knowledge of metaphysics'.[56] Furthermore, the faith response that is made to God's approach is an enabled response: 'God is not present simply as the object of man's response ... our answering love is the very spirit of God working within us. God is present, so to speak, on both sides of the reciprocal relation.'[57] Quick would have agreed with this, though he drew a cautionary 'distinction between the faith which seeks the unceasing cooperation of rational knowledge, and the blind trust which has resigned itself to doing without it'.[58] What Quick calls 'blind trust' is sometimes invoked in relation to the distinction which some draw between 'belief in' and 'belief that'. I have heard it said by eager believers, 'We do not believe *that* certain doctrines are true, but we believe *in* a person, Jesus.' This would seem to imply an existential commitment of an irrational sort, for the speaker disclaims any grounds for believing even that Jesus is worthy of a life-commitment. William Guthrie of Fenwick (1620–65) was wiser in striking the balance thus: 'true justifying faith, which we now seek after, as a good mark of

---

[53] W. G. de Burgh, *Towards a Religious Philosophy*, 54. Kant famously declared that we can have no knowledge of things-in-themselves, the noumenal realm, but only of the phenomenal. In this connection he 'found it necessary to deny *knowledge*, in order to make room for *faith*'. See his *Critique of Pure Reason*, trans. Norman Kempt Smith, (1929), London: Macmillan 1976, 29. Some theologians have pounced upon this as justifying their *religious* understanding of faith, and more than once Tennyson's lines in 'In Memoriam A.H.H.' have been invoked: 'We have not faith we cannot know; For knowledge is of things we see ...' But Peter Baelz rightly pointed out that 'For Kant, faith was no supernatural gift of God but was grounded in the moral experience common to all who deserved the name of rational human beings.' See his *Christian Theology and Metaphysics*, London: Epworth Press, 1968, 13. Tennyson's poem, the first line of which is 'Strong Son of God, Immortal Love', once a fixture in mainline Christian hymnals is not so regularly used today. It is no. 192 in *Congregational Praise*, London: Independent Press, 1951.

[54] See W. G. de Burgh, 'Intelligence in quest of faith', 221; cf. idem, *The Life of Reason*, London: Macdonald & Evans, 1949, 94.

[55] Idem, *The Legacy of the Ancient World*, 527 n. 1.

[56] Idem, *Towards a Religious Philosophy*, 31; cf. ibid., 15.

[57] Idem, *From Morality to Religion*, 259.

[58] O. C. Quick, *Modern Philosophy and the Incarnation*, London: SPCK, 1915, 90.

an interest in Christ, is chiefly and principally an act or work of the heart and will; having presupposed sundry things about truth in the understanding'.[59]

I should now like to offer some very brief reflections on faith and reason, and faith as trust, adding to these the ideas of faith and certainty, faith and proof, and faith and sight. First, Locke observed that, regrettably, reason is sometimes opposed to faith. In his view,

> however *Faith* be opposed to Reason, *Faith* is nothing but a firm Assent of the Mind: which if it be regulated, as is our Duty, cannot be afforded to any thing, but upon good Reason; and so cannot be opposite to it. He that believes, without having any Reason for believing, may be in love with his own Fancies; but neither seeks Truth as he ought, nor pays the Obedience due to his Maker, who would have him use those discerning Faculties he has given him, to keep him out of Mistake and Errour.[60]

The context of these remarks is Locke's broad discussion of reason, in which he refers to belief in the existence of God as being according to reason. It is worth recalling that in his biblical paraphrases Locke, following Paul, also understands faith as trust (*fiducia*),[61] but here he has *assensus* in mind. Among those who took him to task was John Ellis who, with a view to elevating revelation, held that 'the human mind cannot, by any ideas of reflection, or other internal operations, come to the knowledge of God',[62] because our natural faculties are disabled. Quite apart from the noetic effects of sin, however, there is the fact that our minds can never fully comprehend the mystery of God, though, as the Puritans and others steadfastly insisted, we may have a true apprehension of him. As Butler recognized, 'To expect a distinct comprehensive view of the whole subject [of religion], clear of difficulties and objections, is to forget our nature and condition.'[63]

---

[59] W. Guthrie, *The Christian's Great Interest* (1658?), Publications Committee of the Free Presbyterian Church of Scotland, [1951], 55. Two pages later Guthrie observes that 'We often drive people from their just rest and quiet, by making them apprehend faith to be some deep, mysterious thing, and by exciting unnecessary doubts about it, whereby it is needlessly darkened.'

[60] J. Locke, *An Essay Concerning Human Understanding*, IV.17.24.

[61] See his *A Paraphrase and Notes on the Epistles of St. Paul to the Galatians*, etc., ed. A. W. Wainwright, Oxford: Clarendon Press, 1987, I, 136, on Galatians 3: 7. For an account of 'Reason, revelation, faith and Scripture' in Locke and his successors see Alan P. F. Sell, *John Locke and the Eighteenth-Century Divines*, Cardiff: University of Wales Press, 1997, Eugene, OR: Wipf & Stock, 2006, ch. 3.

[62] John Ellis, *Some Brief Considerations upon Mr. Locke's Hypothesis, That the Knowledge of God is Attainable by Ideas of Reflexion* (1743), London: 1837, 29; cf. 129. See also idem, *The Knowledge of Divine Things from Revelation* (1743), 1837 edn, 133.

[63] J. Butler, *Butler's Fifteen Sermons*, introd., W. R. Matthews (1914), London: G. Bell, 1953, 237, in Sermon XV, 'Upon the ignorance of man'.

Hence, for example, the fluctuating puzzlement of Isaac Watts during his student days under the open-minded Calvinist, Thomas Rowe, at the latter's academy at Stoke Newington:

> My Reason should be used as a necessary Instrument to compare the several Parts of Revelation together ... But if an inquisitive Mind overleap the Bounds of Faith, and give the Reins to all our Reasonings upon Divine Themes in so wide and open a Field as that of Possibles and Probables, 'tis no easy Matter to guess where they will stop their Career. I have made Experiment of this in my own Meditations; when I have given my Thoughts a loose, and let them rove without Confinement, sometimes I seem to have carried Reason with me even to the Camp of *Socinus*; but then *St. John* gives my Soul a Twitch, and *St. Paul* bears me back again (if I mistake not his Meaning) almost to the Tents of John Calvin.[64]

My point here is that such doctrinal puzzlement, and the attempt to dissolve it by reasoning, does not necessarily diminish a person's psychological certitude concerning the faith, notwithstanding that his or her reasoning powers may never, given the nature of the enquiries and the capacities of the human mind, find complete intellectual certainty.[65] After all, there is rather more in the New Testament concerning the contrast between faith and sight, than about the alleged contrast between faith and reason. 'Sight is reserved for another world,' declared Richard Sibbes, 'for the church triumphant. There we shall have sight enough; we shall see God face to face.'[66] De Burgh, though not thinking in such eschatologically disjunctive terms as Sibbes, almost concurred: 'In his intellectual life, as elsewhere, man is still a pilgrim, *in* via and not *in* patria; and needs to walk by faith *as well as* by sight.'[67] All of this recalls Hodges' insistence that human reasoning powers necessarily fall short before ultimate questions. Not unconnected with the fact of less-than-absolute-intellectual-certainty is another, namely, that the assurance of faith has more to do with the One of whom we are assured, in whom we have faith/trust, than it has to do with our feelings. In this sense 'Faith is not a means of

---

[64] I. Watts, *Miscellaneous Thoughts in Prose and Verse* (1734), reprinted, Bristol: Thoemmes Press, 1999, 189.

[65] John Heywood Thomas accurately presents Kierkegaard as contending that 'Faith is holding fast the uncertain in passionate certitude, staking my all on the God of my salvation, Who delivers me from the bondage of despair.' See his *Subjectivity and Paradox*, Oxford: Blackwell, 1957, 167. Terence Penelhum has argued that objective uncertainty is not a necessary condition of faith: it may, or may not, co-exist with faith in the sense of subjective certainty. See his *Reason and Religious Faith*, Boulder, CO: Westview Press, 1995, 63–7.

[66] R. Sibbes, *Works*, ed. Alexander B. Groshart, (1862–64), Edinburgh: The Banner of Truth Trust, 1973, 580.

[67] W. G. de Burgh, *Towards a Religious Philosophy*, 2, my italics.

certainty, it *is* certainty – though not of myself and my salvation, but of Christ.'[68] This is why constant attempts to take one's 'spiritual temperature' may be more a sign of fear than of faith.

Precisely because in this life we live by faith, not sight, it must be conceded that, where the greatest questions are concerned, it is possible for people to believe that they are forgiven by God – in which case it would be rational to adopt appropriate attitudes of thanksgiving, relief, renewed commitment – and to be mistaken. 'In other words,' writes Terence Penelhum, 'faith could well involve wholly rational attitudes and yet be mistaken. ... Nor does conceding that believers are rational in trying to change their lives in the ways their faith demands entail that their attitudes and practices are the right ones.'[69] If unbelievers think that the believers' confidence is misplaced, we have what Hodges would call a clash of standpoints.

The Christian faith commitment is commitment to the God who has made himself supremely known in Christ who at the Cross won the victory over sin and the grave. This is an enabled faith which may be inspired, humanly speaking, by gratitude for the Gospel, or penitence, or perhaps a mixture of both. It entails an act of self-surrender, it humbly and gratefully appropriates God's saving grace; but it is not a tool of verification which we wield in order to prove Christian claims.[70] Rather, the constellation of beliefs upon which the faith rests are confirmed in the believer's experience, and the experience is above all that of God, its object. It is not difficult to see in all of this a re-baptism into Christian language of Dilthey's contention that Hodges endorsed: 'The real unit of mental life is not a sensation or a feeling, or even an isolated "intentional act" with its "content", but a total reaction of the whole self to a situation confronting it.'[71]

With this we stand at the threshold of a discussion of world views, standpoints and attitudes. But before finally turning to this I must confess to having held back a particular discussion of considerable importance. All of the themes so far discussed in this chapter are clearly interrelated but when we consider the context in which the four Anglicans articulated them we see at once that the sub-text to all of them concerns the viability or otherwise of metaphysics. Our authors were engaged in a process of adjustment in changing philosophical times, and we must remind ourselves of the ways in which they went about it.

---

[68] P. T. Forsyth, *The Principle of Authority*, 43. For further reflections upon assurance see Alan P. F. Sell, *Confessing and Commending the Faith*, 347–50.

[69] T. Penelhum, *Reason and Religious Faith*, 83. The entire section, 80–85, is relevant and characteristically lucid.

[70] See the important discussion of faith and proof in J. Heywood Thomas, *Subjectivity and Paradox*, 135–41.

[71] Quoted by H. A. Hodges, *Wilhelm Dilthey. An Introduction*, London: Routledge & Kegan Paul, 1944, 43.

V

The four Anglican philosophers were required to chart their course in relation to two currents of thought in particular: the declining influence of the philosophical idealism in which they had been reared, and the scientific mindset as variously represented *inter alia* by empiricism, logical positivism, and the turn taken by ordinary language philosophers and later linguistic analysts from metaphysics in general (in practice if not always in principle). Let us look at each of these in turn.

It must be granted that none of our four philosophers indulged in detailed critiques of idealism; what we find are passing shots across the bows. Thus Matthews set his face against the Hegelian Absolute and the narrow intellectualism it inspired because he thought that it gave inadequate place to the moral consciousness. He also protested against any claimed mystical union with the divine, or pantheizing immanentism, which obliterated the Creator-creature distinction. As to the newer idealists – Croce and Gentile among them – who argued that 'Mind is not substance but activity', this implied, said Matthews, that 'The "nature" which science postulates as the sphere of its inquiries is not an independent order of being having a real existence independent of mind; on the contrary, it is an abstraction made for practical ends from the concrete reality of history, it is in fact a creation of thought',[72] and one which left no criteria for judging the worth of rival interpretations of history; indeed, 'One man's re-living of the past is as good as another's.'[73] On the other hand, Matthews revealed his continuing debt to idealism in holding that religion and philosophy are not radically distinct, and in writing of goodness, beauty and truth, that 'Religion ... is the completion of other forms of the life of the spirit, the climax towards which they tend, so that each of them, when intense and full, passes over into religion.'[74] Nor did he relinquish the idealistic conviction that 'there is no existence apart from mind'.[75]

Quick, likewise, had a bone to pick with post-Hegelian idealism. In face of its immanentism he elevated God's historic *act* in Christ, and he denied that the metaphysical absolute of Bradley, Bosanquet and others could be identified with the Christian Godhead. That would leave us with metaphysics, not religion. Nor does it take much imagination to suggest that Hodges was at one with Dilthey in repudiating Hegel's '*a priori* formalism which makes him treat the movement of life as if it were wholly a movement of ideal principles, and reduce the whole body of historical and social philosophy to one element in a metaphysic of abstract forms'.[76]

---

[72] W. R. Matthews, *God in Christian Thought and Experience*, 128, 129.
[73] Ibid., 151.
[74] Ibid., 24.
[75] Ibid., 151.
[76] H. A. Hodges, *Wilhelm Dilthey. An Introduction*, 65. None of the four philosophical Anglicans was as strident as their contemporary, the (non-birthright) philosophical Quaker, John Macmurray. In *Idealism Against Religion*, London: The Lindsey Press [1944], he declares that because of idealism's 'emotional attachment to ideas rather than to things',

De Burgh, Matthews, Quick and Hodges were united in opposing what might be called scientific methodological totalitarianism. We recall de Burgh's concern that by demarcating the respective provinces of reason and faith, Aquinas and others had paved the way for science to go its own way, regardless of religion. Appreciative of the benefits which had accrued from scientific endeavour, de Burgh was concerned that human moral character had not kept pace with human competence in that field. Wrongly used, the scientific discoveries could be put to dangerous and despicable uses. A further concern of de Burgh's was what might be called the sectarian spirit of the logical positivists within the philosophical guild. He resented the way in which the positivists elevated scientific discourse above metaphysical, aesthetic, moral and religious discourse, regarding the first only as yielding meaningful propositions: that is, propositions that were analytic or, in principle at least, capable of empirical verification. In his opinion cognition, will and feeling were 'integrated, in varying measure, in every human experience';[77] and in any case the positivistic principle did not conform to its own prescription: 'What verification is possible, by sense or by introspection, of the meaninglessness of those sentences which are *ex hypothesi* incapable of verification? Yet the Principle pronounces them to be meaningless.'[78]

Matthews drove directly to the heart of scientific method. Equally impressed by scientific progress, he nevertheless pointed out that science offers but one way of interpreting objects, and it is the way of analysis, simplification and abstraction: 'It concentrates upon that aspect of nature which ... can be counted and measured. ... it abstracts from the other aspects.'[79] Consequently scientific results can seem more definite that those reached in other fields where the concern is no less with truth. Echoing de Burgh, he declared that 'We may use the results of science for any purpose we choose, but science cannot tell us whether our purpose is good or evil.'[80]

Quick was in entire accord: 'the scientific reason fails. For the principle of its order is equally fulfilled whatever value-judgment is to be passed on the cosmic process as a whole. Its very exclusiveness is its undoing. For by including good and evil events indifferently, it excludes from satisfaction that other type of reason

---

'Our Christianity is very sick, and cannot recover until it is cured of idealism. ... The belief that religion and idealism are identical is the cardinal mistake of our contemporary civilization. ... [I]dealism ... institutes a dualism that splits the world in two. ... When idealism makes a conquest of religion, religion becomes concerned with the other life, the spiritual one. ... Idealist religion makes the realization of community impossible by its preoccupation with the idea of a universal community and of its realization.' pp., 8, 6, 10, 11, 22.

[77] W. G. de Burgh, *Towards a Religious Philosophy*, 37.
[78] Idem, *The Life of Reason*, 101.
[79] W. R. Matthews, *Signposts to God*, London: SCM Press, 1938, 15.
[80] Idem, Sermon in the report, 'Service at St. Paul's Cathedral', *Notes and Records of the Royal Society of London*, XVI no. 1, April 1961, 98.

which requires the bringing of all reality under the principle of a order which can definitely be called good.'[81] He added, characteristically, 'The efforts made from the scientific point of view to dispute the belief of religion in a Divine Creator, too often resemble an attempt to prove that music is unreal, on the ground that nothing is learned about it by taking a piano to pieces.'[82]

Hodges regretted the prevalence of the scientific mind-set, according to which anything which was not subject to investigation by scientific methods was viewed askance, and was probably not knowledge at all. He also reminded his readers that no matter how well they are supported by evidence, scientific theories always fall short of logical certitude, and are held provisionally only, always being subject to correction or disproof in the light of further knowledge. He might also have noted that a not inconsiderable part of the history of science is the story of false starts and of conclusions that were eventually shown to be untenable. 'The real conflict', he declared, 'is not between the teaching of science and those of Christianity, but between the spirit and temper of our scientific age and the Christian outlook on life.'[83] Hodges, however, went further than de Burgh, Matthews and Quick when he denied the name of knowledge to theology, holding that 'any cognitive enterprise deserves to be called knowledge in so far, and only so far, as it approximates to the scientific model'.[84] In his view, 'Theology begins only when science has shot its bolt.'[85] To the other three this would have been a concession too far. It is a product of Hodges' epistemological scepticism, and I shall shortly return to this matter. But whether or not there is what de Burgh called 'a world beyond', and whether or not, if there is such a world, we can have knowledge of it, de Burgh, Matthews, Quick and Hodges would all have agreed with H. J. Paton, who said that those who deny that there can be any world other than this 'go too far and become dogmatic in their turn: we are not entitled to say *a priori* that the boundaries of science must be the boundaries of reality'.[86] They would probably have agreed with F. C. Copleston's dry observation concerning such deniers: 'Inability to find any value in metaphysics may very well be an indication of the limits of a man's "world".'[87]

How did de Burgh, Matthews, Quick and Hodges chart their course between the Scylla of waning idealism and the Charybdis of the scientific mindset?

---

[81] O. C. Quick, 'Reason and Christian experience. II. What is reason?' *Theology*, XV, 1927, 251–2.

[82] Idem, *Essays in Orthodoxy*, 17.

[83] H. A. Hodges, 'Christianity in an age of science', in J. H. Oldham, ed., *Real Life is Meeting*, London: The Sheldon Press, 1942, 48.

[84] Idem, *God Beyond Knowledge*, ed. W. D. Hudson, London: Macmillan, 1979, 14.

[85] Ibid., 96.

[86] H. J. Paton, *The Modern Predicament*, London: Allen & Unwin (1955), 3rd impression 1962, S 202.

[87] F. C. Copleston, *Contemporary Philosophy* (1956), London: Burns & Oates, 1965, 76.

With characteristic boldness de Burgh affirmed that 'Man is, above all things, a metaphysical, that is, an ideal-forming, animal; he seeks for reason everywhere, in history as in nature, and his thirst will not be quenched until he find it.'[88] Sounding suspiciously like an older-style idealist, he declared that reason's 'proper end is to know the universe as a single harmonious system', but then, his talk of a spiritual world 'beyond' the world of human experience notwithstanding, he came down to earth and added, 'Unless the claims of man's practical and emotional nature, as well as those of intellect, found satisfaction, the vision would remain discordant *for the intellect.*'[89] Throughout, de Burgh strove to hold together the mundane and the other-worldly, regretting, for example, that 'the ghost of the distinction between the "eternal truths" of mathematics and "matters of fact" (i.e. between values and events) still haunts the sanctuaries (or, shall we say, the graveyards?) of metaphysics.'[90] But although he did not wish to repudiate the empirical realm, de Burgh accorded priority to the *uno intuiti*. We could not, he thought, proceed from the part to the whole; we first have intuitive awareness of the whole, and our subsequent inferential activity is ancillary to that intuition. Accordingly, he faulted both Descartes and the rationalists and Hume and the empiricists for mistakenly thinking of the mind's growth in knowledge on analogy with 'the principle of mechanical composition that had proved so amazingly fruitful in the physical sciences', and for not understanding that that 'method of explanation does violence to the actual nature of the thinking process which is conditions from the outset by an indeterminate and schematic apprehension of the whole'.[91]

Matthews couched his argument in theological terms. While he repudiated Platonism (which makes his nomination for a Cambridge Chair by Inge, that devotee of Plotinus, the more interesting) he stoutly defended the idea of the supernatural. He argued that a supernatural religion 'finds the Eternal to be, not a mere Absolute or Infinite Being or Moral order of the world, but a living, personal Spirit who draws near to man with creative and redemptive purpose'.[92] The negative implication of Matthews's insistence upon the fact that God is a personal, purposive being, was that any metaphysic which thought of God in abstract terms as self-sufficient in and for himself, and as impassible and incapable of change, was untenable. But for all the emphasis upon God's immanence, we also found in Matthews an endorsement of the older view that philosophy and religion are akin in that both 'have as their motive force the desire to pierce behind the appearances to Reality'.[93] This ambivalence suggests that Matthews was a philosopher-theologian between the times, and this lingering commitment to an increasingly outmoded understanding of philosophy (as it became during his lifetime) may in

---

[88] W. G. de Burgh, *The Legacy of the Ancient World*, 499.
[89] Idem, *Towards a Religious Philosophy*, 2.
[90] Idem, *The Legacy of the Ancient World*, 506.
[91] Idem, *The Life of Reason*, 16.
[92] W. R. Matthews, *Essays in Construction* (1933), London: Nisbet, 1936, 40.
[93] Idem, *The Gospel and the Modern Mind*, 129.

part account for his feeling that he was too old to learn the new game of linguistic analysis. He also held to an increasingly queried understanding of religion as being 'the completion of other forms of the life of the spirit, the climax towards which they tend, so that each of them, when intense and pull, passes over into religion'.[94] That the several strands of human experience – the empirical, the moral and the aesthetic – should flow together in mutually supportive ways until they found their goal in religion was precisely the notion that Hodges challenged with his existentialist claim that there is a logical gap, a discontinuity, between all other human experience and religious faith. ... To this point I shall return shortly. For the present I would simply remark that Matthews, the 'liberal' theologian, appears to be more conservative in his understanding of metaphysical method than either de Burgh, Quick or Hodges.

As for Quick, he, like Matthews, though even more determinedly, set his face against Platonist metaphysics. He objected to the identification of the real with the good, because that entailed the dismissal as illusory of most of our present experience. He opposed the idea of the impassibility of God on the ground that this would mean that any union of the human and the divine could occur only by the negation of the human. Furthermore, Platonism could not accommodate an historic incarnation or atonement for, on Platonist terms, such an eruption of the divine into history would necessarily degrade the divine, and Platonic idea that salvation entails the detachment of the individual from the historical world was, said Quick, untenable. As for post-Hegelian idealism, Quick argued that Bradley, Bosanquet and others, by making it 'a matter of logical proof that a mind can only know what is in principle already immanent within it', ruled out 'any doctrine of the self-revelation of God above to Man below ... as superfluous ... [and] self-contradictory'.[95] We were thus left with a 'metaphysical absolute for which the name of Godhead cannot appropriately be used'.[96] He further objected to the way in which idealists such as Edward Caird converted Jesus into the embodiment of the moral ideal and regarded that ideal, not the historic person, as the core of Christianity. He felt that the idealists could not take due account of the reality of evil, which, for them, could only be a stage on the way to a greater good, and consequently, that they played down the need of a remedy for it; and, like Matthews, he abhorred idealism's immanentist, pantheizing, tendency which blurred the Creator-creature distinction and required to be corrected by regarding immanence and transcendence as correlatives. In summary, 'The impossibility of conceiving how real events can ever proceed from pure reason, or how causative happenings can ever be reduced to a mere system of signs, is the brick wall against which idealist philosophy has been running its head from the days of Plato to the days of Hegel and Whitehead.'[97] More generally, Quick contended that the

---

[94] Idem, *God in Christian Thought and Experience*, 24.
[95] O. C. Quick, *Modern Philosophy and the Incarnation*, 65, 66.
[96] Idem, *The Ground of Faith and the Chaos of Thought*, 75.
[97] Idem, *The Gospel of Divine Action*, London: Nisbet, 1933, 25.

metaphysical reason could not demonstrate that the universe as a whole is rational: such a claim was in the nature of an act of faith. He further warned that theologians would be unwise to hitch their wagon to the star of any particular metaphysical system lest the failure of the latter brought the theology tumbling down.

Hodges was in entire agreement with Quick that theology does not arise from 'the speculative ingenuities of metaphysicians, but out of men's commerce with God ... just as physics grows up out of men's commerce with the material world'.[98] More dramatically, he declared that 'Philosophy as we have known it belongs to the period of world history which is going out';[99] and he advised both the world and the Church to have done with 'old [metaphysical] idols'.[100] It is not difficult to detect the influence of Dilthey in some of Hodges' adverse criticism of the older metaphysics. For example, Hodges shared Dilthey's distaste for Hegelian metaphysics because it left the individual and the universal side by side, but unconnected. He further diagnosed the problem of metaphysics as resulting from the way in which such terms as 'force', 'power' and 'necessity' had been understood as naming metaphysical entities, and grammatical forms had been taken as evidence of ontological relations. As a result, he argued, insoluble problems had been created for metaphysics. Unlike his senior colleague, de Burgh, Hodges followed Dilthey in believing that there were no absolute values or unconditional norms of conduct; rather, values are discerned by induction from experience. Here we are at the threshold of that refurbishment of metaphysical statements, to the necessity of which Hodges felt his linguistic analytical colleagues had properly pointed. How might this be done? Hodges answered that ontological propositions needed to be rebaptized as transcendental ones referring not to the world, but to experience, to 'the ways in which we do, or could, regard the world'.[101] By 'transcendental' here Hodges meant precisely not propositions referring to de Burgh's occasionally lingering transcendent realm of experience far 'beyond' and/or 'above' the world of sense experience, of which realm we are alleged to have intuitive apprehensions. At this point Hodges' scepticism came into play. In fact he was here at his most Kantian. When Kant contended that we could have knowledge of the phenomenal realm only, not of the noumenal, and therefore denied that knowledge of reality was possible,

---

[98] H. A. Hodges, 'What is to become of philosophical theology?', in H. D. Lewis, ed., *Contemporary British Philosophy*, Third Series, London: Allen & Unwin, 1956, 218.

[99] Idem, 'The crisis in philosophy,' in F. W. Camfield, ed., *Reformation Old and New. A Tribute to Karl Barth*, London: Lutterworth, 1947, 197.

[100] Ibid., 198.

[101] Idem, *Languages, Standpoints and Attitudes*, 30. Cf. C. B. Daly's argument that from the fact that being and the self are the 'absolute presuppositions' of all knowing and saying it does not follow that we are shut up to metaphysical agnosticism, for being is in, not beyond things, and the self is in, not beyond knowledge. See his 'Metaphysics and the limits of language', in I. T. Ramsey, ed., *Prospect for Metaphysics. Essays of Metaphysical Exploration*, London: Allen & Unwin, 1961, 195.

he was in effect denying that metaphysics had, or could have, any such peculiar subject-matter of its own. But he did not thereby deprive the metaphysician of employment. The positive task of the metaphysician was not to think about a special world, but to think about the structure of our thinking about the ordinary world; not to acquire knowledge of objects beyond our experience, but to clarify the nature and conditions of objects of knowledge within our experience.[102]

Kant may offer his own definition: 'I entitle *transcendental* all knowledge which is occupied not so much with objects as with the mode of our knowledge of objects in so far as this mode of knowledge is to be possible *a priori*.'[103] In other words, Kant is concerned with the conditions of possible experience – with categorial principles, and so was Hodges. W. H. Walsh explains that

> Categorial principles are not read out of, but read into, experience; it is our refusal to give them up in the face of unfavourable evidence which differentiates them from highly general empirical laws. To suppose that they could be arrived at by a simple survey of the facts is ... to fail to understand the part they play in human thinking.[104]

Thus, to give Kant's own example, the proposition, 'everything which happens has its cause' is not analytic, and although it requires to be proved, it is 'a *principle*, not a *theorem* because it has the peculiar character that it makes possible the very experience which is its own ground of proof, and that in this experience it must always itself be presupposed'.[105] The upshot is that, as Dorothy Emmet wrote, the metaphysician's 'word gives form to the experience; it does not copy the structure of the real'.[106] It refers to what we know, not to alleged ethereal ontological realities of which we have no acquaintance. Hodges thus favoured the epistemological-experiential turn in metaphysics, and it is not without significance that Collingwood, on aspects of whose thought Hodges drew, had also made much of categorial principles.

What, now, of the attitude of the analytical philosophers to things metaphysical? In the first place it is important to note that some such philosophers were more hostile towards metaphysics than others. I have already adverted to the logical positivists, but there were others who disdained metaphysics and some, like G. E. Moore, who did not formally repudiate the discipline but concentrated upon

---

[102] Anon., 'Metaphysics', in J. O. Urmson, ed., *The Concise Encyclopaedia of Western Philosophy and Philosophers*, London: Hutchinson, 1960, 263. In this book numerous contributors are listed, but no articles are signed.

[103] I. Kant, *Critique of Pure Reason*, trans. Norman Kemp Smith, 59.

[104] W. H. Walsh, *Metaphysics*, London: Hutchinson, 1963, 169.

[105] I. Kant, *Critique of Pure Reason*, 592; cf. 621, 624.

[106] D. M. Emmet, *The Nature of Metaphysical Thinking* (1945), London: Macmillan, 1966, 227.

the analysis of ordinary language.[107] Whereas de Burgh and Quick made passing references to the analysts and Matthews decided not to pursue them, it was Hodges who was most contemporary with that proliferation of linguistic analysis which characterized the philosophical scene in England during the 1950s and 1960s. He noted the way in which, from Descartes, Hume and Kant onwards ontology had increasingly been overtaken by epistemology as the centre of interest of many philosophers, but that by his time the epistemological problems had proved to be as intractable as the ontological, and hence there was a further shift from the human being as knower to the human being as speaker. He was not opposed to analytical procedures as such. On the contrary, he welcomed the linguistic analysts as 'speaking an important word, which is yet not the final word, about the methods, aims and functions of philosophy'.[108] He felt, however, (a) that philosophy could not finally rest in linguistic analysis because human beings are not merely speakers, but purposeful beings; and (b) that it needed to be recognized that the root cause of the linguistic problems that the linguistic 'therapists' analysed was a confusion of standpoints: 'it is a disorder of intellectual perspectives which sets the use of language wrong'.[109] With this we approach, once again, the question of world views and standpoints.

---

[107] W. H. Walsh was among a number of philosophers who argued that much analytical philosophy of the period was covertly metaphysical. Thus, for example, 'The dictum that "Every thing is what it is, and not another thing", set by Moore on the title-page of one of the most influential philosophical works of the century, has been taken by many of Moore's successors to express a fundamental and unassailable truth. In basing their work on this "truth" it is not extravagant to suggest that they have adopted a distinctive metaphysical point of view.' See his *Metaphysics*, 193–4. He concluded that 'there is no clear dividing line between [analysis and metaphysics] for metaphysicians necessarily engage in analysis whilst analytic philosophers tend to make covert metaphysical assumptions'. Ibid., 194. Similarly, Walter Kaufmann lamented that, for some philosophers, the virtues analysis had become 'ends in themselves. Instead of employing them to sift one's own wheat from one's chaff, one has abandoned any effort to grow wheat.' See his *Critique of Religion and Philosophy*, London: Faber and Faber, 1959, 25. We might expect the Thomist, D. J. B. Hawkins, to (somewhat optimistically) observe that 'It is no longer necessary, perhaps, to meet objections of principle against metaphysics, since anti-metaphysical principles, like that of verification, have a way of turning out to be themselves metaphysical.' See his 'Towards the restoration of metaphysics', in I. T. Ramsey, ed., *Prospect for Metaphysics*, 111. But for examples to show that Walsh and Kaufmann had non-Thomistic supporters, see S. Körner, 'Some types of philosophical thinking' and S. Hampshire, 'The interpretation of language: words and concepts', in C. A. Mace, ed., *British Philosophy in the Mid-Century. A Cambridge Symposium*, London: Allen and Unwin, 1957, 115–31 and 267–79 respectively. H. D. Lewis edited a substantial volume designed to show that *Clarity is Not Enough*, London: Allen & Unwin, 1963. The telling subtitle is, *Essays in Criticism of Linguistic Philosophy*.

[108] H. A. Hodges, 'What is to become of philosophical theology?', 217.

[109] H. A. Hodges, *Languages, Standpoints and Attitudes*, 21.

Our discussion thus far suggests that the four Anglican philosophers were not on all fours in their attitude towards metaphysics. While none of them supposed that their task was to describe in detail the contents of the 'world beyond', the degree to which they thought of that world as intellectually continuous with the world of intellectual discourse varied, and Hodges proposed a discontinuity in that connection, allowing that scientific methods alone yielded what could properly be called knowledge. This did not, however, land him in the anti-metaphysical camp. On the contrary, he felt that metaphysical questions were unsuppressible (however reluctant some philosophers might be to admit it), and in particular that theology, which bristles with such questions, could be taken seriously only if 'the metaphysical mode of thought and speech' were admitted.[110] Again, they all agreed that no dogmatic embargo could be imposed against metaphysical questions, though they differed somewhat as to how such questions were to be construed. They were quick to denounce metaphysical systems that did not appeal to them and, of course, they did this on the basis of views of the world to which they subscribed. Indeed, 'Once it is allowed that every major human activity rests on a theoretical claim, the need for an overall view of the world becomes urgent. That many quite intelligent people manage to get along without such a view is no reason for denying the propriety of trying to arrive at one if we can.'[111] Thus encouraged, I proceed to enquire how de Burgh, Matthews, Quick and Hodges situated themselves *vis-à-vis* world views.

VI

It has been evident throughout this study that de Burgh, Matthews, Quick and Hodges embraced a Christian view of the world. Try as he might to remain faithful to the philosopher's task and to eschew those of the theologian and apologist (and he did not always try tremendously hard), de Burgh could not – or at least did not – keep his deepest convictions at bay. He believed that 'The crudest revelation of God generates of necessity an outlook on men and things, a world-view, which as the mind develops, ripens into a theocentric philosophy';[112] and although his primary objective was to lay the groundwork for such a philosophy, he was prevented by death from producing his desired construction. It is interesting to note, however, that in the last chapter of his posthumously-published Gifford Lectures he declared that 'a Christian philosophy, if such be possible, must be existential'.[113] Although we cannot know how he would have proceeded with this possibility, it would seem that although his Reading successor, Hodges, in his philosophical works tended to reserve his Christian convictions to a coda, he offered careful studies of the limits

---

[110] Idem, 'What is to become of philosophical theology?', 232.
[111] W. H. Walsh, *Metaphysics*, 131.
[112] W. G. de Burgh, *From Morality to Religion*, 150.
[113] Idem, *The Life of Reason*, 197.

of reason and the question of the existential basis of faith. We might say with some justification that he took up where his senior colleague left off. But it was precisely the existentialist emphasis which distinguished Hodges' approach from that of Matthews who, as we saw in connection with metaphysics, thought in more linear terms with religion as the culminating point of a process of argument leading, without the disjunction of a logical gap, from our awareness of the world and our moral and aesthetic experience to faith in God. Thus, for example, he followed Croce in thinking that 'All religion ... has implicit within it a view of the world and cannot therefore be radically distinct from philosophy.'[114] Hodges, I suspect, would regard this as a *non sequitur* (a) because of the logical gap, and (b) because of his recognition that standpoints (the more modest term he used when realizing, against Dilthey, that a view of the world in all its completeness will for ever elude us) may be, and frequently are, in irremediable conflict – another consideration to which, in Hodges' opinion, Dilthey paid insufficient attention. So tenaciously are standpoints held, Hodges argued, that the progress from one to another required not so much a change of mind on certain particular matters, but a conversion. Elsewhere Matthews spoke of religious conversion as 'A change in the whole orientation of the self, and the dominant note of the experience is the feeling that some power, the grace of God, which was not within the resources of the previously existing personality, has caused the transformation.'[115] He applauded Kierkegaard for his insight into these things, and he acknowledged the challenge 'to develop for the first time a philosophy from within Christianity itself';[116] but, as far as I have been able to discover, he did not modify his understanding of the nature and relations of philosophy and theology accordingly. Hence the methodological ambivalence detectable at a number of points in his writings.

Although he did not develop the point in great detail, Quick, when arguing that the metaphysical reason cannot demonstrate that the universe as a whole is rational, invoked 'An act of faith [which] alone can give assurance' of this.[117] He proposed that the rationalist theist show that 'his belief really exhibits a fuller and more inclusive harmony', whereas the religious empiricist must explain that 'the religious fact and experience are unique and inexplicable and manifestly God-given precisely in this, that they shed such wonderful illumination upon the whole plan of reality'.[118] This seems compatible with Hodges' approach. For although Hodges thought that philosophy concluded in scepticism as to metaphysics in general and the realities of the Christian faith in particular, he by no means ruled out post-commitment reasoning on the part of the Christian. But it would be reasoning directed to persuasion, not reasoning with a view to adducing proofs. This was because what was at issue was not simply a balancing out, or an adjudication

---

[114] W. R. Matthews, *God in Christian Thought and Experience*, 90.
[115] Idem, *Reason in Religion*, London: The Lindsey Press, 1950, 15.
[116] Idem, *The Problem of Christ in the Twentieth Century*, 62.
[117] O. C. Quick, 'Reason in Christian experience. II', 252.
[118] Ibid., 253.

between, truth claims; the significance or otherwise of the question whether or not God exists, for example, turned upon a person's basic attitude to life. This attitude comprised the person's hopes, fears and desires, and these 'determine where we look, and how we look, and whether we find what is there to be found'.[119] There is thus 'a will to think, and there is a will to think in certain ways'.[120] Hence, given the impossibility of demonstration, if a person's existential commitment were 'supported by argument, the argument must be of the character of a persuasion, an inducement'.[121] Or, as Walsh put it in relation to a claim to revealed knowledge, 'Argument can and does come in ... but in the last resort it is a matter of inviting the reader to take the principles and see for himself.'[122] As we saw, in Hodges' view a principle, standpoint or attitude 'should open up possibilities of life, experience, and activity'.[123] In the case of Christianity, which presents itself as the way to fullness of life, 'we shall not be judging it by any extraneous standard, we shall simply be asking it to make good its own claims'.[124] Hodges did not further spell out the contents of that orderly, reasoned testimony to which Christians are called; but the theologian, James Richmond, in the light of his case that the words 'fact' and 'real' have at their root the idea of making a difference, made no bones about it and, whilst denying that religious beliefs are meta-scientific theories, declared,

> The theologian should make it clear that there is a 'world' of religious, moral and existential experience, that moral demands, existential decisions and historical events are 'factual', that the dimensions of value, revelation and history are 'real', and that the religious, moral existential and historical approaches to things are 'cognitive', yielding knowledge of 'reality'.[125]

Here one of my doctoral supervisors 'tells it like it is'. He indulges in ontology mixed with epistemology – and why not? C. B. Daly attributed 'metaphysical agnosticism' to two errors:

> First there is the error of thinking that the 'being' lies *beyond* things. In truth, it is *in* things, it *is* things, only we do not notice it; we see things, not their thingness, not the fact that they *are* and are not Nothing. ... Secondly, there is the error of thinking that all knowledge must be clear, distinct, final, leaving its

---

[119] H. A. Hodges, *Languages, Standpoints and Attitudes*, 51.
[120] Ibid., 48.
[121] Ibid., 61.
[122] W. H. Walsh, *Metaphysics*, 181.
[123] H. A. Hodges, *Languages, Standpoints and Attitudes*, 63.
[124] Ibid., 64.
[125] J. Richmond (of blessed memory), *Faith and Philosophy*, London: Hodder and Stoughton, 1966, 214. Cf. Frederick Ferré, *Language, Logic and God*, London: Eyre & Spottiswoode, 1962, 159–66.

solved problems behind like milestones in its march to ever new discoveries. But knowing is not all or nothing; it has an 'open texture'.[126]

Lest any should have been wrongly injected with the view that such ideas ought to be branded heretical by those like Hodges who, in the wake of Kierkegaard, speak of choice, decision, commitment, they will find the antidote in a paper by my first teacher of philosophy of religion. John Heywood Thomas has shown that while Kierkegaard was undoubtedly, even trenchantly, opposed to Hegel's metaphysics he was not opposed to metaphysics as such. On the contrary he proposed his own metaphysics, at the centre of which was the conviction that

> The nature of a truth claim is that it says how things are so that however much we want to insist on the fact that 'truth' relates to what is said it is in the end an ontological rather than a logical or semantic one. ... [Furthermore] By calling attention to the necessary relations of truth – when we speak of moral and religious truth – to persons Kierkegaard was raising a metaphysical problem and not merely one about the self-involving nature of this language. ... *Fragments* contends that the change from error to Truth is like a change from Non-being to Being. The movement from one to the other is not like the idealistic translation of imagination into thought, alternative experiences like looking through plain glasses or looking through glass ones. It is an ontological change.[127]

If we then inquire into the nature of this change as understood within the Christian view of the world, we shall, as I suggested earlier, find ourselves involved in the analysis of such terms as 'conversion', 'regeneration', 'response', 'choice', and 'decision'. We shall also find that just as the ontological claim leads to the analytical task, so the latter, while for legitimate reasons it may bracket the former in the interests of concentrated work, cannot obliterate the metaphysical presuppositions which underlie, and are brought to the surface by, the discourse under review.

VII

As I emerge from an extended period of submersion in the writings of de Burgh, Matthews, Quick and Hodges, I cannot suppress the question, With which of them do I feel in the greatest sympathy? I enjoy being carried along by de Burgh's flowing prose, though I regret that he was taken from us before he had time to explore that existential starting-point for a Christian philosophy to which his travels through morality had led him. Of all the four, and despite his alleged, and claimed, liberalism, and his concern at the way in which idealism could absorb religion into

---

[126] C. B. Daly, 'Metaphysics and the limits of language', 195.
[127] J. Heywood Thomas, 'Kierkegaard's alternative metaphysics', *History of European Ideas*, XII no. 1, 1990, 59, 60.

philosophy, Matthews remained most wedded to the then increasingly challenged idea that the territories of philosophy and religion were in principle identical. In this respect he is the most old fashioned of them all. De Burgh's Reading successor, Hodges, clearly perceived the point at which, where Christian claims are concerned, demonstrative philosophy ran into the sand, but I could wish that he had had more to say about the way philosophy serves apologetics after the existential decision has been made. While agreeing with him that standpoints, and even more world views, are non-demonstrable, and that there is a logical gap between the way of argument and the commitment of faith (*fiducia*), I think that, where apologetics *qua* commendation (and not simply 'defence') of the faith is concerned, more can be made of the insights which inspired the traditional theistic arguments, of our awareness of moral values and aesthetic experience, and of religious experience than is attempted by those whose intellectual starting-point is in revelation as such. In other words, that having adopted the faith stance, one may legitimately and, as it were, retrospectively, gather up the intellectual and experiential pointers to faith and present them not as copper-bottomed confirmations of Christian claims, but as indicators that while demonstration is not possible, those who make such claims are not behaving irrationally, but reasonably in relation to their life experience and their commitment to truthfulness.

As I have elsewhere suggested,[128] Christian apologetics in the sense of witnessing to, and commending, the faith will then appear as a reasoned eclecticism, offered in the hope that others will understand, even if they cannot make the commitment of faith. Indeed, they will do the latter only as God the Holy Spirit opens their eyes. That is to say, the existential choice or decision, though no less ours, is an enabled response to God's prevenient grace. De Burgh saw this very clearly. None of this precludes the 'defence of the faith' against materialism, pantheism, and sundry other 'isms' as undertaken by traditional apologists, but our defence will be undertaken in the context of commendation. It is a task that implies that, over against alternative world views and standpoints, Christians are concerned to make some specific truth claims. It would be unfortunate if Hodges' recognition that standpoints may be in irremediable opposition were taken by Christians as legitimating the fashionable 'broad-minded' attitude encapsulated in the phrase, 'to each his own'. For this would betoken a failure to witness, and a tacit endorsement of the view that one standpoint is as good as another. The bulwark against such a position was erected by Hodges himself. We recall his objection to Dilthey's complacency regarding incompatible world views: 'To live is to act, to act is to choose, and to choose is also to reject',[129] he declared. At the same time, he insisted that 'Our business is to give utterance to the best views we can form, with due

---

[128] See my trilogy on Christian apologetic method, which I have described as a tale of alternative starting-points: *John Locke and the Eighteenth-Century Divines*, *Philosophical Idealism and Christian Belief*, and *Confessing and Commending the Faith. Historic Witness and Apologetic Method.*

[129] H. A. Hodges, *Wilhelm Dilthey. An Introduction*, 105.

modesty born of the consciousness of relativity, but also with confidence that the vigorous interplay of honestly formed and honestly confessed attachments is the right form, and even the only possible form, for a responsible intellectual life to take.'[130] The reference here to relativity cautions us that Hodges' declaration that 'to choose is also to reject' – a characteristic of basic attitudes – is not to be construed as an absolute strong disjunction where inter-human relations and common moral action are concerned. For, as Hodges recognized, a dialectical materialist and a Christian may find themselves allies *per accidens* notwithstanding that their world views are mutually incompatible because their basic attitudes differ. This implies that 'alien' standpoints are not necessarily devoid of worth. There may be, for example – and there frequently is, overlapping common ground where moral issues are concerned, even though the full explanations of the reasons for acting, and the motivations for acting, advanced by a Christian and a Marxist will differ. Again, Christians who testify that 'Jesus Christ is the only Saviour', are, if they are consistent, rejecting all other claims to saviourhood that are, or might be, made. But this does not preclude the recognition of valuable ethical teaching to be found in many religious and non-religious literatures (though it may imply that Christianity is not, in the first instance a body of teaching but the product of a saving act at the Cross). However all of this may be, Christians may draw encouragement from Hodges to make their truth claims with sincerity, conviction and humility, all the while recognizing that those who, for whatever reason, deny the propriety of making truth claims are hoist with their own petard, for they must think that the proposition, 'The making of truth claims is out of order' is true.

On other matters I found Quick seriously wanting on questions of ecclesiastical authority and orders, and deficient in the history and theological principles of historic Dissent. On the other hand, he evinced an ecumenical disposition which was sincere if not always comprehending. Within a narrower range he had a bracing way of making philosophical and doctrinal points, and like Matthews, he did much to reach the 'ordinary man' with Christian teaching. Not for him, however, the psychic adventures of Matthews, or Hodges' interest in angelology. Quick had a deeper grasp of the history of doctrine than Matthews, and whereas Matthews entertained the forlorn hope of credal revision, Quick saw the value of conserving the ancient symbols. Of all of them, Hodges was perhaps the most deferential towards ecclesiastical authority, provided it were not Roman, and that it encouraged that wrestling with the questions of faith to which he devoted so much of his life. He by no means uncritically accepted the deliverances of the past. In particular he, like Matthews and Quick but unlike de Burgh, opposed the doctrine of divine impassibility, and regretted that the idea of ontological unchangeableness had taken precedence over the idea of God's moral steadfastness. All four Anglicans were united in their commitment to the doctrine of the Trinity, their elevation of values, their quest of reasonableness, their post-Kantian metaphysics, and their suspicion of Karl Barth. As contrasted with de Burgh's incarnationalist emphasis,

---

[130] Idem, *Objectivity and Impartiality*, London: SCM Press, 1946, 22–3.

Matthews and Quick gave due weight to both the incarnation and the atonement together, while Hodges placed the Cross at the heart of his understanding of the Gospel (albeit the note of victory was occasionally muted), and with this I am in complete sympathy.

I like de Burgh for the range of his intellect, Matthews for his openness to new truth (however quirky), Quick for the acuteness of his mind, and Hodges for his Christian humanism in which both scepticism and spirituality were appropriately blended. Above all I value their quest of a reasonable faith – a quest which both acknowledges the limitations of reason whilst at the same time refusing to allow its province to be dogmatically constricted by either philosophers or theologians, however 'undogmatic' and 'non-metaphysical' they may suppose themselves to be; and which understands that faith is far more than a matter of assenting to doctrinal propositions.

It is tempting to speculate upon what the reactions of the four philosophical Anglicans might be to some of the now current intellectual fashions. They had reached harbour before the ripples of Reformed epistemology had reached these shores, though I think that they would have been interested in the question of warranted belief. They were also spared the tidal wave of 'postmodernism'.[131] Let us go forward in the hope that in the eternal seminar we may witness a debate between Quick (above all) and a postmodernist. That would be a joy to behold.

---

[131] The inverted commas indicate my feeling that it was an ill day when this horse bolted from its artistic stable to become probably the most denotationally-challenged term ever to gate-crash the philosophical lexicon. I have ventured a few thoughts on it in *Confessing and Commending the Faith*, 132–48.

Bibliography

Allchin, A. M., ed., *We Belong to One Another*, London: Epworth, 1965.
Anon., Review of W. R. Matthews, *God in Christian Thought and Experience*, q.v., in *The Expository Times*, XLII, 1930–31, 66–7.
—, *Congregational Year Book 1932*, London: Congregational Union of England and Wales, 1932.
—, *Who Was Who 1941-1950* and *2001-2005*, London: A. & C. Black.
—, *Congregational Praise*, London: Independent Press, 1951.
—, *Artificial Human Insemination. The Report of a Commission appointed by His Grace the Archbishop of Canterbury*, London: SPCK, 1952.
—, 'Deserved honours' (retirement of W. R. Matthews), *The Times*, 1 January 1962, 11.
—, 'Philosopher and Christian' (obituary of H. A. Hodges), *The Times*, 8 July 1976, 18.
—, *An Agreed Statement of the North American Orthodox-Catholic Consultation, St. Paul's College, Washington DC*, October 25 2003, at http://www.usccb.org/seia/filioque.shtml.
Aubrey, Edwin Ewart, 'Found before the search', a review of W. R. Matthews, *God in Christian Thought and Experience*, in *The Journal of Religion*, XII no. 1, January 1932, 143–44.
Aveling, Francis, *The Psychological Approach to Reality*, London: University of London Press, 1929.
Ayer, A. J., *Language, Truth and Logic*, London: Gollancz, 1936.
Baelz, Peter R., *Christian Theology and Metaphysics*, London: Epworth Press, 1968.
Baillie, John, Review of W. R. Matthews, *Studies in Christian Philosophy*, in *The Philosophical Review*, XXXI no. 2, March 1922, 191–4.
—, *Our Knowledge of God*, London: OUP, 1939.
—, *The Sense of the Presence of God*, London: OUP, 1962.
Balthasar, Hans Urs von, *Herrlichkeit: Eine theologische Aesthetik*, vols. I and II, Einsiedeln: Johannes Verlag, 1961–62.
Barker, H., Review of W. G. de Burgh, *From Morality to Religion*, in *Mind*, NS, XLVIII, April 1939, 221–7.
Bevan, Edwyn, *Symbolism and Belief*, London: Allen & Unwin, 1938.
Bomberger, J. H. A., 'Regeneration', in *Proceedings of the Second General Council of the Alliance of the Reformed Churches holding the Presbyterian System*, Philadelphia, 1880, 543–53.
Bowman, A. A., *Studies in the Philosophy of Religion*, ed. with a Memorial Introduction by Norman Kemp Smith, 2 vols., London: Macmillan, 1938.

Bradley, F. H., *The Principles of Logic*, 2 vols., London: OUP, 1922.
Brown, Stuart, ed., *Dictionary of Twentieth-Century British Philosophers*, Bristol: Thoemmes Continuum, 2005.
Browne, Robert, *A Treatise of Reformation Without Tarrying for Anie* (1582), in A. Peel and Leland H. Carlson, eds, *The Writings of Robert Harrison and Robert Browne*, London: Allen & Unwin, 1953.
Burgh, W. G. de, *The Legacy of the Ancient World* (1923), Harmondsworth: Penguin Books, 2 vols. 1955.
—, Review of C. E. M. Joad, *Return to Philosophy, being a Defence of Reason, an Affirmation of Values, and a Plea for Philosophy*, in *The Hibbert Journal*, XXXIII no. 3, April 1935, 474–8.
—, Review of Bertrand Russell, *In Praise of Idleness, and Other Essays*, in *The Hibbert Journal*, XXXIV no. 4, July 1936, 625–9.
—, *Towards a Religious Philosophy*, London: Macdonald & Evans, 1937.
—, *From Morality to Religion*, London: Macdonald & Evans, 1938.
—, Review of G. Dawes Hicks, *The Philosophical Bases of Theism*, in *Mind*, XLVII, January 1938, 80–86.
—, Review of E. Bevan, *Symbolism and Belief*, in *The Hibbert Journal*, XXXVII no. 1, October 1938, 166–71.
—, *Knowledge of the Individual*, London: OUP, 1939.
—, Review of A. A. Bowman, *Studies in the Philosophy of Religion*, in *The Hibbert Journal*, XXXVII no. 2, January 1939, 335–40.
—, 'Dr. W. M. Childs', *The Portmuthian*, LVI, 2 July 1939, 36–41.
—, 'The right and the good', *Mind*, XLVIII, October 1939, 491–7.
—, Review of E. Westermarck, *Christianity and Morals*, in *Mind*, XLIX, January 1940, 81–7.
—, 'George Dawes Hicks 1862–1941,' *Proceedings of the British Academy*, XXVII, 1941, 405–31.
—, 'Sources of present world-trouble. I. The abuse of knowledge', *The Hibbert Journal*, XXXVIII no. 2, January 1940, 196–206.
—, Review of W. D. Ross, *Foundations of Ethics*, in *The Hibbert Journal*, XXXVIII no. 2, January 1940, 279–80.
—, 'Sources of present world-trouble. II. The idol of humanism', *The Hibbert Journal*, XXXVIII no. 3, April 1940, 307–17.
—, Review of É. Gilson, *God and Philosophy*, in *Mind*, LI, July 1942, 275–80.
—, 'Intelligence in quest of faith', *The Hibbert Journal*, XL no. 3, April 1942, 221–7.
—, Review of *The New Leviathan*, in *The Hibbert Journal*, XLI no. 1, October 1942, 90–92.
—, Review of Frederick Copleston, *Friedrich Nietzsche, Philosopher of Culture*, in *The Hibbert Journal*, XLI no. 4, July 1943, 383–4.
—, Review of Susanne K. Langer, *Philosophy in a New Key: A Study in the Symbolism of Reason, Rite and Art*, in *The Hibbert Journal*, XLII no. 2, January 1944, 183–4.

—, *The Life of Reason*, London: Macdonald & Evans, 1949.
Butler, Joseph, *Fifteen Sermons preached at the Rolls Chapel, and A Dissertation upon the Nature of Virtue, with Introduction, Analyses, and Notes by The Very Rev. W. R. Matthews* (1914), London: G. Bell, 1953.
Cabasilas, Nicholas, *La Vie en Jésus-Christ*, trans. S. Broussaleux, 2nd edn with an Introduction by Dom O. Rousseau, Chevetogne: Collection Irénikon, 1960.
Caldecott, Alfred, *The Philosophy of Religion in England and America*, London: Methuen, 1901.
Calvin, J., *Institutes of the Christian Religion*, trans. Ford Lewis Battles, ed. J. T. McNeill, Philadelphia: The Westminster Press, 2 vols. 1961.
Camfield, F. W., ed., *Reformation Old and New. A Tribute to Karl Barth*, London: Lutterworth, 1947.
Campbell, R. J., *The New Theology*, London: Chapman and Hall, 1907.
Cave, Sydney, *The Doctrine of the Work of Christ*, London: University of London Press, 1937.
—, *The Christian Estimate of Man*, London: Duckworth, 1944.
Chapman, Mark, 'Oliver Chase Quick', in S. Brown, ed., *Dictionary of Twentieth-Century British Philosophers*, q.v.
Cobb, W. F., *Mysticism and the Creed*, London: Macmillan, 1914.
Collingwood, R. G., *The New Leviathan, Or, Man, Society, Civilization and Barbarism*, Oxford: Clarendon Press, 1942.
Copleston, Frederick, *Friedrich Nietzsche, Philosopher of Culture*, London: Burns, Oates and Washbourne, 1942.
—, *Contemporary Philosophy*, (1956), London: Burns & Oates, 1965.
Coutts, James, ed., *A Homage to Ann Griffiths*, Penarth: Church in Wales Press, 1976.
Cunliffe, Christopher, ed., *Joseph Butler's Moral and Religious Thought. Tercentenary Essays*, Oxford: Clarendon Press, 1992.
Dale, R. W., *Christian Doctrine* (1894), London: Hodder and Stoughton, 1903.
Daly, C. B., 'Metaphysics and the limits of language', in I. T. Ramsey, ed., *Prospect for Metaphysics*, q.v., 178–203.
Davey, Cyril J., *The Methodist Story*, London: Epworth Press, 1955.
Davies, Rupert, A. Raymond George and Gordon Rupp, *A History of the Methodist Church in Great Britain*, Peterborough: Epworth Press, vols. 2 and 3, 1978, 1983.
Devenish, Philip E., Review of H. A. Hodges, *God Beyond Knowledge*, in *The Journal of Religion*, LXI no. 1, January 1981, 102–4.
Dickie, E. P., *Revelation and Response*, Edinburgh: T. & T. Clark, 1938.
Dilthey, Wilhelm, *Gesammelte Schriften*, V, Göttingen: Vandenhoeck & Ruprecht, 1924.
—, *Introduction to the Human Sciences*, eds R. A. Makkreel and F. Rodi, Princeton, NJ: Princeton University Press, 1989.
Dimond, Sydney G., Heart and Mind. *Studies in the Philosophy of Christian Experience*, London: Epworth Press, 1945.

Dyson, H. V. D., and John Butt, *Augustans and Romantics* (1940), 3rd revised edn, London: The Cresset Press, 1961.
Eayrs, George, 'The United Methodist Church and the Wesleyan Reform Union', in W. J. Townsend, H. B. Workman and George Eayrs, eds, *A New History of Methodism*, London: Hodder and Stoughton, 1909, I, 481–551.
Ellis, John, *Some Brief Considerations upon Mr. Locke's Hypothesis, That Knowledge of God is Attainable by Ideas of Reflexion*, etc., London: J. Watts, 1743.
—, *The Knowledge of Divine Things from Revelation ... With some Additional Considerations upon Mr. Locke's Essay on the Human Understanding* (1743), London: Thomas Tegg, 1837.
Emmet, D. M., 'The use of analogy in metaphysics', *Proceedings of the Aristotelian Society*, XLI, 1941, 1–26.
—, 'Can philosophical theories transcend experience?' *Proceedings of the Aristotelian Society*, XX, 1946, 198–209.
—, *The Nature of Metaphysical Thinking* (1945), London: Macmillan, 1966.
—, 'The choice of a world outlook', *Philosophy*, XXIII, 1948, 208–26.
Euripides, *Heracles* in *Medea and Other Plays*, trans. John Davie, Harmondsworth: Penguin, 2003.
Evans, Sydney, 'Theology', in F. M. L. Thompson, *The University of London and the World of Learning 1836–1986*, London: The Hambledon Press, 1990.
Ewing, A. C., Review of W. G. de Burgh, *From Morality to Religion*, in *The Hibbert Journal*, XXXVII no. 3, April 1939, 496–9.
Farrer, Austin, 'Revelation,' in B. Mitchell, ed., *Faith and Logic*, q.v., ch. 3.
Ferré, Frederick, *Language, Logic and God*, London: Eyre & Spottiswoode, 1962.
Flew, A. G. N., Review of H. A. Hodges, *Languages, Standpoints and Attitudes*, in *Mind*, N.S. LXIII, January 1954, 112–13.
Forsyth, P. T., *Positive Preaching and the Modern Mind* (1907), London: Independent Press, 1964.
—, *The Person and Place of Jesus Christ* (1909), London: Independent Press, 1961.
—, 'Monism', a paper read before the London Society for the Study of Religion, privately printed, 1909.
—, *The Principle of Authority in relation to Certainty, Sanctity and Society* (1913), London: Independent Press, 1952.
—, *The Church and the Sacraments* (1917), London: Independent Press, 1953.
Franks, R. S., Review of H. A. Hodges, *Christianity and the Modern World View*, in *The Congregational Quarterly*, XXVIII no. 2, April, 1950, 176–7.
—, Review of H. A. Hodges, *The Pattern of Atonement*, in *The Congregational Quarterly*, XXXIII no. 4, October 1955, 367.
Freud, Sigmund, *The Future of an Illusion*, trans. W. D. Robson-Scott, London: L. and Virginia Woolf at The Hogarth Press, 1928.
Galloway, George, *The Philosophy of Religion*, Edinburgh: T. & T. Clark, 1914.
Garvie, A. E., *Memories and Meanings of my Life*, London: Allen & Unwin, 1938.
Gilson, Étienne, *God and Philosophy*, New Haven: Yale University Press, 1941.

Gomme, A. W., Review of W. G. de Burgh, *The Legacy of the Ancient World*, in *The Classical Review*, XXXVIII, November–December 1924, 177–8.
Green, T. H., *Prolegomena to Ethics*, ed., A. C. Bradley, Oxford: Clarendon Press, 1883.
Guthrie, William, *The Christian's Great Interest* (1658?), The Publication Committee of the Free Presbyterian Church of Scotland, [1951].
Gutmann, James, Review of H. A. Hodges, *Wilhelm Dilthey. An Introduction*, in *The Journal of Philosophy*, XLIV no. 22, October 1947, 609–12.
Hampshire, Stuart, 'The interpretation of language: words and concepts', in C. A. Mace, ed., *British Philosophy in the Mid-Century*, q.v., 267–79.
Hart, Trevor A., ed., *The Dictionary of Historical Theology*, Carlisle: Paternoster, 2000.
Hawkins, D. J. B., 'Towards the restoration of metaphysics', in I. T. Ramsey, ed., *Prospect for Metaphysics*, q.v., 111–20.
Hepburn, R. W., *Christianity and Paradox*, London: Watts, 1958.
Herford, R. Travers, *Memorials of Stand Chapel*, Prestwich: H. Allen, 1893.
Heywood Thomas, John, *Subjectivity and Paradox*, Oxford: Blackwell, 1957.
—, 'Kierkegaard's alternative metaphysical theology,' *History of European Ideas*, XII no. 1, 1990, 53–63.
Hicks, G. Dawes, *The Philosophical Bases of Theism*, London: Allen & Unwin, 1937.
Hodges, H. A., in *Phenomenology, Goodness and Beauty (Proceedings of the Aristotelian Society. Supplementary Volume, XI)*, 1932, 84–100.
—, 'British philosophy, 1689-1830,' in H. V. D. Dyson and John Butt, eds, *Augustans and Romantics*, q.v., 100–113.
—, 'Christianity in an age of science', in J. H. Oldham, ed., *Real Life in Meeting*, q.v., 44–51.
—, *Wilhelm Dilthey. An Introduction*, London: Routledge & Kegan Paul, 1944.
—, 'A neglected page in Anglican theology', *Theology*, XLVIII, May 1945, 104–110.
—, *The Christian in the Modern University*, London: SCM Press, 1946.
—, *Objectivity and Impartiality*, London: SCM Press, 1946.
—, 'The crisis in philosophy', in F. W. Camfield, ed., *Reformation Old and New*, q.v., 184–98.
—, in *Things and Persons (Proceedings of the Aristotelian Society. Supplementary Volume*, XXII), 1948, 190–201.
—, 'Art and Religion', *The Church Quarterly Review*, July–September 1948, 131–49.
—, *Christianity and the Modern World View* (1949), 2nd edn London: SPCK, 1962.
—, *The Philosophy of Wilhelm Dilthey*, London: Routledge & Kegan Paul, 1952.
—, *Languages, Standpoints and Attitudes*, London: OUP, 1953.
—, *Angels and Human Knowledge* (1954), reprinted in the One Tradition Series no. 9, Crawley: The Community of the Servants of the Will of God, 1982.

—, *The Pattern of Atonement*, London: SCM Press, 1955.
—, 'What is to become of philosophical theology?' in H. D. Lewis, ed., *Contemporary British Philosophy*. Third Series, q.v., 209–33.
—, *Anglicanism and Orthodoxy. A Study in Dialectical Churchmanship*, London: SCM Press, 1957.
—, "Herbert Arthur Hodges', in Dewi Morgan, ed., *They Became Anglicans*, q.v., 63–71.
—, Review of V. Lossky, *The Mystical Theology of the Eastern Church*, q.v., in *Sobornost*, III no. 24, Spring 1959, 648–50.
—, *Holiness, Righteousness, Perfection*, London: Fellowship of St Alban and St Sergius (1960).
—, Review of N. Cabasilas, *La Vie en Jésus-Christ*, q.v., in *Sobornost*, IV no. 8, Winter 1963, 467–9.
—, *Death and Life have Contended*, London: SCM Press, 1964.
—, 'Methodists, Anglicans and Orthodox', in A. M. Allchin, ed., *We Belong to One Another*, q.v., 30–47.
—, Review of Hans Urs von Balthasar, *Herrlichkeit: Eine theologische Aesthetik*, q.v., in *Journal of Theological Studies*, XVII, 1966, 524–38.
—, 'Ann Griffiths: a note of introduction', *Sobornost*, V no. 5, Summer 1967, 338–41.
—, 'Flame in the mountains: aspects of Welsh Free Church hymnody', *Religious Studies*, III no. 1, October 1967, 401–13.
—, 'The Revd Gilbert Shaw', *Sobornost*, V no. 6, Winter–Spring 1968, 451–4.
—, 'Filioque?', *Sobornost*, V no. 8, Winter–Spring 1969, 559–62.
—, 'Gwenallt', *Sobornost*, VI no. 1, Summer 1970, 25–32.
—, 'Introduction' to James Coutts, ed., *A Homage to Ann Griffiths*, q.v., 5–13.
—, *God Beyond Knowledge*, ed. W. D. Hudson, London: Macmillan, 1979.
—, *God be in my Thinking*, printed for V. J. Hodges, Leominster: Orphans Press, 1981.
Hodges, H. A. and A. M. Allchin, *A Rapture of Praise. Hymns of John and Charles Wesley*, London: Hodder and Stoughton, 1966.
Hodgson, Leonard, *The Grace of God in Faith and Philosophy*, London: Longmans, Green, 1936.
Holt, J. C., *Towards a Christian Philosophy*, London: Nisbet, 1943.
—, *The University of Reading: The First Fifty Years*, Reading: University of Reading Press, 1977.
Hoskyns, Edwyn C., review of O. C. Quick, *The Christian Sacraments*, in *The Journal of Theological Studies*, XXX, October 1928, 86–9.
Hudson, W. D., 'H. A. Hodges (1905–76), prefixed to H. A. Hodges, *God Beyond Knowledge*, q.v., vii–x.
Hume, David, *A Treatise of Human Nature* (1738), London: Dent, 2 vols., n.d.
Inge, W. R., *Diary of a Dean. St. Paul's 1911–34*, London: Hutchinson, 1949.
International Relationships in the Light of Christianity. Lectures by Various Writers, London: The Collegian, 1915.

Iremonger, F. A., *William Temple, Archbishop of Canterbury: His Life and Letters*, London: OUP, 1948.
James, William, *Varieties of Religious Experience*, London: Longmans, Green, 1903.
Joad, C. E. M., *Return to Philosophy, being a Defence of Reason, an Affirmation of Values, and a Plea for Philosophy*, London: Faber and Faber, 1935.
Jones, Rufus M., *Studies in Mystical Religion*, London: Macmillan, 1909.
Kant, I., *Critique of Pure Reason*, trans. Norman Kemp Smith (1929), London: Macmillan, 1976.
Kierkegaard, S., *Philosophical Fragments and Johannes Climacus*, ed. Robert L. Perkins, Macon, GA: Mercer University Press, 1994.
Knight, Marcus, 'Dr. W. R. Matthews', *The Times*, 7 December 1973, 21.
Körner, Stephan, 'Some types of philosophical thinking', in C. A. Mace, ed., *British Philosophy in the Mid-Century*, q.v., 115–31.
Lane, Anthony N. S., *John Calvin, Student of the Church Fathers*, Edinburgh: T. & T. Clark, 1999.
Langley, G. H., Review of W. G. de Burgh, *Towards a Religious Philosophy*, in *The Hibbert Journal*, XXXV no. 4, July 1937, 632–7.
Lejins, P., Review of H. A. Hodges, *Wilhelm Dilthey. An Introduction*, in *American Sociological Review*, XI no. 2, April 1946, 234–44.
Lewis, H. D., *Morals and Revelation*, London: Allen & Unwin, 1951.
—, ed., *Contemporary British Philosophy. Third Series*, London: Allen & Unwin, 1956.
—, ed., *Clarity is not Enough. Essays in Criticism of Linguistic Philosophy*, London: Allen & Unwin, 1963.
Lewis, Saunders, 'Ann Griffiths: a literary survey', in James Coutts, ed., *A Homage to Ann Griffiths*, q.v., 15–30.
Locke, John, *The Works of John Locke in Ten Volumes*, London: W. Otridge, et al., 11th edn, 1812.
—, *An Essay Concerning Human Understanding*, ed. Peter H. Nidditch, Oxford: Clarendon Press, 1975.
Lossky, Nicholas, José Míguez Bonino, John Pobee, Tom Stransky, Geoffrey Wainwright and Pauline Webb, eds, *Dictionary of the Ecumenical Movement*, Geneva: World Council of Churches, 2nd edn, 2002.
Lossky, Vladimir, *The Mystical Theology of the Eastern Church*, London: James Clarke, 1957.
Lucas, Paul, 'Oliver Quick', *Theology*, XCVI, January–February 1993, 4–17.
Lucretius, *De Rerum Natura*, trans. William Ellery Leonard, at http://classics.mit.edu/Carus/-nature_things.html.
MacArthur, Kathleen Walker, Review of W. R. Matthews, ed., *The Christian Faith*, in *The Journal of Religion*, XVIII no. 3, July 1938, 325–30.
McCurdy, Leslie, *Attributes and Atonement. The Holy Love of God in the Theology of P. T. Forsyth*, Carlisle: Paternoster, 1999.

Mace, C. A. ed., *British Philosophy in the Mid-Century. A Cambridge Symposium*, London: Allen and Unwin, 1957.
Macintosh, D. C., Review of W. R. Matthews, *Studies in Christian Philosophy*, in *The Journal of Religion*, III no. 2, March 1923, 214–15.
Mackinnon, D. M., 'Oliver Chase Quick as a theologian', *Theology*, XCVI, January–February 1883, 101–17.
Mackintosh, Robert, *Christian Ethics*, London: T. C. and E. C. Jack, 1909.
—, *Historic Theories of Atonement With Comments*, London: Hodder and Stoughton, 1920.
McLachlan, Herbert, *Essays and Addresses*, Manchester: Manchester University Press, 1950.
Macmurray, John, *Idealism Against Religion*, London: The Lindsey Press [1944].
McTaggart, J. M. E., *Some Dogmas of Religion*, London: Edward Arnold, 1906.
Manning, B. L., *Essays in Orthodox Dissent* (1931), London: Independent Press, 1952.
Manson, T. W., *The Church's Ministry*, London: Hodder and Stoughton, 1948.
Martin, C. B., 'A religious way of knowing', in A. G. N. Flew and A. MacIntyre, eds, *New Essays in Philosophical Theology*, London: SCM Press, 1955.
Matthews, W. R., 'Introduction' to J. Butler, *Fifteen Sermons*, q.v.
—, Review of George Galloway, *The Philosophy of Religion*, in *International Journal of Ethics*, XXV no. 1, October 1914, 116–19.
—, Review of W. F. Cobb, *Mysticism and the Creed*, in *International Journal of Ethics*, XXV no. 3, April 1915, 413–15.
—, Review of *International Relationships in the Light of Christianity. Lectures by Various Writers*, in *International Journal of Ethics*, XXVII no. 1, October 1916, 107–9.
—, *Studies in Christian Philosophy*, London: Macmillan, 1921; 2nd edn., 1928.
—, *The Idea of Revelation*, London: Longmans, Green, 1923.
—, *The Psychological Approach to Religion*, London: Longmans, Green, 1925.
—, 'Three philosophers of religion', *The Church Quarterly Review*, C, April 1925, 122–38.
—, *God and Evolution*, London: Longmans, Green, 1926.
—, *God in Christian Thought and Experience*, London: Nisbet, 1930.
—, *The Gospel and the Modern Mind*, London: Macmillan, 1930.
—, *Seven Words*, London: Hodder and Stoughton, 1933.
—, *The Adventures of Gabriel in his Search for Mr. Shaw, a Modest Companion for the Black Girl*, London: Hamish Hamilton, 1933.
—, 'The Christian ideal for human society', in George A. Yates, ed., *In Spirit and in Truth. Aspects of Judaism and Christianity*, London: Hodder and Stoughton, 1934, 120–31.
—, *The Purpose of God*, London: Nisbet, 1935.
—, *Essays in Construction*, London: Nisbet, 1933; 2nd edn, 1936.
—, *Our Faith in God*, London: SCM Press, 1936.
—, *The Hope of Immortality*, London: SCM Press, 1936.

—, 'The Christian belief in God', in W. R. Matthews, ed., *The Christian Faith*, London: Eyre and Spottiswoode, 1936, 65–93.
—, Anthem: 'Thou hast work for me to do', London: Novello, 1936, reprinted in *The Musical Times*, LXXVII, September 1936, 817–19.
—, *Signposts to God*, London: SPCK, 1938.
—, *The Moral Issues of the War*, London: Eyre and Spottiswoode, 1940.
—, 'Psychical research and theology', *Proceedings of the Society for Psychical Research*, pt. 161, March 1940, 1–15.
—, *Saint Paul's Cathedral in Wartime, 1939–1945*, London: Hutchinson, 1946.
—, 'William Temple as thinker', in *William Temple: An Estimate and an Appreciation*, London: James Clarke, 1946.
—, *The Problem of Christ in the Twentieth Century*, London: OUP, 1950.
—, *Reason in Religion*, London: The Lindsey Press, 1950.
—, 'Voluntary euthanasia', *The Modern Churchman*, XL no. 2, June 1950, 115–18.
—, 'William Ralph Inge 1860–1954', *Proceedings of the British Academy*, XL, 1954, 263–73.
—, *The British Philosopher as Writer*, London: The English Association, 1955.
—, *The Search for Perfection*, London: SPCK, 1957.
—, *The Thirty-Nine Articles. A Plea for a New Statement of the Christian Faith as Understood by the Church of England*, London: Hodder and Stoughton, 1961.
—, Sermon in the report, 'Service at St. Paul's Cathedral', *Notes and Records of the Royal Society of London*, XVI no. 1, April 1961, 95–9.
—, 'Eugenics and the family', *The Eugenics Review*, 1962.
—, *Memories and Meanings*, London: Hodder and Stoughton, 1969.
—, *The Year Through Christian Eyes*, London: Epworth Press, 1970.
— (ed.). *Dogma in History and Thought. Studies by Various Writers*, London: Nisbet, 1929.
—, See Butler, Joseph.
Melanchthon, P., *The Loci Communes of Philip Melanchthon*, trans. Charles L. Hill, Boston: Meador Publishing Company, 1944.
Mitchell, Basil, ed., *Faith and Logic*, London: Allen & Unwin, 1957.
Mitchell, G. Duncan, ed., *A Dictionary of Sociology*, London: Routledge & Kegan Paul, 1968.
Moberly, R. C., *Atonement and Personality* (1901), London: John Murray, 10th reprint, 1932.
Moberly, Walter, 'God and the Absolute', in *Foundations. A Statement of Christian Belief in Terms of Modern Thought*, London: Macmillan, 1922.
Moore, G. E., *Principia Ethica*, Cambridge: CUP, 1903.
Morgan, Dewi, ed., *They Became Anglicans. Personal Statements of Sixteen Converts to the Anglican Communion*, London: Mowbray, 1959.
Morgan, Edward, *John Elias. Life, Letters and Essays* (1844, 1847), Edinburgh: The Banner of Truth Trust, 1973.
Mozley, J. K., *The Impassibility of God. A Survey of Christian Thought*, Cambridge: CUP, 1926.

—, *Oliver Quick as a Theologian*, reprinted from Theology, January–February 1945, London: SPCK, [1945].
Muirhead, John H., *The Platonic Tradition in Anglo-Saxon Philosophy. Studies in the History of Idealism in England and America*, London: Allen & Unwin, 1931.
Murray, Paul D., and Marcus Pound, eds, *Receptive Ecumenism and Ecclesial Learning: Learning to be Church Together*, forthcoming.
Neill, Stephen Charles, *A History of the Ecumenical Movement 1517–1948*, London: SPCK, 1954.
Oldham, J. H., *Real Life is Meeting*, London: The Sheldon Press, 1942.
Oman, John, *The Natural and the Supernatural*, Cambridge: CUP, 1931.
Otto, Rudolf, *The Idea of the Holy*, London: OUP, 1924.
Oulton, J. E. L., *Holy Communion and Holy Spirit. A Study in Doctrinal Relationship*, London: SPCK, 1951.
Owen, H. P., *The Moral Argument for Christian Theism*, London: Allen & Unwin, 1965.
—, *The Christian Knowledge of God*, London: The Athlone Press, 1969.
—, *W. R. Matthews: Philosopher and Theologian*, London: The Athlone Press, 1976.
Parsons, Stephen, Foreword to H. A. Hodges, *God be in my Thinking*, q.v.
Paton, H. J., *The Modern Predicament*, London: Allen & Unwin (1955), 3rd impression, 1962.
Payne, Ernest A., *Henry Wheeler Robison: Scholar, Teacher, Principal. A Memoir*, London: Nisbet, 1946.
Pegis, Anton C., *Basic Writings of Saint Thomas Aquinas*, 2 vols., New York: Random House, 1945.
Penelhum, Terence, *Butler*, London: Routledge & Kegan Paul, 1985.
—, *Reason and Religious Faith*, Boulder, CO: Westview Press, 1995.
Plato, *The Republic*, trans. F. M. Cornford, Oxford: Clarendon Press, 1941.
—, *Apology*, in *Five Dialogues*, trans. G. M. A. Grube, Indianapolis: Hackett, 1986.
Plotinus, *The Six Enneads by Plotinus*, trans. Stephen Mackenna and B. S. Page, at classics.mit.edu/-Plotinus'Enneads.html.
Quick, O. C., 'The humanist theory of value: A criticism', *Mind*, NS, XIX, April 1910, 218–230.
—, 'The value of mysticism in religious faith and practice', *The Journal of Theological Studies*, XIII, January 1912, 161–200.
—, 'Mysticism: its meaning and danger', *The Journal of Theological Studies*, XIV, October 1912, 1–9.
—, *Modern Philosophy and the Incarnation*, London: SPCK, 1915.
—, *Essays in Orthodoxy*, London: Macmillan, 1916.
—, *The Testing of Church Principles*, London: John Murray, 1919.
—, 'Orthodoxy and Dr. Rashdall', *The Commonwealth*, November 1921.
—, *Liberalism, Modernism and Tradition*, London: Longmans, Green, 1922.

—, 'Value as a metaphysical principle', *The Hibbert Journal*, October 1923–July 1924, 123–35.
—, *Christian Beliefs and Modern Questions*, London: SCM Press, (1923), 4th edn, 1936.
—, *Catholic and Protestant Elements in Christianity*, London: Longmans, Green, 1924.
—, 'Goodness and happiness', in A. D. Lindsay, ed., *Christianity and the Present Moral Unrest*, London: Allen & Unwin, 1926.
—, *The Christian Sacraments* (1927), London: Collins Fontana, 1964.
—, 'The Farnham conference on reservation', *Theology*, XIV, March 1927, 167–8.
—, 'Reason and Christian experience. I. Apologetics rational and empirical', *Theology*, XV, October 1927, 182–91.
—, 'Reason and Christian experience. II. What is reason?' *Theology*, XV, November 1927, 245–55.
—, 'Sacramental theory', *Theology*, XX, May 1930, 271–7.
—, *The Ground of Faith and the Chaos of Thought*, London: Nisbet, 1931.
—, *Philosophy and the Cross*, London: OUP, 1931.
—, *The Realism of Christ's Parables*, London: SCM Press, 1931.
—, *The Gospel of Divine Action*, London: Nisbet, 1933.
—, 'The doctrine of the Church of England on sacraments', in Roderick Dunkerley, ed., *The Ministry and the Sacraments*, London: SCM Press, 1937.
—, *Doctrines of the Creed: Their Basis in Scripture and their Meaning To-day* (1938), London: Collins Fontana, 1971.
—, *Christianity and Justice*, London: The Sheldon Press, 1940.
—, *The Gospel of the New World. A Study in the Christian Doctrine of Atonement*, London: Nisbet, 1944.
Quin, Cosslett, Review of H. A. Hodges, *The Pattern of Atonement*, in *Theology*, LVIII no. 426, December 1955, 478–9.
Rahner, Karl, *Theological Investigations*, London: Darton, Longman & Todd, 1969.
Ramsey, A. M., *From Gore to Temple. The Development of Anglican Theology between Lux Mundi and the Second World War. 1889–1939*, London: Longmans, 1960.
Ramsey, I. T., Review of H. A. Hodges, *Languages, Standpoints and Attitudes*, in *The Philosophical Review*, IV no. 17, October 1954, 332–9.
—, *Freedom and Immortality*, London: SCM Press, 1960.
Ramsey, I. T., ed., *Prospect for Metaphysics. Essays of Metaphysical Exploration*, London: Allen & Unwin, 1961.
Reid, Thomas, *The Works of Thomas Reid*, ed., William Hamilton, Edinburgh: MacLachlan & Stewart, 2 vols., 6th edn, 1863.
Richardson, Alan, *A Theological Word Book of the Bible*, London: SCM Press, 1956.
Richmond, James, *Faith and Philosophy*, London: Hodder & Stoughton, 1966.
Robinson, H. Wheeler, *The Christian experience of the Holy Spirit* (1928), London: Collins Fontana, 1962.
Robinson, J. A. T., *Honest to God*, London: SCM Press, 1963.

Robinson, N. H. G., *Faith and Duty*, London: Gollancz, 1950.
—, *The Claim of Morality*, London: Gollancz, 1952.
Ross, W. D., *Foundations of Ethics*, Oxford: Clarendon Press, 1939.
Russell, Bertrand, *Mysticism and Logic, and Other Essays*, New York: Longmans, Green, 1918.
—, *In Praise of Idleness, and Other Essays*, London: Allen & Unwin, 1935.
Sell, Alan P. F., *Robert Mackintosh: Theologian of Integrity*, Bern: Peter Lang, 1977.
—, *Saints: Visible, Orderly and Catholic. The Congregational Idea of the Church* (1986), now from Eugene, OR: Wipf & Stock.
—, *Theology in Turmoil. The Roots, Course and Significance of the Conservative-Liberal Debate in Modern Theology* (1986), Eugene, OR: Wipf & Stock, 1998.
—, *The Philosophy of Religion 1875–1980*, London: Croom Helm, 1988; Bristol: Thoemmes Press, 1996.
—, *Aspects of Christian Integrity* (1990), Eugene, OR: Wipf & Stock, 1998.
—, *Philosophical Idealism and Christian Belief*, Cardiff: University of Wales Press, 1995; Eugene, OR: Wipf & Stock, 2006.
—, *John Locke and the Eighteenth-Century Divines*, Cardiff: University of Wales Press, 1997; Eugene, OR: Wipf & Stock, 2006.
—, *Christ Our Saviour*, Shippensburg: Ragged Edge Press, 2000.
—, *The Spirit Our Life*, Shippensburg, PA: Ragged Edge Press, 2000.
—, *Confessing and Commending the Faith. Historic Witness and Apologetic Method*, Cardiff: University of Wales Press, 2002; Eugene, OR: Wipf & Stock, 2006.
—, *Mill on God. The Pervasiveness and Elusiveness of Mill's Religious Thought*, Aldershot: Ashgate, 2004.
—, *Enlightenment, Ecumenism, Evangel. Theological Themes and Thinkers 1550–2000*, Milton Keynes: Paternoster, 2005.
—, *Testimony and Tradition. Studies in Reformed and Dissenting Thought*, Aldershot: Ashgate, 2005.
—, *Nonconformist Theology in the Twentieth Century*, Milton Keynes: Paternoster, 2006.
—, *Hinterland Theology. A Stimulus to Theological Construction*, Milton Keynes: Paternoster, 2008.
—, 'Clarity, precision, and on towards comprehension: The intellectual legacy of N.H. G. Robinson (1912–1978)', in Ulrich van der Heyden and Andreas Feldtkeller, *Border Crossings. Explorations of an Interdisciplinary Historian. Festschrift for Irving Hexham*, Stuttgart: Steiner, 2008, 267–85.
—, 'Living in the half lights: John Oman in context', forthcoming.
—, 'Receiving from other Christian traditions and overcoming the hindrances thereto: some Reformed reflections', in Paul D. Murray and Marcus Pound, eds, *Receptive Ecumenism and Ecclesial Learning*, q.v., forthcoming.
Shaw, G. B., *The Adventures of the Black Girl in her Search for God, and Some Lesser Tales*, London: Constable, 1932.

Shebbeare, Charles J., 'The evangelical conception of the sacraments', *Theology*, XX, April 1930, 207–15.
Smith, Henry, John E. Swallow and William Treffry, eds, *The Story of the United Methodist Church*, London: Henry Hooks, 1932.
Snaith, Norman, 'Chosen', in Alan Richardson, ed., *A Theological Word Book of the Bible*, q.v., 43–4.
Spens, Will, 'The Christian sacraments', *Theology*, XVIII, January, February and March 1920, 11–18, 78–85, 137–43, respectively.
Spinoza, Baruch, *The Ethics and Selected Letters*, trans. Samuel Shirley, Indianapolis: Hackett, 1982.
—, *Tractatus Theologico-politicus*, ed. Jonathan Israel; trans. Michael Silverthorne and J. Israel, Cambridge: CUP, 2007.
Stebbing, L. Susan, Review of A. N. Whitehead, *Religion in the Making*, in *Mind* NS XXXIX, 1930, 466–75.
Stephenson, A. M. G., *The Rise and Decline of English Modernism*, London: SPCK, 1984.
Stillingfleet, Edward, *A Discourse in Vindication of the Doctrine of the Trinity: With an Answer to the late Socinian Objections against it from Scripture, Antiquity and Reason*, etc., London: J. H. for Henry Mortlock, 1697, reprinted in *The Philosophy of Edward Stillingfleet*, IV, Bristol: Thoemmes Press, 2000.
Stocks, J. L., *Reason and Intuition*, London: OUP, 1939.
Strong, T. B., *A Manual of Theology*, London: A. & C. Black, 1892.
Taylor, A. E., 'The right and the good', *Mind*, NS, XLVIII, July 1939, 273–301.
—, 'William George de Burgh, 1866–1943,' *Proceedings of the British Academy*, XXIX, 1943, 371–91.
Taylor, John, and Clyde Binfield, eds, *Who They Were in the Reformed Churches of England and Wales 1901–2000*, Donington: Shaun Tyas, 2007.
Temple, William, 'Memoir' prefixed to O. C. Quick, *The Gospel of the New World*, q.v.
Thomas Aquinas, see Pegis, A. C.
Thomas, J. M. Lloyd, review of O. C. Quick, *The Christian Sacraments*, in *The Hibbert Journal*, XXVI no. 3, April 1928, 560–63.
Thucydides, *History of the Peloponnesian War*, trans. Richard Crawley, Mineola, NY: Dover, 2002.
Torrance, Thomas F., 'Our witness through doctrine', *Proceedings of the 17th General Council of the Alliance of the Reformed Churches throughout the World holding the Presbyterian Order*, Geneva: Office of the Alliance, 1954, 133–45.
Underhill, Evelyn, *Mysticism. A Study in the Nature and Development of Man's Spiritual Consciousness*, London: Methuen, [1911].
Ure, P. N., 'Professor W. G. de Burgh', *The Times*, 1 September 1943, 7.
Urmson, J. O., ed., *The Concise Encyclopaedia of Western Philosophy and Philosophers*, London: Hutchinson, 1960.
Vidler, A. R., *20th Century Defenders of the Faith*, London: SCM Press, 1965.

Vischer, Lukas, ed., *Spirit of God – Spirit of Christ: Ecumenical Reflections on the Filioque Controversy*, Geneva: World Council of Churches, 1981.
Wach, Joachim, Review of H. A. Hodges, *Wilhelm Dilthey. An Introduction*, in *The Journal of Religion*, XXVI no. 3, 1946, 217–18.
Waddams, H. M., review of O. C. Quick, *The Doctrines of the Creed*, in *Church Quarterly Review*, October–December 1938, 146–53.
Wallace, William, *Lectures and Essays on Natural Theology and Ethics*, ed. Edward Caird, Oxford: Clarendon Press, 1898.
Wallraff, Charles F., Review of H. A. Hodges, *Wilhelm Dilthey. An Introduction*, in *The Philosophical Review*, LV no. 6, November 1946, 702–4.
Walsh, W. H., *Metaphysics*, London: Hutchinson, 1963.
Wand, J., William C., 'Salute to Dean Matthews', *Church Times*, 12 May 1967, 10.
Ward, James, *Psychological Principles*, Cambridge: CUP, 1918.
Ward, W. G., *On Nature and Grace. A Theological Treatise. Book I. Philosophical Introduction*, London: Burns and Lambert, 1860.
Watson, Thomas, *The Mischief of Sin* (1671), Morgan, PA: Soli Deo Gloria Publications, 1994.
Watts, Isaac, *Miscellaneous Thoughts in Prose and Verse, on Natural, Moral, and Divine Subjects* (1734), reprinted Bristol: Thoemmes Press, 1999.
Webb, C. C. J., *Studies in the History of Natural Theology*, Oxford: Clarendon Press, 1915.
Wesley, John, 'Letter on Preaching Christ', in *The Works of the Rev. John Wesley, A.M.*, London: John Mason, 3rd edn, 1830, XI, 480-486.
West, W. M. S., *To be a Pilgrim. A Memoir of Ernest A. Payne*, Guildford: Lutterworth, 1983.
Westermarck, Edward, *Christianity and Morals*, London: Kegan Paul, Trench, Trubner, 1939.
Whately, Richard, *Elements of Logic* (1826), London: B. Fellowes, 1829.
Whitby, G. Stanley, Review of W. G. de Burgh, *From Morality to Religion*, in *Ethics*, L no. 1, October 1939, 116–19.
Whitehead, A. N., *Religion in the Making*, New York: Macmillan, 1926.
Williams, Daniel Day, Review of W. R. Matthews, *The Problem of Christ in the Twentieth Century*, in *The Journal of Religion*, XXXII no. 2, April 1952, 135.
Wittgenstein, L., *Tractatus Logico-Philosophicus* (1922), London: Routledge & Kegan Paul, 1981.

Index of Persons

Abelard, P., 19, 30, 176
Alexander, S. A., 77
Alexander, Samuel, 24, 90, 169
Allchin, A. M., 253, 261, 262
Ambrose, Bert, 5
Anaxagoras, 12, 233
Anaximander, 11
Anaximenes, 11
Anselm, 20, 21, 100, 247
Aristotle, 11, 12, 14–16, 17, 26, 30, 32, 114, 133, 233, 274
Aubrey, E. E., 105
Augustine of Hippo, 18, 19, 32, 179
Aveling, Francis, 86
Averroes (Ibn Rushd), 233
Ayer, A. J., 26, 94, 238

Baelz, Peter, 284
Baillie, John, 42, 52, 81, 93
Balthasar, Hans Urs von, 252
Baring, Thomas, 3
Barker, Ernest, 73
Barker, H., 54
Barth, Karl, 40, 73, 96, 106, 110, 125, 157–9, 276, 277–8, 281, 301
Batstone, Miss, 69
Battles, F. L., 209
Bentham, Jeremy, 216
Berdyaev, N., 96, 277
Bergson, H., 25, 32, 34, 90, 163, 226
Berkeley, George, 214, 215–16, 217, 218
Bernard of Clairvaux, 21, 63
Berthen, Miss, 9
Betts, J. A., 206
Bevan, Edwyn, 19, 32, 57
Binfield, Clyde, 73, 115
Blake, William, 214
Boeckh, Philip August, 231
Boehme, Jakob, 277
Bomberger, J. H. A., 58–9

Bonaventure, 38, 40, 100
Bond, William, 281–2
Bosanquet, Bernard, 39, 161, 288, 292
Bowman, A. A., 53–4
Bradley, A. C., 279
Bradley, F. H., 39, 41, 49, 161, 288, 292
Brinkman, M. E., 268
Brown, Mr., 69
Browne, Robert, 186
Bruno, G., 233
Bryan, Margaret (subsequently Matthews), 72
Bultmann, R., 80
Burgh, Hubert de, 3
Burgh, Maurice de, 3
Burgh, William George de, ch. 2 *passim*, 97, 106, 107, 142, 204, 206, 213, 219, 230, 272, ch. 6 *passim*.
   and Reading University, 1, 5–10
   and students, 8–10
   and Toynbee Hall, 4
   as University Extension Lecturer, 5
   his early years, 1–4
   his works, 7–8
   on analogy, 56–9
   on Christian ethics, 59–61
   on Christian philosophy, 66–7
   on classical thought, 11–16
   on education, 26, 29–31
   on epistemology, 31–43
   on experience, 37, 43
   on faith, 33–4, 39, 40, 42–3, 64
   on God, 40–42, 55
   on history, 41
   on humanism, 26–9, 30
   on idealism, 39
   on logical positivism, 25–6
   on love, 57–9
   on medieval thought, 19–20
   on metaphysics, 31, 42

    on morality, 44–56, 59
    on Neoplatonism, 16–19
    on reason, 31–5, 37, 40, 43, 52
    on religion, 37–9, 52–6
    on revelation, 35–6, 39, 41
    on Russell, 25
    on science, 21–5, 28, 43
    on theistic arguments, 36
    on world views, 63–6
Burnet, John, 7
Butler, Joseph, 16, 34, 99, 131, 132–3, 135, 142, 285
Butt, John, 214

Cabasilas, Nicholas, 256–7
Caird, Edward, 39, 292
Caldecott, Alfred, 71, 72
Calvin, John, 106, 109, 155, 209, 259, 268, 269
Camfield, F. W., 236, 293
Campbell, R. J., 108
Carlson, Leland H., 186
Carlyle, Thomas, 32, 217
Cave, Sydney, 115
Chapman, Mark, 201
Chase Parr, Harriet Bertha (subsequently Quick), 143
Chase Parr, William, 143
Childs, W. M., 6
Chrysostom, John, 54
Clarke, Samuel, 132
Cobb, W. F., 81
Coleridge, S. T., 217, 252
Collier, Arthur, 217
Collingwood, R. G., 48, 97, 231, 250, 252, 294
Comte, A., 27, 220, 224, 233
Cooper, Anthony Ashley, 132, 233
Copleston, F. C., 28, 290
Coutts, James, 263
Cranmer, Thomas, 209
Creed, J. M., 74
Croce, B., 25, 90, 97, 118–19, 288
Cunliffe, Christopher, 133

Dale, R. W., 59–60, 200
Daly, C. B., 293, 298, 299
Dante Alighieri, 21

Darlaston, G. E., 72
Davey, Cyril J., 203
Davidson, Randall, 144
Democritus, 233
Descartes, R., 16, 27, 30, 32, 34, 100, 217, 235, 274, 291, 295
Devenish, P. E., 248
Dickie, E. P., 35
Dilthey, Wilhelm, 204, 206, 207, 213, 217–35, 237, 240, 247, 261, 272, 287, 288, 293, 297, 300
Dimond, S. G., 93
Dionysius the Pseudo-Areopagite, 18
Duncan, Patrick, 5
Dunkerley, Roderic, 191
Dyson, H. V. D., 206, 214

Eayrs, George, 203
Eckhardt, 277
Eddington, Arthur, 25
Elias, John, 276, 281–2
Ellis, John, 285
Emmet, Dorothy, 240, 294
Empedocles, 12
Epicurus, 233
Evans, Ruth, 263
Evans, Sydney, 69
Ewing, A. C., 61–2

Farrer, A. M., 283
Ferré, Frederick, 298
Fichte, J. G., 214, 217
Fischer, Kuno, 231
Flew, A. G. N., 64, 240
Forsyth, P. T., 58, 66, 73, 107, 108, 113, 123, 128, 141, 185, 200, 241, 242, 280, 281, 282, 287
Franks, Robert S., 244, 247, 269
Frazer, James, 104
Freud, S., 87, 208

Galloway, George, 100
Garvie, A. E., 73–4, 115
Gentile, G., 36, 90, 226, 288
George, A. Raymond, 204
Gilson, É., 32, 57, 66
Glover, T. R., 149
Godwin, William, 12

Goethe, J. W. von, 233
Gomme, A. W., 8
Gore, Charles, 72, 108
Grace, Edith Mary, 5
Grace, William Francis, 5
Graham, J. W., 136
Green, T. H., 39, 49, 278, 279
Grey, Edward, 3
Grey, George, 3
Grey, Mary, 3
Griffiths, Ann, 263
Groshart, A. B., 286
Guthrie, William, 284, 285
Gutmann, James, 207

Haldane, R. B., 24
Hamilton, William, 278
Hampshire, S., 295
Hardie, W. R., 4
Harnack, Adolf, 72
Harrison, William, 281–2
Hart, Trevor A., 115
Hartley, David, 217
Hawkins, D. J. B., 295
Headlam, A. C., 70, 71
Hebb, Martin, 72
Hegel, G. W. F., 33, 118, 152, 162, 214, 223, 233, 235, 238, 240, 288, 292, 299
Helmholtz, H. von, 217
Hepburn, R. W., 64
Heraclitus, 11
Herford, R. Travers, 281
Heywood Thomas, John, 286, 287, 299
Hicks, George Dawes, 5, 6, 7, 8, 32, 37
Hippias, 12
Hitler, Adolf, 137
Hobbes, Thomas, 45, 131, 132
Hodges, Herbert Arthur, 65, ch. 5 *passim*, 273, 274, 275, ch. 6 *passim*
    and Reading University, 1, 7, 204–7, 300
    his ecumenism, 210–11, 253–4
    his experience, 211
    his life, 203–13
    his philosophical scepticism, 247–50, 264, 272, 290, 296
    his pilgrimage, 207–13
    his works, 207
    on angelology, 254–6
    on Arminianism, 261–2
    on art and religion, 250–53
    on baptism, 268
    on belief, 241, 246
    on British philosophy, 214–17
    on Calvinism, 261–2
    on Catholicism, 208, 210
    on Christians in the university, 211–12
    on death and eternal life, 269–71
    on Dilthey, 217–35
    on education, 211–13, 228–9
    on ethics, 227–8, 229
    on faith, 268–9, 272
    on holiness, 259–61
    on humanism, 211–12
    on hymns, 261–3
    on linguistic analysis, 237–8
    on logic, 274
    on justification, 267–8
    on metaphysics, 221–3, 238, 272
    on natural and human sciences, 223–6
    on Orthodoxy, 208, 210, 256–8
    on perfection, 259–60
    on psychology, 217–21
    on purgatory, 270–71
    on righteousness, 259–60
    on saving faith, 268–9
    on science, 219, 220, 272
    on science and Christianity, 229–30
    on soteriology, 265–7, 270–71, 272
    on standpoints, 235–40, 272
    on the atonement, 265–7
    on the basis religious presupposition, 243–4
    on theism, 244–7
    on the modern world view, 242
    on the Trinity, 264–5
    on world views, 231–44, 272
Hodges, Vera Joan (née Willis), 203, 205, 206
Hodgson, Leonard, 164
Holland, Henry Scott, 156
Holt, J. C., 5, 6, 9, 10, 204, 205, 206
Homer 13, 161
Hoskyns, Edwyn, 158, 190, 195, 197
Hudson, W. D., 213, 290

Hume, David, 22, 34, 45, 47, 56, 97, 101, 216, 217, 218, 219, 233, 235, 291, 295
Huxley, Aldous, 59
Huxley, Julian, 138

Inge, W. R., 74, 75, 144, 160, 291
Iremonger, F. A., 145

James, William, 32, 147, 151, 152, 153, 168, 199
Jeans, James, 25
Joad, C. E. M., 15
John of Salisbury, 19
John the Scot, 19
Jones, D. Gwenallt, 206
Jones, Rufus M., 152
Joseph, H. W. B., 4

Kant, I., 12, 16, 33, 34, 36–7, 38, 43, 45, 47, 48, 50, 55, 56, 93, 100, 101, 102, 133, 149, 162, 164, 216, 217, 222, 225, 235, 236, 275, 281, 284, 293, 294, 295
Kaufmann, Walter, 295
Kelly, H., 153–4
Kensit, John, 70
Kierkegaard, S. A., 53, 233, 234, 239, 240, 286, 297, 299
Kilham, Alexander, 203
Kingsley, Charles, 156
Kirk, Kenneth, 146
Knight, M., 77
Körner, S., 295

Laird, John, 45
Lane, A. N. S., 209
Lang, Cosmo Gordon, 75
Langer, Susan K., 23–6
Langley, G. H., 64, 65
Leibniz, G. W., 99, 100, 101, 214, 233
Lejins, P., 207
Leucippis, 12
Lewis, H. Elvet, 263
Lewis, H. D., 61, 137, 241, 293, 295
Lewis, Saunders, 263
Lindsay, A. D., 204

Locke, John, 23, 56, 214–15, 216, 217, 218, 278, 285
Loss, Joe, 5
Lossky, Nicholas, 145, 268
Lossky, Vladimir, 257
Lotze, H., 149
Lucas, Paul, 143, 144, 146, 149, 184, 200
Lucretius, 16
Luther, Martin, 96, 155, 259

MacArthur, K. W., 82
McCurdy, Leslie, 73
Macdowell, Dr., 70
Mace, C. A., 295
Macintosh, D. C., 93
MacIntyre, Alasdair C., 64
Mackinnon, D. M., 143, 146, 157, 175, 199, 200
Mackintosh, Robert, 60, 111, 112, 271
McLachlan, Herbert, 281
Macmurray, John, 288
McNeill, J. T., 209
McTaggart, J. M. E., 43
Makkreel, R. A., 225
Manning, Bernard Lord, 191, 192, 197
Mansel, H. L., 106
Manson, T. W., 192
Marsh, Sidney, 70
Martin, C. B., 64
Marx, Karl, 233
Mason, A. C., 9
Mason, H. J. M., 3
Mason, Thomas Monck, 4
Matthews, Barbara, 72
Matthews, Edgar, 69
Matthews, Hubert, 69
Matthews, Michael Harrington, 71–2
Matthews, Olive, 69
Matthews, Philip Walter, 69
Matthews, Walter Bryan, 72
Matthews, Walter Robert, ch. 3 *passim*, 164, 190, 204, 219, ch. 6 *passim*
 and Exeter Cathedral, 1, 74, 75
 and St. Paul's Cathedral, 1, 75–7
 and Westminster Bank, 70
 as Dean and Professor, King's College, London, 72–4
 as Lecturer in Philosophy, 71

as student, 70–71
his children, 71–2
his early years, 69–70
his liberalism, 107–10
his works, 74–5
on apologetics, 91–2
on Articles, 109–10, 128
on Christology, 117–20
on creation, 113–14
on epistemology, 97–8
on ethics, 131–8
on evil, 114–16
on experience, 78–82
on God, 110–13
on humanity, 114
on immortality, 84, 130
on linguistic analysis, 94
on metaphysics, 98
on philosophy and religion, 92–107
on psychology, 83–8
on revelation, 104–6
on science, 88–91, 96, 99
on sin, 116–17, 122
on soteriology, 120–22
on the Church, 126–30
on theistic arguments, 98–103
on the Trinity, 124–6
on world views, 94–5, 96, 99
Maurice, F. D., 156
Melanchthon, P., 276
Míguez Bonino, José, 145
Miletus, 11
Mill, James, 216
Mill, John Stuart, 136
Milton, John, 214
Mitchell, Basil, 183
Mitchell, G. Duncan, 223
Moberly, R. C., 271
Moberly, Walter, 161
Moore, G. E., 94, 134, 294, 295
Morgan, A. E., 7
Morgan, C. Lloyd, 90
Morgan, D., 297
Morgan, Edward, 276, 282
Morris, William, 214
Mozley, J. K., 112, 143, 145, 156, 200, 201
Muirhead, J. H., 217
Murray, Paul D., 254

Myers, Frederic, 83

Nairne, Alexander, 71
Neill, C. S., 145
Nettleship, R. L., 39
Newman, J. H., 150
Newton, Isaac, 214
Nidditch, Peter H., 278
Nietzsche, F. W., 214, 233
Nunn, T. Percy, 70

Oldham, J. H., 290
Olivers, Thomas, 259
Oman, John W., 87
Otto, Rudolf, 78–9, 85, 157, 260, 274
Oulton, J. E. L., 197
Owen, H. P., 35, 58, 69, 77, 102, 118, 124, 131

Paine, Tom, 12
Parmenides, 11
Parsons, Stephen, 203
Pascal, B., 34
Paton, H. J., 290
Payne, Ernest A., 74
Pearson, H. W., 144
Peel, Albert, 186
Pelagius, 19, 171
Penelhum, Terence, 133, 286, 287
Pfleiderer, O., 72
Philo of Alexandria, 247
Plato, 11, 12, 13–14, 15, 16, 17, 19, 21, 38, 45, 55, 129, 149, 152, 162, 217, 233, 281, 292
Plotinus, 16–17, 30, 291
Pobee, John, 145
Pope, Alexander, 30
Pound, Marcus, 254
Powicke, F. J., 73
Price, Richard, 45, 56, 217
Pringle-Pattison, A. S., 162, 164
Protagoras, 12, 13, 233
Pyke, R. Neville, 71
Pythagoras, 11

Quick, Dora, 143
Quick, Frances Winifred, 144

Quick, Oliver Chase, 43, ch. 4 *passim*, 204, 219, ch. 6 *passim*
  and Christ Church, Oxford, 1
  and Durham University, 1
  and ecumenism, 144–5, 188
  his career, 143–7
  his early years, 143–4
  his intellectual stance, 147–8, 159–72
  on apologetics, 166–9
  on apostolic succession, 190
  on authority, 188–9
  on Catholicism, 156–7
  on Christology, 158, 166, 174–8, 201
  on creeds, 151, 172–3, 175, 194
  on ethics, 169–71
  on evil, 162, 169, 173, 179–80
  on Free Churches, 189–90, 192, 200
  on God as Creator, 173–4
  on idealism, 161–3, 200
  on immortality, 181–2
  on impassibility, 148, 150, 175, 176, 200
  on K. Barth, 157–9
  on liberal theology, 148–51
  on materialism, 163
  on metaphysics, 167–8, 171
  on ministerial education, 145
  on mysticism, 151–4, 163
  on natural theology, 164–6
  on Platonism, 159–61, 178, 179, 180, 194
  on Protestantism, 154–6, 180, 184, 187, 200
  on rationalism, 165, 170
  on realism, 169–70
  on reason, 159, 162, 165, 167–8
  on revelation, 159, 165, 166
  on sanctification, 183–4
  on science, 160, 167, 169, 173
  on sin, 153, 158, 173, 178, 179–80, 195
  on soteriology, 153, 174, 179–83, 201
  on the Church, 184–93
  on the Holy Spirit, 183–4, 188
  on theism, 164–8
  on theological traditionalism, 151
  on the sacraments, 157, 190–99
  on the Trinity, 152, 184
Quick, Robert Herbert, 143

Quin, Cosslett, 269

Rabin, Oscar, 5
Rahner, Karl, 52
Ramsey, A. M., 125, 188, 200
Ramsey, I. T., 182, 240, 247, 293, 295
Rashdall, Hastings, 149, 164
Reid, Thomas, 216, 278
Rembrandt, 60–61
Richardson, Alan, 241
Richmond, James, 298
Rickert, H., 228
Ritschl, A., 81, 147, 149
Robinson, H. Wheeler, 73, 74, 78, 83, 190, 195
Robinson, J. A. T., 108
Robinson, N. H. G., 35, 62, 137
Robson, R. Walker, 142
Robson-Scott, W. D., 87
Rodi, F., 225
Rose, Miss, 70
Ross, W. D., 44, 47
Rossetti, D. G., 250
Rouse, Ruth, 145
Rousseau, J-J., 12
Rowe, Thomas, 286
Royce, Josiah, 161
Rupp, Gordon, 204
Ruskin, John, 205, 206
Russell, Bertrand, 24, 25, 59, 99, 103, 171

St. Cedd, Mr., 70
Schelling, F. W. J. von, 214 133
Schiller, F. C. S., 144, 167
Schleiermacher, F. D. E., 64, 78–81, 85, 102, 115, 231–2, 233, 274, 280
Self, Sophia Alice, 69
Sell, Alan P. F., 39, 49, 53, 57, 58, 59, 60, 63, 64, 73, 87, 92, 99, 107, 109, 112, 116, 120, 125, 126, 127, 129, 137, 150, 155, 162, 168, 176, 183, 185, 187, 188, 190, 193, 199, 214, 230, 244, 254, 257, 262, 266, 276, 285, 287, 300
Shaftesbury (*see* Cooper, Anthony Ashley)
Shakespeare, William, 87
Shaw, George Bernard, 29, 139
Shaw, Gilbert, 205

Index of Persons

Shebbeare, Charles J., 194
Shelley, Percy Bysshe, 214
Sheppard, H. R. L. (Dick), 144, 149
Sibbes, Richard, 286
Sibley, Franklin, 7
Sidgwick, Henry, 40, 83
Smith, Adam, 216
Smith, Henry, 204
Smith, J. A., 4
Smith, Norman Kemp, 284, 294
Snaith, Norman, 241
Socrates, 12, 13, 21
Sorley, W. R., 164
Spencer, Herbert, 90, 276
Spens, Will, 196
Spinoza, B., 18, 33, 34, 36, 38, 45, 57, 80, 93, 100, 233, 275
Stebbing, Susan L., 89
Stenton, Doris, 7
Stenton, Frank, 7
Stephenson A. M. G., 107
Stewart, Dugald, 216
Stillingfleet, Edward, 215
Stocks, J. L,. 63
Stone, Lew, 5
Stransky, Tom, 145
Strong, T. B., 71
Swallow, John E., 204

Taylor, A. E., 3, 4, 5, 7, 8, 9, 10, 35, 44–5, 49, 61, 97, 164
Taylor, John, 73, 115
Temple, William, 111, 143, 144, 145, 164, 199, 201
Tennant, F. R., 76, 125
Tennyson, Alfred, Lord, 284
Tertullian, Q. S. F., 96
Thales, 11
Thomas Aquinas, 19, 20, 21, 22, 30, 33, 37, 43, 53, 56–7, 65, 95, 100, 101, 111, 157, 179, 274
Thomas, J. M. Lloyd, 136, 196
Thompson, F. M. L., 69
Torrance, T. F., 269
Townsend, W. J., 203
Treffry, William, 203
Trendelenburg, Friedrich von, 231
Troeltsch, E., 155

Twells, Henry, 163
Tyrrell, G., 150

Underhill, E., 151, 153, 177
Ure, Annie D., 5
Ure, P. N., 5, 10
Urmson, J. O., 294

Van Til, Cornelius, 276
Vidler, A. R., 200
Vischer, Lukas, 265

Wach, Joachim, 207
Waddams, H. M., 154
Wainwright, A. W., 285
Wainwright, Geoffrey, 145
Wallace, William, 43
Wallraff, C. E., 207
Walsh, W. H., 294, 295, 296, 298
Wand, William, 75, 76, 77, 83, 107
Ward, James, 86
Ward, W. G., 24
Watson, E. W., 71
Watson, Thomas, 276
Watts, Isaac, 286
Webb, C. C. J., 57, 66, 111, 164, 275
Wells, H. G., 29
Wesley, Charles, 259, 260, 261, 266, 272
Wesley, John, 203, 261
West, W. M. S., 74
Westermarck, Edward, 23
Whately, Richard, 273
Whitbread, Samuel (1720–96), 3
Whitbread, Samuel (1764–1815), 3
Whitby, G. S., 56
White, H. J., 71, 72
Whitehead, A. N., 23, 24, 89–90, 162, 292
Wilkinson, J. T., 204
Williams, D. D., 120
Williams, William, 263
Willis, Vera Joan (subsequently Hodges), 9
Wittgenstein, L., 94
Wordsworth, William, 214
Workman, H. B., 203
Wright, Francis H., 6

Zinzendorf, N. L. G. von, 259

Index of Subjects

A.I.D., 137–8
analogy, 56–9
angelology, 254–6
Anglo-Catholicism, 146, 156–7, 192
apologetics, 91–2, 99, 140, 141, 166–9, 199, 249, 300
apostolic succession, 190
Arianism, 265
Arminianism, 261–2
art, 38, 97, 107, 250–53
Articles of Religion, 71, 109–10, 128, 145
authority, 27, 123, 128, 140, 164, 188–9, 301

baptism, 193, 195–6, 197, 268
behaviourism, 86–7, 222
belief, 241, 246, 284–5, 302
British philosophy, 214–17
Brown University, 207

Calvinism, 63, 109, 156, 261–2
Calvinistic Methodism, 262
Cambridge University, 5, 6, 69, 74
Catholicism, 63, 156–7, 208, 210, 253, 258, 265, 283
Cheltenham Ladies College, 144
Christ Church, Crouch End, 72
Christ Church, Oxford, 1, 144
Christology, 112, 117–20, 166, 174–8, 201, 264, 265
Church, 65, 123, 126–30, 184–93, 209 n., 210, 249, 252
classical thought, 16–19, 213
Columbia University, 207
conscience, 132–3, 135, 171
creation, 82, 113–14, 173–4
creeds, 142, 145, 151, 172–3, 175, 194, 264–5, 301
Crouch End Congregational Church, 72
Cuddesdon Theological College, 269

death, 269–71
determinism, 46–7
Durham University, 1, 144, 146

ecumenism, 127–8, 144–5, 188, 210–11, 253–4
Edinburgh Faith and Order Conference, 144
education, 26, 29–31, 72–3, 145, 211–13, 228–9
Enlightenment, 23, 258
epistemology, 22, 31–43, 70, 97–8, 218, 255, 273–8, 297–8
ethics, 59–61, 131–8, 169–71, 227–8, 229, 237, 242–1, 277, 279; *see also* 'morality'
Eugenics Society, 137
euthanasia, 138
evil, 114–16, 162, 169, 173, 179–80, 270
Exeter Cathedral, 1, 74, 75
experience, 22, 37, 40, 41, 42, 43, 67, 78–82, 107, 113, 123, 124, 141, 154, 199, 211, 221, 275, 278–81, 292, 300

faith, 20, 32, 33–4, 39, 40, 42–3, 64, 166, 246, 249, 268–9, 272, 275, 277, 282, 284–7, 289, 293, 297, 300, 302
Fellowship of St. Alban and St. Sergius, 208, 259
Free Churches, 189–190, 192, 198, 200, 209

Hackney College, 73
Harrow School, 143
hermeneutics, 232
history, 41, 80, 81, 118–19, 180–81, 225, 231, 242, 283
holiness, 259–61
Holy Spirit, 43, 60, 111, 123, 128, 161, 183–4, 188, 210, 258, 264, 300

humanism, 21, 26–9, 30, 206, 211–12, 217, 302
humanity, 114, 117, 212, 241
human sciences, 224–7, 228–9
hymns, 261–3

idealism, 39, 90, 92, 95, 118, 133, 161–3, 200, 207, 217, 222, 223, 231, 239, 266, 275, 288, 289 n., 291, 292
immanence, 41, 80, 95, 111, 119, 128, 152, 162, 174, 184, 277, 283
immortality, 67, 84, 130, 181–2, 269–71
impassibility, 13, 27, 41, 95, 111–12, 148, 150, 160, 161, 175, 176, 200, 292, 301
incarnation, 41, 58, 65, 110, 117, 118, 121, 141, 148, 150, 153, 158, 160, 161, 177, 201, 260, 265, 266, 272, 278, 283, 301–2
International Missionary Council Jerusalem Conference, 144–5, 201
intuition, 32, 33–4, 131–3, 275

justification, 267–8

King's College, London, 69, 70–74, 76, 77
King Edward VII School, Sheffield, 204

Lausanne Faith and Order Conference, 144, 194
liberal theology, 107–10, 148–51, 299
linguistic analysis, 94, 237–8, 288, 293, 294–6
logic, 274
logical positivism, 25–6, 33, 97, 203, 246, 288, 289, 294
London University, 5, 70, 74, 77, 144
Lord's Supper, 157, 193, 196–7
love, 42–3, 57–9, 111, 112, 113
Lutheranism, 156

medieval thought, 19–20
metaphysics, 27, 31, 33, 38, 39, 42, 91, 96, 98, 113, 118, 154, 161, 167–8, 169–70, 171, 207, 221–3, 226, 231, 233, 235, 237, 238, 243, 245, 247, 249, 255, 260, 264, 272, 279, 281, 287, 288, 289, 291–6, 297–9

Methodist Church, 211, 253, 257–8
Methodist New Connexion, 203
Modern Churchmen's Union, The, 107
Montreal Faith and Order Conference, 210
morality, 31, 44–56, 59, 107, 300; *see also* 'ethics'
mysticism, 105, 151–4, 163, 277

natural and human sciences, 223–7
Neoplatonism, 16–19, 30, 41, 216, 217, 283
New College, London, 73

Orthodoxy, 208, 210, 253, 254, 256–8, 259, 264
Oxford University, 4, 6, 10, 69, 70, 72, 143–4, 146, 204, 207

perfection, 259–60
philosophy of religion, 91–107, 300
Platonism, 28, 41, 48, 95, 159–61, 178, 179, 180, 194, 251, 283, 291, 292
postmodernism, 302
projection, 87
Protestantism, 154–6, 180, 184, 187, 200, 210, 261
psychology, 83–8, 216, 217–21, 223
purgatory, 63, 270–71

rationalism, 106, 152, 165, 170, 214, 275
Reading University, 1, 5–10, 29, 204–7, 300
realism, 169–70
reason, 20, 27, 29, 30, 31–5, 37, 40, 43, 47, 52, 79, 89, 159, 162, 165, 166, 167–8, 273–81, 284, 285, 286, 289, 297, 302
Reformation, 208, 210, 257, 258, 267, 269
Reformed epistemology, 302
regeneration, 58, 195, 276
Regent's Park College, London, 73, 74
religion, 23–4, 37–9, 43, 52–6, 250–53, 279
revelation, 18, 20, 35–6, 39, 40, 41, 42, 57, 70, 95, 104–6, 118, 159, 165, 166, 255, 264, 275–6, 277, 281–4, 286, 298
righteousness, 259–60
Romanticism, 220, 223
Royal Holloway College, 71

sacraments, 157, 190–99, 262, 267, 268
St. Andrews University, 52, 146
St. Boniface College, Warminster, 269
St. Paul's Cathedral, 1, 69, 74, 75–7, 144
sanctification, 183–4
saving faith, 268–9
scepticism, 159, 208, 234, 246–50, 264, 272, 290, 297, 302
science, 1, 20, 21–5, 28, 43, 88–91, 96, 99, 160, 167, 169, 173, 214, 215, 217, 219, 220, 223, 224–7, 228, 229–30, 232, 245, 249, 264, 272, 275–6, 288, 289–90, 296
sin, 41, 116–17, 122, 153, 158, 173, 178, 179–80, 195, 266, 267, 276, 278, 285
Society for Psychical Research, 83, 84
soteriology, 120–22, 140, 148, 150, 153, 160, 162, 174, 177, 179–83, 185, 201, 265–7, 270–71, 272, 302
standpoints, 235–40, 287, 297, 300–301
Stoicism, 16, 28

Tenth Lambeth Conference, 210
theism, 36, 56, 98–103, 140, 164–6, 244–7, 249, 275, 280
Toynbee Hall, 4

transcendence, 41, 95, 111, 119, 152, 184, 277, 282 n.
Trinity, 19, 65, 110, 112, 123, 124–6, 152, 184, 260, 264–5, 301
truth, 40

United Methodist Church, 203–4, 207
United Methodist Free Churches, 203
University Extension system, 5
University of Arizona, 207
University of Maryland, 207
utilitarianism, 50

validity, 190–93, 200
Virgin Birth, 179 n.
vitalism, 90 n.

Wales, 262–3
Westminster Bank, 70
Wilson's Grammar School, 70
Winchester College, 4
Workers' Educational Association, 205
World Council of Churches, 144, 210
world views, 63–6, 94–5, 96, 99, 141, 214, 231–44, 296–9, 300
World War I, 7, 24, 157, 181
World War II, 10, 21, 136–7, 170, 205

www.ingramcontent.com/pod-product-compliance
Lightning Source LLC
Chambersburg PA
CBHW050616300426
44112CB00012B/1521